Tales of the Prophets

(Qiṣaṣ al-anbiyāᵓ)

Muḥammad ibn
ᶜAbd Allāh al-Kisāᵓi

Translated by
Wheeler M. Thackston Jr.

Series Editor
Seyyed Hossein Nasr

GREAT BOOKS OF THE ISLAMIC WORLD, INC.

Printed in the United States of America

Library of Congress Cataloging in Publication Data
al-Kisai, Muhammad ibn Abd Allah, 11th cent.
Tales of the Prophets (*qisas al-anbiya*)

Translation of Q*isas al-anbiya*.
Bibliographical references.
1. Prophets, Pre-Islamic. I. Muhammad ibn Abd Allah.
II. Title.
BP137.T33 1997 297'.1224 77-25941
ISBN: 1-871031-01-X

Cover Design by Liaquat Ali
Cornerstones are Allah and Muhammad connected by *bismillah al-rahman al-rahim* (In the Name of God, the Merciful, the Compassionate)

Logo Design by Mani Ardalan Farhadi
The cypress tree bending with the wind, the source for the paisley design, is a symbol of the perfect Muslim who, as the tree, bends with the wind of God's Will.

Published by
Great Books of the Islamic World, Inc.

Distributed by
KAZI Publications
3023 W. Belmont Avenue
Chicago IL 60618
Tel: 773-267-7001; FAX: 773-267-7002
EMAIL: KAZIBOOKS@KAZI.ORG

Contents

Exordium

Praise be to God Whose bounties are endless, Whose signs are countless, Whose exposition is eloquent. He is the Merciful Whose kingdom is everlasting, the Generous that none resembles. His divine essence is unknown, hidden from every creation. We praise Him with praise fitting only for Him Who made us followers of the master of human beings, the perfect human being, the last messenger, the beacon and the guide of humanity, the ocean of heavenly knowledge who delivered His Lord's message with the utmost eloquence mingled with the fragrance of paradise, an eloquence descending on the hearts of human beings, enlightening them as the early morning dew revives the leaves of the trees, caressing them as the ocean waves caress the sands of the shore.

Recite in the Name of your Lord Who created
. . . . and taught by the pen,
taught the human being that which he knew not.

If all the trees were pens and all the oceans were ink . . . .

Al-Qastallani relates in his book, *al-Mawahib al-ladunniya*, that Prophet Muhammad (ﷺ) said, "God asked me something on the night of ascension and I was unable to answer. Then he put His hands, which defy description, between my shoulders. I felt a coolness which inspired in me the knowledge of the First and the Last."

From God's endless favors come those sincere pious scholars, beloved by God and His prophet; He is satisfied with them and they are satisfied with their Lord. Their deeds were based on the Quran and the sunna; their blood was the ink of their pens; and their hearts were the driving force behind their books, their words were wings for this spirits on the ladders of knowledge. They engraved their works with the light of their inspiration which reflected rainbows of discernment into the hearts of their readers.

Their works are beacons for humanity in understanding the wisdom behind each word of the Quran and its vastness. They recorded all the different meanings and nuances as God taught Adam all the names thereby making human beings his vicegerents on earth. These scholars brought us the secrets behind these eloquent names and letters. They adorned them with the light of their faith and their perfection, words which chase away the love of worldly pleasure and build up love for the hereafter in the hearts of human beings. All their works remind us to leave prohibited actions and urge us to remember our obligations. Their association is paradise and their companionship is happiness. Whoever loves them and loves their works, God and His prophet love. As God said, "*Indeed the friends of God fear not and neither do they grieve*." Their manners consisted in forgiveness, their behavior in mercy, their character in sincerity and their actions in love. Their lives were based on humility and their writings are reflections of themselves. There are no letters, words, phrases or sentences that can describe their endless great works which are like oceans without shores. These scholars are like wild Arabian stallions, unbridled, surpassing one another in expressing the enlightenment of their hearts and in creating a blazing whirlwind of knowledge which shines in the skies of their readers' hearts and blows a fragrant breeze to adorn every part of this creation.

Know, O reader, God said in the Quran, "*And above every knower there is one higher in knowledge*." This means there is no end to knowledge, and that there will always be great scholars, and great books. The Quran is the Word of God which has no limits. The sunna was revealed to Prophet Muhammad (ﷺ) by the archangel Gabriel as an explanation of the Quran without end. And this series of great books is an ocean without end, as it derives its knowledge from the Quran and sunna.

This work is a tremendous undertaking, and those behind it are bringing to humanity the guidance and the light of fourteen hundred years of work preserved in museums, libraries and the homes of scholars. These works are now becoming available to everyone. We hope, as do the administrators of this project, that what we are doing will be in God's way and in the way of Islam and in the way of humanity. We are trying our best to present this wisdom to the seekers of knowledge, understanding, enlightenment, truth and Islam. May Allah bless those doing this work and those reading it. May Allah shower His endless blessings on us and on the reader, and may He shower His endless mercy and prayers on our beloved Prophet Muhammad (ﷺ) and on his family and on his companions forever.

was-salam alaykum wa rahmatullahi

Shaykh Muhammad Hisham Kabbani
Los Altos Hills, California, 1997

Foreword

God's last plenar revelation to present humanity came in the form of a book, al-Qur'ān, which for Muslims is also *the* book and is in fact known also as *Umm al-kitāb* or Mother of All Books. While the peerless majesty of the revelation reduced the first generation of Muslims to silence, the echo of the Noble Book and its encouragement of acquiring knowledge could not but result in a culture which cherished books and honored scholars. This unmistakable emphasis of the Noble Quran on knowledge combined with the synthetic power of Islam to absorb the learning of older civilizations to the extent that they conformed to the doctrine of unity (*al-tawḥīd*) gave rise to a vast and diversified intellectual life which for the past thirteen centuries has produced millions of works dealing with nearly every field of knowledge from the religious sciences, theology and philosophy to the natural sciences, from law to music, and from poetry to politics.

Islamic civilization was a lake into which flowed streams from many civilizations, Greek, Roman, Egyptian, Mesopotamian, Byzantine, Persian, Indian and even Chinese. In this lake the various elements became synthesized into a new body of water which itself became the source for numerous tributaries that have watered the various lands of *Dār al-islām*. Furthermore, Islamic civilization created works which had profound influence upon at least three major civilizations outside of the Islamic world: the Far Eastern, the Indian and the

Western besides creating numerous masterly works whose influence has remained confined within the Islamic world. Such works in both categories contain a precious message for humanity as a whole and need to be made known by the world at large today.

Most treatises in Islamic civilization were written in the language of the Quranic revelation, Arabic, followed by the only other universal language of Islamic civilization, Persian. But important works have also been written in Turkish, Urdu, Bengali, Malay, Swahili, Berber, and numerous other languages including Chinese and during this century even English and French. Nor have all the works in Arabic been written by Arabs nor all the works in Persian by Persians. Numerous treatises in Arabic were written by Persians and later Turks, Indians, Berbers and Black Africans while many books in the Persian language were composed by Indians, Turks and Central Asians. The body of works written within the confines of Islamic civilization belongs to the whole of that civilization and in classical times in fact important books became known rapidly from Morocco to India and later Southeast Asia.

The Great Books of the Islamic World series seeks to make some of the most important works produced in Islamic civilization, primarily in Arabic and Persian, available in English so that these treasures of Islamic thought can be appreciated by those who do not possess the facility to benefit from them in the original languages. The audience to which the series addresses itself is predominantly the Western English reading public, but the series is also meant for Muslims themselves who have facility with the English language and also for non-Muslim non-Westerners who are now becoming ever more knowledgeable in English and who might wish to gain deeper knowledge of the Islamic intellectual universe.

We hope that with the help of God, Exalted is His Majesty, this series will be successfully completed and that by providing a clear and readable translation of some of the great masterpieces of Islamic thought in English, this series will be able to create better understanding of Islam in the world at large and make accessible some of the treasures of traditional thought which, although Islamic in genesis, belong to all human beings who are interested in true knowledge in whatever form it appears.

wa mā tawfīqunā illā bi'Llāh

Seyyed Hossein Nasr
Washington DC
June, 1997

Introduction

Verily we have revealed our will unto thee, as we have revealed it unto Noah and the prophets who succeeded him; and as we revealed it unto Abraham, and Ismael, and Isaac, and Jacob, and the tribes, and unto Jesus, and Job, and Jonas, and Aaron, and Solomon; and we have given thee the Koran, as we gave the psalms unto David: some apostles have we sent, whom we have formerly mentioned unto thee; and other apostles have we sent, whom we have not mentioned unto thee; and God spake unto Moses, discoursing with him; apostles declaring good tidings, and denouncing threats, lest men should have an argument of excuse against God, after the apostles had been sent unto them; God is mighty and wise [Koran 4:163–165].

In the mixed Judeo-Christian and pagan milieu into which it was born in the early seventh century of our era, the Arabic Koran, the scriptural basis of the religion of Islam, was in its own view the final installment, complete and perfect in and of itself, in the long, continuous series of divine revelations that had begun with Adam himself. To men of every age and condition there had been sent prophets and messengers of God to call men onto the righteous path of true religion, "submission (in Arabic, *islām*) to God's will," and to deliver to mankind God's Word; yet in the course of time, due to carelessness and outright hostility to the Word of God, the letter of the revealed texts had been changed and perverted by men to suit their own selfish purposes. The diversity of religions that then prevailed was a direct result of this corruption:

Mankind was of one faith, and God sent prophets bearing good tidings, and denouncing threats, and sent down with them the scripture in truth, that it might judge between men of that concerning which they disagreed; and none disagreed concerning it, except those to whom the same scriptures were delivered, after the declarations of God's will had come unto them, out of envy among themselves [Koran 2:213].

And to every nation there had been sent prophets and apostles to expound the principles of God's religion, each at the proper time and in the language of his community:

We have sent no apostle but with the language of his people, that he might declare their duty plainly unto them [Koran 14:4].

Time and again in the Koran the former prophets, as well as the Prophet Muhammad, are spoken of as having been charged with a dual function, as bearers of glad tidings as well as harbingers of dire threats and warnings for their people.[1] Although some later dogmatic theologians attempted to differentiate between the function of an apostle (*mursal, rasūl*) as scripture-bearing messenger to a particular community of people and that of a prophet (*nabī*) as preacher and follower of the apostles but not to any specific community,[2] since every apostle was also said to be a prophet,[3] the distinction was seldom observed. The Koran, in contrast, maintains that no distinction was to be made among the prophets (see 4:152): the prophets were all members of one "brotherhood," teaching the same monotheistic religion and attempting to save man from his invariable tendency toward sectarianism (see 23:52f.).

Throughout the Koran are numerous allusions to the prophets of Israel, although the histories of few, with the notable exception of Joseph, are treated in a running narrative but are rather introduced sporadically, different episodes in the careers being taken up at different points in the text. The pagan Arabs of Mecca, surrounded as they were by Jewish and Christian tribes and settlements and having extensive commercial contact with Syria to the north and the Yemen to the south, were certainly well acquainted with biblical legends as well as with such Christian lore as apocryphal material on the life of Christ, the Apostles' and saints' legends.[4] In addition, the Judeo-Christian emphasis in the Koran was at first directed primarily at the Christians and Jews themselves, to whom Muhammad felt himself particularly sent until he despaired of reaching them and turned to the pagans.

In the years following the death of the Prophet in 632, with the rapid expansion of the Islamic Empire and the collation of the canonical recension of the Koran and collection of the oral tradition (*hadīth*) of the Prophet and his Companions, the Muslims began to feel the need for explanation of many passages in the Holy Book. It was only natural for them to turn at this juncture for elaboration of the Koranic segments that dealt with the former prophets to those who were most familiar with the traditions of Judaism and Christianity such as ʿAbdullāh ibn Salām (d. 663), originally a Jew from Medina, Kaʿb al-Aḥbār (d. ca. 652), a learned Jewish convert to Islam from the Yemen, and Wahb ibn Munabbih (d. ca. 730), a Yemenite of Persian descent learned in the lore of South Arabia and the history of Israel. The vast majority of legendary traditions on the pre-Islamic nations preserved in the learned literature of Islam goes back to these men.[5]

Even in the learned literature, however, the versions of the majority of the Islamicized prophetic tales were not taken directly from the Old and New Testaments, rather their source was the basically oral interpretation of the stories of biblical characters which has been termed "religious folklore."[6] This genre, which represents much of common Semitic legend and folklore (collections of stories, parables, maxims, and interpretations), and parallels to which can be traced back to the most ancient of Near Eastern mythological literature, has come down to us in Jewish garb as contained in Old Testament apocrypha and as "haggadah" in the Babylonian and Palestinian Talmuds and in numerous midrashic works.[7] The material in Christian guise can be found in the New Testament apocrypha and scattered through the writings of the Church Fathers.[8] Much of this biblical legend also exists in Christian Arabic sources; examples of this type, which, although permeated with Christian prefigurative symbolic interpretation, is remarkably similar at points to the Islamic prophets' tales, are the sixth-century Syriac *Meʿārath Gazzē* (*Book of the Cave of Treasures*), which exists also in Arabic translation as *Maghārat al-kunūz*, the Arabic *Naẓm al-jawhar* by Eutychius, Patriarch of Alexandria (876–939), and the eleventh-century Ethiopic *Book of Adam and Eve*, presumed to have been translated from an earlier Arabic version.[9]

In response to an understandable desire on the part of the

common people, who had no access to the learned literature of the commentators and divines, there arose a parallel tradition of the prophets' legends, a popular genre which served a dual purpose, first of satisfying a pious wish for elaboration on the cursory allusions to the prophets found in the Koran and second of providing a form of entertainment for the masses.

From the first Islamic century there are abundant references to the office of the *qāṣṣ* (pl. *quṣṣāṣ*, "narrator"), whose function initially seems to have been to recite from the Koran and to expound on the readings in the great mosques of the empire, and which as an institution remained virtually unchanged for centuries.[10] Closely connected with the religious establishment, the "narrator" filled a "reputable and influential position."[11] The *qāṣṣ* might perform the duties of the *imām* in leading the congregational prayer and also the function of the *qārī'* in reading from the Koran as well as of the *khaṭīb* in delivering the official sermon, but his prime function was to preach a type of "revivalistic" sermon in which the Koran and Tradition were interpreted and the people were impressed with "fear and hope."[12] The first generation of *quṣṣāṣ* were thoroughly grounded in the religious sciences, as the juridical function of many as well as testimony as to the learnedness and eloquence of many of them shows.[13]

The invectives one meets against the *quṣṣāṣ* from the eighth century onwards were made mainly by the mystics, who criticized them for imitating mystical modes of expression in their preaching while they themselves were no mystics at all.[14] And indeed the sessions of some of those called *quṣṣāṣ al-ʿāmm* ("narrators for the common folk") may have degenerated from the pious level of the early narrators to little more than street storytelling for an indecorous crowd who could be easily charmed by fabulous inventions and a spectacular style of narration. It is not difficult to understand the objection of the mystics on the one hand, who felt that these gatherings were a mockery of their own sessions, and of the divines on the other, who criticized the lack of learning among these tellers of tales who used traditions considered weak and untrustworthy to lend credence to their narratives.[15] Ideally a narrator should augment a Koranic narrative on a given prophet with sound traditions, interpolating as little as possible from his own imagination, and then in homiletic style point out the moral lesson inherent in the story, thereby impressing the people with an example and provoking them to imitate the piety of the former prophets and God-fearing "saints" in their own lives.[16] When a narrator is versed in his material and honest in intention, says Ibn al-Jawzī, "all the people benefit from him. A jurist, or a traditionist, or a reciter of the Koran is not capable of bringing to God a hundredth of the people the preacher is capable of bringing because this latter delivers his exhortations both to the common people and to the elite, but especially to the common people, who scarcely ever meet a jurist, and so they come to him with their questions."[17]

It was not the practice of preaching per se among these narrators that was objected to, for "in so far as the *quṣṣāṣ* served religious ends . . . , they were left alone and undisturbed in their pious work; official theology gladly tolerated these free preachers and popular theologians, who in street or mosque condescended to the level of the understanding of the people."[18] The abuses and excesses of some *quṣṣāṣ*, however, led to such combative measures as governmental edicts against storytellers, along with astrologers and fortunetellers, issued in Baghdad in 892 and again in 896. These street-preachers, claimed the learned, "profaned religious subjects by using them for entertainment and amusement of their audiences; they tried to impress the uneducated populace with piquant etymologies [see, e.g., p. 131 & 210] and other charlatanisms, and endeavoured to give themselves an air of engaging in serious research. Biblical legends embroidered with all kinds of anecdotes were the characteristic contents of their lectures."[19]

In the more learned literature, on the other hand, the vast information gathered on the pre-Islamic prophets then existed either in the form of Koranic commentary, in which case the legends were of necessity broken up, with elaboration and variant accounts given under the verse or group of verses being treated, or in a form such as one must assume the earliest "universal chronologies" and "books of creation" were written. The oldest extant work of this type is the *Tārīkh al-rusul wa'l-mulūk* [*Chronicle of Apostles and Kings*] of Muhammad ibn Jarīr al-

Ṭabarī (839–923) and is a running chronology of all the ancient nations, with their political and prophetic history given in straight chronological order along with variant accounts. In these historiographical accounts, in addition to a certain amount of synthesis on the prophets acceptable to monotheistic Islam, the claims of other, nonmonotheistic nations were also given.[20]

It was not until the fourth Islamic century that the scattered materials on prophetic legend were collected into an independent work; and significantly the first person known to have produced such a book in the heartland of Islam was also a Koranic commentator, Abū Isḥāq Aḥmad ibn Muhammad al-Tha'labī (d. 1036), author of *'Arā'is al-majālis: Qiṣaṣ al-anbiyā'* [*Brides of the Sessions: Tales of the Prophets*],[21] a work which grew out of the mystically oriented circle that acknowledged the Master of Baghdad, Junayd (d. 910), as its founder and which is representative of the learned strain of prophetic literature, replete with citations of authorities and variant traditions. The style of Tha'labī's *Qiṣaṣ* derives directly from Koranic commentary, with the legendary material excerpted and arranged in chronological order, like Ṭabarī's history, from the creation down to the appearance of the Prophet Muhammad, to form an Islamic "prehistory." The result, although thorough, is a choppy, scholastic compilation that neither was designed for nor lends itself to smooth, enjoyable reading or listening. One assumes it was used as a sort of reference manual for preachers.

A slightly different emphasis was placed on the tales by an Iberian contemporary of Tha'labī, Ṭarafī of Cordova (977–1062),[22] who concentrated on the exemplary moral character of the prophets and stressed prophetic admonitions and moral counsels rather than the historical and legendary sides to their careers.[23] This aspect of the legends is indeed given by Tha'labī in his introduction, where he lists five reasons for the revelation of the prophetic tales in the Koran, but he nonetheless follows basically the chronological-narrative approach.

Stating the reasons for, or underlying "wisdom" in God's having related the stories of the former prophets to Muhammad, Tha'labī quotes the Koranic verse 11:120: "The whole which we have related of the histories of our apostles do we relate unto thee, that we may confirm thy heart thereby." Herein, says

Thaʿlabī, lie five "wisdoms" discovered by the sages: (1) Proof of Muhammad's prophecy. Being illiterate and never having spent enough time outside his native Mecca to have acquired such knowledge from the learned, Muhammad received the prophetic history via Gabriel's intermediacy through divine inspiration as a proof to all mankind of his calling as prophet and apostle. (2) Moral example for Muhammad himself. God instructed Muhammad in moral excellence by examples of former apostles, and when he was perfected in the prophetic character, he was praised by God: "Thou art of a noble disposition" [Koran 68.4]. (3) Proof of the supremacy of Muhammad's nation. When shown in the prophetic narratives what had befallen the former nations and how they had been sorely tried by God, Muhammad realized the supremacy of his nation over all the others, since his people were spared most of the suffering inherent in God's trials of the ancients. Furthermore, the Word of the Koran abrogated many of the restrictions and taboos legislated in former times, thereby lightening the burden of faith, as many commentators interpreted the verse "God is minded to make his religion light unto you, for man was created weak" [Koran 4:28, see also 22:78]. (4) As a means of improving the character and mind of the community. Since in many places in the prophetic tales there is mentioned not only the heavenly reward that accrued to the prophets and the righteous but also the torment of the enemies of religion, all the people could derive spiritual benefit by meditating upon the meaning of these stories, as is written, "Surely in the history of Joseph and his brethren there are signs of God's providence to the inquisitive" [Koran 12:7] and "Verily in the histories of the prophets and their people, there is an instructive example unto those who are endued with understanding" [Koran 12:111]. In this respect, a disciple of J̱unayd and leading mystic of Baghdad, Shiblī, used to say, "Let the common people occupy themselves with mere recollection of the tales [of the prophets], but let the élite derive a moral from them." (5) The histories of the prophets were revealed to resurrect the memory of God's apostles, as Abraham prayed, "Grant that I may be spoken of with honour among the latest posterity" [Koran 26:84].[24]

Not long after Thaʿlabī's work was produced in Baghdad and

Ṭarafī's at the western extremity of the Islamic world, a tradition of composing, paraphrasing and translating such works in Persian grew up rapidly in the eastern Islamic lands of Iran and Central Asia. Before 1100 Ibn Khalaf of Nishapur had written an original version of the tales in Persian, by the end of the century several other collections and translations had been made; and from around 1400 on compositions in Turkish too, both in Central Asia and eastern Anatolia, are found.[25] The genre seems to have enjoyed extraordinary popularity in the Persian-speaking world and more especially in Khorasan and Central Asia, perhaps owing to survivals of interest in the pre-Islamic institution of the holy-man in these formerly Buddhist lands.[26] Sufism too, highly cultivated in Khorasan and Central Asia, used the biblical prophets as prototypes of the revelation-bearing prophet-saint and interpreted the prophetic tales as mystical narratives symbolic of the different stages in the progress of the soul toward ultimate reunion with God. The mystical types discovered in the persons of many biblical prophets are reflected in the poetry and prose works of almost all the great Persian-writing Sufis: Sanā'ī, 'Aṭṭār and Rūmī all regularly allude to the prophets in their didactic poetry; and long before Ḥāfiẓ was able to weave exquisitely subtle allusions to these mystical conceptualizations into his *ghazals,* episodes from the prophets' careers had become literary topoi in Persian. To give only a very few of these topoi, we may mention Abraham the Monotheist par excellence in the "fiery rosegarden" as the purified soul freed from the influence of the carnal "Nimrod-self"; Azer, Abraham's father, prototype of the idolator and idol-monger (*butgar, buttarāsh*); the "lost Joseph" (*Yūsuf-i gumgashta*), symbol of Perfect Beauty, and his grieving father Jacob's Abode of Sorrows (*bayt ul-aḥzān*); Moses the worker of miracles, whose "white hand" (*yad-i bayḍā*) is often quoted as a symbol of miraculous prophecy; Solomon, who was given the esoteric knowledge of the languages of all creatures and mastery over men and djinn; and Jesus, the ideal ascetic, whose miraculous messianic breath (*dam-i masīḥ*) could heal all afflictions. Joseph and Zuleikha became one of the standard pairs of lovers, the most famous version of whose story is the *mathnawi* by Jāmī of Herat (d. 1492).

Imported into the Indian subcontinent by Sufi missionaries well acquainted with Persian mystical interpretation of the prophets' legends, versions of these stories abound in all the regional languages of Indian Islam such as Urdu, Sindhi, Punjabi, Bengali, Kachhi, etc. As many of these legends have been assimilated to prior local beliefs, some rather astounding transformations have been made from the "standard" Islamic versions, such as the assimilation of al-Khidr into the personage of a water deity among the inhabitants of the banks of the Indus; and the particularly rich and varied material that can be collected in this respect forms a fascinating corpus for the study of religious and cultural eclecticism. Some of the greatest writers of the regional languages, such as Makhdūm ʻAbdullāh Nāṛiyăwārō in Sindhi, have left *Tales of the Prophets*.[27]

And to bring the prophetic tales down to the present, or near-present, time, one can see that the original and ancient folk aspect that lies beneath the surface of the legends (and sometimes not very far beneath) and which was never completely eliminated even in the most scholarly versions has allowed these "islamicized" legends to reenter the realm of folklore from one end of the Muslim world to the other.[28]

The *Tales of the Prophets*

One of the best-loved versions of the prophetic tales is the *Qiṣaṣ al-anbiyā'* here offered in English translation and composed by a certain al-Kisā'ī, the date of which is highly uncertain, although the prevalent opinion is that it must have been written not long before 1200.[29] It was shortly thereafter translated into Persian by Muhammad ibn Ḥasan al-Daydūzamī under the title *Nafā'is al-ʻarā'is.*[30]

The edition made by Isaac Eisenberg, which is here translated, is not the most complete recension of the Kisā'ī version of the *Tales* extant; and it omits several figures generally included in the Israelite portion of the tales such as Jeremiah and Daniel. As it ends with Jesus, it does not therefore include the Christian saints such as George of Cappadocia, the Sleepers of Ephesus and the Martyrs of Nejran, certain Israelite characters normally interpolated into the "*fatra*" or period between

Jesus and Muhammad such as Samson (although Jonah is normally placed in this *fatra,* he is included in the Eisenberg edition), and the "Masters of the Elephant" (*aṣḥāb al-fīl*) and the usual miraculous events attending the birth and early career of the Prophet Muhammad.[31] As the Eisenberg edition unfortunately lacks variant readings and stemma of the manuscripts he used, one must assume that he followed the oldest available manuscript as the criterion for inclusion and exclusion of the several tales known to be included in later manuscripts. It is quite likely, therefore, that an original version, which did not include these figures, was later expanded on the basis of Tha'labī, Tabarī, or some other more comprehensive compiler.

If not the scholar that was Tha'labī, Kisā'ī was certainly a master storyteller, and his sense of the dramatic value in ending a narrative section at precisely the right moment to heighten an important point in the mind of the listener is exhibited throughout. Although Kisā'ī refrains from doing so, it was at such moments that the preacher might have broken into a moral discourse or urged his audience to ponder the significance of what they had just heard. On a much more mundane level, it must have been at precisely these junctures, when the crowds were most anxious to know "what comes next," that the professional storyteller "made his pitch" and had his *mukawwiz* ("collector") "pass the hat" around before proceeding with the narrative.[32]

In his Preface, Kisā'ī describes the formation of a human fetus in the womb and its entry as a newborn babe into the external world. This is contrasted with the descriptions, typical of the genre, of the "birth" of the world *ex nihilo* by God's Word of command, "Be!" Angelology and cosmology follow with descriptions of the world and natural phenomena, all of which "set the stage" for the climax of God's creativity, the "shaping" of Adam, His most perfect creature. Unlike the rest of creation, all of which was brought into existence by divine fiat, Adam was fashioned by God's own hands and was bestowed with God's own breath of spirit.

Because Adam was given this divine spirit, say the mystics, he therefore, along with all his progeny by inheritance, shares in the mystery of the Godhead through a subtle, spiritual link and is at the same time the microcosm, the center and *raison d'être* of the whole macrocosmic universe. When God then commanded the hosts of heaven to bow down to Adam, it was the spark of divinity contained in him that they were bade to acknowledge. Iblis, however, jealous that, after his eons of faithful worship of God, something could be set over him, vows to sabotage this preferential treatment of Adam and refuses to bow down to a being "made of clay." What he could not see, say some who thus dubbed Iblis the "one-eyed," was the divine part admixed to that clay. Delving somewhat deeper into Iblis' psychology, Farīd al-Dīn 'Aṭṭār, thirteenth-century mystical didact of Nishapur, puts these words into the mouth of Iblis:

> "I know that Adam is not just clay! I will hold my head up to see the 'mystery.' I have no fear!"
> Since Iblis did not bow his head to the ground, he saw the "mystery" from where he lay in ambush.
> God then said to him, "Oh spy! art thou watching the 'mystery' in this place?
> Since thou hast seen the 'mystery' I have secretly inserted, I must do away with thee lest thou speak it abroad in the world!"[33]

Iblis, however, begs a reprieve from God, who dubs him "The Liar" so that man will never believe what he can tell of his "mystery" (*sirr*, a word by which the mystics designated that hidden link that lies deep in the subconscious "heart" of man and through which the connection with the Godhead is capable of being realized).

This episode, so central to the understanding of the subsequent dealings of Iblis with man and of man's relationship with God as well as to the knotty and much disputed problem of free-will and predestination, is one, if not the major, focal point of the creation saga. It provides the background for Iblis' vow of revenge on Adam and his progeny; it relieves the necessity of making Iblis an essentially evil being, a concept abhorrent to Islamic theology and one that smacked of dualism.

Like Iblis, Adam too falls from "grace" because of pride: "a tyrant and a fool" (Koran 33:72), Adam accepted the "trust," the dubious gift of reason and ability to distinguish right from wrong,[34] a quality that at once set him above the unreasoning, ever-obedient angels; but he neglected to seek God's assistance in administering this burdensome trust. Too weak to handle what he had taken on, Adam was duped with the greatest of ease by an appeal through Eve to his vanity. Indeed, Adam's utter naïveté and lack of wisdom are fully displayed in his pathetic "parting shot" at God (see p. 42). Adam is later recompensed, however, for the suffering he has to endure with the gift of contrition and assurance of God's favor and grace toward "all those who with hearty repentance and true faith turn unto him."

With Adam and the "leaves" of holy writ that are given to him through the intermediacy of Gabriel begins the series of books revealed to mankind that will finally culminate in the Koran. The books of God's Word in this series, variously reckoned, are comprised generally of the Books of Adam, Seth, Abraham, Moses (the Torah), David (the Psalter), Jesus (the Gospel), and Muhammad (the Koran).

The sense of continuity developed by the passing of these accumulating "leaves" of Holy Writ from generation to generation echoes a much stronger current of continuity that was cultivated in the Syriac prophetic legends such as the sixth-century reworking of the *Meʿārath gazzē* (*Cave of Treasures*) attributed originally to Ephrem Syrus, where, for example, influenced by the more liturgical orientation of Christianity, the successive generations from Adam serve as high priests and are interred around the Altar of Adam in the Cave of Treasures, Adam and Eve's habitation and resting place. When Noah, Shem, Ham and Japheth bear away Adam's body and the gold, frankincense and myrrh (which had been brought respectively by Michael, Gabriel and Raphael) to save them from the coming Deluge, they pronounce the moving benediction "Pûshw b'shlâmâ" upon the other patriarchs buried in the Cave:

> O holy Paradise, habitation of our father Adam,
> who went forth from thee alive but stripped
> of glory, naked.
> *Remain in peace!*
> Behold, at his death was he deprived of thee
> and cast, with his progeny, in exile into
> this accursed land, where his children pass

their days in pain and sickness, toil, trouble and care.

O Cave of Treasures and Holy Bodies,
Remain in peace!

O habitation and legacy of our fathers,
Remain in peace!

O our fathers and patriarchs,
Remain in peace!

Pray for us, ye who lie in dust, O friends and beloved ones of the Living God. Pray for all those of us who remain of your posterity. Make supplication on your behalf and on our behalf in your prayers, O ye who have propitiated God.

O Seth Patriarch,
Remain in peace!

O Enos Dispenser of Justice,
Remain in peace!

O Cainan, Mahalaleel, Jared, Methusaleh, Lamech and Enoch, servants of God,
Remain in peace!

Cry out in sorrow for us!

O holy mountain,
Remain in peace!

O haven and asylum of the angels,
Remain in peace!

O ye our fathers, cry out in sorrow for us, for ye are today deprived of us; and we will lament in sorrow, for we are cast out into a barren land and our habitation will be among the wild beasts![35]

Long after the waters of the Flood had subsided, Adam was reinterred at the "center of the universe," Golgotha, by Shem and Melchisedek, who remained to minister as priest before the Most High God and to offer up bread and wine on the altar of God.

In Kisā'ī's version, on the other hand, while naturally avoiding such typically Christian symbolic prefigurations, a sense of continuity is maintained by reintroducing "props" throughout the tales. Adam's *tābūt*, for example, which means "coffer" and "sarcophagus," emerges at significant points in the narrative:

it holds the leaves of Adam's Book and is passed down through Seth and successive generations to Noah; it contains carpentry tools used by Noah to construct his ark; it is also the Ark of the Covenant carried about by the Children of Israel. All of the articles of clothing with which Jacob invests Joseph were inherited from the former prophets. Moses' staff, which he takes from Shu'ayb/Jethro, had been brought to Adam from Paradise and passed down to Seth, Idris, Noah, Salih and Abraham. In the Job narrative, Iblis stands on the very rock Cain used to kill Abel. The ram that miraculously appears to be sacrificed in Isaac's stead turns out to be the very ram that Abel offered to God. And the stones which David picks up on his way to do battle with Goliath cry out that they had belonged to his fathers Abraham, Isaac and Jacob.

The major nonbiblical prophets included in the Islamic reckoning are the South Arabians Hūd and Ṣāliḥ, who, although they do not belong to the Judeo-Christian tradition, were easily incorporated into the series of Semitic prophets by virtue of the Arabs' claim to descent from Abraham through Ishmael. The identification of Joktan with the legendary forebear of the Arab tribes, Qaḥṭān, further facilitated this assimilation.

One final observation on Kisā'ī's version of these legends: quite outside what is normally found in the "learned" strain of prophetic tales, Kisā'ī has not failed to include some "fantastic" material of the sort normally encountered in the *Arabian Nights* and similar popular literature. The background story on the Queen of Sheba's lineage, alluded to by Tha'labī, is fully developed, with details of the meeting between Sheba's father and the daughter of the king of the djinn. "Men in those days could see the djinn and go among them," says Tha'labī.[36] It should be remembered that, whereas the prophetic tales have their pious and devotional aspect, Kisā'ī's version is basically designed for popular entertainment and should ideally be recited by a professional raconteur.

A note on the proper names occurring in the Tales

There are three types of names employed by al-Kisā'ī in the *Tales*: "authentic" biblical names, "fabricated" biblical names, and Arabic proper names.

For the authentic biblical names we have, of course, English equivalents (e.g., Hebrew *Mosheh* = Arabic *Mūsā* = English *Moses*; and Hebrew *Yōsēph* = Arabic *Yūsuf* = English *Joseph*). Certain easily identifiable biblical characters have Arabic names slightly deviant from what might be expected from the Hebrew originals, owing to the intermediary of Aramaic-Syriac, through which tongue the Arabs learned the biblical stories, or to analogy with some other similar or associated name; these I have not hesitated to retain in their familiar English form (thus Hebrew *Qorāḥ* = Syriac *Qōrāḥ* = English *Korah,* but Arabic *Qārūn,* by analogy with *Hārūn,* Aaron; Hebrew *Sha'ūl* = English *Saul,* but Arabic *Tālūt,* by analogy with *Jālūt,* from Syriac *Gālūthā* from Hebrew *Galyāth* = English *Goliath*). Others, usually identified in the text by a name familiar from the biblical tradition, are known in Arabic generally by completely different names; and these have been left in their Arabic forms (e.g., *Idrīs,* identified with *Enoch* but confounded with *Hermes,* takes his Arabic name from the Greek *Andreas* or *Esdras*). *Shu'ayb* is identified by the *Tales* with *Jethro* but not in the Koran; therefore, he has been left with his Arabic name. *Iblīs* (< Gk. *diábolos*?), also called "the devil" or "Satan" (Arabic *al-shayṭān*), scarcely figures in the Old Testament; in his role as the Tempter and Leader-Astray, he is a character produced by a later mind more disposed to myth than the author of the Torah (see, e.g., Job 1:6–12; 2:1–7, Mark 1:13, Luke 22:3). As he plays an important part in Islamic lore, as well as theology, he retains his Arabic name.

By "fabricated" biblical names I mean those which cannot be traced to any similar name in Hebrew. They generally belong to quite minor characters or figure only in genealogical listings. As they have been made up in Arabic to sound like genuine Hebrew names, I have transcribed them as the King James translators would have done to retain the "biblical flavor," thus *'Āwīl ibn Lāmīl* becomes *Avel son of Lamel,* and *Shalkhā'* becomes *Shelchah.*

Authentic Arabic names, such as *Mālik ibn Dhu'r*, have been transcribed, but without scholarly diacritical pointing and macrons. All such proper names appear in the Index fully "dotted." The backwards apostrophe for the *'ayn* has been mostly replaced in the text, following the example once again of the King James translators, by an additional "a," thus Ja'far is "Jaafar."

All passages from the Arabic Koran incorporated into Kisā'ī's text have been quoted from George Sale's translation and set in italics for easy identification. Chapter and verse citations, which refer to the standard Egyptian enumeration, follow. The stylistic difference between Kisā'ī's mediæval Arabic and the language of the Koran is immediately apparent: to try and capture this distinction, with the somewhat "archaic" flavor of Koranic Arabic even in Kisā'ī's time, Sale's translation, which first appeared in 1734, removed as it is from nineteenth- and twentieth-century English, seemed the best choice. Few other translations to date have come so near to rendering the force and flow of the Arabic of the Koran without bordering on the ludicrous or the incomprehensible.

NOTES TO THE INTRODUCTION

1. The Koranic term for "bearer of glad tidings," *mubashshir* (e.g., Koran 2:213, 6:48, 33:45, &c.), is probably a loan translation from the Christian conception of the Gospel. It should be remembered that the original signification of "gospel" (Old English *gōdspell*) is precisely "good news" (= Greek *euangélion* = Arabic *bishāra*); the threats and forebodings delivered by the prophet are more in line with the Islamic conceptualization of the Judaic prophetic function.

2. See A. J. Wensinck, *The Muslim Creed*, p. 203f. The Koranic "apostles" are said to be Noah, Lot, Ishmael, Moses, Jethro, Hud, Salih, and Jesus; "prophets," in addition to the above, are Enoch, the Patriarchs, Aaron, David, Solomon, Elijah, Elisha, Job, Jonah, John [the Baptist], and Zacharias. The concept of an apostle as sent to a specific community may be derived from the Christian notion of the Apostles of Christ sent out to all the nations of the earth, hence Arabic *mursal/rasūl* = Syriac *shlīḥā* ("one sent out"), bearing a specific "message" (*risāla*). To be sure, the Arabic *rasūl* also occasionally occurs in the Koran (e.g., 22:75) in the sense of "angel" (cf. the original signification of the Greek *ángelos* ["messenger"] and its Hebrew equivalent, *mal'akh*) but very seldom,

the cognate *mal'ak/malak* being generally preferred. See J. Horovitz, *Koranische Untersuchungen*, pp. 44ff.

3. While, conversely, not every prophet was an apostle, precisely the view of John Chrysostom as quoted in Wensinck, *Muslim Creed*, p. 204. In Shiite tradition a threefold distinction is made among the apostle, the prophet, and the imam. In a reply to Zurāra, the Fifth Imam Abū Ja'far Muḥammad al-Bāqir comments on Koran 19:51 and 54, "wa-kāna rasūlan nabiyyan" ("[Moses] was an apostle ⟨and⟩ a prophet"), saying that "the prophet is one who has visions (*yarā fī manāmih*), hears the voice but does not see the angel (*lā yu'āyinu l-malak*), while the apostle hears the voice, sees the vision and sees the angel." The imam, in contrast, "hears the voice but neither has [the vision] nor sees the angel." The Eighth Imam al-Riḍā wrote in reply to a query from Ḥasan ibn al-'Abbās al-Ma'rūfī that "the difference between the apostle, the prophet and the imam is that Gabriel descends to the apostle, who sees him and hears his words, and communicates the inspiration; the apostle may also have visions like Abraham's. The prophet may hear the words [of Gabriel] and may also see [his] form without hearing the words, while the imam hears the words but does not see the form" (in Abū Ja'far Muḥammad al-Kulaynī, *al-Uṣūl,* I, 176 [translation mine]).

4. E.g., the Christian community at Nejran and the Jewish tribes of Khazraj and Naḍīr at Yathrib (later Medina). For the whole problem of a pre-Islamic Arabic scriptural tradition see A. Baumstark, "Das Problem."

5. Of the first generation of Muslims those who were sought as authorities on questions of primarily Islamic concern were men such as al-Ḍaḥḥāk ibn Muzāḥim (d. 723), Qatāda (679–736), Sa'īd ibn Jubayr (655–714), 'Aṭā ibn Abī Rabāḥ (647–732), and Mujāhid ibn Jabr (or Jubayr, 642–722), authorities on prophetic tradition, Arab genealogy, Arabian chronology and Arabic philology; see Nagel, *Die Qiṣaṣ,* pp. 26–49. On Ka'b al-Aḥbār see I. Wolfensohn, *Ka'b al-Aḥbār*; on Wahb ibn Munabbih see R. G. Khoury, *Wahb b. Munabbih*; see also Nagel, *Die Qiṣaṣ,* pp. 60–68. The knowledge transmitted by that first generation was collected and recorded by men of the second Islamic century such as Ibn Jurayj (699–767), al-Suddī (d. 745), Muḥammad ibn al-Sā'ib al-Kalbī (685–763) and his son Hishām (d. 819), and Muhammad ibn Isḥāq (704–768). Much of these men's work is recorded in the oldest extant chronology of pre-Islamic nations, the *Tārīkh* of Tabarī, as well as in miscellanies by such as Ibn Qutayba (d. 889) and geo-historio-

graphical works by such as Ya'qūbī somewhat earlier still than Tabarī.

6. Although translations of the canonical books of Judaism and Christianity were presumably available in Arabic from the end of the eighth century on (Aḥmad ibn 'Abdullāh ibn Salām [fl. ca. 800] is said to have translated "the Torah, the Gospels, the books of the prophets and apostles from the Hebrew, Greek and Sabæan into Arabic" [Ibn al-Nadīm, *Fihrist*, p. 22]) and occasional quotations from biblical translations are met with, these certainly do not form the basis for the legendary material.

7. On Old Testament apocrypha see R. H. Charles, *The Apocrypha and Pseudepigrapha*. For a list of some well- and lesser-known midrashim see D. Sidersky, *Les Origines*, pp. 3ff. For a survey of studies on haggadic sources for and parallels in Islamic legend see B. Heller, "La Légende biblique" and "Récits et personages bibliques." The parallels that can be shown in almost every instance between the Islamic and Judaic legends have been omitted entirely in the present study; Ginzberg's masterly *Legends of the Jews* is generally available for comparison.

8. For New Testament apocryphal material see E. Hennecke, *New Testament Apocrypha*.

9. For Syriac and Arabic texts and German translation of the *Me'ārath Gazzē* see C. Bezold, *Die Schatzhöhle* and A. E. W. Budge, *The Book of the Cave of Treasures* for English translation and general introduction. On Eutychius see Sezgin, *GAS*, I, 329 and Graf, *GCAL*, II, 32–35. A translation of the *Book of Adam and Eve* was made from the Ethiopic by S. C. Malan, q.v.

10. Pedersen, "The Islamic Preacher," pp. 232ff.; Massignon, *Essai*, pp. 163ff.

11. Pedersen, "The Islamic Preacher," p. 235.

12. Cf. the *qāṣṣ* as *"khaṭīb al-yaqẓa"* as opposed to the *khaṭīb* proper who read the *khuṭba* in Ibn al-Jawzī, *al-Mudhish*, p. 200, and Pedersen, ibid., 235. Note that most of the early *quṣṣāṣ* were classed as "ascetics" (*zuhhād, nussāk, 'ubbād*) and that during the course of the eighth century the ascetics were urged not to isolate themselves from everyday life but rather to engage in exhortation of the people and to deliver tearful sermons to excite the people to contrition (whence they were sometimes called *bakkā'ūn*, "weepers") with eschatological depictions (see Massignon, *Essai*, p. 165f.).

13. E.g., Ibn al-Nadīm (fl. 985), author of the *Fihrist*, mentions the beauty of the narrations (*qiṣaṣ*) of an influential theologian at Basra, Abū 'Umar Muḥammad al-Bāhilī (d. 912); and at Bukhara,

where only students of jurisprudence and Koranic commentators delivered sermons (Pedersen, "Islamic Preacher," p. 236).

14. Pedersen, "Criticism," p. 222.

15. Ibn al-Jawzī lists six reasons for which the people of earlier generations had criticized the *quṣṣāṣ*: (1) they had not been customary (*sunna*) in the time of the Prophet and were thus condemned; (2) the "stories of the ancient people were seldom authentic, especially those that were related concerning ancient Israel, while at the same time the Revelation [of the Koran] . . . was fully adequate"; (3) a preoccupation with storytelling had tended to distract some people from the more important religious sciences; (4) the stories contained in the Koran, augmented by Tradition, had rendered stories of uncertain authenticity superfluous; (5) some people introduced elements into their stories that corrupted the minds of the people; and (6) most of the *quṣṣāṣ* were not learned enough to distinguish the true from the false and therefore propagated false material unwittingly if not by design (*Kitāb al-quṣṣāṣ*, text p. 10, trs. p. 96f.).

16. Ibn al-Jawzī's *al-Mudhish*, a manual on preaching, purports to instruct in the principal techniques necessary to the preacher. Its five divisions treat respectively (1) how to read correctly and gramatically from the Koran; (2) how to interpret the words of the Book, especially how to distinguish the "abrogating" (*nāsikh*) and "abrogated" (*mansūkh*) portions thereof, and how to relate Koranic passages to Tradition; (3) the different branches of the science of Tradition; (4) how to extract and relate material from history books; and (5) in two parts, (a) on the prophetic tales and (b) one hundred examples of sermons of exhortation. The twelfth chapter of his *Kitāb al-quṣṣāṣ* is also devoted to "Directives for the *Qāṣṣ* in the Conduct of his Meetings," pp. 136–147, trs. pp. 218–234.

17. Ibn al-Jawzī *Kitāb al-quṣṣāṣ*, trs. p. 230.

18. I. Goldziher, *Muslim Studies*, II, 153.

19. Ibid., p. 156.

20. According to reports given by the historiographer Maqdisī (*al-Bad' wa'l-tārīkh*, III, 1ff.), there are said to have been 124,000 prophets, among whom 315 were apostles. According to Ibn' Munabbih, the five "Hebraic" apostles were Adam, Seth, Idris (Enoch), Noah, and Abraham, while the five "Arab" apostles were Salih, Hud, Ishmael, Shuayb (Jethro), and Muhammad. The prophets of Israel were one thousand in number from Moses to Jesus, some of whom heard the voice [of Gabriel], some of whom received their inspira-

tion in dream-visions, and some of whom were addressed directly by God (see n. 3). Further, according to Ibn Munabbih, one hundred and four books had been revealed to man, among them the Book of Seth, the Book of Enoch, the Book of Moses (which is the Torah), the Book of David (the Psalter), the Book of Jesus (the Gospel), and the Book of Muhammad (the Koran); others add the Book of Adam (see also Ibn al-Nadīm, *Fihrist*, p. 22 for substantially the same traditions reported by Aḥmad ibn ʻAbdullāh ibn Salām).

The prophets mentioned by name in the Koran are: Abraham, Isaac, Jacob, Noah, David, Solomon, Job, Joseph, Moses, Aaron, Zacharias, John [the Baptist], Jesus, Elijah, Ishmael, Elisha, Jonah, Lot, Muhammad, Hud, Salih, Shuayb (Jethro), Dhū'l-Kifl, and ʻUzayr (Ezra); those not mentioned by name but allusions to whom were later identified are: Samuel b. Elkanah, Ezekiel b. Buzi, Jeremiah, the Patriarchs (Reuben, Simeon, Levi, Judah, Issachar, Dan, Naphtali, Gad, Assher, Zebulun, and Benjamin), and three Apostles of Jesus, John, Thomas and Simon. To these those "learned in the traditions of the ancients" add: Seth b. Adam, Moses b. Menasseh b. Joseph, Dhū'l-Qarnayn, Balaam b. Beor, Joshua b. Nun, Caleb b. Jephunneh, Būshāmā [? the same as Kisā'ī's "Josephus"] b. Caleb, Isaiah b. Amoz, and [St] George [of Cappadocia]. The Jews and Christians add the following: Daniel, ʻAylā (?), Mīshyāīl (?), ʻĪlūq (?), Habbakuk, Hosea, Joel, Amos, Obadiah, Micah, Nahum, Zephaniah, Haggai, Zechariah, and Malachi. Other apostles known from Antioch were Barnabas, Lucius, Matthias (? Māthānīl), and Agapus. Three "pseudoprophetesses" (*mutanabbiyāt*) known are Mary Magdalene, Anna daughter of Phanuel, and Abigail. A tradition from Abū Hudhayfa [author of a *Book of Creation*] adds Samson, Adaryāsīn (= Adarnásēs?), the Sleepers of Ephesus (*ahl al-kahf*), and al-Khiḍr.

Again from Ibn Munabbih is a tradition that there were twenty-three prophets in Sheba, one of whom was named Ḥanẓala ibn Afyūn [usually Ṣafwān] al-Ṣādiq, and one prophet during the period between Jesus and Muhammad in Arabia named Khālid ibn Sinān al-ʻAbsī.

The Magian prophets are said to have been Jamshid, Gayumarth, Fereidun, Zoroaster, and Behâfarid. The prophets of Harran are given as Orani, Agathodæmon, Hermes, and Solon the grandfather of Plato. Another two ancients who claimed prophecy to be knowledge and practice were Socrates and Aristotle. Hindu "prophets" listed are Bahabud, Shiva of the Kābalites, Rāmān, Rāwan, and Nāshid; the Brahmins had a "prophet" named Mahādur. Dualist "prophets" are four in number, Bardaisan, Abū Shākir, Ibn Abī'l-'Awjā', and Bâbak the Khurramite.

The Muslims were not only interested in the narrative history of the early prophets but also in the relative chronology of the ancient nations and in dating world history from the creation. In his *Muḥāḍarat al-abrār* Ibn 'Arabī gives a number of traditions relating to the chronology of the ancients: according to Ibn 'Abbās the period from the creation of Adam to the appearance of the Prophet Muhammad was 5575 years. al-Kalbī breaks down this period as follows: Adam-Noah, 1200 years; Noah-Abraham, 1100; Abraham-Moses, 575; Moses-David, 1179; David-Jesus, 1365; Jesus-Muhammad, 600 (= 6019 years), while al-Wāqidī reckons the period to be 4600 years. Based on Muḥammad ibn Isḥāq the breakdown is Adam-Noah, 1200; Noah-Abraham, 1142; Abraham-Moses, 575; Moses-David, 569; David-Jesus, 1365; Jesus-Muhammad, 600 (= 5451), while Ibn Munabbih calculated 5600. According to the chronology of the Persian magi the period was 4182 years, 10 months and 19 days; the Jews make it 4640 years, and the Greek Christians 5772+ years. In another account, the "Aṣḥāb al-Rīḥān," who did not believe in prophets (? perhaps Sabæans such as the "Aṣḥāb al-Rūḥāniyyāt" [see al-Shahrastānī, *al-Milal wa'l-niḥal,* pt. 2, p. 64f.]), reckoned 3725 Persian (solar) years and 349 days from the Deluge to the Hegira (Ibn 'Arabī, *Muḥāḍarat al-abrār,* p. 120f.).

21. Numerous printings; citations here refer to Beirut edition (al-Maktaba al-Thaqāfiyya [197?]).

22. Abū 'Abdullāh Muḥammad b. Aḥmad b. Muṭarrif al-Kinānī, to whom is ascribed a *Qiṣaṣ al-anbiyā'* described briefly by Levi della Vida (*Elenco,* p. 258); for list of contents see Nagel, *Die Qiṣaṣ,* p. 167.

23. Nagel, *Die Qiṣaṣ,* p. 106.

24. Tha'labī, *'Arā'is al-majālis,* p. 2f.

25. The oldest extant version of the prophetic tales in Persian is by Ibn Khalaf of Nishapur, presumed to have been written in the fifth century of the Hegira (before 1100), the text of which has been edited by Ḥabīb Yaghmā'ī and published in the Persian Texts Series, No. 6 (Teheran: B.T.N.K., 1961). If the *Qiṣaṣ al-anbiyā' wa-siyar al-mulūk* of "Shaykh Muḥammad Ḥuwayzī (or Juwayrī)" really dated from the date given, 963, it would be not only contemporaneous with Tha'labī and Ṭarafī but also one of the oldest surviving works in Persian; unfortunately the date is most certainly a forgery. Lithographs have been done at Tabriz in 1279/1862, 1281/1864 and 1290/1873 and at Teheran in 1284/1867; see Storey,

I, i, 158. Another presumably early work is the *Qiṣaṣ al-anbiyā* by Aḥmad b. Muḥammad b. Manṣūr al-Arfajnī based on the *Takmilat al-laṭā'if wa-nuzhat al-ẓarā'if* of Abū Muḥammad 'Abd al-'Azīz al-Jasrī. Contemporary with Ibn Khalaf was Abū Naṣr al-Bukhārī, who wrote after 1082 at Balkh a large work on the prophets entitled *Tāj al-qiṣaṣ,* which contains his Koranic commentary *Anīs al-murīdīn* and should probably be considered in that category (see Storey, I, i, 29 §2 and 159 §196). In the tenth century an Arabic work entitled *Ma'aṣī al-anbiyā'* ("Disobediences of the Prophets") was written in Samarqand, but the book was said to be so full of heretical notions that it was burnt. Perhaps based to some extent on this work was the *'Iṣmat al-anbiyā'* ("Impeccability of the Prophets") of Abū'l-Ḥasan Muḥammad al-Bashāghirī, of which no copy survives; an abridgement, however, still in Arabic, was made by Nūr al-Dīn Aḥmad al-Ṣābūnī of Bukhara (d. 1184), which was very popular and was translated into Persian by Ṣābūnī's pupil, Abū 'Abdullāh Mas'ūd al-Ṣarrāf, in 1212 and entitled *Ḥiṣaṣ al-atqiyā' min qiṣaṣ al-anbiyā'* ("Portions of the Pious from the Tales of the Prophets"). Around this same time Daydūzamī's translation of Kisā'ī's version was made, and another collection was done for the Seljuq Abū'l-Muẓaffar Ibrāhīm by 'Imād al-Dīn Maḥmūd Faryābi (d. 1210) and called *Maqāṣid al-awliyā' fi maḥāsin al-anbiyā'* ("Intentions of the Saints on the Virtues of the Prophets"). Būshanjī's Arabic work was also translated into Persian by one Muḥammad b. As'ad of Tustar, the sole MS. of which is dated 1330. Thereafter the versions proliferate, especially during the sixteenth and seventeenth centuries.

There are no Turkish versions of the Tales known to have been made before the fourteenth century either in Central Asia or in Anatolia, and the first two versions extant today are almost exactly contemporary: Rabghūzī's *Qiṣaṣ al-anbiyā',* written in 1310 in Central Asia, is an adaptation of the tales from the creation down to and including the martyrdom of Husayn, grandson of the Prophet Muhammad, at Kerbela in 680, while the earliest eastern Anatolian *Qiṣaṣ* is a translation of Tha'labī, one of the few books of the time to be translated from Arabic and not Persian, made during the first decade of the fourteenth century. A unique MS. of the translation is preserved in Bursa, Ulu Cami No. 2474. Rabghūzī's *Qiṣaṣ* has been reproduced in Copenhagen; see also S. Malov, "Légendes musulmanes." Other versions extant are either paraphrases of this initial copy or new translations most likely made from the Persian translation of Kisā'ī.

26. See I. Goldziher, "The Influence of Buddhism."

27. A. Schimmel, "Sindhi Literature," p. 19.

28. For folkloristic aspects of the prophetic tales for the older period see R. Basset, *Mille et un contes,* vol. III, R. Paret, *Die Geschichte des Islams &c.,* and E. Westermarck, *Survivances païennes*; for North Africa see especially E. Doutté, *Magie et religion* and Pérès & Bousquet, *Coutumes, institutions et croyances*; for Palestine see T. Canaan, *Mohammadan Saints*; for Iran see H. Massé, *Croyances et coutumes*; for India see M. L. Dames, *Popular Poetry* and Wm. Crooke, *Popular Religion.*

29. The oldest surviving manuscript copy of Kisāʾī's *Qiṣaṣ* is the British Museum MS. dated 617/1220 (Or. 3054, see Rieu, *Supplement,* No. 497), and Storey is of the opinion that the work was not composed long before that date (Storey, I, i, 161 §200). The Berlin MS. cannot have been written before the end of the fourth Islamic century, when the latest authorities cited therein (al-Ḥusayn b. Muḥammad al-Dīnawarī, d. 393/1003, and al-Muʿāfī b. Zakariyā, d. 390/1000, neither of whom appears in the Eisenberg edition) died, thus placing that redaction sometime after 1000 (Ahlwardt, *Verzeichnis,* No. 1021). In agreement with Ahlwardt and Brockelmann, Nagel identifies the author of *Qiṣaṣ,* formerly wrongly identified as the grammarian ʿAlī b. Ḥamza al-Kisāʾī, with Abū Jaʿfar Muḥammad b. ʿAbdullāh al-Kisāʾī, author of a work on cosmology and natural phenomena entitled *ʿAjāʾib al-makhlūqāt,* which genre is not now believed to have been produced before the end of the twelfth century (Nagel, *Die Qiṣaṣ,* 137–140).

30. See Storey, I, i, 161 §200. Ḥājjī Khalīfa's comment that this work was a recension of Thaʿlabī must mean that the title was adapted from Thaʿlabī's *ʿArāʾis al-majālis* (*Kashf al-ẓunūn,* 1328). The Paris MS. dated 673/1274 is definitely translated from the Kisāʾī Arabic version (see Blochet, *Catalogue,* I, 366).

31. In Thaʿlabī's *Qiṣaṣ* Solomon is followed by the tales of Nebuchadnezzar, Hosea, Jeremiah, Daniel, Ezra, Luqmān the Sage, Balok, Dhūʾl-Qarnayn/Alexander; sections are also given on Jesus' apostles and their acts. There are also included earlier sections on Samuel and Eli, Dhūʾl-Kifl, and Ezekiel.

32. See. I. Goldziher, *Muslim Studies,* II, 159.

33. ʿAṭṭār, *Manṭiq al-ṭayr,* lines 3256–3259 and ff. [translation mine].

34. Thus ʿAzīz al-Dīn Nasafī, *al-Insān al-kāmil,* 252. See also ʿAbd al-Karīm al-Jīlānī, *al-Insān al-kāmil,* pt. 2, p. 48.

35. C. Bezold, ed., *Die Schatzhöhle*, Syriac and Arabic texts pp. 88–91 [translation mine].
36. Tha'labī, *Qiṣaṣ*, 278.

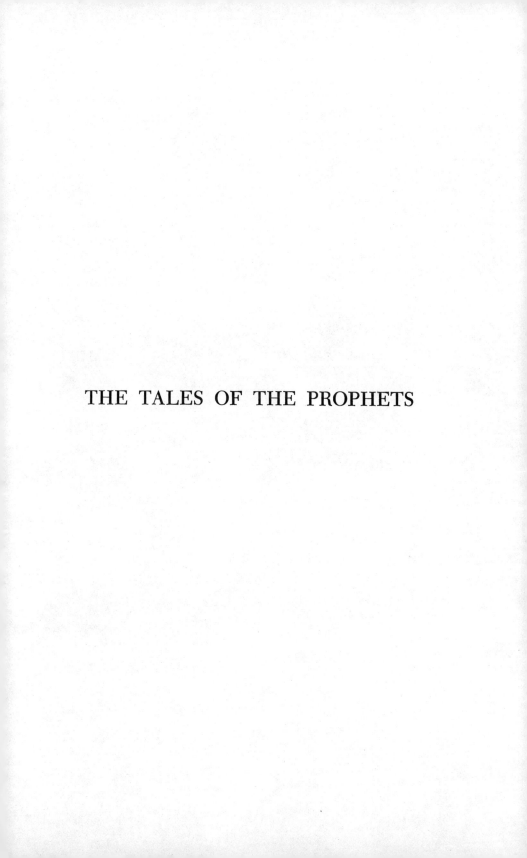

THE TALES OF THE PROPHETS

Prologue

The learned and venerable scholar Muhammad ibn Abdullah al-Kisa'i has said:

Praise be to God, who has caused creatures to germinate as living organisms, gave them life from a state of death, gathered them together from a state of dispersal, and moved them from layer to layer. He then made them embryos from blood clots, split them apart and rent them asunder, bound them about with sinews, inserted in them stalks, fixed in them veins like flowing rivers, brought forth upon them flesh, and caused blood to spring forth; then He fashioned them into bodies, and enveloped them with skin. He breathed the spirit into them, beginning with the cranium, established in them movement and rest, and made in them well-ordered ribs and harmonious organs. In them He created the five senses, that knowledge of the perceived and perception of the tangible be clear to them, then He sent them forth with limited excellence, that it keep them to their reckoned purpose. He caused milk to flow abundantly for their sustenance, inclined hearts favorably toward them as a natural disposition, bestowed them amply with favor, and raised them up to knowledge that they might attain perfection and distinguish truth from error. He charged them with no more than they could endure and burdened them with no more than they could bear; and He urged them to discern and taught them by example, that they might know that God is capable of every thing and that God's knowledge encompasses all things.

Praise therefore be to Him who is the master-builder and object of admiration, who created you, fashioned you and set you in order; in whatsoever form He pleased He made you.

Blessed be God, the Most Excellent Creator; and His prayers and peace be with the best of all His creation, Muhammad, Seal of the Prophets, Apostle of the Lord of the Universe, and with his house and companions all!

In this book have I gathered what should properly attract the attention concerning the creation of heaven and earth, the djinn and mankind, and the conditions of the prophets according to such reports as have reached us. After having worked diligently on it and tested what is near to and far from being agreeable with the truth, this is what I have set down. As for what was contrary to the truth, the offense belongs to the one who first wrote it. And what is my prosperity save through God, in whom have I verily put my trust, who is my Recompense: how excellent is trust in Him!

1. *The Tablet and the Pen*

Ibn Abbas[1] said: The first thing God created was the Preserved Tablet, on which was preserved all that has been and ever shall be until the Day of Resurrection. What is contained thereon no one knows but God. It is made of white pearl.

Then, from a gem, He created a Pen, the length of which would take five hundred years to traverse. The end of it is cloven, and from it light flows as ink flows from the pens of the people of this world. The Pen was told, "Write!" And, as the Pen trembled because of the awesomeness of the proclamation, it began to reverberate in exaltation, as thunder reverberates. Moved by God, it flowed across the Tablet, writing what is to be until the Last Day, whereat the Tablet was filled and the Pen ran dry. And he who is to be happy shall be, and he who is to be wretched shall be.

2. *The Creation of Water*

Ibn Abbas said: After that, God created in the backbone of the heavens and the earths a white pearl with seventy thousand tongues to glorify Him. With each of these tongues it glorifies Him in seventy thousand languages.

Kaab said:[2] It has eyes so large that if the towering mountain peaks were cast into them, they would be like flies on the surface of the Great Sea.

Then God spoke to the pearl; and, because of the majesty of the proclamation, it trembled so much that it became moving water, with waves swelling and crashing against each other.

In time, however, everything became lax in praising God except water, which has never ceased to glorify God, for its act of exaltation is its quaking and movement. For this reason God preferred water over any other created thing and made it the basis for creation, as He hath said: *And we made every living thing of water. Will they not therefore believe?* (31.30) Then the water was told, "Be still!" And it was still, awaiting God's command. This is limpid water, which contains neither impurity nor foam.

3. *The Creation of the Canopy and the Throne*[3]

Then, from a green jewel, God created the Canopy, neither the magnificence nor the light of which can be described. And the Canopy He placed on the surface of the waters.

Wahb said: There is no book of the ancients in which the Canopy and the Throne are not mentioned. God created them from two great jewels.

Kaab said: The Canopy has seventy thousand tongues, each of which glorifies God in diverse languages. And it was upon the waters, as He hath said: *His throne was above the waters* (11.7).

Ibn Abbas said: Every builder first lays the foundation and then raises the roof; but God created the roof first, for He created the Canopy before the heavens and the earths.

Then God created the winds and gave them wings, the number of which only God knows. He commanded them to bear up the waters; and it was done. Then the Canopy rested upon the waters, and the waters upon the winds.

Then God created the bearers of the Canopy, which are today four in number. On the Day of Resurrection He will add four more, as He hath said: *And eight shall bear the throne of thy Lord above them, on that day* (69.17). They are of a magnificence that does not admit description, and each of them has four faces. The face like that of man intercedes for the sustenance of human kind; the face like that of a bull intercedes for the sustenance of beasts of burden; the face like that of a lion intercedes for the sustenance of wild beasts; and the face like that of an eagle intercedes for the sustenance of birds.

Ibn Abbas said: The Throne is of a jewel which is the generic opposite of the jewel from which God created the Canopy.

Wahb[4] said: There are angels bended on their knees and standing, bearing up the Canopy on their shoulders. Occasionally they grow so weak that the Canopy is borne only by the Might of God. The Throne is made from the light of the Canopy. It is said that the Throne is God's knowledge.

It is also said that the Canopy is God's knowledge of His creation, but this is invalid in view of what Abu Dharr al-Ghifari[5] has related on the authority of the Apostle of God: "I asked the Apostle of God, 'Which is the best verse in the Koran?' 'The Throne-verse,' he answered. Then he added, 'In comparison to the Throne, the seven heavens are like a patch of clothing thrown into an open plain. And the Canopy is as superior to the Throne as the plain is to the patch.' "

Kaab al-Ahbar said: Then God created a great serpent to surround the Canopy. Its head is of white pearl and its body is of gold. Its eyes are two sapphires, and no one can comprehend the magnitude of this serpent except God. It has forty thousand wings made of different kinds of jewels, and on each feather there stands an angel holding a jeweled lance, praising God and blessing His name. When this serpent extols God, its exaltation overwhelms that of all the angels. When it opens its mouth, the heavens and the earths are lit by the lightning that flashes. Were not this serpent tempered by extolling God, it would strike down all created things with the might of its voice.

It is said that the serpent greeted our Prophet Muhammad on the night of his ascent into heaven and gave him glad tidings concerning himself and his community.

The Canopy is the Canopy of Might and Majesty, and the Throne is the Throne of Glory and Splendor; but God has no need of them, inasmuch as He was neither *on* a place nor *in* a place before they were brought into existence.

4. *The Creation of the Earth, the Mountains and the Seas*

Kaab al-Ahbar said: When God wished to create the dry land, He commanded the wind to churn up the waters. When they had become turbulent and foamy, waves swelled and gave off vapor. Then God commanded the foam to solidify, and it became dry. In two days He created the dry land on the face of the waters, as He hath said: *Say, do ye indeed disbelieve in him who created the earth in two days?* (41:9). Then He commanded these waves to be still, and they formed the mountains, which He used as pegs to hold down the earth, as He hath said: *And we placed stable mountains on the earth lest it should move with them* (21:31). Were it not for the mountains, the earth would not have been stable enough for its inhabitants. The veins of these mountains are connected with the veins of Mount Qaf, which is the range that surrounds the earth.

Then God created the seven seas. The first is called Baytush and surrounds the earth from behind Mount Qaf.[6] Behind it is a sea called Asamm, behind which is a sea called Qaynas, behind which is a sea called Sakin, behind which is a sea called Mughallib, behind which is a sea called Muannis, behind which is a sea called Baki, which is the last. These are the seven seas, and each of them surrounds the sea before it. The rest of the seas, in which are creatures whose number only God knows, are like gulfs to these seven. God created sustenance for all these creatures on the fourth day, as He hath said: *And he provided therein the food of the creatures designed to be the inhabitants thereof, in four days; equally, for those who ask* (41:10).

There are seven earths.[7] The first is called Ramaka, beneath which is the Barren Wind, which can be bridled by no fewer than seventy thousand angels. With this wind God destroyed the people of Ad. The inhabitants of Ramaka are a nation called Muwashshim, upon whom is everlasting torment and divine retribution. The second earth is called Khalada, wherein are the implements of torture for the inhabitants of Hell. There dwells a nation called Tamis, whose food is their own flesh and whose drink is their own blood. The third earth is called Arqa, wherein dwell mulelike eagles with spearlike tails. On each tail are three hundred and sixty poisonous quills. Were even one quill placed on the face of the earth, the entire universe would pass away. The inhabitants thereof are a nation called Qays, who eat dirt and drink mothers' milk. The fourth earth is called Haraba, wherein dwell the snakes of Hell, which are as large as mountains. Each snake has fangs like tall palm trees, and if they were to strike the hugest mountain with their fangs it would be leveled to the ground. The inhabitants of this earth are a nation called Jilla, and they have no eyes, hands or feet but have wings like bats and die only of old age. The fifth earth is called Maltham, wherein stones of sulphur hang around the necks of infidels. When the fire is kindled the fuel is placed on their breasts, and the flames leap up onto their faces, as He hath said: *The fire whose fuel is men and stones* (2:24), and *Fire shall cover their faces* (14:50). The inhabitants are a nation called Hajla, who are numerous and who eat each other. The sixth earth is called Sijjin. Here are the registers of the people of Hell, and their works are vile, as He hath said: *Verily the register of the actions of the wicked is surely in Sijjin* (83.7). Herein dwells a nation called Qatat, who are shaped like birds and worship God truly. The seventh earth is called Ajiba and is the habitation of Iblis. There dwells a nation called Khasum, who are black and short, with claws like lions. It is they who will be given dominion over the Gog and Magog, who will be destroyed by them.

* * *

And the earth was tossed about with its inhabitants like a ship, so God sent down an angel of extreme magnitude and strength and ordered him to slip beneath the earth and bear it up on his shoulders. He stretched forth one of his hands to the East and the other to the West and took hold of the earth from end to end. However, there was no foothold for him, so God created from an emerald a square rock, in the middle of which were seven thousand holes. In each hole was a sea, the description of which is known only to God. And He commanded the rock to settle beneath the angel's feet. The rock, however, had no support, so God created a great bull with forty thousand heads, eyes, ears, nostrils, mouths, tongues and legs and commanded it to bear the rock on its back and on its horns.[8] The name of the bull is al-Rayyan. As the bull had no place to rest its feet, God created a huge fish, upon whom no one may gaze because it is so enormous and has so many eyes. It is even said that if all the seas were placed in one of its gills, they would be like a mustard seed in the desert. This fish God commanded to be a foothold for the bull, and it was done. The name of this fish is Behemoth.[9] Then He made its resting place the waters, beneath which is the air, and beneath the air is the Darkness, which is for all the earths. There, beneath the Darkness, the knowledge of created things ends.

* * *

Next God created the Soul Rational (*'aql*) and said to it, "Draw nigh!" and it drew nigh. Then He said to it, "Draw back!" and it drew back. "By My Majesty and Splendor," God said, "I have not created anything so beloved to me as thee. Through thee I shall take away and through thee shall I give. Through thee I shall reward and through thee shall I punish."

When asked how sin affects the beauty of the Soul Rational, the Prophet said, "God forgives its sins, and the excellence of the Soul remains intact. It shall surely enter Paradise." He also said, "The one possessed of Reason is truthful, long of silence, and men are spared his evil. On the Day of Judgment God will not punish the rational man as He will punish the ignorant one, who lies with his bold tongue about what does not concern him, even though he be able to read and write."

The Prophet also said, "Nothing adorns the servant of God more beautifully than Reason, and nothing is more odious than ignorance."

Abu Hurayra said:[10] "He whose sorrow is great today will rejoice tomorrow, and he whose joy is great today will sorrow tomorrow. Anyone who thinks that one person is better than another by any criterion except good health is ignorant. On the Day of Resurrection the rational man will attain degrees which those who fast and pray will not, and those who strive most truly are those who are the most rational."

It is said that Kaab al-Ahbar's last advice to his son was this:

"O my son, there is nothing better than reason adorned with knowledge, or knowledge with piety, or piety with certainty, or certainly with compassion, or compassion with politeness, or politeness with humility, or humility with godliness, or godliness with right guidance. So, my son, be possessed of these qualities and you shall excel the great among men."

5. *The Creation of the Heavens and the Angels*

Ibn Abbas said: Then God commanded the vapors emanating from the waters to rise up into the air. In two days He created from them the firmament. In four days He created what is between the sea and the firmament. Then the heavens were ripped apart from the earth out of fear of the majesty of God. And there were seven heavens and seven earths, as He hath said: *Do not the unbelievers therefore know, that the heavens and the earth were solid, and we clave the same in sunder* (21.30). And, as He hath said: *And he formed them into seven heavens, in two days* (41.12), from the rising of the sun and moon and stars.

The first heaven is of emerald and is called Birqi': its inhabitants are angels shaped like cows. God made one angel, named Ismael, the guardian. The second heaven is of ruby and is called Faydum: its inhabitants are angels shaped like hawks; the angel in charge of them is named Michael and is the guardian of this heaven. The third heaven is of topaz and is called Awn: its inhabitants are angels in the shape of eagles, and the angel responsible for them is named Saadiael. The fourth heaven is of silver and is called Arqlun: its inhabitants are angels shaped like horses, and the angel in charge of them is named Salsael. The fifth heaven is of red gold and is called Ratqa: the inhabitants are angels that look like the houris, and the angel in charge of them is called Kalkael. The sixth heaven is of white pearl and is called Rafqa: its inhabitants are angels that look like children, and the angel responsible for them is named Shamkhael. The seventh heaven is of light that glows like pearl and is called Gharibya: its inhabitants are angels in the form of men, and their warden is called Razqael.[11]

Kaab al-Ahbar said: These angels never cease glorifying and praising God, be they standing, sitting, kneeling, or prostrate, as He hath said: *They praise him night and day; they faint not* (21.20).

Abdullah ibn Salam said:[12] They are cherubim and seraphim, aligned and encompassing, kneeling and prostrate. Among them are those who stand between mountains of light on a high place and exalt Him and bless His name.

Wahb said: Above the seven heavens are veils in which are so many angels that they do not even know each other. They praise God in divers tongues, like peals of thunder.

Ibn Abbas said: Above the veils are angels whose legs have pierced as far as a five hundred years' journey below the seven heavens and earths. Their feet extend like white banners below the seventh and lowest earth.

Kaab said: Gabriel is the most exalted of the angels and is known as the Faithful Spirit. He has six wings, on each of which are a hundred wings, and behind these are two green wings he spreads only for the destruction of towns. All of his wings are of various jewels. Moreover, he has full whiskers, flashing teeth, white skin, and black hair. His body is as white as snow, his feet are enveloped in light, and his face fills the horizons.

Aïsha said:[13] "Kaab, I have heard the Prophet of God say, 'O Lord of Gabriel and Michael and Israfel, forgive me!' Now I have heard tell of Gabriel and Michael in the Koran, but tell me about Israfel."

"O Mother of the Faithful," said Kaab, "I will tell you about him and others. As for Israfel, he is a great angel with four wings. with one wing he barricades the East, with the second the West; with the third he blocks what is between heaven and the earth, and with the fourth he has veiled God's magnitude. His feet are below the seventh and lowest earth, and his head reaches to the pillars of the Throne. Over his head is a tablet made of a jewel. Whenever God wills to act directly among His servants, He commands the Pen to write on the Tablet, which sweeps down to Israfel and comes to rest before his eyes. Finally it comes to Gabriel, who is closer to the world than Israfel, and he executes whatever God has commanded, as He hath said: *That God might accomplish the thing which was decreed to be done"* (8.44).

* * *

Kaab said: Beyond the Visited House are angels whose number no one knows save God, in charge of which God placed an angel with seventy thousand tongues to praise Him.[14] Above him are other angels, and above these are even greater angels. Between them is a veil so that those who are below will not be scorched. Above these are the greatest angels, from whose mouths fall burning embers when they praise God. From these embers God creates angels that fly through the air praising Him, and between the angels are veils so that those below will not be burnt by these embers. Above all of these is an angel in the form of man. Were God to give him permission to swallow the heavens and the earths, he could easily do so. He is the spirit about whom God hath said: *The day wherein the spirit Gabriel and the other angels shall stand in order, they shall not speak in behalf of themselves or others, except he only to whom the Merciful shall grant permission, and who shall say that which is right* (78.38). Above him are angels of even greater magnitude and who praise God even more.

Ibn Abbas said: God has angels who roam about in the air and gather in places where *dhikr* and prayer are held.[15] They guarantee the prayers of Muslims, and no one save God knows their number.

* * *

It is related that the Prophet said to Gabriel one day, "Gabriel, I should like to see you in the most magnificent form that God created for you."

"Beloved of God," said Gabriel, "I have such an awesome form that neither you nor anyone else could bear to see it without falling down in a swoon."

"But I want to gaze upon you in your greatest form," insisted the Prophet.

"Where then do you want to see me?" asked Gabriel.

"Outside Mecca, in the valley."

"Beloved of God," said Gabriel, "the valley is not big enough."

"Then on Mount Arafat."

As the Prophet was headed for Arafat, suddenly there came a great rustle and clashing, and a face was blocking out the horizons. When the Prophet looked, he fell down in a swoon. Gabriel resumed his former shape and came to the Prophet, embraced and kissed him, and said, "Fear not, Beloved of God, for I am your brother Gabriel."

"You spoke the truth, Gabriel," said the Prophet. "I did not suspect that any of God's creatures had such a form!"

Then Gabriel said, "O Beloved of God, if you were to see Israfel, you would think *my* form but small and insignificant!"

* * *

Kaab al-Ahbar said: In the seventh heaven is the Fiery Sea, in which are angels who hold jeweled spears. Each spear is a year's journey long. God made an angel named Michael—whom no one but God himself could describe—warden over this sea. Were Michael to open his mouth, the heavens would be like a mustard seed in the deep sea by comparison. Were he to reveal himself to the people of heaven and earth, they would be consumed by his light. He is in charge of the Fiery Sea and its angels.

Kaab said: As for the Angel of Death, his name is Azrael, and his abode is in the heaven of this earth. God created for him the same number of helpers as those who shall taste death. His legs are on the borders of the seventh and lowest earth, his head is in the seventh and highest heaven at the Last Partition, and his face is turned toward the Preserved Tablet. He has three hundred and sixty eyes, in each of which are three eyes; he has three hundred and sixty tongues, in each of which are three tongues; he has three hundred and sixty hands, in each of which are three hands; and he has three hundred and sixty feet, in each of which are three feet. He has four wings: one in the East, one in the West, one at the Last Partition, and one under the limits of the seventh and lowest earth. He gazes on the Preserved Tablet, and all creation is depicted before his eyes. No creature's soul is taken except after his livelihood is exhausted and his purpose fulfilled. The souls of the faithful he seizes with his right hand and places in Illiyyin; the souls of infidels he seizes with his left hand and places in Sijjin until Doomsday.[16]

6. *The Creation of the Sun and Moon*

Wahb said: Then God created the sun and the moon. The sun. He created from the light of the Throne, and the moon He created from the light of His veil.

Kaab used to say that on the Day of Resurrection the sun and the moon will be led like bulls and hurled into Hell. When Ibn Abbas heard this, he grew angry and said, "Kaab has lied. God praised the sun and the moon, saying, *He likewise compelleth the sun and the moon, which diligently perform their courses, to serve you* (14.33). How then can they be cast into Hell?"

Wahb ibn Munabbih said: God entrusted the sun and the moon to angels who send them out for a while and draw them back for a while, as He hath said: *God causeth the night to succeed the day, and he causeth the day to succeed the night* (22.61). Therefore,. what is subtracted from one period is added to the other.

The people of the Torah say that God began to create on a Sunday and finished on a Saturday, whereupon He sat on the Throne; therefore, they have adopted that day as a holiday. The Christians say that the beginning fell on a Monday and the end on a Sunday, whereat He sat upon the Throne; therefore they have adopted that day as a holiday.

Ibn Abbas said: The beginning was on Saturday and the end on Friday. God rested on Friday, so for that reason we have made it a holiday.

The Prophet said that Friday is the mistress of the days of the week and is greater in God's view than *Id al-Fitra* and *Yawm al-Adha*.[17] Friday has five significances: on that day Adam was created, the spirit was breathed into him, he was married on that day, and on that day He took him unto Himself. Also on that day is a time during which God's servants ask their Lord for nothing He does not grant (a variant report adds: . . . so long as it not be a thing forbidden).

And on that day will Doomsday commence.

7. *The Creation of Paradise and Hell*

Ibn Abbas said: Then God created Paradise, which consists of eight gardens. The first is the Abode of Splendor and is made of white pearl; the second is the Abode of Peace and is of ruby; the third is the Garden of Refuge and is of emerald. The fourth is the Garden of Eternity and is of yellow coral; the fifth is the Garden of Grace and is of white silver; the sixth is the Garden of Paradise and is of red gold. The seventh is the Garden of Tranquility and is of pungent musk. The eighth is the Garden of Eden and is made of glimmering pearl. It has two gates and two portals made of gold, the distance between which is the same as the distance between heaven and earth. Its edifices are made of alternating silver and gold bricks, its tile is musk, its dust is ambergris, its grass is saffron. Its palaces are made of pearl and the chambers therein are of sapphire; the gates are made of gems.

Ibn Abbas said: The best rivers of Paradise are six. The first is the River of Mercy, which flows through all of the gardens. The pebbles in it are pearls, and its water is whiter than milk and sweeter than honey. Then there is the River Cawthar, on the banks of which grow trees of pearl and sapphire. This river is for our Prophet Muhammad, as God hath said: *Verily we have given thee al Cawthar* (108.1). Next is the River of Camphor, the River Tasnim, the River Salsabil, then the River of Rahiq-makhtum. Beyond these are rivers the number of which only God knows, for they are more numerous than the stars in the sky; and likewise the mansions found therein.

The eight gardens have gates of gold set with precious stones. Engraven on the first gate is:

THERE IS NO GOD BUT GOD
MUHAMMAD IS THE APOSTLE OF GOD.

On the second gate is inscribed:

THE GATE OF THOSE WHO PRAY THE FIVE PRAYERS WITH COMPLETE ABLUTION AND WITH ALL THE PRINCIPAL PARTS OF THE PRAYERS.

On the third is:

THE GATE OF THOSE WHO GIVE ALMS READILY AND WILLINGLY.

On the fourth is written:

THE GATE OF THOSE WHO ENJOIN JUSTICE AND FORBID INJUSTICE.

Over the fifth is written:

THE GATE OF THOSE WHO HAVE RIDDED THEMSELVES OF PASSION.

On the sixth gate is:

THE GATE OF PILGRIMS OF THE MAJOR AND MINOR PILGRIMAGES.

On the seventh is:

THE GATE OF THOSE WHO STRIVE IN THE WAY OF RELIGION.

And on the eighth is written:

THE GATE OF ASPIRANTS WHO CAST DOWN THEIR GAZE & PERFORM GOOD WORKS SUCH AS HONORING THEIR PARENTS AND FULFILLING FAMILIAL OBLIGATIONS.

Through these gates enter those who have performed works in accordance with the inscriptions.

Inside are beautiful, white-skinned, dark-eyed houris, whose beauty no one could describe except He who created them. Also in the gardens are beautiful houris, the likes of whom no eye has seen nor ear heard, nor has the likes of them ever occurred to the mind of man. There is also that which satisfies the soul and gives pleasure to the eye, and there is favor such as will never cease or end. This God has prepared for His pious and devout servants.

A Description of Hell.

Wahb ibn Munabbih said: There are seven gates to Hell, and it would take five hundred years to travel between any two of the seven. Through each gate are seventy thousand kinds of torture: cords, fetters, shackles, chains, poisons, hot water and bitter fruit.

The first is Gehenna. The second is Laza, which is for idolators. The third is Hutama, which is for the Gog and Magog and infidels like them. The fourth is Saïr, which is for the devil, as God hath said: *For whom we have prepared the torment of burning fire* (67.5). The fifth is Saqar, which is for those who do not pray and give alms, as He hath said: *What hath brought you into hell? They shall answer, We were not of those who were constant at prayer, neither did we feed the poor; and we waded in vain dispute with the fallacious reasoners; and we denied the day of judgment, until death overtook us* (74.42-47). The sixth is Jahim, which is for Jews, Christians and Majians. The seventh is Hawiya, which is for hypocrites, as He hath said: *The hypocrites shall be in the lowest bottom of hell fire* (4.145). This is all taken from His word: *It hath seven gates; unto every gate a distinct company of them shall be assigned* (15.44).[18]

Ibn Abbas said: Paradise is to the right of the Throne and Hell is to the left, and it has seven heads.

Kaab al-Ahbar said: It has seven layers, seven gates and seven heads, each of which has thirty-three mouths. In each mouth are innumerable tongues which praise God in various manners. There are trees of fire, the thorns of which are like long spears and blaze with flame. Upon them are fruits of fire, and on each fruit is a serpent which takes the infidel by his eyelashes and lips and strips off his skin down to his feet. There are also Myrmidons that hold iron bludgeons, on the ends of each of which are three hundred and sixty rods of fire such that neither the djinn nor men could bear even one. Over them are nineteen angels, as God hath said: *It scorcheth men's flesh: over the same are nineteen* (74.29-30) who do not disobey God and carry out their orders.

8. *The Creation and Beginning of the Djinn & Iblis' Period of Worship*

Wahb said: When God created the fire of Samum, which is a heatless, smokeless fire, He created the father of the genii, Jann, from it, as He hath said: *And we had before created the genii of subtle fire* (15.27).

God made the first Jann an enormous creature and called him Marij.[19] From him he also created a mate called Marija. Then Marij lay with Marija, and she bore him a son called Jinn, from whom branched out the tribes of the djinn. Iblis the Accursed also sprang from this race. Jann produced males and Jinn females. The males were mated to the females, and they grew to number seventy thousand tribes, ever-increasing until their number was like unto the sands of the desert. Iblis married a woman from the offspring of Jann, called Ruha daughter of Shalshael son of Jann, and she bore twins, first Balaqis and Qutruba, and then Faqtas and Faqtasa. The children of Iblis multiplied until they became innumerable, and they crawled on their faces like tiny specks, ants, gnats, locusts and birds. They inhabited caves, wastelands, gardens, hills, roads, dumps, lavatories, wells, rivers, crannies, cellars, and every dark and evil place until all regions of the earth were filled with them. Then they appeared in the form of oxen, mules, asses, camels, cattle, sheep, dogs and lions.

When the land had become filled with the offspring of Iblis the Accursed, God caused the offspring of Jann to inhabit the air below heaven and the children of Jinn the first heaven. He commanded them to worship and obey Him, as He hath said: *I have not created genii and men for any other end than that they should serve me* (51.56).

Then God told the angels, "I have created two abodes, one from my Mercy and the other from my Wrath. Gaze upon them both." The angels' eyes became fixed upon Gehenna and, seeing its pillars and strata and all the different types of torture there, they asked God to tell them for whom it was. God caused the fire to speak and it said, "I was created as a habitation and torture for the treacherous and those who deny God's unity." Then the angels gazed upon Paradise and all that God had provided therein for its inhabitants.

"Our God," they said, "for whom hast thou created this abode?"

God commanded Paradise to speak in answer, and it said, *"Now are the true believers happy"* (23.1).

"Then it has been created for us," they said, "for we are the believers."

But Paradise added, *"Who humble themselves in their prayer, and who eschew all vain discourse, and who are doers of alms-deeds and who keep themselves from carnal knowledge of any women except their wives, or the captives which their right hands possess (for as to them they shall be blameless: but whosoever coveteth any woman beyond these, they are transgressors): and who acquit themselves faithfully of their trust, and justly perform their covenant; and who observe their appointed times of prayer: these shall be the heirs, who shall inherit Paradise; they shall continue therein for ever"* (23.2–11). And the angels knew for certain that it had been created for beings other than themselves.

Then God said to them, "I have created this abode for those who obey Me from among those whom I shall create by mine own command and with mine own hands, into whom I shall breathe my spirit, before whom I shall cause my angels to prostrate, and whom I shall prefer over all my creation." Thus He spoke.

* * *

Heaven boasted to the earth, saying "My Lord has raised me above you, and I am the loftiest creation, the dwelling-place of angels. In me are the Throne, the Canopy, the Pen, the sun, the moon, and the stars. In me are the storehouses of mercy and from me divine inspiration descends to you."

"O my God," cried the earth, "thou has stretched me out flat and hast entrusted me with the growth of trees and plants and with springs. Thou hast anchored the mountains on my back and hast created upon me all kinds of fruits. Heaven boasts to me of the angels who glorify thee that dwell in her. I have been overtaken by wilderness, and there is not a creature upon me to make mention of thee."

"Be still!" the earth was told, "for I shall create from thy dust a form which shall have no equal in beauty. I shall provide it with reason and speech and shall teach it of mine own knowledge and shall cause my angels to descend to it. Then from it shall I fill thy womb and loins and thy east and west. So take pride, O my earth, and boast to my heaven of that." And the earth was happy, and she was white and immaculate, as though of gleaming silver.

* * *

Then the djinn looked down upon the earth and saw the wild animals, predatory beasts and crawling things that were in it and asked to let them alight upon it. He gave them permission to do so on condition that they worship Him and not disobey Him. They made these promises unto Him and descended, seventy thousand clans in number. They worshipped God truly for a long time, but then they began to disobey and shed blood, so that the earth cried for help against them, saying, "My God, I would rather be empty than have upon my back those who disobey thee."

"Be still!" said God to the earth, "for I shall send them an apostle."

Kaab al-Ahbar said that the first prophet God sent to the genii was Amir ibn Umayr ibn al-Jann, but they killed him. Then He sent Saïq ibn Naïq ibn Marid, and they killed him also. This continued until He had sent eight hundred prophets, one a year for eight hundred years; but they killed them all. Since they had denied all the apostles, God told the children of Jinn, who dwelt in the sky, to descend to the earth and wage war against the children of Jann. They descended, Iblis the Accursed among them, and fought the children of Jann until they had driven them into a corner of the earth; and they worshipped God truly.

Since Iblis' worship was greater than that of any of them, God raised him to the heaven of the earth, where he worshipped God for a thousand years and was called The Worshipper.[20] Then God raised him to the second heaven and continued to elevate him until he had reached the seventh heaven. It is said that he was in the first heaven on Saturday, the second on Sunday, the third on Monday, and so on until Friday, when he was in the seventh heaven. So every day he worshipped God in a different heaven, and each of those days was equivalent to a thousand years.

Iblis held an exalted station among the angels. Whenever Gabriel and Michael and the others passed by him, they would say, "God has given this servant an ability to obey God such as He has given to no angel."

* * *

Long ages afterward, God commanded Gabriel to alight upon the earth and take a handful of dust from the East, the West, the plains, and the mountains so that He might fashion a new creation destined to be the best of all creatures. Iblis learned of this and, coming down, stood upon the midst of the earth and said, "O Earth, I have come to you as an advisor."

"What is your advice, O chief of the ascetics?" asked the Earth.

"God wishes to fashion from you a creature which He will prefer over all His creation, but I fear that the creature will disobey God and will be tormented in Hell," said Iblis. "Gabriel has been sent down to you to gather dust. When he comes, make him swear not to take anything from you."

Therefore, when Gabriel alighted upon the Earth, she cried out, "O Gabriel, for the sake of Him who sent you to me, take not anything from me, for I fear He will fashion from me a creature who will disobey Him and will be sent to torment in Hell." Gabriel trembled at this oath and returned without taking anything from the earth and informed God, who is all-knowing. Then God sent Michael to bring a handful of dust, but he fared no better than Gabriel. Then God sent Azrael, the Angel of Death; and when he was about to take the handful of dust, the earth swore as she had to Gabriel. The Angel of Death, however, said to her, "By the Might and Majesty of my Lord,

I shall not disobey Him in anything He commands me to do." Then he took from all places, the pleasant, the sweet, the salty, the bitter, the aromatic and the noxious, and from all colors (and all the children of Adam are created from that very dust). When the Angel of Death returned with the handful of dust, he stood in his place for forty years without speaking. Then the Voice of God came to him, asking, "O Azrael, what have you done?" (and God is, of course, all-knowing). The angel told Him what happened to him with the Earth, and God said, "By my Might and Majesty, verily shall I fashion a creature from what thou hast brought and verily shall I give thee dominion over the taking of its soul, because of thy little compassion."

Then God put half of that measure of earth in Paradise and half in Hell. God, be He exalted, spoke, saying:

"I AM GOD WHO DESTINES. FOR ME NO ONE DESTINES."

9. *The Creation of Adam*

Wahb ibn Munabbih said: God created Adam's head from the first earth, his neck from the second, his chest from the third, his hands from the fourth, his belly and loins from the fifth, his thighs and buttocks from the sixth, and his legs and feet from the seventh. He called him Adam because He created him from the surface (*adīm*) of the earth.

Ibn Abbas said: God created him from the climes of the world: his head from the dust of the Kaaba and his chest from the dust of the desert, his belly and loins from the soil of India, his hands from the east and his feet from the west.

Wahb ibn Munabbih said: God created in him nine doors, seven in his head, which are the two eyes, two ears, two nostrils, and mouth, and two in his body. In his nostrils God created the faculty of smell, in his mouth the faculty of taste, in his hands the faculty of touch. He created in his eyes the faculty of sight, in his ears the faculty of hearing, and in his feet the faculty of walking. In his mouth He created for him a tongue, by means of which he might speak, and also four middle incisors, four canine teeth, four eyeteeth, and sixteen molars. Then in his neck He placed eight vertebrae and in his back fourteen; on the right side He placed eight ribs and on the left seven, one crooked, with the foreknowledge that from it He would create Eve. Then He created the heart and placed it on the left side of the chest. He created the stomach in front of the heart, and He made the lungs like fans for the heart. The liver He created and placed on the right side and established in it bitterness. The spleen He created on the left side, subservient to the liver. He created the kidneys, one above the liver and the other above the spleen. Between the kidneys and below the rib cartilage of the chest cavity He placed the diaphragms and inserted the ribs into them.

He created the bones: one in the shoulder, one in the chest, two in the forearms, five in the palm and three in every finger except the thumb, in which there are two. In the hips He placed two bones, in the thighs two, in the knee two, in the leg two, in the heel two, in the foot ten, and in every toe three, except the big toe, in which there are two. Then He inserted in him the vessels, the major one of which He made the aorta, the home of blood, from which blood gushes throughout the body. The vessels are various: there are four which feed the brain, four the eyes, four the ears, four in the nostrils, four in the lips, two in the temples, two in the tongue, two for the teeth, two for the molars. Two vessels transport blood from the brain to the kidneys and two veins lift cold blood from the kidneys to the brain; seven feed the neck, seven the chest, ten the belly, and the rest of the veins feed the rest of the body and they are so numerous that no one but God knows their number. The tongue is an interpreter, the eyes are two lamps; the ears are for hearing, the nostrils are for breathing; the hands are like two wings, and the feet are for walking. In the liver is compassion, in the spleen is mirth, in the kidneys are guile and deceit; the lungs are a fan, and the stomach is a storehouse. The heart is the dean of the body—when it is corrupt, all of the body is corrupt; when it is sound, all of the body is sound.[21]

Wahb ibn Munabbih said: When God had created Adam in this form, He commanded the angels to bear him to the gate of Paradise, where the angels passed to and fro. At that time he was merely a body without spirit, as He hath said: *Did there not pass over man a long space of time; during which he was a thing not worthy of remembrance?* (76.1) (that is, he was not a shapen thing).

Kaab said: The angels marveled at the strangeness of his form and figure, for they had never seen anything like him. Iblis looked at him for a long time before saying, "God has created this thing for some great purpose. Perhaps He himself has gone inside it." Then he said, "This is a weak creature: it has been made of clay and is hollow. And what is hollow must have food."

Iblis is reported to have said to the angels one day, "Do you not know that God prefers this creature to you?"

"We obey the command of our Lord and do not disobey Him," they said.

Iblis, however, retorted, "If this thing be preferred to me, I shall disobey Him; if I be preferred to it, I shall destroy it!"

10. *The Entrance of the Spirit into Adam's Body*

Kaab al-Ahbar said: Adam's spirit is not like the spirits of the angels or of any other creature, for it is a spirit preferred by God over all His creation, as He hath said: *When, therefore, I shall have completely formed him, and shall have breathed of my spirit into him; do ye fall down and worship him* (15.29). God hath also said: *They will ask thee concerning the Spirit: answer, The Spirit was created at the command of my Lord* (17.85).

God bade the spirit to be immersed in all the lights, then He commanded it to enter Adam's body with praise and without haste. The spirit, seeing a very narrow entrance and narrow apertures, said, "O Lord, how can I enter?"

It was told, "Enter reluctantly and exit reluctantly." So the spirit entered from the cranium into the eyes. Adam then opened his eyes and looked at his clay body. He could not speak, but he saw inscribed on the pavilion of the Throne:

THERE IS NO GOD BUT GOD † MUHAMMAD IS THE APOSTLE OF GOD IN TRUTH.

Then the spirit reached his ears, and he could hear the angels adoring God round about him. Then the spirit began to turn in his head and brain, while the angels gazed upon him, waiting to be commanded to prostrate themselves. Iblis, however, kept his opposition secret in his heart.

God had informed the angels before creating Adam, as He hath said: *And remember when thy Lord said unto the angels, Verily I am about to create man out of dried clay, of black mud, wrought into shape; when, therefore, I shall have completely formed him, and shall have breathed of my spirit into him; do ye fall down and worship him* (15.28-29).

Then the spirit reached Adam's nose and he sneezed. The sneeze opened the blocked passages, and Adam said, "Praise be to God Who Is Now and Ever Shall Be." This was the first thing spoken by Adam.

Then the Majestic One called to him, saying, "Thy Lord has compassion upon thee, O Adam. From this I created thee, and my mercy is everlasting for thee and thine offspring so long as they say as thou hast said."

Ibn Abbas said: Nothing irritates Iblis more than the words, Bless you, when someone sneezes.

Then the spirit moved through Adam's body until it reached his legs. And Adam became flesh, blood, bones, veins, nerves, and bowels, except his feet, which remained clay. He tried to stand but was unable, which is the meaning of His Words: *Man is created of precipitation* (21.37).

When the spirit reached the legs and feet, Adam stood up erect. It is said that the spirit took five hundred years to permeate throughout Adam's body and that it was on Friday at sunset that it was completed.

On the authority of Jaafar ibn Muhammad al-Sadiq:[22] The

spirit was in Adam's head a hundred years, in his chest a hundred years, in his loins a hundred years, in his thighs a hundred years, and in his legs and feet a hundred years.

11. *The Prostration of the Angels before Adam*

Wahb said: When Adam stood erect, the angels saw that he appeared to be of glistening silver. Then God ordered them to prostrate themselves. The first to hasten to bow down before him was Gabriel, then Michael, then Israfel, then Azrael and all the other angels.

Ibn Abbas said: The prostration before Adam was on Friday at midday, and the angels remained prostrate until dusk, wherefore God made that day a holiday for Adam and his descendants until the Day of Resurrection. God answers prayers on that day and its eve, a period of twenty-four hours. Every hour God releases seventy-thousand prisoners from Hell.

Iblis, however, refused to prostrate himself before Adam out of pride and jealousy. *God said to him, "What hindereth thee from worshipping that which I have created with my hands? Art thou elated with vain pride? Or art thou really one of exalted merit?" Iblis said, "I am more excellent than he: thou hast created me of fire, and thou hast created him of clay* (38.76f.). Fire consumes clay and I have worshipped thee under the shadow of heaven with the cherubim, the seraphim and all the hosts and company of heaven."

Then God said, "I knew through my eternal knowledge that my angels would obey me and that thou wouldst disobey me. The length of thy worship will be of no avail: for I have known from all time what thou wouldst do. I have stripped thee of all goodness until the end of eternity and have made thee accursed, outcast, a devil, damned and abhorred!" With this, his countenance was transformed into that of the devil.[23] The angels, gazing upon his evil appearance and smelling his abominable stench, fell on him with their spears, cursing him and saying, "Accursed! Accursed! Damned! Damned!" The first to stab him was Gabriel, followed by Michael, Israfel and the Angel of Death and the hosts of angels. Iblis ran from them until they cast him into the Fiery Sea; and the angels of the Fiery Sea hastened upon him with their spears, which were made of fire, and they continued to stab him until they reached the Euphrates, where he disappeared from their sight.

And the angels trembled and the heavens quaked at the audacity of Iblis.

12. *The Inspiration of the Names to Adam*

God taught Adam the names of all things (2.31) so that he knew all languages, even the language of the snakes and frogs and all things that were on land and in the sea.

Ibn Abbas said: Adam spoke seven hundred languages, the best of which was Arabic.

Then God commanded the angels to carry Adam on their shoulders so that he might be higher than them. As they marched along the highways of heaven, they said, "Blessed! Blessed! We shall always obey you."

When the angels were assembled in rows, Adam passed before each row and said, "Peace be with you!"

"And with thee peace," they answered, "and the mercy of God and His blessings, O Chosen of God and His élite, the marvel of His creation!"[24]

Ibn Abbas said: In the highest level of heaven they erected for Adam ruby and emerald domes.

As Adam passed by the gatherings of angels and the station of the prophets, he mentioned each one and also his companions by name. Then the angels returned him to his Lord.

13. *Adam Rises up to Preach*

Then God commanded Gabriel to call the angelic hosts to gather before Adam so that he might address them. Gabriel, therefore, called out; and the hosts of the heavens assembled in twenty-thousand rows, each row more splendid than the last. But Adam's voice was low and did not reach them, so they placed him on the Pulpit of Honor, which had seven stairs.

That day Adam was wearing a robe of silk brocade as delicate as air, and he had two tresses studded with jewels and scented with musk and ambergris. On his head was a bejeweled crown of gold with four points, on each of which was a great pearl so radiant that the light of the sun and the moon was extinguished. On his fingers were the Rings of Honor, and about his waist was the Girdle of Favor. He radiated a brilliant light, which shone in every corner of Paradise.

Adam stood on the pulpit in all that radiance, and God taught him all names and gave him a staff of light. The angels were dazzled and said, "Our God, hast thou created anything more beautiful than this?" And God said, "My angels, this one, whom I created with my own hands, is unlike any I created by fiat."[25]

Adam mounted the pulpit and saluted the angels, saying, "Peace be with you, O angels of my Lord, and the mercy of God and His blessings!"

And they answered, saying, "And with thee peace, O Chosen of God and Marvel of His creation!"

Then a cry rose to him from God, saying, "O Adam, for this have I created thee: this greeting is a salutation for thee and thy progeny until the Day of Resurrection."

Wahb said that this greeting did not spread among any people but that they were safe from torment.

It is related on the authority of Ibn Abbas that the Apostle of God said, "Shall I not direct you to a deed which, if you do it, shall cause you to enter Paradise?" Those with him said, "Yes, O Apostle of God." Then the Prophet said, "Distribute food, openly declare peace and pray for me at night while the people are asleep. And you shall enter Paradise with peace."

Ibn Abbas said that when a believer salutes his brother believer, Iblis weeps and says, "O woe is me!" The two who have then saluted each other shall not be parted until they die.

Then Adam began to address the heavenly host. The first thing he said was, "Praise be to God." And that became customary for Adam's children. Then he cited the knowledge of the heavens and the earths. After lauding God with words inspired to him by God, he mentioned what sorts of creatures God had made in the world. Thereupon God said to the angels, *Declare unto me the names of these things if ye say truth* (2.31) (that is, the names of the creatures Adam had mentioned). But the angels were unable to do so and said, *"Praise be unto thee; we have no knowledge but what thou teachest us, for thou art knowing and wise"* (2.32).

God said, "O Adam, tell them their names" (2.33). And Adam informed them of the name of every thing God had created on land and in the sea, even the pearl and the gnat. And the angels were astounded.

Then God said, *"Did not I tell you that I know the secrets of heaven and earth, and know that which ye discover, and that which ye conceal?"* (2.33) (that is, what was kept secret in Iblis' disobedient heart).

Then Adam descended from the pulpit, and God increased his beauty and radiance. God caused a bunch of grapes to draw near to Adam, and he ate it; and that was the first food of Paradise Adam had eaten. When he had finished, he said, "Praise be to God." God said, "For this have I created you, O Adam. It is to be a custom for you and your children to observe until the end of the ages."

Slumber then overcame Adam and he slept, for there is no rest for the body except in sleeping. The angels, alarmed, said, "Sleep is the brother of death: this one will surely die!"

When Iblis heard that Adam had eaten food, he rejoiced and said, "I shall lead him astray!"

* * *

Wahb ibn Munabbih said that one of the signs of death is sleep and one of the signs of resurrection is wakefulness.

The children of Israel asked Moses, "Does our Lord sleep?"

And God said unto Moses, "O Moses, were I to sleep, the heavens would tumble to earth and the universe and all its contents would pass away altogether."

Ibn Abbas said, "The Jews asked our Prophet Muhammad about this, and God revealed to him: *God! there is no God but he; the living, the self-subsisting: neither slumber nor sleep seizeth him* (2.255). Then they said, 'O Muhammad, do the people of Paradise sleep?' He said, 'They do not sleep, because sleep is the brother of death; neither do they die. Likewise the people of Hell neither sleep nor die or grow old; rather they are ever in torment.' "

14. *The Creation of Eve*

While Adam slept, God created Eve from one of his left ribs, which was crooked. She was called Eve (*Ḥawā*) because she was made from a living being (*ḥayy*), as He hath said: *O men, fear your Lord, who hath created you out of one man, and out of him created his wife* (4.1).

Eve was as tall and as beautiful as Adam and had seven hundred tresses studded with gems of chrysolite and incensed with musk. She was in the prime of her life. She had large, dark eyes; she was tender and white; her palms were tinted, and her long, shapely, brilliantly colored tresses, which formed a crown, emitted a rustling sound. She was of the same form as Adam, except that her skin was softer and purer in color than his was, and her voice was more beautiful. Her eyes were darker, her nose more curved, and her teeth whiter than his were.

When God had created her, He seated her at Adam's side. Adam saw her in his sleep on that long-ago day and loved her in his heart.

"O Lord," he asked, "who is this?"

"She is my handmaiden Eve," He said.

"O Lord," asked Adam, "for whom hast thou created her?"

"For one who will take her in trust and will persevere in thanks for her," said God.

Then Adam said, "O Lord, I will take her on one condition, that thou marry me to her." And so Adam was married to Eve before entering Paradise.

It is related on the authority of Ali ibn Abi Talib[26] that Adam saw her while he was asleep and that she spoke to him, saying, "I am the handmaiden of God, and you are the servant of God. Seek my hand from your Lord." Ali also said, "Do not hold marriage to be a good thing, for women can control themselves neither for profit nor for loss; nonetheless, you hold them in trust from God, so do them no harm!"

On the authority of Kaab al-Ahbar: Adam saw her in a dream. When he awoke he said, "O Lord, who is this who was so kind to me when she drew near?"

"This is my handmaiden," said God, "and thou art my servant, O Adam. I have not created anyone nobler in my sight than you two, for you have obeyed me and worshipped me. I have created for you an abode and called it Paradise: whosoever enters therein shall be my friend in truth, and whosoever enters not therein shall be my enemy in truth."

Adam grew alarmed and said, "O Lord, dost thou have enemies? Thou art the Lord of the heavens and the earth."

"Had I willed all of creation to be my friends I should have done so," said God, "but I do what I will and I decree what I desire!"

"O Lord," said Adam, "this thy maid Eve, for whom hast thou created her?"

"O Adam," said God, "I created her for thee that thou be content with her and that thou not be alone in my Paradise."

"Lord," said Adam, "marry her to me."

"O Adam," said God, "I will marry thee to her on one condition: that thou teach her the precepts of my religion and be thankful to me for her." And Adam accepted.

A chair of pearl was placed for Adam. When he sat down, the angels gathered about, and God told Gabriel to betrothe them. The sponsor was the Lord of the Universe, the betrother Gabriel, the witnesses the angels, the groom Adam and the bride Eve. So Eve was married to Adam on condition of obedience, piety and good works; and the angels showered them with the coins of Paradise.

Abdullah ibn Abbas said: Proclaim marriage, for it is the custom of your father Adam. There is nothing more beloved to God than marriage and nothing more hateful in his sight than divorce. When the believer performs the major ritual ablution, Iblis weeps and says, "This servant of God has been cleansed of his sins, yet has satisfied his desire and upheld the custom of his father Adam."

Then God said to Adam, "Mention my favor towards thee, for I have made thee the marvel of my creation and have fashioned thee as a man, according to my will, and have breathed into thee from my spirit. I have caused the angels to bow down before thee and to bear thee on their shoulders. I have caused thee to preach to them and have loosened thy tongue to speak all languages. I have placed thee among those who extol on the pulpit of contentment. Thou wert a preacher to the Pure Ones, the cherubim, the seraphim, the divine and the hosts of heaven. For thee I did all this as a source of pride and honor. I made Iblis a devil and cursed him when he refused to prostrate himself before thee. I gathered my grace in my handmaiden Eve for thee, and there is no favor, O Adam, better than a pious wife. Two thousand years before I created thee I built the Abode of Eternal Life so that you two might enter therein under my covenant and trust."

15. *The Epoch Wherein Adam Held the Trust*

God had offered this trust to the heavens and the earths before the angels, saying, *We proposed the trust unto the heavens, and the earth, and the mountains* (33.72). The terms of the trust were that they do sufficient good and punish evil-doing, but they refused to accept it.

Then the trust was offered to Adam, and God said, "If thou art obedient I shall reward thee with good things and shall give thee eternal life in Paradise. If thou break my covenant I shall expel thee from my abode and shall hand thee over to torment in Hell."

"O Lord," said Adam, "I accept thy covenant and thy trust and commandment."

The angels were greatly astonished that Adam accepted the trust, as He hath said: *We proposed the trust unto the heavens, and the earth, and the mountains: and they refused to undertake the same, and were afraid thereof; but man undertook it: verily he was unjust to himself, and foolish* (33.72).

Ibn Abbas said that between the time Adam accepted the trust and the time he ate from the tree was no more than the time between afternoon and evening.

* * *

Then God portrayed Iblis to Adam and Eve for them to gaze upon his form. To them He said, *"Verily this is an enemy unto thee, and thy wife: wherefore, beware lest he turn you out of paradise; for then shalt thou be miserable"* (20.117). Then He said to Adam, *"O Adam, dwell thou and thy wife in the garden, and eat of the fruit thereof plentifully wherever ye will; but approach not this tree, lest ye become of the transgressors"* (2.35). And Adam accepted the terms of the trust in their entirety.

God spoke to Gabriel,[27] saying, "Go to Ridwan, the warden of Paradise, and tell him to bring Adam's horse, which I created five hundred years before I created Adam himself."

Kaab al-Ahbar said: God created Adam's horse from camphor, musk and saffron, and there was not in heaven a beast, save the Buraq,[28] more beautiful than Adam's horse.

Wahb ibn Munabbih said: The Buraq excels all the other beasts of Paradise just as our Prophet Muhammad excels all the other prophets. And as for Adam's horse, it was created from the musk of Paradise, mixed with the Elixir of Life. Its mane was of coral, its forelock was of sapphire, and its hooves of topaz.

Gabriel came to Ridwan,[29] and Ridwan opened the gates of the gardens and called out, "O Maymun, draw nigh!"[30] And it came, praising and glorifying with jubilation, until it stood before Gabriel. It was fitted with a saddle of emerald and topaz and bridled with reins of sapphire, and it had wings of different sorts of gems. Gabriel led it to Adam, and Adam marveled at its beauty. With Gabriel holding the stirrup, Adam sat on its back and said, "Praise be to God, who has rendered these things serviceable to us!"

"You have done well, O Adam," said the horse, "for no one may ride me except a thankful servant of the Lord."

God then called to Adam, saying, "Thou hast given thanks for what thou wast given by saying, 'Praise be to God!' "

Eve was given a camel which God had brought into being by saying, "Be!" Then, with Eve mounted on the camel and Adam upon the horse, they went to Paradise, Eve riding behind, the angels on all sides, and the cherubim and heavenly hosts lined up with their spears and banners, right to the gate of Paradise, where the angels were commanded to make Adam halt.

"O Adam," said God, "thou hast gazed upon the congregation of the heavens. Hast thou seen any who resemble thee in beauty of form?"

"O Lord," replied Adam, "I have not seen among them anyone who resembles me, nor has anyone been given such as thou hast given me, so praise be to thee! How great thou art!"

"O Adam," said the Lord, "thou art nobler in my sight than them, since thou hast obeyed me and hast been content to accept my trust and hast not been unjust or unfaithful."

In all of this Adam accepted the trust but did not ask his Lord for protection or help, for which God held the angels in witness.

* * *

Adam and Eve were crowned, diademed and honored. When they entered Paradise, not an angel, bird or tree failed to extol them. The horse stopped with Adam at the stations of the prophets and others in Paradise. And when they stood in the midst of Paradise, in the Garden of Eden, he looked and beheld a dais of pearl with seven hundred pillars of different kinds of gems and many quilts. On the dais was a carpet of silk brocade, and about the carpet were piles of musk and ambergris. Atop the dais were four domes, the Dome of Contentment, the Dome of Pardon, the Dome of Eternity, and the Dome of Honor. Then the dais itself cried out, "Verily, I, O Adam, was created for you, and for you was I adorned." Adam and Eve, after having gone around all of Paradise, dismounted and sat on the dais. Grapes and fruits of Paradise were offered them, and they ate. Afterward they withdrew to the Dome of Honor, which was the most ornate of the domes, then to the Dome of Contentment. To the right of the dais was a mountain of musk and to the left a mountain of ambergris, and the Tuba tree shaded the dais.[31]

When Adam wished to draw near Eve, the domes lowered their curtains over the dais, and the gates were closed and hid them.

Adam remained with Eve in Paradise for five hundred of the years of this world in extreme happiness and under the most favorable conditions, and Adam used to descend from the dais and walk in the fields of Paradise with Eve behind him, dragging her silken brocades. Whenever they proceeded from mansion to mansion, the angels would shower them with the coins of Paradise until they returned to their dais.

* * *

Iblis feared the angels because of the vilification they had given him with their spears, so he moved about in hiding from them. While he was creeping around Paradise, a loud voice said, "O people of heaven, I establish Adam and Eve in Paradise under the trust and covenant. I permit them everything that is in Paradise, except the Tree of Eternity. If they approach it and eat from it, they will be among the unjust!"

16. *The Peacock's Conversation with Iblis*

When Iblis heard this, he rejoiced and said, "I shall certainly have them expelled from that kingdom, seeing they have been forbidden something!"

Slinking stealthily along the highways of heaven, at the gate of Paradise he found the peacock, who had just come out. The peacock had two wings, which, when outspread, resembled a lotus tree, and an emerald tail, on each feather of which was a white jewel that shone like the sun. His beak was of a white stone, his eyes of topaz. He was the most beautiful bird of Paradise in voice and form, and he outdid them all in singing the glory of God. He used to go to the highest station of the seven heavens, whenever it came to his mind to do so, and his exaltation would reverberate throughout Paradise.

When Iblis saw him, he drew near and spoke to him in a soft voice, saying "O bird, wonder of creation, most beautiful of colors, most pleasing of voice! Which of the birds of Paradise are you?"

"I am the peacock," he said. "What is it to you? You, who look like a fugitive, or as though afraid of some pursuer."

"I am one of the angels of the highest station of the assembly of cherubim who never for one moment cease praising God, not even long enough to gaze upon Paradise and what God has put there for its inhabitants. Do you think you could get me into Paradise?" said Iblis. "In return, I shall teach you three words. Whoever says these words will never grow old or ill and will never die."

"What do you mean?" said the peacock. "Do the people of Paradise *die*?"

"Yes," he replied, "they die, they grow old, and they suffer illness—unless they have these words." And he swore by God that it was true.

The peacock, trusting him and not believing that anyone would swear by God if he were lying, said, "Oh! I am desperately in need of these words, but I fear Ridwan will find me out. I will send you the serpent, who is the mistress of the beasts of Paradise, and she will let you in."

17. *The Serpent, and Iblis' Entry into Paradise*

The peacock walked hurriedly off to Paradise and told the serpent all that had happened.

"How greatly do you and I need those words!" said the serpent.

"I promised I would send you to him," said the peacock. "Go out to him before he passes you over for another!"

Kaab said that at that time the serpent was shaped like a camel and, like the camel, could stand erect. She had a multicolored tail, red, yellow, green, white, black, a mane of pearl, hair of topaz, eyes like the planets Venus and Jupiter, and an aroma like musk blended with ambergris. Her dwelling was in the aqueous Paradise, and her pond was on the shore of the River Cawthar. Her food was saffron, and she drank from that river; and her speech was exaltation of God, the Lord of the Universe. God had created her two thousand years before he created Adam, and she had told Adam and Eve about every tree in Paradise.

That day the serpent went out and saw Iblis, just as the peacock had described him. Iblis drew near her and spoke with a soft voice, as he had done with the peacock. "Make me a promise about what you say!" said the serpent. And Iblis swore by God to her, just as he had done with the peacock.

"That will suffice," she said, "but how can I let you into Paradise?"

"I see a wide opening between your fangs," said Iblis. "I know it is big enough for me. Let me get in, and I will teach you the words."

"If Ridwan finds out where you are, what shall I do?" asked the serpent.

"You have my word that I will be responsible so long as you are with me," Iblis promised. "Don't be afraid!"

Ibn Abbas said that she asked him, "If I am carrying you in my mouth, how shall I speak if Ridwan speaks to me?"

"Don't worry," said Iblis. "I have the names of my Lord. If I pronounce them, neither Ridwan nor any of the angels will perceive you or me." (And all the angels were inattentive to their conversation; but Eve, meanwhile, had missed the serpent.)

Iblis kept on in this manner until the serpent had confidence in him. She opened her mouth, and Iblis jumped in and sat down between her fangs (thus the fangs of snakes became poisonous until the end of the ages). Then the serpent closed her mouth and entered Paradise. Ridwan did not say anything to her, because it had all been foreordained.

When the serpent reached the middle of heaven, she said to him, "Get out of my mouth now before Ridwan sees you!"

But Iblis spoke from the serpent's mouth, saying, "O Eve, Beauty of Paradise, haven't I been with you in Paradise and told you about everything that is here? Haven't I told the truth in all I have said to you?"

"Yes," said Eve, "I have only known you to be truthful in your speech."

"Eve," said Iblis, "tell me what God permitted to you of this Paradise and what he forbade you." And she told him what God had forbidden them.

"Why did your Lord forbid you the Tree of Eternity?" asked Iblis.

"I do not know," said Eve.

"But I know!" cried Iblis. "He forbade it to you because He wanted to make you like that slave whose place is under the Tree of Eternity and whom God brought to Paradise two thousand years before you!"

Eve jumped up from her dïas to look at the slave, whereupon Iblis lept out of the serpent's mouth like a streak of lightning and sat down under the tree. Eve saw *him* and thought he was the slave. Calling to him, she asked, "Who are you?"

"I am a creature of my Lord, who created me from fire. I have been in this Paradise two thousand years. He created me, as He created you two, with his own hand and breathed his breath into me. He caused the angels to bow down before me, then He established me in Paradise and forbade me to eat from this tree. I did not eat from it until one of the angels, who swore to me that he was giving me good advice, told me to do so, saying that whosoever ate from it would have everlasting life in Paradise. I trusted him and ate from it. As you can see, I am still in Paradise and have been safe from old age, illness, death and expulsion." Then he added, as God hath said: *"Your Lord hath not forbidden you this tree, for any other reason but lest ye should become angels, or lest ye become immortal"* (7.19). Then he cried to her, "Eve, eat from it! It is good and edible–of the fruits of Paradise! Hurry and eat before your husband Adam, for whoever eats first will have precedence over his companion."

Then Eve said to the serpent, "You have been with me since I entered this Paradise, but you have not told me anything about this tree." And the serpent was silent, fearing Ridwan and desirous of the words Iblis had promised to teach her.

Ibn Abbas said: Were it not for her alarm over death, she would not have desired the words; but she did what she did.

Thereupon, Eve, bright with good news, came to Adam and told him of the serpent and the person who had sworn to her that he was giving her sound advice, as He hath said: *And he swore to them, saying, "Verily I am one of those who counsel you aright"* (7.20). Then destiny was added to Iblis' speech and vow.

So Eve drew near to the tree. It had innumerable branches, and on each branch were ears that contained seeds like Tell Hujur (or, as it is also said, like ostrich eggs). They had a fragrance like musk and were whiter than milk and sweeter than honey. Eve plucked seven ears from seven branches of the tree, ate one and hid one away; the other five she took to Adam.

It has been related from Ibn Abbas that Adam had nothing to do with the act, neither in denial nor in acquiescence, but that it was predestined, as He hath said: *When thy Lord said unto the angels, I am going to place a substitute on earth; they said, Wilt thou place there one who will do evil therein, and shed blood? but we celebrate thy praise, and sanctify thee? God answered, Verily I know that which ye know not* (2.30).

Then Adam took the ears from her hand, having forgotten the covenant binding upon him, as He hath said: *But he forgot; and we found not in him a firm resolution* (20.115), that is, he did not keep the covenant and tasted of the tree as Eve had done, as He hath said: *And when they had tasted of the tree, their nakedness appeared unto them* (7.22).

Ibn Abbas said: And by Him in whose hand is my soul, no sooner had Adam tasted one of the ears of grain than the crown flew off his head, his rings squirmed off his hand and everything that had been on both him and Eve fell off—their clothes, jewelry and ornaments. Each article, as it flew from them, cried out, "O Adam! O Eve! Long may you sorrow and may your affliction be great! Peace be with you until the Day of Resurrection, for we made a covenant with God that we should clothe only obedient, humble servants."

Then the dais rose from the carpet and flew into the air, crying, "Adam the Chosen has disobeyed the Most Merciful and has obeyed Satan!"

And the pearls which were in Eve's tresses fell off, and the belt fell open from her waist, saying, "May your affliction be great and may you sorrow long!" Then, none of their clothing remained on them, and they hurriedly began to cover themselves with leaves, when their Lord called to them, saying, *"Did I not forbid you this tree: and did I not say unto you, 'Verily Satan is your declared enemy'?"* (7.22)

Ibn Abbas said that God warned the children of Adam when He said: *O children of Adam, let not Satan seduce you, as he expelled your parents out of paradise* (7.27).

He caused each of them to look upon the evil of his companion, and they became dismayed. Then Iblis hastened to flee in secret along the highways of heaven. Adam cried out aloud, but there was not a single thing in Paradise that did not shout after him, saying, "O disobedient!" The inhabitants of Paradise averted their gaze from them and said, "O Lord, expel them from thy Paradise!"

Adam's horse Maymun said, "O you deluded one, thus was the covenant between you and your Lord?!" The leaves of the trees also fell from them so that they were not able to cover themselves with anything. When Adam came near a tree, it would shout at him, saying, "Go away from me, O disobedient one!"

The dove which had shed light on Adam's crown drew near and said, "O Adam, where is your crown, your jewels, your finery? O Adam, after beauty and magnificence, you have come to be cursed!" And every thing shouted rebuke after him from all sides, and the angels also; and he looked at them with longing and regret.

When they had heaped blame and censure upon him, he fled; but when he reached the acacia tree, it turned to him, seized him with its branches and cried out at him, "Where are you fleeing, O disobedient one?"

Adam stopped, frightened, a fugitive, realizing that torment had descended upon him, and said, "Have mercy, O Most Merciful!"

Eve was desperately trying to cover herself with her hair, but it kept exposing her. When she had rallied against it, it cried out to her saying, "O you whose evil is so obvious, how can you cover yourself, having thus disobeyed your Lord?" With that, she sat down and hid her face in her knees so that no one could see her. She was under the tree and Adam was left standing, caught by the acacia tree.

Then the Awesome One shouted to Gabriel, "O Gabriel, dost thou not see how Adam, the marvel of my creation, has disobeyed me?" And Gabriel quivered with fear of God and fell down prostrate. The pillars of the Throne fell still and said, "Praise be to thee! Praise be to thee! Most Glorious! Most High! Clemency! Clemency!"

Thereupon the Awesome One called out to Adam, who fell down in a swoon of terror. When he came to, he said in a weak voice, "Thy will be done, my Lord and Master!"

Then God said to him, *"O Adam, did I not forbid you this tree: and did I not say unto you, Verily Satan is your declared enemy?"* (7.22)

"O Lord," cried Adam, "thou didst not teach us that anyone would swear by Thee to a lie!"

18. *The Expulsion of Adam from Paradise*

Then, with his Lord's permission, Gabriel came and, grabbing hold of Adam's forelock, freed him from his entanglement in the tree.

"O angel," said Adam, "treat me gently, for you were my friend before."

"I am not gentle to anyone who has disobeyed his Lord," said Gabriel. "Where would you be, Adam, if the myrmidons approached and were told to seize you, fetter you, and take to the raging fire? Where would you be, Adam, if the Warden of Hell were to vent his wrath upon you? If he showed his face to the people of heaven and earth, they would melt away just as lead melts in fire. Were his voice made manifest to solid mountains, they would be scattered about like atoms. O Adam, when he shouts at the people of Hell, the layers of Hell tremble and blaze up and burn. O Adam, do you not know that Hell is the destiny of anyone expelled from Paradise, unless God have compassion?" And while Gabriel enumerated the favors God had shown him and the punishments for his disobedience, Adam trembled and quivered with fear until the discourse was completed.

Then Adam began to make signs to Gabriel and said, "Let me flee from Paradise, for I am ashamed before my Lord."

"Where will you flee?" asked Gabriel. "Your Lord is the Nearest of the Near and perceives those who flee."

"O Gabriel," said Adam, "permit me one parting glance at Paradise." So Adam looked to the right and to the left, but Gabriel did not leave his side until they had come near the gate of Paradise.

When Adam had one foot outside the gate, the Voice of God called, "Gabriel! Stop him at the gate of Paradise!" Then the Awesome One called, saying, "O Adam, I created thee to be a thankful servant, not an unbelieving slave!"

"O Lord," cried Adam, "by thy Splendor I beg thee to restore me to the dust from which thou createdst me, and I shall be dust as I first was."

"O Adam," said God, "how can I restore you to dust, when I have known for all eternity that I would fill the earth and Hell from thy loins."

And Adam was silent.

19. *The Address of Eve*

Then Eve was called: "O Eve!"

"Here I am, my Lord and Master," she replied. "My finery is gone, misery is upon me, and I am left naked. Nothing from Paradise will cover me, O Lord of the Universe."

"And who has stripped from thee the blessings and the finery which were upon thee?" she was asked.

"My God and Master, it is mine own sin, which I was made to do," she said. "Iblis led me astray with his deception and evil whisperings and swore to me by thy Majesty that he was advising me well. I never thought that anyone would swear by Thee if he were lying."

"Depart now from Paradise, deceived forever henceforth," said God. "I make thee deficient in mind, religion, ability to bear witness and inheritance. I make thee morally malformed, with glazed eyes, and make thee to be imprisoned for the length of the days of thy life and deny thee the best things, the Friday congregation, mingling in public, and giving greeting. I destine thee to menstruation and the pain of pregnancy and labor, and thou wilt give birth only by tasting the pain of death along with it. Women shall experience more sorrow, more tears shall flow from them, they shall have less patience, and God will never make a prophet or a wise person from among them."

"O God," cried Eve, "how can I leave Paradise? Thou hast denied me all blessings."

Then the Voice of God cried out: "Leave! For I have bent the hearts of my servants in sympathy with thee."

Ibn Abbas said: God created affection and familiarity between men and women, so keep them at home and be kind toward them insofar as you are able; for every woman who is pious, worships her Lord, performs her religious obligations, and obeys her husband will enter Paradise.

Then God called to Eve, saying, "Depart! for I expel through thee those with whom I shall fill Paradise: the prophets, the pious, the martyrs, those who will be pardoned, and those among your progeny who pray for and ask forgiveness for you two."

Kaab al-Ahbar said: Whenever a male or female believer prays for forgiveness for Adam and Eve, God bestows forgiveness upon him; and Adam and Eve rejoice and say, "Lord, this person has asked forgiveness for us and has prayed for us. Therefore pray thou for him, grant him absolution and increase him in thy sight in innocence and godliness."

Abu Hurayra said: Anyone who does not pray for them whenever mentioning their name has been undutiful towards them.

Hasan al-Basri said: Say, "O God, pray for Adam and Eve the prayers of thy angels, and give them contentment until thou makest them content. Give them in our stead the best reward thou givest a mother and father on their child's account."

When Eve was commanded to depart, she lunged forth at one of the leaves of Paradise (the length and breadth of which only God knows) in order to cover herself; but when she took it, it fell from her hands and said, "O Eve, you are in grave deception. O Eve, nothing from Paradise will cover you after you have disobeyed God!" Then God commanded the leaf to respond to her request, and she covered herself with it. Gabriel then grasped her by her forelock and cast her out of Paradise.

When she saw Adam, she cried out. "O woe is me, Gabriel!" she said, "Please let me look at Paradise!" So he permitted her, and Eve turned to Paradise in anguish. Then she departed and stood outside, the angels by her side.

20. *The Expulsion of the Peacock from Paradise*

Then the peacock was summoned, and the angels stabbed him until his feathers fell out. Gabriel dragged him forth, saying, "Leave Paradise forever! So long as you shall live, you shall always be accursed."

His crown was stripped from him, and Gabriel drove him naked from Paradise, save the few feathers left on his lame wings.

21. *The Expulsion of the Serpent from Paradise*

Then the serpent was summoned, and the angels dragged her on her belly until her legs were deformed. She became elongated, malformed and deprived of the power of speech, mute and forked-tongued.

"May God have mercy neither on you nor on any who has mercy on you!" said the angels as they dragged her past Adam, stoning her from all sides.

* * *

It is related that the Prophet said: "He who kills a serpent will have seven blessings, and he who leaves it alone, fearing its evil, will have no reward. He who kills a viper will have one blessing."

Ibn Abbas said, "Verily, to kill a serpent is better in my opinion than to kill an infidel."

* * *

Then Adam was expelled from Paradise. Gabriel sent him out into the heavens, and Eve was veiled from his sight. The angels gazed upon Adam in his nakedness and were terrified. "Our God, our Lord," they said, "is this Adam, the marvel of thy creation? How mean and small he is! Do not make him eternal, but have mercy upon him, O Most Merciful."

With that, Adam put his right hand on top of his head and his left hand over his navel, and his tears flowed like rivers over his cheeks. As he passed before the angels, they rebuked him for breaking his Lord's trust and covenant, and they heaped upon him much abuse and mentioned the favor God had shown him.

"O angels of my Lord," cried Adam, "have mercy upon me. Do not rebuke me, for what I did was destined to me by the foreknowledge concealed on the Preserved Tablet."

This is indicated by the Word of God: *I am going to place a substitute on earth. They said, Wilt thou place there one who will do evil therein, and shed blood? but we celebrate thy praise; and sanctify thee? God answered, Verily I know that which ye know not* (2.30).

22. *Harut and Marut*[32]

Presently the angels fell silent and increased their rebuke no more, except for Harut and Marut, who continued to heap censure, reproach and revilement upon Adam. They had indeed been the very first to calumniate him, for when God hath said, *"I am going to place a substitute on earth,"* Harut and Marut said, *"O Lord, wilt thou place there one who will do evil therein, and shed blood? but we celebrate thy praise, and sanctify thee"* (2.30). And God knew from this that they were jealous of Adam.

They continued to speak evil of him until God afflicted them and punished them on Adam's account, as has been mentioned in the Word of God: *Verily I know that which ye know not.*

* * *

Harut and Marut were bound and shackled in a well in the land of Babylon, there to remain until the Day of Judgment.

It is also said that they were merely prohibited from rising up to heaven but remained as they were.

* * *

In the days of Idris,[33] Harut and Marut went to him and said, "We committed one mistake and are forbidden to go up to the heavens. Can you beseech God on our account to overlook our mistake?"

"How can I know if He will overlook such a thing?" asked Idris.

"Implore Him on our behalf," they said. "If you see us, then your prayer will have been answered. If you do not see us, then we will have been destroyed."

So Idris made himself ritually pure, prayed two *rak'as* and called upon God.[34] Then he turned to where Harut and Marut had been and, not seeing them, knew that punishment had befallen them and that they had been wrenched from their place to the land of Babylon in Iraq.

Then they were given a choice between punishment in this world and punishment in the next world. They chose that of this world, for it is the Abode of Impermanence. There, in the land of Babylon, they were placed upside down in a well until the Day of Judgment.

* * *

When the angels saw what had befallen Adam and his wife, they wept out of compassion and begged forgiveness for those on the earth, as He hath recorded the angels' words: *O Lord, thou encompassest all things by thy mercy and knowledge; wherefore forgive those who repent, and follow thy path, and deliver them from the pains of hell* (40.7).

Ibn Abbas said that magic came from Harut and Marut, as He hath said: *They taught men sorcery . . . So men learned from those two a charm by which they might cause division between a man and his wife; but they hurt none thereby, unless by God's permission* (2.102), that is, by God's determination.

* * *

When the angels' censure of Adam had become too much, God commanded Gabriel to bid the angels assemble in ranks.

They arranged themselves in rows, with Adam standing in their midst, and God cried out to him, "O Adam, say: 'Here I am my Lord and Master. Thou seest me, but I see thee not. Thou are all-knowing of hidden things.' " Then God said, "O Adam, I have known that I would not excuse those who are disobedient unless they repent, and towards those who do repent shall I be gracious with my mercy.

"O Adam, were I to create in the fullness of the earth servants who then disobeyed me, I should set them down in the station of the disobedient. Were the inhabitants of the heavens and the earth, the mountains and the seas to disobey me, I should make Hell their dwelling place, and I should not care.

"O Adam, how little do creatures mean to me when they disobey me, and yet how noble are they in my sight when they are obedient.

"O Adam, I fashioned thee in such a way that none of the angels resembles thee. I breathed into thee mine own breath and caused the angels to prostrate themselves before thee. I caused thee to dwell in Paradise and gave thee my handmaid Eve in marriage. I taught thee all names and caused thee to know all things and all places. I raised thee up to address the angels and caused thee to be borne on their shoulders.

"O Adam, how hast thou forgotten thy pact with me and obeyed mine enemy Iblis?"

"O Lord," said Adam, "thou hast done all of that, and I cannot describe thy goodness towards me. But, O Lord, this disobedience of mine was immutable by virtue of thine own pre-eternal knowledge. I am thy feeble slave, encompassed by thy fetter and thy will. My forelock is in thy hand: thou canst twist it as thou willst. Have mercy upon me, O Most Merciful!"

"O Adam," said God, "for this have I created thee. Disobedience has come through my decree, my omnipotence and my will, which have existed in my pre-eternal knowledge."

Then Adam said, "O Lord, by the right of him to whom thou hast given highest honor, cannot my fall be lessened?"

And the Voice of God cried, "O Adam, who is he by whose right thou makest this petition?"

"My God and Master," replied Adam, "he is thy chosen one, thy charge, thy beloved Muhammad, who is the Light thou hast established before my eyes, for I have seen his name written on the Canopy of the Throne, on the Preserved Tablet, on the Book of Heaven, and on the portals of Paradise. I know, O Lord, that thou hast expelled me from Paradise and that thou desirest to bring me together with my enemy Iblis, so how may I be protected from him and how may I have strength to ward him off?"

"O Adam," said God, "verily thou canst ward him off by declaring my Unity, which is that thou sayest, 'There is no god but God † Muhammad is the Messenger of God.' Moreover, these words are like a shooting star to my enemy and thine.

"O Adam, I have caused thy dwelling place to be the mosque. Thy food is all that is lawful and over which my name has been pronounced. Thy drink is what I have caused to flow from the springs in my earth. Let thy battle-cry be my name and thy clothing what thou weavest with thine own hand."

"O Lord," said Adam, "give me more!"

"I shall not take away repentance from thee, or from thine offspring," said God, "so long as they repent to me."

"O Lord," said Adam, "give me more!"

"I shall forgive thee and thy children and shall not take anything against you into account," said the Lord.

23. *Iblis' Query*[35]

After Adam, Iblis spoke, saying, "O Lord, thou madest me covetous. Thou didst lead me astray, and thou madest me a devil. All that was in thy foreknowledge. *O Lord, respite me, therefore, until the day of resurrection.*"

God said, "Verily thou shalt be one of those who are respited until the day of the determined time" (which is announced by the first blow on the trumpet) (30.80ff).

Then Iblis said, *"Because thou hast depraved me, I will lay wait for men in thy straight way; then will I come upon them from before, and from behind, and from their right hands, and from their left; and thou shalt not find the greater part of them thankful"* (7.16f).

God said, "Get thee hence, despised, and driven far away: verily whoever of them shall follow thee, I will surely fill hell with you all" (7.18).

"Lord," said Iblis, "thou hast given me reprieve. Where then is my dwelling to be?"

"When you descend to the earth," said God, "your dwelling will be places of filth!"

"What shall I read?" asked Iblis.

"Poetry and song!"

"What will call me to prayer?"

"Musical instruments!"

"What will be my food?"

"That over which my name is not pronounced!"

"What will my drink be?"

"Wine!"

"Where will I dwell?"

"Public baths!"

"Where will be my gathering place?"

"Markets!"

"What is my battle-cry to be?"

"My curse!"

"What is my garment to be?"

"My Wrath!"

"What is my prey?"

"Women!"

"By thy Might and Splendor," said Iblis, "then I shall put love of women into the hearts of men!"

"O Accursed," said God, "God shall not take repentance away from the heart of mankind until he gurgles with death. Depart thou hence! For thou art accursed, and the curse shall remain upon thee until the Day of Judgment!"

24. *Adam's Query*

Adam said, "O Lord, this Iblis, to whom thou hast given reprieve and who has sworn by thy Might to ensnare my children, how may I avoid his deceits?"

"O Adam, said God, "I have bestowed upon thee three qualities. The first is for myself, and that is that thou worship me and not associate anything with me. The second is for thee, and it consists of good deeds, be they large or small. For every one good deed thou wilt receive tenfold, for ten a hundredfold and for a hundred a thousandfold, and these I keep in store for thee and pile them up like towering mountains. If thou commit one evil deed it shall be repaid in kind. If thou ask my forgiveness, I shall forgive thee, for I am the all-forgiving, the merciful. The third is between me and thee, which is that thou pray and I answer. Stretch forth thy hands and call upon me, for I am nigh and responsive."[36]

When Iblis heard this he shrieked with envy of Adam and said, "Lord, how can I ensnare Adam's children?"

"Accursed one," he was told, "urge them on with your cavalry and troops. Share in their wealth and children and promise them provisions.

"O Lord, said Iblis, "give me more!"

"There shall be no child born to Adam," said He, "but that there shall be seven born to you."

"Give me more!" said Iblis.

"I increase you that you run the very course of the blood in their veins and dwell in their very breasts!"

"On what condition shall I then alight upon the earth, O Lord?" asked Iblis.

"On condition of despair of my mercy, for I shall fill Gehenna with you and with all those who follow you!" said God.

* * *

Wahb said: But the children of Adam fell short of Iblis' expectation in all he asked his Lord, for his partnership in possessions was limited to unlawful things and his partnership in children was limited to those produced by fornication and adultery, for they made marriage a pleasant thing and shunned fornication and mentioned God's name in every instance. Whenever Iblis hears someone praising God, he melts like lead in fire.

Wahb ibn Munabbih said: God gave this community two chapters, and whoever reads them before sunrise and after sunset escapes the devil, who bays like a dog. These two chapters are called *al-Mu'awwidhatayn*.[37]

Ibn Abbas said: When the chapter *al-Ikhlāṣ* was revealed,[38] Gabriel came and said, "Muhammad, before this day you have continually feared for your community. Now, however, we are at peace with regard to your community, for no one will read this chapter with certainty of recompense without entering Paradise. And there will be a veil between him and the devil." In the Prophetic Tradition it is said that whoever reads this chapter a thousand times will be safe from having his eyes put out, being stoned, earthquake and drowning.

* * *

When Adam finished his petition, he passed along and, seeing the serpent, said, "Lord, this serpent, who aided my enemy Iblis against me, how then shall I have stamina against it?"

"O Adam," said God, "I cause it to dwell in dark places and its food to be dirt. Whenever you see one, crush its head!"

Wahb ibn Munabbih said: Had Iblis not sat between its fangs, it would not have been poisonous. Kill it wherever you find it.

Ibn Abbas said: The snake, the scorpion and the wasp were transformed into poisonous animals.

* * *

Then the peacock was told that his dwelling was to be river banks, his food plants of the earth, and that love for him would be placed in human hearts so that he would not be killed or beaten.

25. *Eve's Query*

Then Eve began to question, saying, "My God, thou didst create me from a crooked rib-bone. Thou didst create me deficient in reason, religion, ability to bear witness and in inheritance. Thou hast afflicted me with impurity and denied me the right to assemble at the Friday congregational prayer and further burdened me with divorce and bearing children. I beseech thee, O Lord, to grant me something as Thou has granted these others."

"Verily," said God, " I have given thee life, mercy and kindness. I decree such a reward for thee, upon performance of ritual ablutions after menstruation and birthing, that, were thou to see it, it would give thee satisfaction. Furthermore, if a woman die during childbirth, her place shall be among the ranks of the martyrs."

"That is sufficient for me," said Eve.

* * *

Ibn Abbas said: There is no woman repudiated but God gives her the wages of a martyr for each repudiation. If she gives birth and is sound, she shall be told, "God has forgiven you your past sins, be they as vast as the ocean." If a woman dies in childbirth, she dies a martyr and will be rejoined to her husband in the hereafter and will be exalted over the dark-eyed houris seventyfold.

* * *

When their lots had been meted out, they were commanded to descend to the earth, as He hath said: *Get ye down, the one of you an enemy unto the other; and there shall be a dwelling place for you on earth, and a provision for a season* (2.36, 38) (the "dwelling place" is the grave and the "season" the Day of Resurrection).

Adam went down by way of the Gate of Repentance, Eve by the Gate of Mercy, Iblis by the Gate of Malediction, the peacock by the Gate of Wrath, and the serpent by the Gate of Ire. This was in the late afternoon.

* * *

Ibn Abbas said: From these gates descend repentance, mercy, malediction, wrath and ire.

Wahb said: God created Adam on Friday, and on that very day he entered Paradise, where he dwelt for half a day, which was equivalent to five hundred years. Adam came down between noon and dusk and descended through a gate called *al-Mubarras,* which is the terminus of the Visited House.

Mujahid said: Adam descended through the Ascension Gate.

Amr ibn al-As said:[39] Adam descended through the Gate of Mercy, which shall be open to all who repent until the Day of Resurrection, when it will be closed and repentance will no longer be possible.

Kaab said: Adam came down to India, on top of a mountain called Serendip, which surrounds India. Eve came down to Jidda, Iblis to the land of Maysan, the peacock to Egypt, and the serpent to Isphahan.[40]. God separated them one from another so that they were unable to see each other. On the day of his fall, Adam had only a leaf from the garden that had stuck to his body; the wind, however, carried it off to India, where it became the source of perfume.

Thereupon Adam wept day and night for a hundred years. He did not raise his head toward heaven until God had caused aloe-wood, ginger, sandalwood, camphor, ambergris and all types of scents to grow from his tears. And the valleys became filled with trees.

Eve too wept, and from her tears God caused carnations and herbs to grow.

The wind carried Adam's voice to Eve and Eve's to Adam, and each thought that he was near the other, although between them were distant lands.

Ibn Abbas said: Eve remained fixed in the heavens for a long time, so she put her hands on her head, thus transmitting that custom to her daughters until the Day of Resurrection.[41]

Wahb said: When Adam stood erect his head was in the heavens and he could hear the angels praising God, so he praised along with them. It was then that God caused his hair and beard to grow, as before he had been bald and his head had glistened like silver.

26. *The Story of the Eagle and the Fish*

Wahb said: The first to learn of Adam's fall was the eagle, who came and wept with him.

Kaab al-Ahbar said: The eagle, a wild creature of the earth, came down one day to the seashore, where he saw a fish floundering in the water. The eagle came to the edge of the water, spoke to the fish and made friendly overtures to it, to which it responded, having had no friend prior to that. And the two became constant companions.

When the eagle learned of Adam's fall, he told the fish, "Today I saw a strange creature that "contracts" and "expands," stands and sits, comes and goes."

"If what you say is true," replied the fish, "then there has come that with which neither you on the land nor I in the sea can dwell. This is farewell for us."

It is found in the Prophetic Tradition that the fish said to the eagle, "You inform me of a strange creature who eats and drinks. If you are telling the truth, then he will drive me from my sea and you from your land."

Wahb said: When God sent Adam down to the earth, an angel cried out, saying, "O Earth and all that dwell therein, there has descended to you a man who forgot [*nasiya*] his pact with his Lord, and God calls him 'human' [*insān*]." When the eagle heard this, he went to the fish and told him what he had heard. The two were alarmed and said one to the other, "This is farewell between us. Woe to the inhabitants of the land and sea on account of this 'human'!"

* * *

Adam continued weeping prostrate until the birds and beasts had drunk from his tears and trees had grown and fixed their roots in the earth. Along with Adam wept all the beasts and animals.

When the animals and beasts saw him, however, they fled from him and said, "Adam, we inhabited this earth before you, but now you have frightened us, made us wild, caused us to weep and occasioned us great sorrow." From that day forward the beasts were no longer friendly to human beings, and all the birds also dispersed from him, except the eagle, who sorrowed and wept along with him.

Then Adam saw his beard and said, "Lord, what is this thing? I did not see it while I was in Paradise."

"This is on account of thy transgression," he was told. "It has changed your appearance that you may know male from female."

Then the flocks, birds and wild beasts in the hills, thickets and mountains wept, and the very earth became heavy laden with Adam's sorrow.

Wahb ibn Munabbih said: Adam wept so much that the angels, the cherubim and seraphim also wept in sympathy and said, "Our Lord God, lessen the fall of Adam, thy Chosen One, for he has sorrowed to the bottom of his heart over his sin!"

Ibn Abbas said: Were Jacob's weeping for Joseph and David's weeping for his transgression to be placed on one side of a balance along with that of all creation and Adam's weeping on the other side, Adam's would outweigh them all, for he wept for more than one hundred years.

Then Adam sat for another hundred years, not raising his head toward heaven out of shame before his Lord.

Wahb said: After Adam had ceased his hundred years' weeping, some of his tears remained on the earth, and the birds and beasts drank from them. His tears had a fragrance like that of musk, which is why there is so much perfume in India.

Kaab said: He wept for three hundred years, never raising his head toward heaven and all the while saying, "O God, how could I gaze at the heavens, whence I descended naked and disobedient?" God caused the animals to speak in consolation of Adam for his disobedience, and there was not a single animate being that did not go to him.

27. *A Description of the Locust*

Qatada said:[42] The first thing to console Adam was the locust.

Kaab said: God created the locust from clay and put the Great Name of God on its wings. It is one of God's soldiers, and there is nothing more numerous than the locusts.

Sa'id ibn al-Musayyib said:[43] With some of the clay left over from Adam, God created the locust.

Makhul said:[44] We were in Taif around Ibn Abbas' table, and a huge locust lighted on it. Ikrima took it, and Ibn Abbas said, "Look at its wings." When he looked he saw some black spots. Ibn Abbas said to Muhammad ibn al-Hanafiyya, "My cousin, I was told by my father that the Apostle of God said that these black dots in Syriac mean, 'I am God † There is no god but Me † The Punisher of tyrants † I have created the locust a soldier in my army † Through him to destroy any of my creatures I will.' "

Wahb said: The locust multiplies in a country only when God is displeased with its people. Rid a country of them by asking God for forgiveness. To kill it is a transgression, and to leave it alone is a good deed.

Mujahid said:[45] There are nine thousand kinds of locusts, some of which are as big as hawks and eagles. God has entrusted them to an angel, who knows every kind and how each praises God. Whenever God wills to destroy a nation, He commands that angel to send the locusts, and in the twinkling of an eye they devour everything that nation possesses, even the gates.

Jaafar ibn Muhammad said: God created locusts as big as wild beasts which no one except Solomon has seen. God sent them to Pharaoh and his people for one hour, and they devoured forty parasangs. Seventy thousand kinds, yellow, green, red, black and all colors, clustered around Solomon to praise God and bless His name.

* * *

When the animals came to Adam, they consoled him and forbade him to weep. They also commanded him to praise God and bless His name.

Then Adam ceased to weep.

28. *Adam's Repentance*

Thereupon God said to Gabriel, "Adam, the marvel of my creation, has caused the heavens and earth to weep, has mentioned none other than me and has called upon none but me. His transgression has grieved me, yet he was the first to praise me and the first to call upon me by my Beautiful Names.[46] Verily I am the all-merciful, and my mercy takes precedence over my wrath. I have decreed that my mercy shall reach all who call upon me truly repentant of their sins and making humble entreaty.

"These are words I have designated for Adam so that he may have repentance to lead him from darkness into light. Descend therefore to him, Gabriel, and give him my greetings. Wipe away his tears and teach him these words."

Gabriel took the words from his Lord and, surrounded by a great light, descended with them to Adam. Smiling and bearing glad tidings, he said, "Peace be with you who have wept and grieved much!" But, because he was so choked with emotion, Adam did not hear him. So Gabriel cried out in a loud voice, "Peace be with you, Adam. Your repentance has been accepted, and your transgression is forgiven." Then he spread his wings over Adam's face and breast until he ceased weeping.

Hearing the voice, Adam said, "Here I am, my friend. Do you address me with the Cry of Wrath or the Cry of Favor and Forgiveness?"

"Nay, Adam," answered Gabriel, "with the Cry of Favor and Forgiveness. You have caused the inhabitants of heaven and earth to weep, but here are words, which are words of mercy."

* * *

Kaab said: The words were those spoken by Jonah in the fish's belly: *There is no God, besides thee: praise be unto thee! Verily I have been one of the unjust* (21.87).

Abdullah ibn Umar said they were these words:[47] *O Lord, we have dealt unjustly with our own souls; and if thou forgive us not, and be not merciful unto us, we shall surely be of those who perish* (7.23).

Abdullah ibn Abbas said they were these words: *There is no*

God, besides thee: praise be unto thee! Verily I have been one of the unjust. There is no God, besides thee: praise be unto thee! O Lord, I have dealt unjustly with mine own soul and have done evil. Forgive me, O thou best of those who forgive (21.87). These are the words spoken by God in His Book.

* * *

And Adam learned words of prayer from his Lord, and God turned unto him, for he is easy to be reconciled and merciful (2.37).

Wahb said: Whoever says these words will be forgiven seventy years' sins. There is no servant of God who says them with humility but that he will shed his sins and be as he was the day he was born.

* * *

When Adam prayed with these words, he was told, "Adam, thou art truly my friend, for I have forgiven thee thy transgression. Ask and it shall be given thee."

"My God," he said, "forgive any of the faithful among my children who does not associate anything with thee, and forgive any servant who desires thy forgiveness using these words." When Adam spoke thus, his voice was carried to the distant horizons; and the earth, the mountains and the trees set up a great clamor, saying, "Adam, God has given you relief and has blessed you through your repentance."

Then God commanded these words to be taken to Eve, and the breeze carried them to her. Thus she too received the glad tidings and said, "No one will hear these words but that God will have made them forgiveness and mercy, for He is the Most Merciful." Thereupon she spoke the words and fell down in prostration.

When Adam had accomplished his prostration he was told, "Lift up thy head." When he lifted up his face, the veil of light was raised, the gates of heaven were opened to him, and a voice cried out announcing repentance and absolution. "Adam," he was told, "God has accepted your repentance!"

* * *

Adam then tried to stand up but could not, for his feet had become fixed in the earth like roots, so Gabriel plucked him out as one would a tree. Adam cried out loud with the pain that seared his body and said, "Thus does transgression act on those who commit it!"

The angels gazed upon him and saw that his tears had dug furrets in his cheeks. "Adam," they said, "what has changed you after such magnificence and beauty? Where is the Light of Paradise? Where are the Garments of Contentment?"

Adam answered, "This is what my Lord promised when He said, '*Verily we have made a provision for thee, that thou shalt not hunger therein, neither shalt thou be naked: and there is also a provision made for thee, that thou shalt not thirst therein, neither shalt thou be incommoded by heat*' " (20.118f).

"Leave Adam alone!" Gabriel said to the angels. "Censure him no more for his transgression, for God hath erased his sins." And the angels then sought forgiveness for him.

Gabriel then struck the earth with his wings, and a spring gushed forth more redolent than musk and sweeter than honey. As Adam bathed himself in that water, he said, "Praise be to God for this water and for every condition. O God, purify me from my transgression and relieve me of my anxiety." Gabriel clothed him with two robes of heavenly brocade.

To Eve God sent Michael, and he gave her the glad tidings of repentance and forgiveness and garbed her. She said, "Praise be to God for His excellence and sanction." When she learned that her repentance had been accepted, she removed herself to the seashore and bathed herself and said, "Has not God accepted my repentance? When then shall I find Adam?" And she began to weep out of longing for Adam. Every drop of her tears that fell into the sea was transformed into pearl and coral.

When she returned to her dwelling place, she began to look for Adam, who was at the time asking Gabriel about her. He was told that God had accepted her repentance and would bring them together in the most noble of all places, Mecca. He also told him that God commanded him to build there His House, which is the Kaaba, which he should circumambulate and in which he should offer prayer as he had seen the angels do at the Visited House, There He would offer him Iblis to stone as the angels had done when he refused to prostrate himself.[48]

Adam laughed and lept up, his head in the sky. Therefore,

God commanded the angels and animals to draw near him, to greet him and congratulate him on the acceptance of his repentance. God also commanded Gabriel to put his hand on Adam's head to reduce his height. Adam, however, was grieved when he could no longer hear the angels' glorification of God; but Gabriel said, "Grieve not, for God acts as He pleases!"

Then Adam was commanded to build a house to resemble the Visited House for him and his children to circumambulate. Gabriel said, "Adam, God will rejoin you to your wife and from your seed will produce progeny until the Day of Resurrection." God commanded Adam to go with Gabriel to the spot of the Sacred House in Mecca. Wherever Adam put his feet along the way, that place became fertile, while between his steps remained desert. When he reached the spot, he built Mecca. Thus the first village to be built was Mecca and the first house was the Glorious Kaaba.

Then God spoke to Adam, saying, "Build now My House, which I placed on the earth two thousand years before I created thee. I have commanded the angels to aide thee in building it. When thou shalt have completed it, circumambulate, shout hallelujah, glorify me and bless my name, and lift up thy voice in proclaiming my oneness, in praising me, and in thanking me. Grieve not over thy wife, for I shall join thee to her in the bowers of my House, which I shall make the Great *Qibla,*[49] the *qibla* of the Prophet Muhammad, who shall be the greatest source of honor for thee. I know what thou feelest in thy heart for Eve and she in hers for thee, so when thou seest her, be kind to her, for I have destined her to be the mother of boys and girls."

Falling down prostrate before his Lord, Adam said, "O God, what thou hast told me of the excellence of this House and its ritual is sufficient for me."

29. *Mankind Undertakes the Covenant*

Ibn Abbas said: God spoke to Adam, saying, "Adam, I desire to make a covenant with thy progeny, who are in thy loins." The angels gathered around Adam in their various forms, and Adam was overcome with fear and trembling. Gabriel lept and clasped Adam to his breast, as the valley began to tremble and quake with fear of God.

"Be still, O valley!" cried Gabriel, "for you are God's first witness to the covenant God is making with the descendants of Adam." And the valley, with God's permission, was still.

Then God touched Adam's loins with his Right Hand of Might and said, "Adam, look upon those who appear from thy loins!"

The first to appear was our Prophet Muhammad, who advanced rapidly and said, "Here am I, O Lord." Then he stood to the right, saying, "I am the first to testify to thy Oneness and to confirm my obedient service to thee. I testify that thou alone art God, there is no god but thee; and I testify that I am thy servant and thine apostle!"

Then the second rank of apostles replied, one after the other, in all their light and splendor. They hastened to the right side and stood below our Prophet Muhammad. Then came the party of believers, some proclaiming God's Oneness and affirming their faith in Him, and stood below the prophets.

Then, with his Left Hand of Might, God touched Adam's loins. The first to appear was Cain son of Adam and after him the "people of the left," who stood to the left, their faces black.[50]

"O Adam," said God, "look upon these thy children that thou mayest know them according to their appearance and time." He looked at the people on the right and laughed and blessed them, but when he looked at those on the left he cursed them and turned away his face.

Then God asked them to speak, saying, *"Am I not your Lord?"* (7.172).

They answered, "Yea: we do bear witness and affirm."[51]

Ibn Abbas said: The people on the right answered immediately, but those on the left hesitated before answering.

Then God said, "O angels, bear witness that the progeny of Adam have indeed confirmed that I am their Lord, with whom they will not associate anything and whom they will not deny. Bear witness also that Adam has blessed those on the right and cursed those on the left. The people on the right will, by my mercy, be in my Paradise. The people of the left will be in Hell, for they deny me my due."

Then, as He had brought them forth by his Might, God replaced the two groups into Adam's loins.

Wahb ibn Munabbih said: On the Day of Resurrection, when all created beings are brought forth for the passing of judgment, Adam will be told to send one group to Paradise and the other to Hell. He will know them by sight as he saw them in the world. Then he will give forth a mighty shout, which all will hear. Approaching them, he will say, "Have you forgotten your covenant with your Lord? Have you forgotten that you testified that He is the One, the All-Victorious?"

They will answer, *"Verily we were negligent as to this matter"* or, *"Verily our fathers were formerly guilty of idolatry"* (7.172f) (meaning Cain, the first to disobey his Lord, who killed his brother Abel). Then they will shout, *"O Lord, show us the two that seduced us, of the genii and men, and we will cast them under our feet, that they may become most base and despicable"* (41.29) (meaning Iblis the Accursed and Cain son of Adam). Thereupon Adam will take nine hundred and ninety-nine from his left for Hell and one from his right for Paradise.

"O Lord," Adam will then ask, "have I faithfully executed what I was commanded to do?"

"Yes," he will be told. "Now, by My mercy, enter My Paradise!"

* * *

Mujahid said: There is not a single soul upon the earth who does not know that God is his Lord and that the devil is his enemy. There is not a single polytheist who does not tell his children, "We found our fathers of a certain community and are only imitating their example."

Wahb ibn Munabbih was asked why the children of polytheists will be tormented in Hell, since they previously confirmed their faith and were infidels no more. "Because," he answered, "their confirmation was accompanied by hesitation, as they were among the people of the left, whose involuntary faith God does not accept, as He hath said: *Whatsoever is in heaven and on earth worshippeth God, voluntarily or of force* (13.15). Hast thou not heard His saying: *And the companions of the right hand (how happy shall the companions of the right hand be!) And the companions of the left hand (how miserable shall the companions of the left hand be!)* (56.8f). Those on the right hand are those who confirmed first, and those on the left hand are those who hesitated to confirm, as He hath said: *Our word hath formerly been given unto our servants the apostles*" (37.171).

* * *

An angel then approached Eve, who was seated by the sea, and said, "Take these your garments, go forth and enter the Sanctuary in submissiveness to your Lord." He gave her a chemise and a veil from Paradise and turned away while she was putting on the chemise and covering herself with the veil. She entered the Sanctuary from the east of Mecca on a Friday in the month of Muharram, weeping over the loss of her beauty and comeliness. Then the angel sat her on Mount Marwa (which was so named because womankind [*mar'a*] sat there). Eve entered the Sanctuary seven days prior to Adam.

Adam entered from the west of Mecca. When he had gone up onto Mount Safa, the mountain cried out, saying, "Welcome, O Chosen of God" (and it was thus called Safa because Adam was known as the Chosen [*ṣafwa*] of God).[52]

Then Adam cried out to his Lord, saying, "Here am I. Here am I. Thou hast no partner. Here am I. Praise, glory and the kingdom are Thine. Thou hast no partner. Here am I" (and it became part of the ritual to say these words during the major and minor pilgrimages).[53]

God answered him, saying, "Adam, today have I sanctified Mecca and all that surrounds it, and it shall be sacred until the Day of Resurrection" (that is, those who enter therein become so sanctified that they will not burn in Hell).

"O Lord," said Adam, "thou has promised me that thou wouldst join Eve and me in this place. Where is she?"

"O Adam," came the reply, "she is before thee on Mount

Marwa. Thou art on Mount Safa. Look upon her, but touch her not until thou hast performed the rites of pilgrimage." Adam then went down to Eve, and they met and rejoiced, for, as Eve was setting out from Marwa and Adam from Safa, they had seen each other across the valley. They met during the day and spoke of Paradise and the primeval fate that had befallen them. By night Eve returned to Marwa and Adam to Safa, where they remained until the month of Dhu'l-Hijja, when Gabriel came to Adam and taught him the pilgrimage rites.

Encompassing the Sanctuary was a ruby dome with four doors, Adam's Door, Abraham's Door, Ishmael's Door, and Muhammad's Door. Gabriel placed the House at the Kaaba, and there were seventy thousand angels with him that day. The world shone in splendor from the light of the House.

After Gabriel taught him the rites, Adam rose and was vested with the pilgrimage garb. Gabriel took him by the hand and circumambulated the House seven times, taught him all the rites of pilgrimage and made him stand at all the stations. Afterwards he returned him to the House and commanded him to circumambulate seven times. When he had finished, Gabriel said, "This is sufficient for you, Adam. You are absolved, your repentance has been accepted, and your wife has also been absolved. Pray to your Lord to heed your prayer." Adam then prayed for all believers who ascribe no partner to God and asked Him to edify the House with His visitation, and God granted his prayer.

Adam went to Eve, with the angels aligned in ranks and saying, "God grant you mercy, Adam! We have performed the pilgrimage to this House two thousand years before you." Adam and Eve came together on a Friday eve, for which reason, to the exclusion of all other nights, He grants coition on Friday eve. And Eve conceived that very night.

Kaab said: Eve did not conceive until after she had menstruated. When she first experienced it, she was frightened; but Adam said, "It is in fulfillment of your Lord's promise to afflict you with impurity. But Eve," he continued, "where is your beauty and comeliness? You have been transformed."

"It is on account of my transgression," she said. So Adam denied her the right to pray during the days of her menstrual period until the blood should have stopped. Then there came unto her an angel, who stood before the well of Zemzem and said to Adam, "Run about in this place!" When he ran, the earth, with God's permission, burst forth with a spring filled with water that was colder than ice, sweeter than honey and more redolent than musk. Eve wished to drink the water, but Adam said, "Do not drink until God gives me permission." Eve bathed in it, however; and from her tresses the musk spread throughout the earth.

Then God spoke to Adam, saying, "If thou build not up this habitation, none of thy children will do so." Therefore, Adam built it up and constructed for himself a dwelling in which he and his wife could take refuge. After that he began to cultivate, sow seeds and dig wells for water, as animate beings can live only by eating and drinking. Gabriel brought him a seed the size of an ostrich egg, as soft as butter and as sweet as honey. He also brought him from Paradise two oxen and iron. When Adam saw the seed, he cried out, "What am I to do with this seed, which caused my expulsion from Paradise?"

"Adam," said Gabriel, "this is your sustenance in the world, as you chose it in Paradise. It shall be your food and the food of your children in the world."

* * *

Sa'id ibn Jubayr said:[54] Someone asked Ibn Abbas about the prophets' trades. He answered, "Adam was a cultivator, Idris a tailor, Noah a carpenter, Hud and Salih merchants. Abraham was a cultivator, Ishmael a hunter, Isaac a shepherd, Jacob a shepherd, Joseph a king. Job was a rich man, Jethro and Moses shepherds, Aaron a minister to his brother. Elijah was a weaver, David a maker of chain-mail, Solomon a king. Jonah was an ascetic, Zacharias a carpenter, John a hermit, Jesus a wanderer. Our Prophet Muhammad was a warrior for God, a blessing to the faithful and a torment to infidels."

* * *

Then Gabriel said to Adam, "Arise, till the soil and sow seed! I have brought you this iron to be worked into a hammer and anvil. This is fire I bring you: I have plunged it seventy times into water so that it has become tempered and calm. I have concealed it in stone and iron, and it will come out only when you beat rock against iron. Then make a knife to slaughter what you desire. Over it utter the name of God; otherwise it is unlawful. Make a shovel to dig what you desire and to plow to till the earth. Make also a yoke, for you will not be able to plow until you have a yoke."

Wahb ibn Munabbih said: The first things Adam made of iron were an anvil, tongs, a hammer and other tools he needed. After these he fashioned tools for carpentry. He made a yoke and set out to plow. Gabriel brought him a ram from Paradise, which he slaughtered and the flesh of which he and his wife ate. Then he was commanded to make shears, which he used to strip the wool from the ram, which he spun into thread, wove into cloth and fashioned into two cloaks, one for him and one for Eve. When they put on the cloaks and felt the coarseness of the wool, they wept out of longing for Paradise and the embroidered and brocade clothes they had had there. "Adam," he was told, "this is the clothing of the devout in this world. Silk and brocade are for men in the hereafter; only arrogant men, who will not have such a portion in the next, wear them in this world." Then God sent down to Adam one pair of every thing that is on the face of the earth.

Kaab al-Ahbar said: The one that brought the seed to Adam was Michael. When Adam saw him and not Gabriel, he was alarmed and said, "Which of my Lord's angels are you? Where is Gabriel the Trusted of God?"

"Adam," he said, "I am Michael, who am entrusted with seeds, rain, trees and fruit. There is nothing about me to cause you alarm. Rise and plow the earth, sow seed and channel the water, for thereby will you gain your own livelihood, that of your wife and children and of every living thing on earth." Adam took the ear of grain and wept over it until it was wet with his tears. Then Michael said to him, "Adam, therein are three qualities: first, there is not a seed that grows in the earth that does not praise God for a long time, and the reward for its praise accrues to the sower; second, the soul that eats therefrom has it as a votive offering, for God has destined it as a reward for the almsgivers; third, whatever is taken in season or out, before it ripens, prolongs the sower's life, and he is blessed by this my gift. Adam, blessings are seven; six are in cultivation of the soil and one in all else."

Adam took the red oxen, which had been created by God's fiat, put the yoke on their necks and plowed and sowed until he was exhausted. "You have bequeathed this exhaustion to me," he said to Eve.

"Adam," said Michael, "be patient until it reaches maturity, and you reap the harvest, for then you will gather it in, thresh and winnow it. When you have finished that, extract from it what is due the day it is reaped. Gather it with praise and thanksgiving, grind it, knead it and bake it. Then you will eat it when you are exhausted from the sweat of your brow, and you will know what it is to be tired and exhausted."

Indeed Adam did all this with severe exertion until he had baked and eaten, whereupon he said, "Praise be to God from beginning to end. Praise be to God for what He hath ordained and decreed."

Kaab al-Ahbar said: Seeds remained large during the days of Adam and his son Seth, down to the time of Idris. When the people turned faithless, seeds shrank from the size of ostrich-eggs to a smaller size. Then, in the days of Pharaoh, they became smaller still. In the time of Elijah, when they disbelieved, seeds became the size of chicken eggs (and it is said, of the heathercock) and remained thus until the time of Jeremiah. When they killed John son of Zacharias and the days passed until the appearance of Nebuchadnezzar, they became the size of hazel-nuts and remained so until the days of Ezra. However, when the Jews called Ezra the son of God, they shrank to the size of chick-peas. Thus they remained until the days of Jesus; but, when the Christians called Jesus the son and his mother the wife of God, they shrank to what you see today.

Kaab added: And they will soon diminish to the size of grains of millet.

Wahb ibn Munabbih said: When Adam had run the two oxen, God caused them to speak, saying, "Adam, how far it is between the two abodes, the one in which you were before and this, the abode of toil, exhaustion and exertion! You have bequeathed these things to yourself and to us too!" Adam wept bitterly and prayed for blessing and good health for the two oxen; and God placed in them and their offspring a benefit for humans until the Day of Resurrection.

Adam would stand by his fields and ask, "When will they ripen?" From the fields he would hear a voice say, *"Man is created of precipitation"* (21.37).

Wahb said: The fields were as thick as palm groves, and each ear of grain was ten cubits long and glistened like silver. The winds blew over the fields, the north wind exuding fragrance and the south wind exercising care. Then Adam harvested and Eve gathered in the crops. The angel taught Adam to thresh and winnow, and God sent the morning breeze to separate the wheat from the chaff. Then he was taught to mill, knead and bake. All this he did, and then he and Eve ate and drank water, whereupon they were afflicted with wind and rumbling in their bellies and belching, as their bodies had been changed and grown heavy. "We ate in Paradise," each said to the other, "but we did not experience anything like this!"

When their bellies had grown too heavy, the angel commanded them to go into the desert for the call of nature. When they saw that in themselves, they wept bitterly and said, "This is what our sins have bequeathed to us!"

The angel ordered them to cleanse themselves with clay and to wash. He taught them ablutions, and they performed them in the Islamic manner. Then he commanded them to pray, and the first prayer Adam prayed was the noon prayer, just as it was the first prayer our Prophet Muhammad prayed when he was divinely called in Mecca.

30. *The Cock God Gave Adam*

One day Adam was so occupied that he neglected his prayers, because he did not know when the times for prayer were. Therefore, God gave him a cock and a chicken. The cock was white and had small feet—like the great bull.[55] It would strike its wings together at prayer-time and say, "Glory be to Him whom all things glorify. Glory be to God, and praise, O Adam,—the prayer! May God have mercy upon thee!" And Adam, knowing it to be time for prayer, would perform his ablutions and prayers. This cock's nest was over the door of Adam's house; and, whenever Adam came out to plow and cultivate the soil, the cock would praise and bless God's name. When it raised its voice against Iblis, it was louder than a storm.

Ibn Abbas said: Iblis' favorite bird is the peacock; the most hateful to him is the cock. Have many cocks in your homes, for the devil does not enter a house in which there is a white cock.

Wahb ibn Munabbih said: All cocks sprang from this one.

Kaab said: Whenever a cock crows at dawn, a voice cries from Paradise, saying, "Where are the humble? Where are those who kneel down? Where are those who praise God humbly? Where are those who glorify God? Where are those who seek forgiveness at dawn? Where are those who worship the One God?" The first to hear this is an angel in heaven, himself in the form of a cock, with white feathers and down, whose head is beneath the Gates of Mercy on the Sublime Throne and whose feet are in the roots of the Seventh Lower Earth and whose wings are always spread. When he hears that cry from Paradise, he beats his wings once and says, "Praise be to Him who hath created mercy that extendeth to every thing. Who doth not long for thy Paradise, O God of heaven and earth?"

Makhul said: "Of the things of this world I love only four: a horse on which I can fight for God; a sheep on whose milk I may breakfast; a sword which I may strike left and right; and a cock to wake me for prayer." Then he was asked what he knew of the cock. "By God," he said, "it is more humble than the humble and makes more mention of God than any who mention His name. It is more vehement against the devil than a blazing meteor."

Qatada said: "There are more cocks in heaven than any other bird, and God has a cock on the Throne. Whenever it praises God, so do all cocks on the earth. Therupon demons are vanquished and their plots go in vain. Whosoever believes in God and in His prophet and in the Last Day, let him honor the cock. From all the birds Adam chose the cock and the dove; from all the grazing beasts he chose the ewe; and from all the beasts of burden the camel."

Adam planted trees until all the fruits upon the earth sprouted and the earth sent forth her flowers. Adam longed for Paradise and wept, and he ate from the vegetables and plants of the earth.

Wahb ibn Munabbih said: The first vegetable Adam planted was endive. The first aromatic plant he planted was henna, then myrtle and then the others.

31. *Eve's First Conception*

Then Adam lay with Eve on a Friday eve, and she conceived twins, a male and a female. In the eighth month she aborted, and this was the first miscarriage in this world. Then she again conceived male and female but was likewise afflicted, and Adam and Eve were grief-stricken. Then she conceived for the third time, as He hath said: *And when he had known her, she carried a light burden for a time, wherefore she walked easily therewith* (that is, until her pregnancy was obvious). *But when it became more heavy, she cried upon God their Lord, saying, "If thou give us a child rightly shaped* (that is, if this pregnancy ends sound), *we will surely be thankful"* (7.189).

Iblis came to Eve and said, "Do you want what is in your womb to live?"

"Yes," she replied.

"Then name him Abdul-Harith," said Iblis, as He hath said: *Yet when he had given them a child rightly shaped, they attributed companions unto him, for that which he had given them* (7.190) (that is, they gave Iblis association in the name by calling him Abdul-Harith, for the Harith is Iblis).[56]

When she gave birth to a healthy child, she called him Abdul-Harith. An angel came to them with God's permission and asked them, "Why did you call this babe by that name?"

"So he would live," said Eve, whereupon the angel said, "Why did you not name him Abdullah, or Abdul-Rahman or Abdul-Rahim?" Adam and Eve became extremely frightened and said, "We do not need this child." So God caused it to die.

Eve again conceived twins, male and female; and when she bore them she called them Abdullah and Amatullah. Then she conceived another pair of male and female twins and called them Abdul-Rahman and Amatul-Rahman. She continued to bear until she had given birth to twenty sets of male and female twins. Then she bore the prophet of God Abel and his sister, then Cain and his sister, then Siboë and his sister, then Sandal and his sister.[57] She continued to give birth until she had borne one hundred and twenty times, each time to male and female twins. And they begat generations and multiplied.

32. *Adam's Mission*

Ibn Abbas said: Then God appointed Adam apostle to his progeny and, on the first night of Ramadan,[58] designated him for divine inspiration, saying, "Adam, this is the month for those of thy children who stand, kneel and prostrate themselves in prayer. Adam, this is the month in which God extends His mercy and His blessings. Every hour of the day and night God releases seventy thousand slaves from Hell. In this month was Paradise adorned, and during this month are the new-born fashioned. Adam, dost thou think that thy children can obtain my mercy by abstaining from food and drink? Nay! not until they also repent to me with penance during this my month."

Kaab al-Ahbar said: Then, on the first night of Ramadan, God revealed to Adam twenty-two leaves, on which were several chapters written in disjointed letters, none of which were joined together. This was the first book God revealed to Adam. It contained a thousand words, comprising duties, traditions, legislation, the foreboding threat, and accounts of this world.

In it God showed him the actions of the people of every age, their shapes and careers, their kings and prophets and what they would do upon the earth, even their food and drink.

Adam looked upon all of that and knew what his children would do after him. And Adam read it to his children.

Then God commanded him to write it with the pen, so he took sheepskins and tanned them until they were soft. On them he wrote the twenty-eight letters which are in the Torah, the Gospel, the Psalms and the Koran:[59]

Alif — I AM GOD † *ONE GOD* † *THE ETERNAL GOD* † *HE BEGETTETH NOT* † *NEITHER IS HE BEGOTTEN* † *AND THERE IS NOT ANY ONE LIKE UNTO HIM* (112)

Be — Creator of Heaven and Earth

Te — HE is One in HIS Kingdom † All things are humble before HIS Greatness

The — The Ever-Constant † Never to pass away

Jim — HE is Beautiful in Action † HE is Magnificent in Speech

Ha — HE is Clement to those who disobey † Praiseworthy to those whom HE hath fashioned

Kha — Omniscient of the origin of things † Creator of every thing

Dal — Judge on Doomsday † HE judges whom He hath created

Dhal — Possessor of the Greatest Excellence † Possessor of the Glorious Throne

Ra — Lord of all creatures † The Sustainer † The Clement † The Merciful † The Compassionate

Zayn — The Planter without seed † The Increaser of those who thank HIM † Who hath adorned everything with HIS Mercy

Sin — Quick to punish † The Hearer of prayer † Quick to respond to those who call upon HIM

Shin — Harsh in punishment † The Witness of everything † Who witnesses every secret

Sad — The Eternal † Who keeps HIS Promise † The Patient with those who disobey HIM

Dad	The Light of the Heavens and the Earth † Who hath guaranteed forgiveness to HIS prophets and Mercy to HIS faithful servants
Ta	Blessed be the obedient who are sincere in HIM † The Tuba for those who obey HIM
Za	HE hath made HIS Affair Manifest † Those who love HIM are victorious in Paradise
Ayn	The All-Knowing † The All-Cognizant † Who Knows hidden things † Who is Sublime in HIS Lordship
Ghayn	Succourer of those who seek aid † The Self-Sufficient † Who is never impoverished
Fa	The Doer of what HE wishes † The Unique in HIS Kingship † Who hath no Director over HIM
Qaf	The Self-Existing † Who superintends what profiteth every Soul † The All-Powerful † The Victorious
Kaf	The Kind † Who WAS before any thing † Who SHALL BE after every thing † The Driver-away of every affliction
Lam	To HIM belongeth what is in Heaven and on Earth † To HIM belongeth Creation and Command
Mim	King of the Day of Judgment † The Watcher † The Self-Magnifying † The Praiseworthy † The Giver of Grace † The Free from the predication of Before and After
Nun	The Light of Heaven and Earth † Whose Hell is kindled for those HE will torment
He	Right Guidance from error for those to whom HE hath willed Right Guidance
Waw	Friend to Believers † Woe unto those who disobey HIM † There is no god save HIM
Ya	HE Knoweth what is in Heaven and Earth and what is between the two and what is hidden in the breasts of men

When these letters had been revealed, Adam learned them and taught them to his son Seth, who transmitted them by inheritance until they came to Enos, then to Cainan, then to Mahalaleel, then to Jared, until God sent Enoch the Younger (who is Idris), to whom He revealed fifty pages, on which these same letters were written. Idris wrote them, and he was the first to write with the pen after Enos the son of Seth. Idris then taught them to his children and told them, "My children, know that you are Sabæans. Learn, then, the art of writing in your youth that you may profit thereby in your old age." Thus the Sabæans had books, as He hath said: *Christians and Sabæans* (2.62). And they passed down the Books of Seth and Enoch and the Book of Adam until the time of Noah and Abraham. After God gave him victory over Nimrod, Abraham migrated to the land of Syria, the land of his forefathers. When he reached the land of Harran in Mesopotamia, he found a group of Sabæans reading the ancient books and believing in them. "My God," said Abraham, "I did not think that anyone, other than me and those with me, believed that thou art One." "Abraham," said God, "the earth is not void of people to uphold proof of God!" God then commanded Abraham to call them to his religion; but they refused, saying, "How can we believe in you when you do not read our book?" Therefore God caused them to forget the knowledge and books they had preserved, and they realized that Abraham was a prophet sent by God. Abraham read to them the books they had studied, and some of them believed. The Sabæans became divided amongst themselves, and some of them believed in him (and they were the Brahmites) and stayed with him, while others remained in their old religion in the land of Haran and did not migrate to Syria with Abraham. They said, "We are of the religion of Seth, Enoch and Noah," and called themselves the Noachites.

Then Abraham opened Adam's coffer, where he found the Book of Adam and the Books of Seth and Enoch. There were also the names of every prophet sent by God after Abraham, and he said, "Verily, blessed be the seed of him from whom these prophets spring." And God said, "Abraham, thou art their father, and they are thy children." For this reason Abraham is called Father of the Prophets.

* * *

Then God revealed the ancient letters to Adam, who fasted during the month of Ramadan, prayed prodigiously and glorified God. When the day for breaking the fast came, Adam was told to request what he wanted. "My God," he said, "for myself

I ask thee to forgive me my sin. For my children I ask thee to forgive all who fast in observation of this month." And God granted him this request.

33. *The Story of Cain and Abel*[60]

Then Adam called his two sons Cain and Abel, whom he loved the most of all his children, and reminded them of all the grace God had shown him since his very beginning, how he had disobeyed, how he had repented and how God had accepted his repentance. Then he said, "I want you two to offer a sacrifice to your Lord: perhaps He will accept it from you."

Abel was a shepherd; so he took from among his flocks the finest, fattest ram and sacrificed it.

Cain was a farmer; so he took from the best grain and placed it as an offering. Then a white light, which had neither heat nor smoke, came down from heaven and burnt Abel's offering and consumed it. As Cain's offering was not consumed, envy of his brother entered his heart and he said, "His children will lord it over my children after me." And he worked himself up to the point of killing Abel, as He hath said: *Relate unto them also the history of the two sons of Adam, with truth. When they offered their offering, and it was accepted from one of them, and was not accepted from the other, Cain said to his brother, "I will certainly kill thee." Abel answered, "God only accepteth the offering of the pious; if thou stretchest forth thy hand against me, to slay me, I will not stretch forth my hand against thee, to slay thee; for I fear God, the Lord of all creatures"* (5.27f).

As they were headed back from Mina, the place of sacrifice, to the dwelling of their father Adam, Abel walked in front of Cain. Cain took a large rock, struck his brother on the head and killed him. Then he paced around him, sorry for what he had done, as He hath said: *But his soul suffered him to slay his brother, and he slew him; wherefore he became of the number of those who perish* (5.30).

Then there appeared two ravens, who fought together; and one slew the other. The victor scratched the earth with its feet to dig a hole, into which it dragged the dead one and buried it. Thus Cain said to himself, *"Woe is me! am I unable to be like this raven, that I may hide my brother's shame?" and he became one of those who repent* (5.31).

* * *

When the two were late in returning, Adam set out to look for them, found Abel slain and was stricken with grief. The earth was drenched with Abel's blood, and the trees and flowers of the surrounding area had withered. It is said that he recited this poem:[61]

The land and all who inhabit it are changed;
The face of the earth is transformed, and hideous.
Everything which has taste and color has changed;
The happy mien of that lovely face is dimmed.
Cain has killed Abel, his brother:
Alas! for that face that shone like the morning.

* * *

Then Adam carried his son Abel over his shoulders, his eyes weeping and his heart full of sorrow. He and Eve wept over him for forty days, until God spoke to him, saying, "Cease your weeping, for I shall give you another child as pure as Abel, who shall produce prophets and apostles." So their sorrow passed away, and they came together in the Tabernacle of Glad Tidings, where Eve conceived Seth. When her time was accomplished, she gave birth and saw that he was just like Abel and did not differ from him in any way. She called him Hibatullah,[62] and from his face shone the Light of our Lord Muhammad. The angels brought the good news of Seth's birth to Adam.

When Seth had grown and come of age, God sent him a twig of the heavenly lote-tree (which is made of pearl),[63] which had a fragrance like musk. Seth had a dark mole on his right shoulder,[64] and God granted him children during his father Adam's lifetime.

34. *The Circumstances of Adam's Death*

Abdullah ibn Abbas said: Adam planted trees and tilled the soil until all the earth was cultivated. When his days were accomplished, God said to him, "Adam, thine appointed time hath drawn nigh. Make thy bequest to thy son Seth" (who was then four hundred years old).

"Lord," asked Adam, "what is death?"

"It is a decree I have ordained for all my creation. It is, O Adam, more bitter than mortal poison: it taketh away the freshness and beauty from the face and speech that the body return to what it was in the bowels of the earth; then the earth devoureth the flesh, blood, bones and all parts of the body until it be restored to clay as it was in the beginning. Thus shall I do to thee, O Adam, that thou return to dry clay. Then shall I resurrect thee and thy progeny and shall requite thee and them according to your deeds. I have known from all time, O Adam, that I should cause every creature I have created to taste death."

Adam cried aloud with the anguish of death. The Earth answered him, saying, "O Adam, the day He took a handful of dust from me to create you, my Lord promised me that He would return to me every particle taken from me." Fear of death overcame Adam.

* * *

Ibn Abbas said: There was not a single prophet or apostle who did not hate the cup of death except our Prophet Muhammad, who said, "How blessed is he who is reverted to my Lord and Paradise and the Sublime Place and the Prepared Cup!"[65]

* * *

Ibn Abbas said: When God showed Adam his progeny for making the covenant, Adam looked at every one of them. He saw among them one whose light shone brilliantly and said, "O Lord, which of my children is this?"

"O Adam," he was told, "this is thy child David."

"How many years hast thou allotted him, O Lord?"

"Sixty years have I allotted him."

"How many hast thou allotted me?"

"A thousand years."

"O Lord," said Adam, "I would give David forty years of my life."

"Wouldst thou do that?" asked God.

"Yes," said Adam. Therefore the angels were witnesses, and it was written down against him.

When God told Adam that his appointed time was nigh, Adam said to the angels, "But my life is not yet completed!"

Thereupon he was told, "Thou gavest forty years of thy life to thy child David."

"I did *not!*" said Adam to the angels.

"Thou didst indeed, O Adam," said God. "I have given thee one thousand years and thy son David one hundred."

Thus Adam was the first to deny in the face of proof.

Ibn Abbas said: God commanded that witnesses be always present, saying: *And have witnesses when ye sell one to another* (2.282).

* * *

Then God spoke to Gabriel, Michael, Israfel and the Angel of Death and told them to descend to Adam to make certain that he gaze upon the face of death.

35. *A Description of Death*

God sent Death to him in the form of a beautiful ram, which spread out its wings so far that only God knows where they reached, and the earth was filled with the wings. Death has certain wings it spreads only for angels, wings for prophets, wings for the devout, and wings for infidels and hypocrites (upon these no one can gaze without falling down in a swoon).

* * *

Kaab said: As for the wings that are spread for believers, they are studded with all sorts of gems and inscribed with phrases of mercy; the wings it spreads for others, however, are inscribed with curses and various types of torment.

* * *

When Adam looked upon the form and countenance of Death, he fell down in a swoon. The angels bore him up on their shoulders and sprinkled his face with the Water of Life until he awoke from his swoon. All the while perspiration dripped from his brow in yellow beads, like saffron.[66] Then he said, "My God, how awful is Death and how terrible his appearance! I am amazed, my God, at anyone who takes advantage of his lifespan when Death is just behind him. Is this just for me, or for all creatures?"

"O Adam," said God, "this is for all my creation. By my Glory, I shall cause all my creatures to taste death, down to every atom and gnat and what is even smaller than those, until all creation shall have disappeared and there remain only I. As for Adam's progeny, they too shall taste death in accordance with their deeds, which will determine their reward or punishment. The souls of the faithful will be in Illiyyin and the souls of the infidels in Sijjin until Doomsday,[67] when all souls shall be sent back to their bodies to be resurrected and gaze upon me, all of them crowded together. Then they shall be dispersed to be rewarded or punished, every good deed tenfold and every evil deed singly."

36. *Adam's Bequest & Eve's Death*

Then, when God commanded Adam to make his bequest, he summoned his son Seth and said to him, "My son, I am about to depart this life to rejoin my Lord. See that you, my son, do not turn loose of the firm handhold,[68] which is the act of witnessing that there is no god but God, and affirming faith in Muhammad, the lord of the ancients and of those yet to come, prince of the prophets and apostles. Thus I saw written on the

Canopy of the Throne and the gates of Paradise, the layers of the heavens and the leaves of the Tuba tree. This is my bequest to you."

Then he added, "My son, God made manifest my progeny from my loins that I might be made to know them and everything about them. Now I have entrusted them to your seed, and I shall show you, my son, their forms that you may also witness them." God had given Adam a white cloth from Paradise and placed it in the coffer,[69] which He now commanded Adam to open. Adam took out the cloth and spread it out. Upon it were the forms of the prophets and pharoahs, rank after rank; and the first of the prophets was Seth and the last Muhammad. He looked at the pharoahs, all of whom were descended from Cain's seed, while the best, the prophets and the pious, were from Seth's seed. Having seen all this, he was commanded to fold the cloth and put it back into the coffer.

Then he took a handful of hair from his beard, placed it in the coffer and said, "My son, so long as this hair remains black, you shall be victorious over your enemies; but, when it grows white, then know that you are about to die: make your bequest to the best of your children, as I have done to you. Know also, my son, that God will take my spirit at the same hour in which He created me (which is the best hour on Friday). When the time comes, go out of the tabernacle and listen to the consolation of the angels. My son, God will transmit shrouds for me from heaven, and Gabriel and the other angels will take charge of washing my body. Regard well how they do it and learn so that it may be a custom for your children after you. Gabriel, Michael, Israfel, the Angel of Death and host after host of the cherubim will pronounce the prayers over me. When they have finished, you too pray over me and seal my tomb with the pronouncement of peace."

Then he took his ring from his finger, gave it to Seth and resigned the coffer to his care, saying, "My son, know that God will give you the reward of the warriors of God, for you will wage war against your brother Cain and God will grant you victory over him."

Then he added, "My son, I lusted after one of the fruits of Paradise, and my Lord promised me He would feed me from it.

Go out and see what angels you meet and mention to them my behest." Seth went out and found an angel, one of the guardians of Paradise called Nuriael, who had brought with him some of the fruit of Paradise. When Seth brought it, Adam said, "My son, God will not fail at the appointed time." And that was on Thursday.

The next day, Friday, at the same hour in which God had created Adam, between midday and the time the imam finishes his prayer,[70] God commanded the Angel of Death to descend to Adam in the form in which he appeared to no other except Muhammad and to take with him the Nectar of Separation, to give it to him to drink, to take the spirit He had breathed into him and to inform him that had He made anyone in this world immortal, it would have been Adam.

The Angel of Death descended along with Gabriel, Michael, and many other angels carrying their banners. The Great Throne was also taken out of Paradise for Adam and was placed between heaven and earth. Paradise spread banners over its turrets and it was bedecked. The angels unfurled their flags on the gates of heaven in expectation of Adam's spirit.

Adam raised his eyes toward heaven and gazed upon the honors done for him. The Angel of Death entered and said, "Peace be with you, O Father of Mankind. Do you recognize me?"

"Yes," said Adam, "you are the Angel of Death. What are you commanded to do?"

"I am commanded to give you this draught to drink that you may taste death," said the angel.

"I hear and obey my Lord's command," said Adam; and the angel gave him death to taste from the draught of Paradise, as God had commanded.

Seth was standing at the door to the tabernacle, awaiting the angel's condolences. Gabriel approached, and Adam said to him, "Welcome, my friend and companion!"

"O Adam," said Gabriel, "I have come to give you glad tidings. Lift up your countenance to heaven!" When Adam raised his head, he saw all above him, in the heavens, angels standing with their wings spread, and in their hands banners of honor and flags of glad tidings. His child Abel was represented to him standing between heaven and earth and crying,

"Hasten! Hasten! Greatly have I longed for you, father!" Then the Angel of Death gave him the Nectar of Separation. He drank it and departed this life.

Gabriel consoled his son Seth by saying, "God has exalted your purpose and has blessed your father by the honor bestowed upon him."

"We are God's, and unto him shall we surely return," (2.156) said Seth.

"Well said, O Hibatullah!" cried Gabriel. "May you and all who say thus be treated with kindness upon the affliction that comes from God." Then Gabriel washed Adam's body with water of Paradise and wrapped him in shrouds from Paradise. When he had finished, Gabriel told Seth to come forth and pray over his father, so he came forward and prayed, with Gabriel, Michael, Israfel and all the innumerable hosts of angels standing behind him. It is said that he pronounced the Great Exaltation over his father seven times.[71] Then the angels of heaven prayed and after them the beasts of the earth, standing in rows. They laid him in a grave, his head at the site of the Kaaba and his feet stretched out.

Ibn Abbas said: Pray for your father Adam, then weep over him at the mention of his name, for God created him in a beautiful form and preferred him over all creation. He taught him all names and taught him also seventy thousand chapters of knowledge. Verily Paradise prays for Adam out of longing for him, and there was not a thing upon the face of the earth or in the heavens that did not weep over Adam the day he was expelled from Paradise.

Eve's Death

And Eve did not know of Adam's death until she heard the birds and beasts weeping and saw the sun eclipsed. Rising in terror from her place, thinking that what had happened to Abel had also befallen Seth, she went to Adam's tabernacle. Not finding him there, she screamed.

Her son Seth came to her and said, "Mother, cease weeping and be consoled by God, for my father, having tasted death, has gone to his Lord. He commanded me not to tell you until after his burial. You must be patient."

Eve rent her clothing, cried out and beat her face and breast (a habit she bequeathed to her daughters until the Day of Resurrection). Then she remained by Adam's tomb for forty days, never tasting sleep. Afterwards the angels descended to her and told her that her time had drawn nigh, and she knew that they spoke the truth.

She grew seriously ill and so remained until the angels wept out of compassion for her. The Angel of Death descended and gave her the draught he had given Adam, and she departed this life.

Her daughters washed her body and wrapped her in a shroud from Paradise. She was buried alongside Adam, and it is said that her tomb is at Jidda.

Thereupon the guardianship passed to Seth, and the sons of his father obeyed him. The coffer and the steed, Maymun, also passed into his hands. This steed was so well known that when it neighed all the beasts of burden would respond by extolling God.

37. *Seth Fights Cain*

Then God commanded Seth to fight his brother Cain, who had withdrawn to another region of the earth and built it up. He had taken one of his sisters, named Lebuda, whom he loved, and had by her many children, whom God wanted to make Seth's slaves. So, accompanied by all his children, Seth went out, girt with a sword (he was the first to gird himself with a sword). Before him the angels carried ruby staffs that lit the night like daylight. That day Seth wore a white robe that God had given him; round about him were angels, and before him was raised a white banner that stretched from the east to the west.

When he began to march in this battle array, Iblis hastened to Cain to inform him and order him to beware, but Cain was so perplexed that he did not know what was happening until

Seth had arrived and cried out, "Cain! What think you of that which God hath wrought? This is the reward of him who killed his own brother without cause. O Cain! killing an inviolate soul is a more grievous thing in God's sight than the end of the world."

Cain met him with his children and progeny, and they fought. Cain was overthrown in battle, and Seth took him prisoner along with a number of his children. This was the first war among the children of Adam.

The angels came to Cain and fettered him with black chains from Gehenna, bound his hands to his neck and drove him in disgrace to his brother Seth. Cain said, "Seth, remember the bond of kinship between us!"

But his brother reviled him and said, "There exists no bond between us after you killed your brother unjustly!" So saying, Seth kept him in his domicile before delivering him in bondage to the angels, who took him to the sun's well in the west, where he remained facing the sun until death took him, and he died an infidel, his offspring passing into bondage to Seth and his children.

* * *

After that, Seth built more than a thousand cities, in each of which was a lighthouse on which was emblazoned the words, There is no god but God: Adam is the Chosen of God: Muhammad is the Beloved of God.

Seth and his children commanded that which was just and forbade that which was unjust, until the whole earth flourished and was filled with their exaltation and prayer.

God revealed to Seth fifty pages of scripture, which he and his progeny read and from which they learned without enmity, hatred, envy or degeneracy among them. Therefore, Iblis envied them and was desirous of gaining dominion over Seth and his children; but he had no power against them until he discovered the rancor of women and Seth's fondness for them.

Adam had arranged Seth's marriage before his death, but now Iblis appeared to him in the form of a beautiful woman, wearing not a little jewelry.

"Who are you?" asked Seth.

"I am a woman sent you by your Lord for you to marry," said Iblis, "and I am not of the children of Adam."

"My Lord has not commanded me to do any such thing, nor has He told me of you," said Seth. "Furthermore, I think you are none other than Iblis the Accursed!"

"Praise God!" said he, "I am not Iblis, but one of the women of Paradise. Do not disobey your Lord: marry me!" And he made himself so attractive to Seth that he almost seduced him, but the angels cried out, "O Prophet of God! this is your enemy who caused your father's expulsion from Paradise. Do not obey him!" And Seth grabbed Iblis and was about to kill him when Iblis said, "Let me go, Seth! You cannot kill me. My Lord has granted me respite until the Day of Resurrection, but I give you my word I shall not show myself to you again." Therefore Seth let him go, and Iblis caused him no trouble after that.

* * *

Then Enos was born to Seth, whom he resembled, and Seth gave him his place, surrendered the coffer to him and charged him with fighting Cain's children. Then he died at the age of nine hundred and twenty, and Enos stood at the head of Seth's children. Then Enos made his bequest to his son Cainan, and Cainan to his son Mahalaleel, and Mahalaleel to his son Jared, to whom was born Enoch, who is Idris.

38. *The Prophet Idris*[72]

Idris was like his forefather Seth, after whom he was the first to write with pen and paper. He occupied himself with worshipping God and communing with pious men until he had come of age, when he withdrew to be by himself in devotion. In that respect he rose above all the men of his time. God made him a prophet and revealed thirty pages of scripture to him. Moreover, he inherited the Book of Seth and the coffer of Adam.

He earned his livelihood by manual labor and was a tailor; he was the first to sew clothing. With every stitch he would glorify God and bless His name. If once in a while he took a stitch and neglected to praise God, he would take it out and sew it again with praise.

When he was forty years old, God made him a messenger to the sons of Cain, who were giants on the earth and so preoccupied with frivolity, singing and playing musical instruments that none of them was on guard.[73] They would gather about a woman and fornicate with her, and the devils would make their action seem good to them. They fornicated with mothers, daughters and sisters and mingled together. On the encouragement of devils, they had adopted five idols in the likeness of Cain's children and called them Wadd, Suwaa, Yaghuth, Yauq and Nasr, which were also the names of Cain's children.[74]

God sent them Idris to order them to worship Him and profess him God's messenger. So he called them and forbade them to do unjust actions. He divided his time into two: for three days of the week he preached to the people to worship God, and for four days he devoted himself to God's service and every day performed good works of a sort that none of Adam's children had ever done.

Ibn al-Azhari relates on the authority of Wahb that Idris was the first to take up weapons and fight in the service of God, to fight the children of Cain.[75] He was the first to wear clothing, for before his time they wore skins. He was the first to set down weights and measures and to record the elements of astronomy.

* * *

Idris greatly desired to enter Paradise, but he had seen in books that no one may enter therein unless he die and be sent there, so he struggled with his people for God's sake and worshipped Him truly.

While he was worshipping God, the Angel of Death appeared to him in the shape of an extremely beautiful man. "Who are you?" asked Idris.

"I am one of God's servants," he answered, "who worships Him like you. I want to accompany you. Would you allow it?"

Idris gave him permission to accompany him; and that day

they were together until evening, when they chanced upon a shepherd grazing some sheep.

"Why don't we take one of this man's sheep to feast on tonight?" asked the Angel of Death.

"How could we feast on what is not lawful to us?" said Idris. "Leave it, for He whom we have taken as our companion will not leave us without sustenance." When night fell God provided them with food, and Idris ate, but the Angel of Death did not.

They rose and passed the night in prayer. They spent the second day in the same fashion. On the third day Idris said, "You have been my companion for two days and nights, yet I have not seen you eat anything. Nevertheless, you seem to me to be diligent in worshipping God, strong of body, beautiful of face and pleasant of odor."

"O prophet of God," he said, "thus have I always been."

"Who are you?" asked Idris.

"I am the Angel of Death," he said.

"Have you become my companion to take my spirit?"

"No," said the angel, "for my Lord did not command me to do that. Had He commanded, I would not have delayed even a twinkling of an eye. But He did command me to accompany you."

"I have a request for you," said Idris. "I want you to take my spirit."

"Why do you want that?" asked the angel. "For death entails untold agony."

"Perhaps God will bring me back to life afterward," said Idris, "and then I shall be more diligent in worshipping Him."

"Then what you desire, O prophet of God, is to taste death twice," said the angel. "'But I can only take your spirit at God's command. Ask your Lord!"

Then God made himself known to the Angel of Death, saying, "I know what is in the heart of my servant Idris. Take his spirit!" Therefore the Angel of Death took his spirit, and God immediately brought him back to life. Afterwards he was so earnest in his devotion that he fasted and prayed more than any of the people, and the Angel of Death became his comrade and would come often to him.

Once Idris said to the angel, "Can you cause me to stand before Hell so that I might gaze upon it?"

"Why do you want to do that?" the angel replied. "Hell has terrors you could not bear. I have not the means of bearing them either. However, I will take you near there, but God knows best why you need this." So the Angel of Death took him and stood him on the path of Malik, the Guardian of Hell. When Malik saw him standing there, he made such a grimace that Idris' soul nearly departed his body. God spoke to Malik, saying, "By my Splendor and Awesomeness, my servant Idris will never be made to see anything so evil as this grimace of yours. Return to him and carry him to the brink of Hell so he may see what is there."

Malik returned, led him to the brink of Hell and shouted to the guards to stir up the layers of Hell. Idris gazed upon these horrors, the shackles, the torments, the fires, the pitch, the snakes and scorpions; and had Got not given him the strength, he would have been struck unconscious. Then Malik took him to where he had been before, and the Angel of Death came to him and carried him back to the earth. Thereafter he lived in constant worship of God and until the end of his life neither slept nor ate from fear of the torment he had witnessed.

* * *

One day he came to the Angel of Death and said, "Can you cause me to enter Paradise so I might look upon it?"

"Paradise is forbidden all people," the angel said. "No one in this world may enter therein before death, for the inhabitants of Paradise do not die. Nonetheless, your request is for God. I shall bear you and seat you before Ridwan, the Guardian of Paradise. Ask him to grant your wish."

When they reached Paradise, Ridwan and the heavenly host approached, looked at Idris and asked the Angel of Death, "Who is this?"

"This is the prophet Idris," he said, "one of the people of the earth. He desires to look upon the people of Paradise so that his diligence in worshipping his Lord may increase."

"That is up to my Lord," said Ridwan.

"I know what my servant Idris desireth," said God to Ridwan.

"I have therefore commanded a branch of the Tuba tree to bend down close to him. He shall grasp hold of it and be brought into Paradise."

Idris sat on the highest branch and, entering Paradise, saw the marvels of grace contained therein.

"Now come out!" said Ridwan.

"Does he who enters in come out again?" asked Idris, disputing with Ridwan. The guardian wanted to send the Angel of Death to him, but the Angel said, "I have not the power to take his spirit now."

"O Angel of Death," said Idris, "God has given you the power to take my spirit once, and you have done it. You cannot do it again. You took my spirit, and God brought me back to life. I also entered and saw Hell. The ordinance my Lord has decreed for all His servants is that they die and approach Him. He has said: *Every soul shall taste of death* (3.185), and I have already tasted it. He hath also said: *There shall be none of you but shall approach near the same: this is an established decree with thy Lord* (19.71). And: *Eternal therein.* Now that I have entered Paradise, I shall not leave!"

"O Lord," said the Angel of Death, "Idris is in a place wherein I cannot enter, and I have no means of taking his spirit."

"My servant Idris hath disputed with thee," said God. "Leave him in my Paradise and trouble him no more!" Therefore Idris remained in Paradise with God's permission, which is in accord with His Word: *And remember Idris in the book; for he was a just person, and a prophet: and we exalted him to a high place* (19.56f).

39. *The Story of Noah*

Before he was raised up into heaven, Idris left on earth a child named Methuselah, who married a woman called Methuselcha, who bore him a son with such great strength and might that he could take a huge tree and pluck it out by its roots with his bare hands. From his face the light of our Prophet Muhammad shone, but he concealed his faith from his own people.

One day, going out into the wilderness, he came upon an extremely beautiful woman, around whom sheep were grazing. He was delighted with her and asked her name.

"My name is Cainush, daughter of Rakel son of Avel son of Lamech son of Cain son of Adam," she said.

"Do you have a husband?" he asked.

"No," she answered.

"How old are you?"

"One hundred and eighty years old," said she.

"Had you reached your maturity," he said, "I would marry you" (maturity in those days was at two hundred years).

When she asked who he was, he did not tell her he was of the children of Seth because of the enmity that existed between the children of Seth and the children of Cain. All he said was, "I am one of those to whom the unlawful is not permitted."

"I thought you were not going to pay me any heed," she said, "but now that you want to marry me, I will tell you that I am actually two hundred and twenty years old. Go to my father and ask for my hand." So he went and was engaged to her by her father, whom he satisfied with a sufficient amount of money. He married her, and she bore him Noah.

Wahb said: At the time of his birth, Noah's mother bore him in a cave because she feared the treachery of a king who ruled at that time.

After Noah's mother had given him birth, she desired to move freely again. Noah spoke to her and said, "Have no fear on my account, mother; for He who created me will watch over me."

She went to her home, leaving Noah there for forty days, after which his father Lamech died. The angels took Noah, adorned and painted with kohl, to his mother, who rejoiced over him and undertook his upbringing until he reached maturity.

Noah was possessed of reason, knowledge and a beautiful voice. He was tall and stout and resembled Adam. He had a broad forehead, an oval face, beautiful eyes, a stout neck, a lank belly, fleshy thighs and calves, an erect stature and graceful feet. He pastured his people's sheep for a period of his life and also learned carpentry, so he led an easy existence. However, he began to despise his people because of their idolatry.

* * *

Their king was named Darmesel son of Avel son of Lamel son of Enoch son of Cain, who was a mighty tyrant and the first to drink wine, gamble, sit on thrones, commission work in iron, brass and lead, and to adopt clothing spun with gold. He and his people worshipped five idols, Wadd, Suwaa, Yaghuth, Yauq and Nasr, which were the idols of Enoch's people. But they increased the number of their idols until they had one thousand seven hundred, an idol for each of them.

To house these idols, Darmesel ordered an alabaster house to be built, a thousand cubits long and a thousand cubits wide. He also commissioned thrones of gold and silver, laid with magnificent carpets, whereupon the idols were placed, and crowned with diadems studded with pearls and rubies. And there were slaves to serve the idols and glorify them.

When Noah saw all that, he hated to be near them and withdrew into the wilderness. He did not mingle with them or go among them during their festivals until the time known to God arrived for sending Noah as a prophet to his people.

40. *Noah's Mission*

Noah's mission began when God commanded Gabriel to descend to Noah and give him the glad tidings of his prophethood and apostleship to his people.

Descending to earth, Gabriel said, "Peace be with you, Noah!"

"And with you peace," he answered. "Who are you, O noble man?"

"I am Gabriel. I bear your Lord's greetings and tidings that He has made you a prophet to your people." Drawing near, he clothed Noah with the garb of God's warriors, bound his head with the Turban of Victory, girt him with the Sword of Splendor, and said, "Go to Darmesel son of Avel son of Lamel and his people and call them to worship God!" Then he departed and ascended back into heaven.

Noah went to his people that very day, which was one of their festivals. From the time of Cain it had been customary for them to take out their idols on their festival days, to mount them on thrones and to make burnt offerings to them. While the sacrifices were being burned, the people would fall down before the idols. Then they would drink wine, beat tambourines, dance and, without modesty or shame, fornicate like beasts with the women.

That very day Noah came to them. They were in seventy groups, each group uncountable because of the great multitude. When he stood before them, he raised his face to heaven and said, "My God, I ask thee to grant me victory over them!" He pushed between them until he stood in their midst and, as they were about to bow down before the idols, put his fingers in his ears and cried out, " O people, I have come to you with advice from your Lord: I call upon you to worship and obey Him. I forbid you to disobey Him. Fear God and obey Him!" As his voice pierced the hearing of all from east to west, the idols toppled from their pedestals, the people quivered with fear of Noah's cry, and Darmesel fell from his throne. When he awoke from his swoon, he hastened to mount his throne.

"Children of Cain," he addressed them, "whose voice is this? I have never heard it before."

"Sire," they replied, "this voice belongs to one of us who is called Noah son of Lamech. He was away for a while, and now his madness has waxed."

"What does he say?" asked the king.

"He calls us to believe in his Lord and forbids us to worship these idols."

Darmesel grew angry and gathered his people, saying, "Bring him to me!" When his aides had brought Noah and stood him before him, the king asked, "Who are you? Woe unto you who have spoken evil of our gods!"

"I am a messenger of the Lord of the universe," said Noah.

"I advise you to believe in God and shun these atrocities and idols."

"Noah," said Darmesel, "you do not know what you are saying. We do not believe in you because you are bereft of your reason. If you are possessed by demons, we will heal you. If you are afflicted by poverty, we can remedy that too."

But Noah spoke to them, saying, "O people, there is no madness in me, nor have I any need of what you have to give! The kingdom is God's the One, the All-Victorious. All I need is for you to say that there is no god but God and that I, Noah, am God's apostle."

Darmesel grew angry and said, "Noah, today is our festival and killing is not permitted; otherwise we would kill you so painfully that no one else would ever have the audacity to say such things!"

It is said that the first person to believe in him was a woman called Amorah, whom Noah married and who bore him three sons, Shem, Ham and Japheth, and three daughters, Hasura, Mayshura and Mahbuda. Then another woman from among his people, called Walia bint-Mahwil, believed in him. He married her and she bore him two sons, Japheth and Canaan; but she proved a hypocrite and reverted to her old religion.

* * *

Every day Noah would go out into the valleys where the people were and call upon them to worship God and to cease their disobedience, and Darmesel left him alone on the basis that he was mad. The people would come out of their houses and beat him until he swooned. Then they would drag him by the feet and throw him on the refuse heaps. When he came to, he would go back and be treated the same way. This continued for three centuries (reckoning one hundred years to the century), with Noah constantly struggling against them and calling them to worship God. Women and children would gather around him and beat him until he fainted. When he awoke he would wipe his face, pray two *rak'as* and say, "By the Glory and Splendor, may my patience be increased that I may endure that with which they afflict me!"

* * *

The king Darmesel died; and his son Julian, who was even haughtier and more tyrannical than his father, assumed sovereignty.

The fourth century came, and Noah called them, as he had the others, to God; but they beat him, slapped him and reviled him, saying "Get away from us, liar!" They would also put their hands over their ears so they could not hear him. He would go away and then return and point to the course of the sun and moon as proof. He mentioned the layers of heaven and earth and the miracle of their creation, but they only increased in pride, as He hath said: *And whensoever I call them to the true faith, that thou mayest forgive them, they put their fingers in their ears, and cover themselves with their garments, and persist in their infidelity, and proudly disdain my counsel* (71.7).

They would gather rocks on the roofs so that when Noah passed by they would pelt him until he fell down, more dead than alive. Then they would throw him on the refuse heap, and the birds would gather around him, fan him with their wings and rouse him with water sprinkled on his face so that he could return to the people. But they payed him no heed and said, "Woe unto you, Noah! It does not pain you when we beat you. When we make light of you it does not drive you from us. Were you speaking the truth when you claim to be God's prophet, you would be immune to the evil we do you. It is madness that drives you to do all this."

"There is no madness in me," Noah would answer, "but you are an ignorant people. I called to your fathers and grandfathers until they died, and now they are repenting in torment for their lack of faith. Believe in me and tomorrow be saved from the painful torment, for He will forgive you your sins and will postpone the terrible end."

Thus was Noah's condition for six generations. With the seventh generation the king Julian died and was succeeded by his son Tophredius, who was as haughty as his father and grandfather.[76]

By night Noah would stand before the idols and cry out at the top of his voice, saying, "O people, say that there is no god but God and that I, Noah, am God's prophet and apostle. Leave your idolatry!" And the idols would topple over on their heads. Thereupon the people would come and beat Noah and trample on his stomach until blood gushed from his nose and he vomited blood because of the pain.

"This will be your reward, Noah," they would say, "so long as you remain among us!"

When they were about to die, they would bequeath half their property to the idols and their servants and half to their own children and family, whom they would pledge not to believe in or obey Noah. They would also take their sons to Noah and tell them, "Son, look at this man: my father brought me here and warned me of him as I am now warning you. He is a lying sorcerer."

Whenever Noah asked them to take him to Tophredius, they said, "Noah, we realize that you are mad; otherwise we would have put you to death in a hideous fashion!" And all the while he preached to them, they only grew more oppressive and prideful.

Then the earth set up a great clamor before the Lord, saying, "My God, what makes thee tolerate such corrupt people to walk upon me, to eat the fruits of thy trees and to worship other than thee?"

The birds and beasts also said, "Our God, were thou to command us, we would pluck them out and destroy them!" And every living thing cried out to the Lord in complaint of their haughtiness, disbelief and tyranny. And Noah called on his Lord to destroy them.

* * *

Kaab said that neither would the cocks crow for them nor would the doves brood on their eggs.

* * *

While Noah was calling to his people, there was a man, great among his own, called Wasi, and his son Jarud. The man said, "Son, know that this man is a liar." And the boy reached down, filled his hand with dirt and threw it in Noah's face. His eyes filled with dust, Noah said, *"Lord, leave not any families of the unbelievers on the earth: for if thou leave them, they will seduce thy servants, and will beget none but a wicked and unbelieving offspring* (71.26f). With this, the gates of heaven were opened to Noah's plea, and the angels were entrusted with it.

Then God said to Noah, *"Make the ark in our sight"* (11.37). When Noah realized that they were to be drowned, he wanted some, if not all, to believe; but God said, *"Verily none of thy people shall believe, except he who hath already believed: be not therefore grieved, for that which they are doing* (11.36). I have known from all time, a thousand years before creating heaven and earth, that I would destroy the earth by flood."

* * *

It is said that Noah was so called because he wailed (*nāḥ*) for his people.

41. *Noah's Ark*

Thereupon, knowing for certain of their impending destruction, Noah ceased to call his people. When he had determined to construct the ark, he called for Adam's coffer, which contained carpentry tools such as a saw, an axe, a drill and other things. God spoke to him and told him to build the ark in his people's land and to make it one thousand cubits long, five hundred broad and three hundred deep. He sawed wood into planks and pegs, on each of which was the name of one of the prophets, and they shone like the stars, except for the one with the name of Muhammad, which shone as brightly as the sun and the moon together.

Gabriel taught him how to construct the ark, and Noah built it with the help of his children and his faithful followers. All the people made fun of him and said, "Noah, first you take up prophecy. Now you have taken up carpentry. We complain of drought, and you are building for a flood. All this is caused by your madness."

But Noah said, *"Though ye scoff at us now, we will scoff at you hereafter, as ye scoff at us; and ye shall surely know on whom a punishment shall be inflicted"* (11.38f).

By night the people came and set fire to the ark, but it caused no damage. As they left, they said, "This is part of your sorcery, Noah."

Noah spent a month building the ark. He made its head like a peacock, its neck like an eagle, its face like a dove, its tiller like a cock's tail, its beak like that of a falcon and its wings like a hawk's.On every feather of the wings he hung multi-colored jewels, and to the tiller he attached a great mirror with a great light. Then he covered the whole with pitch and, instead of ropes, secured it with iron chains. He divided it into seven stories, each storey with a door; and on these doors he hung lamps. Og son of Anak helped him carry the planks.

When he had finished construction, it became infested with worms, of which he complained to God. "The ark will not be sound," said God, "until thou drive into it four pegs on which are written the names of Muhammad's companions, Abu Bakr, Omar, Othman and Ali." When this was done, the ark was sound.

Then God caused the ark itself to speak, with the people looking on and listening. "There is no god but God," it said, "and Noah is God's prophet. Whosoever boards me will be saved; whoso shuns me will be destroyed, and only the devout will enter me!"

"Now do you believe?" Noah asked his people.

"This is the least of your sorcery!" they replied.

* * *

Noah asked God to allow him to make a pilgrimage, which He permitted. When he had departed, the people decided to burn the ark; but God commanded the angels to bear it up into the sky, where it stayed, suspended between heaven and earth, with the people looking at it but unable to do anything to it. Still they took no heed of the miracles they saw.

When Noah completed the pilgrimage, he cried out to God to curse his people. The angels were entrusted with his curse, and God heard him, as He hath said: *And remember Noah, when he called for destruction on his people, before the prophets above-mentioned: and we heard him, and delivered him and his family from a great strait* (21.76).

When Noah completed the pilgrimage rites, he turned and saw Adam's kiln to the right of the Kaaba and asked God if it could be moved to his house. God told the angels to carry it to Noah's house, which was then where the mosque of Kufa stands now.

* * *

Noah returned from the pilgrimage, and the ark was let down from the sky.

42. *The Deluge*

Then God told Noah to call the birds and beasts of every description so that his voice would reach them. Noah stood on the roof of his house and cried out, "Beasts that graze, beasts that wander, beasts of prey, livestock scattered and birds of the air, come to the ark and be delivered!" His cry reverberated from east to west and from plain to mountainside, and these creatures came in groups.

Noah said, "I have been commanded to take into this ark one male and one female of every species." When he said this, they all became fearful; and all those to whom God had given permission to be taken aboard were stricken with fright, except those who were human, who were eighty men and women.

At that time the snake was huge, as big as a mule; the scorpion was as big as a lion is today, and the lion then was as big as an elephant. Gabriel struck the lion with his wing and said, "Be fatigued and listless." He also struck the snake's mouth, and its fangs fell out. He struck the scorpion, and its stinger was cut off so that it could not harm any of the humans in the ark.

The signal for the deluge was the boiling over of Adam's kiln, and Noah waited for that to happen. When the new moon of the month of Rajab shone in the sky, a voice cried from the kiln, saying, "Arise, Noah, and take into your ark two of every species."

Through the first door he took the men and Adam's body, which was still fresh and unchanged, except for his fingernails, which had grown dark for lack of fresh air. He also took Adam's coffer, in which were the prophet's staffs, numbered at three hundred and thirteen by the will, upon each of which was written its owner's name. Through the second door were taken the women, among whom were Noah's wife and daughters. Eve's body was also taken in. Through the third door were taken beasts of burden and grazing animals. Through the fourth door were taken species of birds and flying and nonflying crawlers. Through the fifth door went wild beasts with fangs and claws. Through the sixth door went the male and female elephant and the male and female lion.

During all this time Noah stood on the deck of the ark, saying, *"Embark thereon, in the name of God; while it moveth forward and while it standeth still"* (11.41). And everyone who boarded said, "In the name of God" and took his seat; and all their voices were raised in praise and celebration of God.

The donkey, however, was slow in mounting the ark because Iblis was hanging on to his tail. When Noah said, "Get in, you devil!" the donkey went in along with Iblis, whom Noah asked, "Who let you into my ark, O Accursed One?" " You did, Noah," he answered, "when you said, 'Get in, you devil!' Therefore you must take me."

"Then tempt none of the people of my ark!" said Noah.

"I will not; but I shall seduce them when they leave your ark," replied Iblis. "Noah, ask your Lord if He will forgive me."

Noah did ask the Lord, who answered, "His penance is to bow down before Adam" (meaning Adam's coffin).

When Noah told him this, he said, "I did not bow down to him when he was alive and in Paradise. That I bow before him in this world now that he is dead is a thing that will never be!" So Iblis sat at the ship's tiller, and God told Gabriel to command the wardens of the waters to send them forth in measureless amounts and to strike the waters with the Wing of Wrath. Gabriel struck the waters, and springs and wells gushed up profusely; the kiln boiled over, the sky poured down rain, and the waters met as ordained; the water of the sky was dark and that of the earth light. The waters broke freely, and the waves battered against themselves, with the angels in their midst causing lightning and thunder; and the deluge inundated from all sides and every place, the angels of wrath churning it up with their wings. And God commanded the angels of the earth to hold the world lest it be pulled loose from its moorings.

The devils that had hidden themselves inside idols and seduced the people by speaking with the idols' tongues began to crawl out when they saw the deluge coming, but the angels smote them with their wings and prevented them from escaping so that they were drowned along with the idols.

God commanded the angels to lift the Kaaba into the sky. At that time the Black Stone was whiter than snow; it is said that it became black from fear of the deluge. According to another report it turned black because of the sinfulness of God's servants.

The waves tossed high, as God hath said: *And the ark swam with them between waves like mountains: and Noah called unto his son, who was separated from him, saying, "Embark with us, my son, and stay not with the unbelievers."*

He answered, "I will get on a mountain, which will secure me from the water."

Noah replied, "There is no security this day from the decree of God, except for him on whom he shall have mercy." And a wave passed between them, and he became one of those who were drowned (11.42f).

The ark sailed left and right but did not go beyond the regions of Noah's people, and God told it to protect its passengers as a mother protects her child, lest they feel the waves and terrors. God then commanded the regions of the earth to go round Noah, whereat Noah opened the doors and began to read the Books of Seth and Enoch.

The people in the ark could not tell day from night except by means of a white bead: when its light diminished they knew it was day, and when its light increased they knew it was night. The cock also crew at dawn, by which they knew it to be the break of day.

Wahb ibn Munabbih said: Whenever the cock crew it would

say, "Praise be to the Blessed King. Praise be to Him who hath taken night away and brought the dawn of a new creation. To prayer, O Noah! God will have mercy upon thee."

* * *

The earth became one layer under the water; and no rocks, mountains or trees were visible, for the water had risen forty cubits above the mountains. The ark traveled until it reached Jerusalem, where it stopped and spoke, with God's permission, saying, "Noah, this is the place of Jerusalem, wherein the prophets of your seed will dwell." Then it went to the place of the Kaaba, circled it seven times and pronounced the Great Labbayk, as did Noah and all those aboard. Then the ark passed on, and whenever it stopped it would say, "This is such-and-such a place." It rounded the East and the West, then headed back to the region of Noah's people. When it stopped it said, "O prophet of God, do you not hear the rattling of chains on the necks of your people?"

Thus the ark roamed for six months, from Rajab to Dhu'l-Hijja, after which it came to rest on Mount Al Judi. God spoke to heaven and earth and said, *"O earth, swallow up thy waters, and thou, O heaven, withhold thy rain." And immediately the water abated, and the decree was fulfilled, and the ark rested on the mountain Al Judi; and it was said, Away with the ungodly people* (11.44).

The sky was cleared of rain, the earth swallowed up the water on its surface, and Noah thought of his son Canaan and of his having drowned. When he could endure it no longer, he spoke and said, *"O Lord, verily my son is of my family; and thy promise is true"* (11.45) (that is, God's promise to save Noah and his family).

But God spoke, saying, *"Verily he is not of thy family"* (that is, he was not a believer).

* * *

Ibn Abbas said: No prophet's wife was treacherous by corruption: the treachery of Noah's wife was that she told her people he was mad; the treachery of Lot's wife was that she pointed out the guest.[77]

* * *

Noah opened one of the doors in the ark, looked at the earth and saw that it was white. He asked God what the whiteness was and was told, "It is the bones of your people who denied me."

It is said that Noah mourned for his people, but God said to him, "Why dost thou grieve for a people thou didst call time and again but who did not answer thee. Thou didst call down destruction upon them, and I responded to thy prayer by destroying them in accordance with their deeds. As for the young, I knew that were I to leave them they would do no good. I made creation only that it might worship me, and when they disobey in disbelief I destroy them and care not!

"Noah, I have known from all time that I should not again torment anyone with flood and drowning until the Day of Resurrection, for I have set my rainbow, which thou seest in the sky, as a guarantee for the people of the earth against deluge."

Noah rejoiced and sent out a dove, saying, "Go see how much water remains on the face of the earth." The dove passed over the east and the west and hastened to return, for Noah had charged it with haste, and said, "O prophet of God, the earth is destroyed and likewise all the trees, except the olive, which is green as usual." Noah had sent a raven before; but it was slow in returning, so he sent the dove.

Then God said, *"O Noah, come down from the ark, with peace from us, and blessings upon thee, and a part of those who are with thee"* (11.48). So Noah and those with him in the ark came out.

God restored day and night, the sun, the moon and the stars, and also the trees and plants as they had been. He commanded them to avoid eating carrion, blood, pork and anything over which other than the name of God be pronounced at slaughter, and not to kill a soul when forbidden by God, except by right.

The birds and beasts dispersed to the various regions of the earth. Then God commanded Noah to build, and he built a village below Mount Al Judi called Qaryat al Thamanin, which is the Village of the Eighty, after their number; and it was the first village to be built after the deluge.[78]

Noah set out all the trees he had taken with him in the ark, and they took root and gave fruit, except the vine, which was slow; but it too finally bore fruit.

Noah divided the earth among his sons, Shem, Ham and Japheth. To Shem he gave the Hejaz, the Yemen, Syria and Mesopotamia; and he is thus the father of the Arabs. To Ham he gave the West; and he is the father of the blacks. To Japheth he gave the East; and he became father to the Turks.

Then God told Noah to return Adam's coffer to the place from which he had taken it, and he did as God commanded.

43. *Noah's Curse on Ham*

It is said that one day Noah came to his son and said, "My son, I have not slept since I boarded the ark, and now I desire to sleep my fill." So saying, he put his head on Shem's lap and went to sleep. Suddenly a gust of wind uncovered Noah's genitals; Ham laughed, but Shem jumped up and covered him.

When Noah awoke he asked, "What was the laughter?" Shem told him what had happened, and Noah grew angry with Ham.

"Do you laugh at your father's genitals?" he said. "May God change your complexion and may your face turn black!" And that very instant his face did turn black. Turning to Shem, he said, "You covered your father: may God shield you from harm in this world and have mercy on you in the next! May He make prophets and nobles of your progeny! May He make bondswomen and slaves of Ham's progeny until the Day of Resurrection! May He make tyrants, kings and emperors of Japheth's progeny!"

And God knows best.

44. *Noah's Bequest to Shem*

Kaab al-Ahbar said: God sent Noah as an apostle to his people when he was two hundred and fifty years old, and he remained among them a thousand years less fifty.

When his time had come, he called his son Shem and said, "I charge you with two things and forbid you two others. One of the two with which I charge you is the Profession of Faith, 'There is no god but God,' for this Profession will rend asunder heaven and earth, and nothing can veil it. Were you to place the Profession on one side of a balance and heaven and earth on the other, the Profession would outweigh. The second thing is that you increase saying 'Praise be to God' and 'Praise Him,' for He is the repository of all reward.

"As for the two I deny you, one is polytheism and the other is reliance on anything other than Him."

When he had finished his bequest, the Angel of Death came to him and said, "Peace be with you, O prophet of God."

Noah, quaking in fear of him, said, "And with you peace. Who are you? My heart was terrified at the sight of you, and my mind unsettled at your words!"

"I am the Angel of Death," he said, "and I have come to take your spirit. Why then this unrest? Have you not had your fill of this world throughout the length of your days?"

"O Angel of Death," replied Noah, "all that has passed of my life in this world is no more than a house with two doors, one by which I entered and the other by which I exit." So saying, Noah turned to the left and to the right but could see none of his children. The Angel of Death handed him a cup in which was a potion and said, "Drink this that your fear may be stilled." Taking it, Noah drank and fell dead.

* * *

Ibn Abbas said: When God gathers all creatures for the execution of the Last Judgment, the first community He will call for reckoning will be Noah's community, who will be asked, "How did you answer the apostle [i.e., Noah] who was sent to you as a prophet?" They will say "Noah neither came to us nor called us. He did not exhort us to do justice or forbid us injustice. If God sent him to us, he was concealed from us and kept his advice from us." Then Noah will be told, "Arise and confront thy people with proof, for they have denied thee." He will say, "My God, thou knowest best concerning this, and thou are sufficient as witness; for verily I delivered the message to them. *I have called my people night and day; but my calling only increaseth their aversion* (71.5f). I called their fathers and grandfathers, and their history was heard by the prophets after me down to the Seal of the Prophets and his community." Then God will say to Muhammad, "What hast thou in evidence for thy father Noah?" Muhammad will rise and say, "*We heretofore sent Noah unto his people; and he tarried among them one thousand years, save fifty years: and the deluge took them away, while they were acting unjustly*" (29.14). Noah's people will say, "Muhammad, how can you testify against us, for you came after us and we before you?" God will say, "O miserable ones, this is the testimony given against you by my beloved Muhammad: it is from my message to him!" And they will be ordered to Hell as the first community to enter therein. Then there will be brought to Noah one of the camels of Paradise, which he will mount. With the angels before him, he will go to the gates of Paradise but will not enter until after Muhammad.

45. *The Offspring of Ham, Shem & Japheth*

Kaab al-Ahbar said: When Noah died, Ham lay with his wife; and God opened his gaul-vesicle and that of his wife also so that they mingled and she conceived a black boy and girl. Ham despised them and said to his wife, "They are not mine!"

"They are yours!" said his wife, "for the curse of your father is upon us." After that he did not approach her until the children had grown, when he again lay with her, and she bore two more black children, male and female. Ham knew that they were his, therefore he left his wife and fled.

When the first two children grew up, they went out in search of their father; but when they reached a village by the edge of the sea, they stayed there. God sent desire to the boy so that he lay with his sister, and she conceived. They remained in that village with no food except the fish they caught and ate. Then she gave birth to her brother's children, a black boy and girl.

Ham, meanwhile, returned seeking the two children and, not finding them, died soon afterwards of anxiety over them. His wife also died, and the other two children set out in search of their brother and sister until they came to a village by the shore, where they stayed. Then they joined the other two along with their own two children. They remained there and each brother lay with his sister, begetting black male and female children until they multiplied and spread along the shore. Among them are the Nubians, the Negroes, the Berbers, the Sindhis, the Indians and all the blacks: they are the children of Ham.

* * *

Japheth went to the east, where he was given five sons, Gomer, Tiras, Meshech, Asaph and Seqoel. From Gomer descend the Slavs, the Greeks and their subdivisions; from Tiras, all the Turks and Khazars and their races; from Meshech, the races of the Persians; from Asaph, Gog and Magog; and from Seqoel, the races of all the Armenians.

* * *

Shem was also given five sons. Arphaxad, the eldest, is the father of all the Arabs, who are the tribes of Rabia, Mudar, Asmad, Iyad and al-Yaman. Lud became the father of Amalek, Tasm, Jusham and Luqaym. Asshur is the father of al-Bayas, a people in the Yemen in Hadramaut who have but one eye. Elam is the father of Ad the First of Amalek, Yamlah and al-Sulakha, who have no heels. Aram is the father of Ad and Thamud, Ad being the son of Uz son of Aram, from whom branch the tribes of the Arabs. The native land of Ad was from Hadramaut to the sandy desert called Ramal-alij. The tribe of Thamud settled in the land of Kus, a land of many trees, where they lived for seventeen years. Then they moved to the Hejaz from Wadi al-Qura and built lofty palaces.

And each race began to worship what it pleased. Some worshipped idols, some the sun and moon and stars, some rocks, or whatever seemed true and heartfelt, according to how Iblis had seduced that person.

Thus they remained for a long time, not knowing holy writ, until God sent Hud as a prophet to Ad.

* * *

Kaab was asked for a description of Ad and replied, "Were I to tell you of its splendors and miraculous works, I fear you would call me a liar, and thus you would be committing a sin. I shall tell you only of the Torah, the Gospel, the Psalms and the ancient books. Know that in the beginning there were twelve male children of Ad son of Uz son of Aram son of Shem son of Noah, and they were Shaddad, Shadid, Mārid, Marīd, Saïd, Jundub, Tubba',[79] Sadd, al-Dahm, Luqma, Luqaym and Ghalib. From them branched out twelve tribes, Ramal, Wafd, Sawadd, Samad, al-Abbud, al-Kanud, al-Jahhud, al-Saud, Awj, Jahada, Munafidh and Munhil, numbering more than seven hundred thousand. And God gave them power He has given to no one else."

46. *The Prophet Hud*

Wahb ibn Munabbih said: The greatest king of Ad was Khuljan ibn al-Dahm ibn Ad; and he had three idols, Sada, Hird and Haba, in the service of which he had placed one man for every day in the year. Among these, the noblest and best was called Khulud ibn Saad ibn Ad. When he was asked why he had not married, since he had reached the accustomed age, he replied, "Because in a dream I saw coming out of my loins a white chain, which had a light like the light of the sun. I heard a voice saying, 'Look well, Khulud, for when you see this chain come out of your loins again, marry the girl you will be commanded to marry.' So, although to this day I have not seen the chain again, I am determined to marry only when I do see it." So saying, he hastened to the sanctuary of the idols to pray for prosperity in marriage; but, when he tried to enter, he could not; whereupon he heard a voice say, "Khulud, marry the daughter of your uncle!" While he was asleep, suddenly the chain came forth from his loins.

When he awoke he went to his cousin, spoke for her and was married to her. When he had lain with her, she conceived Hud the prophet.

The ponds and rivers, the birds and beasts, wild and tame, rejoiced at the conception of Hud. The trees of the tribe of Ad became green and brought forth fruit out of season by the blessing of Hud. And when his mother's days were accomplished, he was born on a Friday.

* * *

One day, while he was at prayer, his mother saw him and asked, "My son, whom are your worshipping?"

"I am worshipping God, who created me and all creation," he answered.

"Do you not worship the idols?" asked his mother.

"Those idols bring neither harm nor profit," he said. "Neither do they see nor do they hear."

"My child," she said, "worship your God, for the day I conceived you I saw many strange things. When I was delivered of you in the valley there were dry trees that became green and bore fruit. When I put you on a black rock, it became whiter than snow. Then I carried you home and saw a man whose head was in the sky and whose feet were in the vast expanses of the earth. He took you from me and raised you up to a people in the sky whose faces were white. Then they returned you to me, and on your head were rays of light and on your arm was a green pearl. I heard one of them say, 'God has made you a prophet.' So act accordingly with what has appeared to you."

* * *

Kaab al-Ahbar said: When Hud was forty years old, God spoke to him, saying, "O Hud, I have selected thee as a prophet and have made thee a messenger to the tribe of Ad. Go therefore to them and fear them not. Call upon them to witness that there is no god but I alone, who have no partner, and that thou art my servant and my messenger."

Hud set out to his people on the day of their great festival, when they were dispersed among the sandy regions called Ramalalij. Their king, Khuljan, was seated on a golden throne with the crown of his grandfather, Ad ibn Uz, on his head.

"O my people," said Hud, *"worship God: ye have no other God than him"* (7.65). So saying, he let out a great shout; and from afar the wild beasts and lions drew near and said, "We are at your service, O Hud. Inform us and have no fear."

But the hearts of the people were filled with fear: their faces turned pale, and they shuddered. A man from among them, called Omar ibn Ahla, said, "We wish you would describe your God to us. What are his features like, his form, his length? Is he made of gold or silver?"

Hud described God's majesty. When he had finished his speech, the king said to him, "Do you think your Lord is more powerful than we are, considering the multitude of our numbers and the strength of our forces? Or do you not know that there are born to us every day and night one thousand two hundred male and female children?" As God hath said: *Did they not see that God, who had created them, was more mighty than they in strength?* (41.15).

The first person to believe in Hud that day was Junada ibn al-Asim, forty of whose cousins also believed.

Hud retired to his house. The next day he went out to the people and said, "O people, listen to my words. Do not exchange the favor of God for infidelity. Know that the wide earth is too narrow for the wrath of God." But the people rebuked him and cursed him, so he withdrew from them. He continued to indulge them, however, for a long time. Then God caused the women's wombs to become barren, and not a single woman among them bore a son or daughter.

* * *

A man called Marthid ibn Saad approached Hud and said, "Hud, I have come to you with a problem. If you can tell me what it is before I tell you, then you are truly a prophet."

"Marthid," Hud said, "yesterday while sleeping with your wife, you lay with her. Then you said to her, 'You are pregnant.' She said to you, however, 'I am not pregnant.' "

"That is it," said Marthid. "But tell me, O prophet of God, is my wife pregnant or not?"

"Yes," said Hud, "she is indeed. She will bear you two sons, who will be believers. Moreover, she will bear ten times, each time two sons, and they will be of my nation." Marthid fell upon Hud, kissed his head and became one of his closest friends. He went off to tell his wife, and she too believed and became one of the pious.

Next, a man called Nuhayl ibn Khalil became a believer. Hud tried day and night to restrain his people, but they neither listened nor mended their ways. When he had thus passed a long time, he withdrew from among them and occupied himself with worshipping his Lord.

Whenever Hud wished to curse them, he would consider their great number and say to himself, "Perhaps they will believe." He never ceased warning them until he had been calling them to worship God for seventy years, but still they had no faith.

* * *

Kaab al-Ahbar said: When their disbelief and injustice had increased, Hud went out to the Valley of Noah, performed the ablutions and prayed twenty *rak'as,* then lifted his gaze to heaven and said, "O God, thou knowest that I have preached my message, but they do not believe. O God, I ask thee to strike them down with famine and drought. Perhaps then they will believe. If they do not, then I ask thee to destroy them through torment such as no one has been destroyed before or will afterwards."

God answered his prayer and commanded him and any who believed along with him to depart from the people. Then God took away the rain and caused the earth to shrivel up, and no green thing grew in their fields and their beasts died; but they bore all this with patience for four years, until, despairing of themselves, they were about to believe. Thereupon the king, Khuljan ibn al-Dahm, called for the leaders and said, "It has reached us that you are determined to enter into Hud's religion because of the plight you are now in. You must not do such a thing, even if you be eating sand and drinking urine. If this suffering has afflicted us because of the multitude of our sins, why then have the wild beasts and animals of burden, which have no sin, been afflicted as much as we?" Thus they resolved that this condition could not persist, but Hud called out to them from a mountain-top, saying, "O children of Ad, if you have faith in your Lord, I will ask Him to send the heavens to you to pour down rain and to cause the earth to send forth her fruits."

* * *

Ibn Abbas said that in those days it was the custom, when a people was afflicted from heaven or from an enemy, to take offerings to the Sanctuary of the Kaaba and to ask God for release from suffering. They would enter the Sanctuary mounted on she-camels adorned with diverse jewels.

In accordance with this custom, they chose from among the noblest people seventy men. Seven were chosen from these to lead groups of ten, and their names were Qayl, Luqman, Jahlama, Ubayl, Marthid ibn Saad (who believed in Hud), Amr, and Luqaym. While they were departing from their land, they heard a voice saying, "Despair and misery for you, O House of Ad! You shall perish, and a destructive, shifting, icy gale, turbulent with dust, will descend upon you." They paid no attention to the voice, however, and went along their way. Marthid rode ahead and sang,

> Ad have disobeyed their prophet and have thirsted:
> The sky gives them no moisture.
> Fate and affliction have arrived and the judgment
> of God: passion has conquered
> Ad. Verily Ad is the most evil people: may they
> be destroyed and may there remain no trace
> of them!
> I shall not depart the religion of Hud by the might
> of the ages: Or annihilation will come.

While Marthid ibn Saad was thus mounted on his camel, suddenly a host of angels greeted him and said, "Welcome, O Marthid!" They took him down from his camel and seated him on another one they had with them. He rode with the angels through the sky until they reached the Sanctuary, where they said, "Our God and Master, give thy prophet Hud victory over his people and hasten their destruction."

When the delegation arrived seeking entrance into the Sanctuary, they heard a voice saying,

May God vanquish the delegation of Ad:
Ad is the most evil people of perdition.
The delegation has traveled to pray for rain:
May they quench their thirst with hot water!

* * *

The king of Mecca at that time was called Muawiya ibn Bakr, who was an Amalekite; and his sister was Hudhayla, the wife of Luqaym. The delegation descended at his house and remained there for one month, eating and drinking, and forgot what they had come for. When news of this reached their own king, Khuljan, he sent to Muawiya asking him to order them to pray for rain. But Muawiya was loathe to ask them to leave his house, although it is said that all this hospitality had grown burdensome for him. Therefore, he sent them two slave-girls, called the Two Locusts, who were singers in his service. He said to them, "While they are eating and drinking, sing to them and make them desirous of praying for rain." So when they had eaten and drunk, the two girls sang,

Come forth, O Qayl! Woe unto you! Rise up and murmur!
Perhaps God will grant us a wispy cloud,
Wherein there be a slight rain to wet the hills and
give the plain and the regions of Kama to drink,
And water the land of Ad: verily Ad are thirsty—
They are unable to speak;
Because of great thirst neither grand lord nor slave
has hope.
So they say, O delegation of drunks, remember your
tribe who are parched with thirst.

When they heard what the slave-girls said, they bathed themselves, put on clothes not soiled by wine, approached the Sanctuary and draped it with their robes; but the Sanctuary would not accept them.

Marthid said, "God, the Lord of this House, will not accept a gift except from a true believer."

One of the men said,

O Abu Saad, you are of the tribe of Abu Ad.
Your mother is of Thamud.
Shall we abandon the religion of our noble and meritorious fathers,
And follow the religion of Hud?

Then another of them came forward and said, "O Lord of Ad, give drink to Ad, for thou hast mercy on thy slaves and givest drink to the gardens and all the country."

"O God," said Marthid, "we do not come to thy Sanctuary but for an earth in need of water and a community in need of response from thee. Thou wilt not be niggardly in thy providing. O God, send torment to those who believe not!"

God commanded the angel of the clouds to spread over them three clouds, one white, one red and one black. On the black cloud was the angel entrusted with the Barren Wind. When they saw these clouds they rejoiced but were told, "O Qayl, choose for your people one of these three clouds!" He chose the black one and was told, "O Qayl, you have chosen the black cloud, in which are ashes and lead. Ad shall perish to the last from the heat!" The cloud moved until it had emerged from Wadi al-Mughith. When the people of Ad saw it, they said, "This cloud has come to give us rain!"

Then God commanded the angel of the clouds to open a portion of that cloud for the Barren Wind by spreading a wing for each of the tribes of Ad.[80] Gabriel then said, "O wind, be a torment to the people of Ad and a mercy to others!"

On the first day the wind came so cold and grey that it left nothing on the face of the earth unshattered. On the second day there was a yellow wind that touched nothing it did not tear up and throw into the air. On the third day a red wind left nothing undestroyed. And the wind kept on blowing over them for eight unhappy days and seven hapless nights. On the eighth day the tribes lined up and began to shoot arrows at the wind, saying, "We are mightier than you, Lord of Hud!" Thereupon the wind ripped them apart and went into their clothing, raised them into the air and cast them down on their heads, dead. The wind snatched their arrows and drove them into their throats. Thus it continued until there was left of them only their king, who remained to be shown what had become of his people. He fended the wind with his chest and said,

Only Khuljan himself remains:
  Woe to you on this terrible day!
There is no sense in being frightened:
  The very foundations are afflicted.
Sons and thrones are destroyed!

Then the wind entered his mouth and came out his posterior, and he fell down dead. The wind hurled the palaces together and killed all the women and children that were in them. It passed on to the Sanctuary and raised them into the air and cast them down on their heads, dead. As God hath said: *And when our sentence came to be put in execution, we delivered Hud, and those who had believed with him, through our mercy* (11.58).

Hud and those believers who were with him traveled to the Yemen, where they camped. They remained there for two full years, then death took him and he was buried in the Hadramaut.

* * *

Kaab al-Ahbar said: "One day I was in the Prophet's Mosque during the caliphate of Othman ibn Affan. A man entered the mosque, and everybody stared at him because of his height.

" 'Which of you is the Prophet's cousin, Ali ibn Abi Talib?' he asked.

"We sent to inform Ali; and when he came they exchanged greetings. Ali asked, 'Who are you?'

" 'I am from the Hadramaut,' he said.

" 'Do you know the lote-tree from the leaves of which drops fall as red as blood?' asked Ali.

" 'O Abu Hasan,' he said, 'you are asking about Hud's grave!'

" 'Yes,' said Ali.

" 'In my youth I went with a group of lads of my own people, and we traveled through the land of the sandy desert until we reached a high mountain, in which were many caves. One of us, who knew of Hud's grave, had us enter a cave; and we went to the end of it. There we found a huge rock stacked on top of another rock, and between the two was an opening through which only a thin man could pass. As I was the thinnest of the group, I entered and found a throne of red gold on which sat a dead man. I touched his body; he was Hud. I looked at him and saw that his eyes were large and his eyebrows met. He had a wide forehead, an oval face, fine feet and a long beard. He had never known affliction. Over his head was a rock shaped like a board, on which were written three lines in Indian letters. The first of these said, "There is no god but God; Muhammad is God's messenger." On the second was written, "God has commanded that none be worshipped but He: do good to your parents." And on the third was written, "I am Hud ibn Khulud ibn Saad ibn Ad, God's apostle to the tribe of Ad. I came to them with the message, and they denied me. God took them with the Barren Wind. After me shall come Salih ibn Kanuh, whose people shall be obstinate. The Great Cry shall take them, and they shall be left in their region lying on their breasts.'

"Ali said, 'You have spoken the truth. But have you any news of Thamud?'

" 'No,' he said, 'I know nothing of them, O Prince of the Faithful.' "

47. *Salih ibn Kanuh and His People, the Tribe of Thamud*

Kaab al-Ahbar said: After God destroyed the people of Ad, Thamud inhabited the land. They were a nation of ten tribes, each of which was composed of ten thousand men, under each of whom were ten thousand others, not counting the women;

and they were of great might and consequence. They dwelt in al-Hijr between the Hejaz and Syria in Wadi al-Qura; and their king was named Jandaa ibn Amr ibn al-Qayl. They carved their houses, each of which was one hundred cubits long and one hundred cubits deep, out of rock in the mountains; and they covered them with plates of iron, riveted with nails of brass.

After many years, a large number of them gathered before the king and said, "Sire, we desire to adopt a god for ourselves to worship, such that not even Ad or Noah's people had." As he gave them permission to do this, they went out to a mountain thereabouts and made an enormous idol with the face of a human, the neck of a mule, and the hands and feet of a horse and plated it with gold. On its head they placed a golden crown studded with jewels, and they made a sacrifice to it and bowed down to it.

The king then commanded a house of alternating bricks of gold and silver to be constructed for the idol, and the roof was gold-plated and studded with jewels. Around this building he had other buildings constructed for other idols, and in these he commanded gold lamps to be suspended from silver chains. The idol was then placed on its throne along with all the other idols on their smaller thrones. The man consecrated to the idol was called Rabab ibn Saghir of Ad. Another man of the nobility of Thamud was consecrated to serve the idols, and his name was Kanuh ibn Ubayd.[81] Old men worshipped the idols until they became senile, and youths worshipped until they grew old. In spite of all this, they flourished and prospered as a people; their livestock gave birth twice a year, and their trees bore fruit twice a year.

One day, while the people were in the idol-temple, Salih's seed moved in his father's loins and emitted a blinding light. A voice cried out, "This is the light of Salih! *Truth is come, and falsehood is vanished* (34.49). This is Salih ibn Kanuh, by means of whom God will rectify corruption!" Kanuh grew so terrified that he went to the great idol to bow down before it; but the idol lowered its head, and the demon spoke from inside it, saying, "O Kanuh, in your loins is a prophet. The earth is illuminated by the light of your seed." So saying, the idol toppled over on its face, and the crown fell from its head.

When news of this reached the king, he ordered Kanuh killed. However, God struck blind those charged to kill him and caused their hands to wither. He also sent an angel to bear Kanuh away and put him in Wadi al-Ashjar, where he remained asleep for a hundred years. In his place they appointed another servant for the idols, who was called Daud ibn Amr.

* * *

Raum, Kanuh's wife, wept grievously over the loss of her husband. One night while she was weeping, something landed in the courtyard of her house. When she went out to see what was there, she saw a bird in the shape of a raven with a white head, green back, black belly and red feet and beak. On its neck was a pearl on a golden chain.

"O bird," she said, "how beautiful you are! You must have escaped from your owner."

"I have not fled my owner," said the bird, "but am the raven God sent to Cain when he killed his brother Abel. It was I who showed him how to conceal the atrocity he had committed against his brother. As for my white head, it turned white when I saw Cain kill Abel; my feet and beak are red because I dipped them into the blood of Abel the Martyr. My back is green because it has been touched by the angels and the houris, as I am one of the birds of Paradise. Would you like me to lead you to your husband Kanuh? I know where he is."

"Who could possibly do such a thing for me?" she asked. "He has been gone a hundred years!"

"Do not deny the possibility," said the bird, "for God is capable of all things." Then, girting herself with a sword, she followed the bird. God hemmed up the distance so that she reached her goal in a short time and she found Kanuh asleep.

"O Kanuh ibn Ubayd!" cried the bird, "rise up by the might of God, who quickens the dead!" Kanuh stood up, saw his wife and embraced and greeted her. God then cast passion for her into his heart, and he lay with her, whereby she conceived Salih. And God sent down the Angel of Death to take Kanuh's spirit. Raum followed the bird back to the land of Thamud.

* * *

When her months were accomplished, she gave birth on a Friday eve, the *Ashura*. It is said that even from his crib Salih never ceased to praise and glorify God until he had grown to maturity.

When he was twenty years old he heard a great clamor and asked his mother what the commotion was. "My son," she said, "this is a king called Malkin, who raids us once a year and takes our possessions. This commotion is from his soldiers." When he heard this, he girt himself with his father's sword and went out to the people and shouted at them. God put such terror in their hearts that some died on the spot as a result of his cry and others turned and fled. Salih plundered their possessions and their livestock and returned to his mother.

* * *

When Salih was forty years of age, Gabriel descended to him and gave him the tidings of his apostleship. "Go to Thamud," he said, "and command them to say that there is no god but God and that you, Salih, are the servant and apostle of God. Also command them to cease worshipping idols!"

Salih came among his people on the day of their festival, when they set up their idols, adorned them with finery and offered them a sacrifice. "O people," cried Salih, "I have come to you as an apostle, and I call upon you to witness that there is no god but God and that I, Salih, am the apostle of God." And he delivered his entire message.

"O Salih," asked the king, "how is it that your Lord has singled you out of all of us as an apostle? Are there not among us more noble than you?"

"God's grace comes to whomever He wills," answered Salih. Some of the people believed in him, and some did not.

Salih then built for himself and for those who believed in him a mosque, in the construction of which he had the assistance of an angel and one of his cousins. At the door he planted the Tree of Felicity, which Gabriel had brought from Paradise and at the roots of which God caused a spring of sweet water to flow.

Salih never ceased calling his people to God for one hundred years, but they only increased in pride and disbelief. Then he decided to curse them; and, going out to a nearby mountain, he began to pray. On the mountain he saw a cave, from which light was streaming. Upon entering, he saw a throne covered with multicolored tapestries. He threw himself on the throne and slept for forty years, during which time no one knew where he had gone.

* * *

When the forty years had passed and Salih had awoken, he set out in search of his people. "O Salih," a voice cried to him, "because you were hasty in cursing your people, God struck your ears and you slept for forty years. Now go to your people and call them to obey God. Be not in haste, for your Lord is not hasty." As Salih realized what was expected of him, he fell down and prayed for forgiveness.

He went among his people and called out, saying, "My people, say that there is no god but God and that I, Salih, am God's apostle and prophet. My people, I was sent to you once before, and now this is the second time." When he spoke, the idols toppled down on their faces and the beasts spoke, saying, *"Truth is come, and falsehood is vanished"* (34.49).

"Who are you?" asked King Jandaa.

"I am Salih ibn Kanuh," he replied.

"Salih was among us for a long time," he said, "but he disappeared forty years ago. You are not Salih, but a lying sorcerer."

Now the king had a vizier named Harbil ibn Luqaym, who said, "Salih, we realize that you are advising us in what you say, but we do not need your advice. Go away from us!"

Turning to him, Salih said, "O Harbil ibn Luqaym, you shall die at such-and-such a time, and along with you your household and children. Your mother and father will also die in the al-Ghadd river. However, if you have faith in God, he will restore you to life; and you will be a proof to the people of Thamud." Thereafter Harbil and his family and children believed in Salih.

When the time Salih had mentioned came, Harbil and his family and children all died. Salih came to their graves and brought them back to life with God's permission. When the people saw this, they only disbelieved all the more and said, "This is nothing but sorcery!"

"O tribesmen of Thamud," said Salih, "I am God's apostle to you all. Believe in me that you may be saved from torment!"

"Salih," said the people, "we want you to perform a miracle. Make a she-camel come out of this white rock!"

"That is simple for my Lord," said Salih. "Describe how the camel should be."

Daud ibn Amr, the servant of the idols, stepped forward and said, "O Salih, if you be a prophet, produce a camel whose colors are dark red, pure yellow, unmixed green, intense black and pure white. Let her face be ablaze with lightning; let her grumbling be rumbling like thunder; let her gait be as stormy as a gale. Let her be a hundred cubits tall and a hundred cubits broad; let her have four udders, let her give water, milk, wine and honey!"

Then a man called Bahir ibn al-Shakir jumped forth and said, "O Salih, produce for us a camel and let her be slender, tall, wide- and black-eyed, with brown eyelids. Let her have foam and a hump. If you produce her thus, then we will believe in your apostleship."

Yet another man, called Labin ibn Jawwas, advanced and said, "O Salih, produce for us a camel with golden feet, silver legs, an emerald head, ruby eyes and coral ears. In place of the hump let there be a dome of pearl with four pillars studded with rubies and sapphires."

"O Salih," said the king, "produce for us a camel with fibers, blood, bones, veins, sinews and hair. Let her, moreover, be thick-skinned, pitch black and snow white. Let her give pure milk. Let her young follow her, and let her speak and bear witness that you are an apostle and that your Lord is one."

Salih faced his people and said, "If I produce such a camel, will you then believe in God?" And they agreed on condition that she give cold milk in the summer and warm milk in the winter such that when the sick drink it they be cured and the poor made rich.

"If I produce such a camel, will you then believe in God?" repeated Salih.

"Yes," they said, "on condition that she not graze in our pasture lands but on the tops of mountains and in the bottoms of valleys and leave what grows on the surface of the earth for our own flocks. Furthermore, she may have water on alternate days with us. At dusk she is to come into our region, call each of us by name and give him however much milk he wants without having to be milked."

"You have made many stipulations," said Salih. "Now I impose one stipulation, and that is that no one ever ride her or throw stones or shoot arrows at her. Let also no one prevent her from drinking or grazing."

"So be it!" they said.

Salih concluded pacts with them and then performed two *rak'as*. As he prayed to God, the rock shook and trembled; and the people heard a rumble like thunder. Out of the air they saw come hurling down like a falling star a dome of ruby with four emerald doors suspended by coral chains. It settled on the rock, which began to moan as women do in childbirth. Birds gathered around it, shading it with their wings and sprinkling water on it from their beaks. Then the camel could be seen revolving inside the rock as a child does in its mother's womb. The rock split open, and a camel as large as a mountain emerged and stood before Salih. In her eyes were rays of light, on her were reins of pearl; from her hump to the tip of her tail was seven hundred cubits, and she was seventy cubits broad. She had four udders, each of which had twelve nipples, ten cubits apart. Each of her legs was one hundred and fifty cubits long. She cried out, saying, "There is no god but God; Salih is God's apostle." Gabriel came and rubbed her belly, whereupon a kid emerged identical to her.

The king and many of the nobles believed in Salih; but the rest of the people allied themselves with Shihab, the king's brother, and made him king in Jandaa's place.

* * *

The camel went out to the mountain summits, and the branches of every tree she passed bent down for her to eat. She went down afterwards to the valley bottoms and grazed, leaving whatever grew on the surface of the ground for the flocks of Thamud. At dusk she entered the city and cried out intelligibly, saying, "Whoever wants milk, let him come forth!" And the people would come out of their houses with pans to place under her udders, and she filled them all, no matter how much they wanted. Subsequently she would return to Salih's mosque and glorify God until dawn, when she again went out to pasture. Thus was her daily schedule.

The people had a well from which they drank. On her day the camel came to the well, lowered her head and drank. On the camel's day the people drank milk; on their day they drank water and stored some for the next day, as He hath said: *She shall have her portion of water, and ye shall have your portion of water alternately, on a day appointed for you* (26.155). When anyone who opposed Salih drank her milk, he would have a seizure of itching and pox; but her milk was nourishing and healthy for those who believed.

48. *The Slaughter of the Camel & the Destruction of Thamud*

Kaab al-Ahbar said: Among the people was a woman named Unayza bint Umayra, whom everybody called Umm-Ghanam because she had so many sheep. She also had four daughters of true beauty and grace. There was another woman named Saduqa bint al-Muhayya, who also owned many flocks.

Saduqa went to a man called Khubab and said, "Would you like to have me as a wife?"

"How could that be?" he asked.

"I want you to slay the camel," she said. But he refused. Then she approached a cousin of hers called Musaddi ibn Muharrij and offered herself to him on condition that he slay the camel, and he accepted.

Unayza went to Qidar ibn Salif, the most hideous man of the tribe of Thamud, flat-nosed, blue-eyed, with large nostrils, and stocky. She offered him her eldest daughter on condition that he slay the camel, and he accepted.

As God hath said: *And there were nine men in the city, who acted corruptly in the earth, and behaved not with integrity* (27.48). Qidar and Musaddi went with the other seven, whose names were Hudhayl, Sallad, Rabbab, Qalam, Sabit, Amir and Samaan, all armed with swords and intent upon slaying the camel. And this was on a Wednesday.

When the camel came to the well, Qidar threw a spear and wounded her in the girth. All the rest also cast their spears and drew near her, swords in hand, as she fell to the ground. Qidar struck her with his sword once on the head, once on the neck and once on the flank and said to his companions, "Cut up her flesh for yourselves!" So they hacked her to pieces and ate and drank. Her kid escaped and ran to the summit of a mountain, where it raised its head toward heaven and cursed the tribe of Thamud.

When news of this reached Salih, he and his faithful followers wept; and God said to him, "Warn thy people of a torment for three days."

Salih said to his people, "Woe betide you! You have slain your Lord's camel. I bring you therefore tidings of a torment from God which will descend upon you for three days."

When the people awoke the next morning, they saw that in every place the camel had dwelt there were springs of blood bubbling up. Their faces and clothing also began to turn yellow and increased in intensity until their faces were the color of saffron. The nine who had slain the camel said, "Salih is shortening our lives. Let us kill him and be rid of him!" Under the cover of darkness they set out to slay him, but Gabriel hurled a rock at each of them and killed them all. The next morning the people saw their friends murdered and were certain that it was of Salih's doing. They gathered together to go to his mosque to kill him, but God commanded him to leave the mosque. He therefore departed and went to one of his people, a man called Baïd and spent the night at his house.

When the people came to the mosque and did not find Salih there, they departed. The next morning, however, they found their faces had turned red; and the morning after their faces were black as coal. They dug a pit for themselves, their wives and children and hid themselves inside, waiting for the torment to come. On the fourth day God told Gabriel to command Malik, the warden of Hell, to send sparks from beneath the earth to burn and destroy their palaces and dwellings.

Gabriel descended and ordered Malik to do as God had commanded. Then Gabriel spread the Wing of Wrath and began to cast down upon them embers the size of mountains, while the angels sang, "Holy! Holy!" He seized the extremities of the region of Thamud and shook it, with all its houses and palaces therein. The people felt the quake and the shock, but they still did not believe.

Then Gabriel gave a great shout, and black clouds rolled in, pouring down torrents of fire on the houses. At the end of seven days, everything was charred to ashes.

On the eighth day the clouds passed away, the sun came out, the earth was stilled and the fires died down, with God's permission. Salih and his people took what possessions they could manage and gathered the bones of the camel and her kid and put them in a golden coffer. They went to Palestine, where they dwelt until Salih went to God's mercy. His grave is well known there.

* * *

Kaab al-Ahbar said: Thereafter the people divided into two groups, one of which went to the land of Aden and were known as the Lords of the Unused Well. The other group went to the Hadramaut and were known as the Lords of Mashid Palace, which Shaddad ibn Ad built and plastered against the wind. But when the palace was finished he died, never having dwelt in it. He was so powerful that he could pull up a tree by its roots and eat enough for twenty men. He was so enamored of women that he married more than seven hundred virgins, each of whom bore him a boy and a girl. When he sat atop his palace with his wives, he would order everyone who passed by, be he who he may, to be killed. God destroyed him, his household and his people with the cry of Gabriel; and his palace remained in ruins, no one daring to enter. It is said that there was a huge serpent there whose groaning, like that of a sick person, could be heard.

* * *

As for the Unused Well, it is in Aden. Since the people were perpetually deprived of rain, they had to carry water from great distances. God gave them this well on condition that they worship him as is His due. They constructed the well of rocks and made a basin around for each of their tribes. Each tribe had a rope, a bucket and a basin. They had a king to lead them, and when he died they mourned him greatly. Iblis came to them and said, "O remnant of the tribe of Thamud, why do I find you deprived of happiness?"

"Why should we not be sad," they replied, "when we have lost our king, who was good to us?"

"This king of yours has not died," said Iblis, "but has been occulted and will so remain until you deify and worship him."

"How can we see and hear him?" they asked.

"I will lead you to him," said Iblis. "When you see him, bow down to him; and he will speak to you."

Iblis made an image in the likeness of the king and set it upon the king's throne. When the people approached, the demon inside it said, "O remnant of the Thamud tribe, why do I see you weeping?"

"We cannot endure the loss of you, sire," they said.

"You lie in what you say!" said the demon. "I was among you for four hundred years, and not one of you once bowed down to me."

"Sire," they replied, "if we could see your face, we would worship you."

Thereupon Iblis cast off the veil from his face, and no one could deny the resemblance to the king. They fell down prostrate and inclined themselves to him. And they adopted him as a god, besides God.

Among them was a man of Salih's lineage called Hanzala. When he saw what they were doing, he left their country and went to Mecca, where he worshipped his Lord. He heard a voice saying, "O Hanzala, go to your people, command them to worship God and forbid them to worship idols." He therefore went among his people in the land of Aden and called them to worship God; but they rebuked him and killed him, whereupon God at once caused the well to cease functioning, and they could not find even a drop of water in it. Gabriel gave forth the Cry of Wrath, and they all died.

* * *

As for the Lords of al-Rass, they built a large city in the Hadramaut and their king was named al-Rass.[82] They were believers and worshipped God, but Iblis diverted them from their worship of God and ordered them to worship idols and to commit sodomy with women and children, which they did. When this abomination increased among them, God sent them an apostle called Safwan, who called them to obey God and warned them of punishment. He remained among them for a long time preaching to them, but they would not be preached to until God tormented them with famine and hunger. When the prophet's words became too much for them, they killed him and burned him in a fire. Thereupon Gabriel gave forth a cry, and they all dried up; and no one remained in their land who did not turn into black rock.

49. *The Children of Cush and Nimrod*

Kaab al-Ahbar said: Among Ham's progeny were a boy called Cush son of Qatran and his brother Reu. They were tyrants in the land and could not be resisted. Cush was stronger than his brother, dark-complexioned, blue-eyed, of a mighty physique and had fingernails like lion's claws. One day he went out with his army touring the east and west, waging war, fighting, pillaging and plundering. At last he came to a place called Cuthah-rabba in Iraq, which abounded in rivers and trees. Summoning his astrologers, he said, "This city seems agreeable. See if it would be suitable as a dwelling for us."

"Give us three days' time," they said. And on the fourth day they came before him and said, "Sire, we have discovered through our knowledge of the stars that in this place there will come to be a magnificent king who will rule from east to west."

Cush smiled and said, "I am that king." Then he ordered that site to be built up, and fine palaces and ornamented assembly halls were constructed. He ordered them to make gardens and to channel rivers. There he dwelt for a long time, and God gave him a child named Canaan and another named al-Hasir.[83] Canaan was mighty and powerful and so expert in hunting that when he screamed at the beasts, their ferocity would be subdued and they would fall down on their faces.

Then Cush died, and the kingdom passed to al-Hasir.

* * *

Once, while Canaan was in the wilderness, he saw a woman tending some cows. He tried to entice her to sin, but she rebuked him. He grew too much for her, however; so she finally said, "My husband will be returning from the other direction. If he sees you with me, he will kill both of us!"

Canaan laughed and said, "Is there anyone on the face of the earth who can match me? I am Canaan son of Cush!"

The woman laughed and said, "Do not talk of kings, for you are a mere hunter." And while they were talking, her husband approached, cried out to Canaan, slapped him on the face, threw him down on his back and jumped on his chest to kill him. Canaan curried his favor so that he forgave him; then Canaan jumped up, picked him up and dashed him to the ground, killing him. Coming near the woman, whose name was Shelcha the Shepherdess, he lay with her and took her to his house.

* * *

The wars between the children of Japheth and the children of Cush grew more numerous, and al-Hasir conquered the Japhethites and reigned over them.

* * *

Canaan sent a message to Jawhar ibn Sarabil seeking his daughter in marriage, but he refused and said, "You are not of the lineage of kings. You are a mere hunter." Canaan grew angry at this and came to his brother al-Hasir to inform him of what Jawhar had said.

"My brother," he said to him, "I ask you to give me charge

of the army so that I can go against Jawhar ibn Sarabil, take his daughter by force, and kill him."

"My brother," answered al-Hasir, "Jawhar is one of the lords of the Japhethites. I cannot help you to kill him."

Canaan grew angry and seized al-Hasir by his feet, dragged him from his throne and killed him. Thus he gained possession of the kingdom.

Thereupon he set out for Jawhar's land, bore off his daughter and married her. Then Telah, Jawhar's son, gathered his forces and set out to fight Canaan. A mighty battle raged between them, but Canaan was defeated, whereupon he went to Og son of Anak, the king of the giants, seeking his help against Telah. Og agreed to help him, and Canaan set out with seventy thousand men to wage war against Telah, whom he took prisoner after killing his men. Thus he gained possession of his wealth and kingdom.

* * *

One night in a dream Canaan saw a man severing his neck and saying "O accursed of the people of the earth! God has delayed the time when I shall drive you from tyranny and judgment!" When he awoke he told his dream to the astrologers, who said, "Your dream indicates a newborn child at whose hand will come your destruction. His mother has conceived him already."

When he saw that Shelcha the Sheperdess had conceived that very day, he was determined to kill her and the child in her womb; but he heard a voice saying, "Calm yourself, Canaan, for you have no power to kill him!" And when he heard that, he put off killing her.

When her months were accomplished, she was delivered of a black, flat-nosed boy. Then, suddenly, a thin serpent came out of her womb and entered the boy's nose. Shelcha was terrified and told Canaan, who said, "Woe unto you, Shelcha! Kill him, for he is accursed!"

"I would have no peace of mind if I were to kill him," she said, "for he is my son and my darling."

"Take him then," said Canaan, "and cast him in the wilderness so that he may die of hunger and thirst." Therefore she set out into the wilderness, where she came upon a shepherd grazing cattle.

"Take this child and raise him," she said to him, "and he will be your slave." The shepherd therefore took the child and placed him among the cattle, but they shunned him and scattered left and right. No matter how many times the shepherd herded the cattle together, they would not come near the boy. Then the shepherd's wife came, and he told her about the child.

"This child is cursed," she said. "Kill him!" But the shepherd refused. His wife, however, took him to a fast-flowing river, threw him in and departed, thinking that he had drowned. The river cast him out onto the bank, and God sent a tigress to suckle him until some people chanced upon him, took him in and brought him up. They named him Nimrod because of the tigress [*nimra*] that had suckled him.

When he reached manhood, he took to highway robbery, raided towns and cities, stole the people's money and took their women captive. When a large number of degenerates had gathered around him, he entered Cuthah-rabba and waged war against Canaan, whom he defeated and whose neck he severed, unaware that he was his own father. After he had taken possession of Canaan's kingdom, he raided the kings of the earth one by one until he gained victory over all the lands. Then he marched with seventy thousand warriors against the king of the West, whose name was Barshush, and killed him. Then he marched against the king of the East, whose name was Ghizar, whom he also defeated and slew. Then he marched against the king of the Yemen and killed him, then to China and the Hadramaut, until he had slain many kings, the last of whom was Bihat, the king of India.

Upon his return to Cuthah-rabba, he summoned the master-carpenter and architect, Terah son of Nahor, and ordered him to build a magnificent house. Terah constructed for him a square palace, a thousand cubits in length and breadth. The walls he made of pearl and the floor of silver, the roof of sandal-wood and the gates of ivory. Inside he caused rivers of milk and honey, wine and water to flow, and trees of silver and gold were planted along the borders. He put many assembly-halls in it, in each of which was a portrait of Nimrod. When he had finished, Nimrod was so pleased with it that he made Terah one of his boon-companions and his grand vizier.

Nimrod became so haughty and tyrannical that he claimed godship. In addition he wanted to learn star-gazing, the science that God had given to Idris. When Idris was translated into heaven, this science was taken by his successor, a devout man named Hermes; and the faithful had continued to learn it until Nimrod's time.

One day, while walking in one of his pleasure-parks, Nimrod found a group of ascetics, clad in wool and hair shirts, and asked them who they were.

"We are what remains of Idris's people, and we worship God in this place," they told him.

Nimrod ordered them into his palace, where he said to them, "You have two choices: either enter into my religion or teach me knowledge of the stars."

"We will teach you what we know," they answered.

When he had learned something from them, Iblis appeared to him in the guise of an old man and said, "You have occupied yourself with learning about the stars, but I know something more than they do."

"What is that?" asked Nimrod.

"Sorcery and soothsaying," said Iblis; and he taught him those sciences. Then he said, "The kings of old had their own gods to worship and other idols for the people. As you are the greatest and noblest of them, you should build an idol for yourself apart from those of your people." Therefore Nimrod summoned Terah and ordered him to construct seventy idols of gold in his own image. Then he ordered his people to build idols for themselves; and everyone constructed an idol in his own likeness. Terah also built for Nimrod a golden idol, seven cubits high and two cubits broad, with ruby eyes and an emerald nose. On its head he placed a golden crown studded with pearls and called it Dilun.[84] Then he built for it a throne of ivory and aloe-wood.

Nimrod ordered sacrifices to be made to the idol, and the people worshipped idols until they knew nothing else.

*   *   *

One day when Nimrod mounted his throne, he heard a voice say, "Wretched be he who is ungrateful to Abraham's God!"

To Terah, who was standing beside him, he said, "Terah, who is Abraham?"

"I do not know," he answered.

Some time later, while Nimrod was contemplating the beauty of his palace, he heard a voice say, "O Nimrod, be not deceived by this palace of yours! Where shall you flee from Abraham and his God?" And Nimrod was vexed.

Then one day he went out hunting. When he was all alone, there came a voice, which said, "O Nimrod, do not be deceived by the lions, elephants and weapons you have collected, for they will be the first to be avenged of you." Nimrod returned anxiously to his palace and went to his idol Dilun. Bowing down, he asked about Abraham. The idol said, "Despair, O Nimrod! for Abraham will wrench your kingdom from you, unless you believe in him and his Lord." Nimrod sacrificed seven hundred bulls, sheep and cows to the idol.

* * *

One day, while Nimrod was in the courtyard of his palace, two white birds descended from the air and hovered before him. One of them said, "You and your kingdom are doomed! I am a bird of the East, and this is a bird of the West. We bring you tidings that Abraham's God will destroy you by Abraham's hand." Then they flew away.

Nimrod summoned Terah, who, upon hearing the story, said, "Sire, I think these were no more than rebellious genii who covet your position." But that night Nimrod had a terrifying dream. When he awoke, he summoned the astrologers and said, "I dreamed of a man from whose eyes came forth a light as bright as the sun. He wore two white garments and in his hand was a black stalk. He kicked me with his foot and said, 'O Nimrod, which would you prefer: to believe in Abraham's Lord or to have me shatter your crown?' Then he plucked out my right eye, and I began to cry for help; but no one would come to my assistance. Then the man said, 'Be you blind in eye and in heart!' Then he left me. This is what I saw."

The dream-interpreters said to him, "Sire, such terrifying

dreams may be produced by various foods. Do not let it trouble you." But when they had gone away they said to each other, "This dream indicates the passing of his kingdom and his own destruction."

* * *

One day while he was seated on his throne, an angel came to him in the guise of a man carrying a white vial in his right hand and a black vial in his left.

"Who let you into my house?" asked Nimrod.

"The Lord of the House let me in," he replied. "These two vials are a parable for you: this is Paradise, and this is Hell. Choose whichever one you desire." As the angel was departing, he struck the two vials together and said, "Your kingdom is doomed."

* * *

That night Nimrod had another dream and, summoning Terah, said, "Terah, in my dream I saw the moon rise from your loins and cast its light between heaven and earth. Then I heard a voice saying, *'The truth is come and falsehood is vanished'* (17.81). And I looked at the idols and saw that they were trembling."

"Sire," said Terah, "on earth I am like unto the rising moon because of my great devotion to the idols."

* * *

Then, while Nimrod was asleep seated on his throne, he had another dream, from which he awoke in fright. Summoning the people of his realm, he said, "I see miracles from Terah. Were he not one of the élite of my realm, I would say that he is my enemy, for I saw growing from his loins a green branch covered with clusters of grapes. Then twigs sprouted from the branch and twined around the east and the west and the heavens, and not one of my subjects was left who did not bow down before that branch—even my own palace and throne and all that is in my palace."

* * *

Afterwards Nimrod went to sleep and dreamed of a man standing with the sun in his right hand, the moon in his left, and all the stars between his hands. Then the man said, "Worship the Lord of heaven and earth!" whereupon the throne convulsed and threw him down.

Then Nimrod went to sleep again and had another terrifying dream. When he awoke he sent for the soothsayers and dream-interpreters and said to them, "I had a horrible dream. If you conceal its true meaning from me, I will have you tortured and thrown to the lions."

"What did you see, sire?" they asked.

"I saw a beam of light more brilliant than the sun and the moon. In this beam I saw a nation descending from and ascending into heaven. Then a man, among the most beautiful of that nation, stood in the light, and the people were saying to him, 'May God grant you victory, and through you may He revive the earth.' This was my dream."

"Give us a day and a night," they said; and he granted their request. But when they were with Terah, they said, "The king's dream indicates a child, born of those closest to him, who will inherit all the earth and whose name will be revered to the skies from east to west." Terah accompanied them to give the king their interpreation of the dream, which was, "He will come to you with neither weapons nor army."

Nimrod smiled and said, "If the matter be thus, then it will be simple."

"The child will come from the lineage of those closest to you," said the interpreters.

"There is no one closer to me than my son Cush, and there is no one I honor more than my vizier Terah," said Nimrod, who thereupon ordered his son Cush's throat cut and every woman with child watched, so that all male children born were to be killed, while the females were to be left alone: Thus it was until, in the course of seven years, he had slaughtered one hundred thousand babes. Then he called the astrologers and told them to see if his enemy had been killed or not.

"Sire," they said, "his mother has not yet conceived him." Confident in this knowledge, he had the slaughter ceased for a time, but later resumed; and he had so many babes slain in their mothers' arms that all creatures set up a great clamor to God.

Then God informed the angels of the birth of Abraham, the Friend of God, and they heralded it with great glorification.

50. *The Story of Abraham*

Now Terah went to his wife and informed her of what had happened.

"I will tell you of something stranger still," she said, "for I ceased to be fertile a long time ago, but today I menstruated and do not know what is wrong."

"Keep this matter concealed," he said, "and do not let news of it reach the king!" And she remained thus until she had again become pure.

Then Terah heard a voice saying, "Your wife's youth has been restored to her that she may produce the brilliant light which is in your seed." Thereupon an angel appeared and said, "O Terah, return and give up the trust which is in your seed." He returned to his house but dared not approach his wife. The next morning, however, there was a dazzling light shining from his face.

"Do you not see this light?" he asked his wife.

"Yes," she said, "and I, who was a barren old woman, have become a fertile girl."

Terah made sacrifices of animals, food and drink to the idols, thinking that they ate and drank. During the night devils came to devour the food, but they were frightened away by angels. The next day Terah was grieved to find the food still there and thought the idols were angry with him. Standing before the idols, he worshipped them to placate them. As he was slow in returning home, his wife came to the temple to find him. Overcome with desire, he lay with her in the temple itself, and she conceived Abraham. Thereupon the Kaaba fell down prostrate and spoke, saying, "There is no god but God alone who hath no partner." The idols were all toppled and the beasts beat the ground with their tails at the conception of Abraham; and his star rose over the extremities of the earth and shone like the sun and the moon together. Nimrod, seeing the star, asked the astrologers about it; and they said, "Sire, this star indicates that the child at whose hand will come your destruction has been conceived by its mother." Thereupon Nimrod had so many children killed that their number cannot be reckoned; but Abraham continued to increase in beauty and light in his mother's womb until four months had passed, when his mother had a vision of a fire reaching from beneath her skirt to the heights of heaven and spreading throughout the world.

When nine months had passed with Abraham in his mother's womb, Nimrod had a terrifying dream and awoke in fright. Calling for his astrologers, he said, "Last night I saw a smokeless fire descend from heaven, approach the door of my palace and say, 'Nimrod, say with me, "There is no god but God; Abraham is the apostle of God!" Otherwise I will burn you up.' Then it came near me and scorched me."

"This dream indicates a boy at whose hand will come your destruction," said the astrologers. "Make certain you slay him the moment he is born." Therefore Nimrod and the people of his realm strove to seek out all children and kill them.

When they came to Terah's house they asked his wife, "Have you conceived a child?"

"I have not been with child at all," she answered. God blinded them to Abraham, who would move to the other side of his mother whenever they touched her. As it was not apparent to them that she was with child, they left her.

When her birth pains commenced, an angel came and said, "Come with me to the Cave of Light, where Idris and Noah were born." There she found carpets, pillows and birthing implements, and God eased her pain.

She gave birth to Abraham on Friday night, the tenth of the month of Muharram. When Abraham was delivered, he stood erect and cried out at the top of his voice, "There is no god but God alone who hath no partner!" And his voice carried to the East and the West. Then Gabriel cut the umbilical cord, immersed him in the waters of the rivers of al-Ridwan and clothed him in a white garment. When he rubbed his mother's breast it flowed with milk and honey. When he sucked his fingers, his thumb flowed with honey, his index finger with wine, his middle finger with milk, his ring finger with cream and his little finger with water.

Abraham's mother returned home, her mind at ease concerning her child. On the third day she left her house in secret, headed for the cave. When she saw lions and wild beasts at the entrance to the cave, she became anxious and thought her child had surely perished. Entering the cave, however, she found him on a silk-brocade carpet and his eyes painted with kohl. Realizing that he was protected by his Lord, she returned home. Subsequently she visited him once every three days.

When four years had passed, Gabriel brought him a garment from Paradise and gave him the Nector of Unity to drink so that he would never associate anything with God.[85]

"Now go forth from the cave, victorious," said Gabriel, who preceded him with a golden staff.

God hath said: *And thus did we show unto Abraham the kingdom of heaven and the earth, that he might become one of those who firmly believe. And when the night overshadowed him, he saw a star, and said, This is my Lord; but when it set, he said, I like not gods which set. And when he saw the moon rising, he said, This is my Lord; but when he saw it set, he said, Verily if my Lord direct me not, I shall become one of the people who go astray. And when he saw the sun rising, he said, This is my Lord, this is the greatest; but when it set, he said, O my people, verily I am clear of that which ye associate with God: I direct my face unto him who hath created the heavens and the earth; I am orthodox, and am not one of the idolaters* (6.76ff). Then he began to repeat over his heart, his tongue, and all parts of his body the Profession of Sincerity, which is, "There is no god but God alone who hath no partner." And God commanded the wind to bear the Great Profession to the ears of all creatures, which were thereby occasioned bewilderment and fright; and Nimrod was terrified.

God then caused an angel to descend to Abraham and say, "Rise up, O Abraham, and go to your father and mother. Fear not! and remember your Lord morning and evening!"

Gabriel and Abraham stood together before the door of a

house, and Gabriel said, "Abraham, this is your parents' house. Enter therein and greet them." So saying, Gabriel left and ascended into heaven.

Abraham sought permission to enter and was invited in by his father. When he entered, Terah saw his beauty; and Usha came and embraced him, saying, "By the might of Nimrod, it is my son!"[86]

"Mother," said Abraham, "do not swear by the might of Nimrod, for might and majesty belong to God, who created me, shaped me, raised me, preserved me and guided me aright."

Terah was thunderstruck by his words and exclaimed, "My son, have you a lord other than Nimrod, who possesses the kingdom of the earth in its breadth and length?!"

"Father," said Abraham, "my Lord, who created heaven and earth, has no partner!"

News of Abraham reached Terah's relatives, who began to argue against him and threaten him with Nimrod's punishment; but he vied with them and made mention of the greatness of his Lord.

* * *

"Mother," Abraham asked one day, "am I more handsome or is Nimrod?"

"You are, my son. He is black, cross-eyed and flat-nosed."

"If he were the creator, then he would not look like that, would he?" asked Abraham.

"Abraham," said his father, "do not speak ill of our king and god, for it is he who created you and me."

Abraham grew angry and exclaimed, "May you be wretched, old man!"

Terah rose and went to Nimrod, bowed before him and said, "Sire, the child you feared is my son—my son, that is, inasmuch as he was born in my house, and quite without my knowledge. Now he has come to me as a youth, but he claims to have a lord other than you."

Nimrod, trembling with fear, asked, "How long has he been with you?"

"For three months," said Terah.

"Bring him to me!" said Nimrod to his aides, who seized Abraham and brought him before Nimrod.

Nimrod had decorated his palace and assembly halls in a marvelous manner, and Abraham turned to the left and to the right and said, "O God, make me victorious over them!" Then, turning to the people, he said, "My people, *what do ye worship* other than God?" (26.72ff)

They answered, "We worship idols."

"Do they hear you, when ye invoke them?" asked Abraham. *"Or do they either profit you, or hurt you?"*

They answered, "But we found our fathers do the same."

Abraham described God and, turning to his father said, *"And forgive my father, for that he hath been one of those who go astray"* (26.86).

Then Nimrod approached him and said, "Abraham, follow my religion and worship me, for it is I who created you and have given you substance."

"You lie!" said Abraham. "My creator and my sustainer is God, other than whom there is no god!"

The people were speechless, but slowly a liking for Abraham crept into their hearts.

Nimrod said to Terah, "This child of yours is young and does not know what he is saying. Take him and show him kindness. Perhaps he will recover his senses."

So Terah took him by the hand and said, "My son, since you are in my debt, I want you to vend idols as your brother does."

"But how can I sell what I despise?" asked Abraham. Nonetheless he was given a large and a small idol to sell. He would go out with two boys to carry the idols and would say, "Who will buy that which neither harms nor benefits?" And no one would take them from him. Then he would immerse the idols in water and say, "Drink!" and pull the ropes attached to their legs to draw them out of the water. The people would stare, but no one dared to say anything to him.

When an old man came asking him to sell one of the idols to him, Abraham said, "Old man, I have been sitting here scoffing at them. They are not to be worshipped." So the old man went to his brother Aaron, from whom he bought an idol. As he was carrying it on his back, it fell and broke; so he came back to Aaron and said, "You sold me a broken god."

"What are you going to do with the broken god?" asked

Abraham. They went to Terah, who said, "Take it and worship it. I give you permission to do so."

Then an old woman came to Abraham and asked him to sell her an idol. He took out the two idols for her and said, "Take the big one. There is more of it for firewood and kindling."

"I don't want it for kindling," she said. "I want it to worship. I had a god, but it was stolen in a bundle of clothing."

"A god cannot be stolen," said Abraham. "Were it really a god, it would have protected itself and your clothing too. If, however, you worship the Lord of heaven and earth, He will restore your clothing."

"When I see my bundle I will believe," she said. So Abraham prayed to his Lord, and suddenly the bundle, brought by Gabriel, appeared before him.

"Here is your bundle," Abraham told her, "and inside is your idol." The old woman took the bundle, broke the idol with a stone and believed in Abraham's God. After this she went about the city of Cuthah-rabba saying, "O people, worship God, who created you and has given you substance."

When news of the old woman reached Nimrod, he ordered her hands and feet to be cut off. When it was done, Abraham prayed her to be patient; and God sent down the angels to her with a green tabernacle. "Woman," said the angels, "rise and enter this tabernacle." They gave her a draught from Paradise to drink, and God restored her hands and feet and also her youth and beauty. Then she entered the tabernacle and rose into the air until she stood above Nimrod and said, "I am she to whom you did what you did. Woe unto you, Nimrod! My lot is Paradise, but yours is Hell!"

Then more than a thousand of the people of Cuthah-rabba believed in Abraham. Nimrod ordered them to be rounded up and thrown to the lions, but none were eaten. Then they were thrown to the dogs, but they would not devour the people either.

When Abraham had completed his fortieth year, Gabriel descended to him and said, "Your Lord has sent you to Nimrod the Accursed. Fight him and fear him not, for I shall protect you and shall give you victory over him."

Abraham stood at Nimrod's gate and shouted at the top of his voice, "O people! Say that there is no god but God and that

I, Abraham, am God's apostle." Nimrod was terrified and, trembling with fright, called for his viziers and patriarchs, whom he seated in the assembly halls; he also summoned his army with their weapons and instruments of war and drew up his lions and elephants in ranks on his right and left. Then Abraham mentioned God, and the lions, elephants, beasts and dogs became humble and submissive before him. Again he cried out, "O people! Confess that there is no god but God, creator of every thing!"

When one of the viziers asked him who he was, he said, "I am Abraham, son of Terah, apostle of the Lord of the Universe. I call you to worship Him."

"Who is your Lord?" they asked.

"He who created all people."

"My kingdom is greater than His!" said Nimrod.

"You lie!" said Abraham. "All kingdom and dominion belong to the Lord of the Universe."

With that, Nimrod's throne shook and said, "You do lie, Nimrod, enemy of God. It is God who has created all creation."

There was in Nimrod's palace a cock that now approached and said, "Nimrod, Abraham is the apostle of the Lord of the Universe, and what he says is the truth." And it too followed Abraham.

Next came a cow of great beauty that said, "Enemy of God, were I given leave by my Lord, I would gore you so that afterwards you would never be able to eat again!" Nimrod ordered the cow to be slain, but God restored it to life and caused two wings to grow from it; and the cow flew into the air.

Abraham turned and saw a slave-girl in the palace. She was nursing Nimrod's small daughter. Suddenly the girl lept from her mother's lap, faced Nimrod and said, "Father, this is God's prophet Abraham." And Nimrod ordered her cut to pieces.

"One of my tokens of prophecy," said Abraham, "is the power to call these lions, elephants and dogs and to have dominion over them. I can command your throne to topple you. I can command your crown to fly from your head, and I can command your palace to fall in on top of you. Verily God is not incapable of anything; He is capable of all things."

"What do you know of His power?" asked Nimrod.

"My Lord is he who giveth life, and killeth," (2.258) said Abraham.

"I give life, and I kill," said Nimrod.

"How can you do that?" asked Abraham.

"I set free from prison men sentenced to death, and I kill men not sentenced to die."

"My Lord does not give life or cause death thus," said Abraham. "He quickens the dead and He causes death to the living yet kills them not. But, O Nimrod, *God bringeth the sun from the east, now do thou bring it from the west." Whereupon* Nimrod *was confounded.* Then Abraham called upon his Lord and said, *"O Lord, show me how thou wilt raise the dead"* (2.260).

God said, "Dost thou not yet believe?"

He answered, "Yea, but I ask this that my heart may rest at ease."

God said, "Take therefore four birds."

Abraham took a white cock, a black raven, a green dove and a peacock, killed them, cut off their heads, mixed up the blood and feathers and scattered their flesh on four mountains tops. He then called them, and the heads went out of his hands, each to its own body, saying, "There is no god but God; Abraham is God's apostle to Nimrod and his people."

Nimrod then ordered Abraham to be bound and thrown into prison deep beneath the earth, and the guards put him in the remotest place. The angels, however, brought him food and drink from Paradise, and when he rose for prayer at night the light that encompassed him shone up to the heavens.

Abraham told the prisoners the story of Paradise and Hell. Once a man came and said, "Abraham, I am an Arab and the son of a king. We were four brothers, but the king grew angry with us and imprisoned me here and my brothers in the east, in the west and in the Yemen. Can your Lord reunite us?" Abraham performed the ablutions, rose and prayed two *rak'as* and called upon God. Suddenly the two brothers from the east and west fell from the air in front of their brother, whereupon everyone in the prison marveled. When the news reached Nimrod, he called for the brothers and asked, "Who brought you together with your brother and loosened your chains?"

"Our God did this through the prayer of Abraham," they answered.

Nimrod called for his sorcerers and said, "I want you to bring the other brother from the Yemen."

"Sire," they said, "we are not capable of such a task."

Then Nimrod said to Abraham, "Bring me the brother who is in the Yemen the same way you brought these two." Abraham prayed to his Lord, but God told him that the brother had died and now lay in his grave. When Abraham told them, they did not believe him.

"Pray to your Lord to bring us his grave!" said Nimrod.

Abraham prayed, and God commanded the angel entrusted with the earth to cleave the ground before Abraham, and the grave opened beneath their feet.

"This is the grave of your brother," he said to them.

"If what you say be true," they said, "pray your Lord to bring him back to life so that we can see him and speak to him." Abraham prayed, and suddenly the grave was split open and the man stepped forth, blazing in flame, and said, "This is the retribution of him who worshiped idols and was ungrateful to his Lord."

* * *

A man called Harith, along with many of the people, believed in Abraham. Nimrod ordered the believers thrown into the fire, but it did not harm them.

"If you speak the truth, accursed one," said Harith, "then order your viziers to be cast into the fire and you make it easy for them!"

Nimrod grew angry and called for fire and oil, into which he had them cast, and they were all burned to ashes. God sent a white cloud, which rained down upon them living waters, which caused their flesh and bones to grow back and brought them back to life. Springing forth and standing erect, they confessed the greatness of God.

Nimrod ordered them imprisoned with scorpions and snakes, where they remained for forty days; but God kept the snakes and scorpions from them and caused the narrow space where they sat to seem a great expanse.

Usha, Abraham's mother, came to Nimrod and wept, asking him to pardon her son. Nimrod did pardon him and let him go from his cell along with those who had believed with him.

Nimrod called for Terah and said, "I realize that your son is a sorcerer. I would like to have someone like him in my palace. Take him with you to the idol-temple and be kind to him. Perhaps his heart will soften toward us, and I will crown him with the diadem of honor and will marry him to my daughter. He shall be my own grand vizier." So Terah took Abraham by the hand and led him from Nimrod's palace.

When they had reached the middle of Cuthah-rabba, Abraham shouted, "O people, confess that there is no god but God and that I, Abraham, am God's apostle!"

But they denied him and said, "What you bring us is sorcery."

* * *

Then God took away the rain from them, and Nimrod was left in dire straits. He had all the available grain and food gathered up and stored in underground warehouses, estimating that he had enough for his people.

Abraham went outside the city to a sand dune and called his Lord to turn the sand into food for the faithful. God granted his prayer and made it food of Paradise, from which the believers took as much as they wanted; and the infidels took from Nimrod until his supply was exhausted, whereupon the people began to incline to Abraham.

One day, while Nimrod was standing at the gate of his palace, Abraham came near carrying a bag of wheat he had brought from the sand dune.

"Abraham," called Nimrod, "what have you there?"

"Food," answered Abraham. "My Lord has provided sustenance for me and for all who believe in Him and in me." Nimrod ordered him to open the bag; and, putting in his hand, he drew out red sand. Then Abraham put in his hand and drew out grains of wheat the size of pistachio nuts. On each grain was written, "A gift from the Magnificent to Abraham the Friend."

"You have corrupted my people," said Nimrod. "Go from my land!"

"I have more right to this city than you," said Abraham, "for it has been the land of my fathers and forefathers from all time. Your father Canaan came and settled here by force." And Abraham departed to his house.

* * *

Each year the people of Cuthah-rabba had a festival during which they went far out of the city and worshipped for several days. Afterwards they would return, and Nimrod would parade with the lords of the realm in magnificent array. When that festival approached and they were about to leave the city, they said to Abraham, "Are you not coming with us to the festival?"

"Verily I shall be sick," said Abraham (meaning because of their idolatry). *And they turned their backs and departed from him* (37.89f) to their festival so only the infirm and children were left in the city. Abraham entered the idol-temple, where the people had put tables of food before the idols.

"Why don't you eat, see or speak?" Abraham asked the idols. Then, taking an axe, *he turned upon them, and struck them with his right hand* (37.93), breaking the arm of one, the leg of another, the head of yet another—until he had shattered them into pieces, as God hath said: *He brake them all in pieces, except the biggest of them* (21.58) around the neck of which he hung the axe, mashed its face into the food that was before it and returned home.

When the festival was over and the people returned, they entered the temple and saw what Abraham had done to their idols. *They said, "Who hath done this to our gods? He is certainly an impious person." And certain of them answered, "We heard a young man speak reproachfully of them: he is named Abraham"* (21.59ff).

They said, "Bring him therefore before the people, that they may bear witness against him." When he was brought before the assembly, they said unto him, "Hast thou done this to our gods, O Abraham?"

He answered, "Nay, that biggest of them hath done it: but ask them, if they can speak."

And they said, "Verily thou knowest that these speak not."

Abraham answered, "Do ye therefore worship, besides God,

that which cannot profit you at all, neither can it hurt you? Fie on you: and upon that which ye worship beside God!"

The people said, "O king, burn him as he has burned our hearts." Now Nimrod had an iron furnace; and, whenever he grew angry at any of his subjects, he would order it to be lit, and the subject would be cast into it alive to be melted like lead. He ordered this furnace to be lit, and Abraham was thrown in. As the fire did him no harm, he was taken out again. Then Nimrod ordered a great pit dug and so much wood brought in by beasts that the animals themselves refused to carry the wood, all except the mule (as punishment for which God caused it to be sterile).

Wood was gathered for four years by men, women, children and slaves. Then they set torch to it. The flames lept up, and the smoke rose to a height of four hundred cubits so that when even a bird flew over, it was burnt and fell dead. However, they could discover no device whereby they could get Abraham into the fire. Iblis appeared to them in the guise of an old man and asked, "Why are you so perplexed?" They told him why, and he said to them, "Construct a catapult," which he taught them how to do. When it was ready, they put Abraham naked into the pan of the catapult, whereupon the sky and the earth and the angels set up a great noise, saying, "Our God, here is thy servant and apostle about to be cast into the fire!"

"If he calls upon you for aid," said God, "then do you help him. If he calls upon me, verily I am the succorer of those who seek aid."

Abraham prayed to his Lord to give him victory over his enemy, and the angels encompassed the pan of the catapult so that when they tried to lift him they could not.

"If you want him to rise up," said Iblis to them, "then bring ten women, strip them naked and expose their private parts." This they did, and the angels left the catapult, whereupon they hurled him forty cubits into the air, where Gabriel met him and said, "Abraham, have you any request?"

"From you, no," said Abraham. "God is my keeper: how excellent is his guardianship!"

Then God said, *"O fire, be thou cold, and a preservation*

unto Abraham" (21.69) (Ibn Abbas said this means "cold" from the heat of the fire and "preservation" from the cold).

The fire therefore became cool and its heat vanished. Gabriel brought a golden throne and clothed Abraham with garments from Paradise.

Nimrod saw in the midst of the fire a man seated on a throne and clad in green clothes, and on his right and left two men of extreme beauty and around about him a great multitude. "How many have you cast into the fire?" asked Nimrod. "One or a hundred thousand?"

"Only Abraham," they replied.

"Then who are those people around him?" asked Nimrod, and they were astonished.

"Go to him," said Nimrod, "and make him swear to you by God that he will come out to you." They made him swear, and he came out, wading through the fire, which did not burn him at all.

"Your magic is indeed marvelous," said Nimrod.

"It is not magic," replied Abraham. "It is the might of God!"

"Then I will go up into the heavens and kill this God of yours," said Nimrod, who then ordered a cube-shaped ark built, with two doors, one opening to the sky and the other to the earth. He also ordered four eagles to be starved for three days. He took two iron rods and nailed them to the sides of the ark; on the end of each rod he hung a piece of meat and fastened the eagles by their middles to the rods. Taking a bow and a quiver of arrows, he climbed into the ark and closed the doors. When the eagles raised their heads, saw the meat and realized what it was, they flew upwards, carrying the ark with them, and rose high, high into the air. Then Nimrod told his vizier to open the door and see how the earth appeared. Opening it, he said, "I see it as though it were but a village." Then he opened the door that gave to the sky and cried, "It looks just as it did when we were on the ground." He closed the door, and the eagles rose higher and higher until they grew tired and were about to drop with the ark, at which point an angel in the sky met the ark and said, "Woe unto you, Nimrod! Whither do you think you are going?"

"My destination is Abraham's God, with whom I am going to do battle. How much distance remains between Him and me?"

"Between the earth and the heaven of the world the distance takes five hundred years to traverse, and the canopy of heaven is of a like distance. There are seven heavens, and the height of each is like the height of the heaven of the world." When the vizier heard that, he fell down to the earth in a swoon, and Nimrod was left by himself in the ark. Then he took the bow and, placing an arrow in it, said, "If I cannot reach you, O God of Abraham, this arrow will!" And he shot the arrow into the air (and it is said that it returned to him smeared with blood), whereupon he exclaimed, "I have killed the God of Abraham!"

Now Gabriel struck the ark with one of his wings and cast it into the sea, from which the waves churned it up and left it on the shore. Nimrod emerged from the ark and found that his beard and hair had turned white.

From there he wandered from town to town until he came to Cuthah-rabba, which he entered by night. The next morning the people came to him but did not recognize him at first because of his white hair.

When the news of Nimrod's return reached Abraham, he went to Nimrod and said, "How did you find the might of my Lord?"

"I killed your Lord," said Nimrod.

"My Lord is too magnificent for you even to engage in battle with Him," said Abraham, "but do you think it is within your power to fight me tomorrow?" Nimrod assented and gathered his armies, while Abraham went out into the desert with seventy of his companions. Then God sent gnats down on Nimrod's army and the whole world was filled with them. They caused the death of so many people that the rest went into their houses, lit fires and locked their doors, all of which they did to no avail.

A gnat fell on Nimrod and came to rest on his beard. He was about to kill it when it entered one of his nostrils and crawled up to his brain and began to gnaw at his flesh, marrow and blood, praising God. Forty days passed during which Nimrod could not sleep, eat or drink, so he had an iron bar made with which he ordered his aides to strike his head, for every time they struck him the gnat would be still.

Those who struck his head were of only the highest rank;

but, after forty more days had passed, one of the viziers, a man of enormous strength, struck his head so hard that his skull split in two, and the gnat emerged like a chick from an egg, saying, "There is no god but God; Abraham is the apostle of God and His Friend."

Nimrod died in a most horrible manner; and God visited earthquakes upon his people, and their city was pulled down around them. God hastened their souls to Hell and made their everlasting abode miserable.

51. *Abraham's Migration to the Sacred Land*

Kaab al-Ahbar said: Then Abraham gathered together those of his companions who had believed in him and set out for Syria. He traveled until he came to the city of Harran, where he dwelt for a time. There reigned a king named Harran, who believed in Abraham and gave him his daughter Sarah in marriage.

From there he went to Jordan, where there was a king named Zadok, who summoned Abraham and asked who he was.

"I am Abraham, Friend of God," he said. Then the king asked who the woman was.

"This is my sister," said Abraham.

"Marry her to me!" commanded the king.

"She is forbidden to marry an infidel," he said, 'for she is a believer."

"If you do not give her to me in marriage," said the king, "I shall take her from you by force!" And he ordered Sarah brought to him. Abraham prayed to God, and when the king stretched out his hand toward her it withered and stuck to his neck.

"This is your just retribution," said Sarah, "because you were wrathful toward the Friend of God and his wife."

"Are you his wife?" asked Zadok.

"Yes," she answered.

"Then I am sorry for what I have done," he said, "and am repentful. Ask Abraham to pray to his Lord to forgive me." Abraham prayed to his Lord and was told that the king would not be set free unless he submit his kingdom to Abraham and depart. When told this, the king agreed and gave his land to Abraham.

52. *Hagar and Ishmael*

The king had an extremely beautiful daughter named Hagar, whom he gave to Sarah.

At this time Gabriel came to Abraham and bore him tidings that God would bless him with two sons. One was to be born of Sarah, and from his loins would issue many prophets; the other one was to be born of Hagar, and from his loins would issue one prophet whose name would be Muhammad, the Seal of the Prophets. Now since Sarah was old and had never given birth, she gave her handmaiden Hagar to Abraham so that God might give him a child by her. Abraham lay with her, and she conceived.

When her months were accomplished, she was delivered of Ishmael, from whose face radiated the Light of our Prophet Muhammad like the moon. Sarah, however, was grieved because she had no child of her own. When seven years had passed, Sarah could no longer bear to see Abraham with Hagar, and jealousy in her heart caused her to say to him, "O Prophet of God, I do not like having Hagar in the house with me. Remove her to some other place—wherever you wish." As God told him to take Hagar and Ishmael to the Sacred Land, Abraham took them and settled them near the Kaaba, which was at that time in a million pieces, relics of the Deluge.

There Abraham said to Hagar, "Remain here with my child, for thus have I been commanded."

"Upon whom shall I rely?" asked Hagar.

"Upon your Lord," answered Abraham, who turned to the right and to the left, but, seeing no one, said, *"O Lord, I have caused some of my offspring to settle in an unfruitful valley, near thy holy house, O Lord, that they may be constant at prayer. Grant, therefore, that the hearts of some men may be affected with kindness toward them, and do thou bestow on them all sorts of fruits, that they may give thanks. O Lord, thou knowest whatsoever we conceal, and whatsoever we publish"* (14.37f). Then Abraham returned home, leaving them there.

* * *

When the heat became unbearable, Hagar saw a tree where the Well of Zemzem was to be, over which she suspended a robe to shade them from the heat of the sun. As they had finished the water in the jug they had with them and were thirsty, Hagar did not know what to do. First she ran in the direction of Safa in search of water and then towards Marwa, crying, "Our God, do not destroy us by thirst!" Then Gabriel descended to them bearing tidings of relief, whereupon she went to Ishmael, who was scratching the earth with his finger; there the Well of Zemzem sprang up, and she fell down prostrate in thanks to God. Hagar said, "It is abundant water [*zamzam*]," from which it took its name. Then she gathered stones around the spring lest the water flow away; had she not done that, the water would have flowed across the face of the earth from east to west.

There they remained until a caravan approached from the Yemen headed for Syria. When they saw birds hovering above Hagar and her child, they were perplexed and said, "Birds hover only over water and inhabited places." Drawing near, they found Hagar and Ishmael beside a well of sweet water. "Are you a human being or from the genii?" they asked her.

"I am Hagar," she answered, "handmaiden of Abraham, Friend of God, and this is my son by him. God has brought forth this well for my son."

"We have come with our people, and we used to dwell there familiarly with you. Would you deny us water?"

"It is God's," she said, "for God's creatures to drink." So they returned with their people and herds and stopped at the Sacred Land.

When Ishmael came of age, he married a noble woman of that tribe; and Hagar died.

* * *

Abraham longed for his son Ishmael. When he had taken leave of Sarah, who gave him permission to go, Gabriel brought him a horse from Paradise, which he mounted and rode to the Sacred Land. Entering his son's house, he said, "Peace be with you, O people of this dwelling," but the woman said nothing to him save to ask what he wanted and to tell him that the master of the house was away. Abraham said to her, "When your husband comes, tell him to change the threshold of his house." Then he returned to Syria. When Ishmael returned from hunting, his wife informed him of what had happened. "Go rejoin your people," he told her, and she departed.

Ishmael then married a woman from Jurhum called Hala, daughter of Imran ibn al-Harith, who bore him Kedar and his twin Nebaioth, then Zaynab and Amram, Aramel and Adiar, Ketur and Tablud, Massa and Mutin, and Lisan and Sharabah, twelve children in all, six sets of twins.[87]

* * *

When Abraham again longed to see Ishmael, Gabriel brought him a horse to mount and, with Sarah's leave, he approached the Sacred Land, where, entering Ishmael's house, he said, "Peace be with you, O people of this dwelling."

Ishmael's wife replied, "And with you peace, O noble man. Come in, for the master of the house is away but will return shortly."

"Have you any food?" asked Abraham. The woman replied that she did and brought him bread, a plate of sliced meat, a cup of water and some roast fowl, upon which he dined. Then she washed his head and annointed it with oil.

"When the master of the house comes," said Abraham, "give him my regards and tell him to hold fast to the threshold of his house." And he departed.

When Ishmael returned his wife told him what had happened, and he said to her, "Now you have become nobler in my sight because you have honored Abraham. You are that threshold of which he spoke."

* * *

A third time Abraham longed to see Ishmael, after having been separated from him for twenty-three years, so he set forth and found him.

God spoke to Abraham, saying, "Build the Sacred House!" But Abraham did not know what dimensions to make it, so God sent a cloud the size of the Kaaba and told him to dig foundations not to exceed the size of the cloud, as He hath said: *When Abraham and Ishmael raised the foundations of the house, saying, "Lord, accept it from us, for thou art he who heareth and knoweth"* (2.127).

Then Gabriel took them to Mina, where they prayed the midday, afternoon, evening and night prayers, and spent the night. When they awoke they prayed the dawn prayer. Then they were taken to Mount Arafat, where they prayed the midday and afternoon prayers, and passed on to al-Mawqif, where they greeted the *qibla* by pronouncing the Great Exaltation and *du'a* prayer until the sun set. From there they were taken to al-Muzdalifa, where they slept. When they awoke, they went to Mash'ar al-Haram and then returned to Mina, where each of them cast seven stones, for it was there that Satan was shown to them. And with the casting of each stone Satan wandered throughout the earth.

Then Gabriel taught them their ritual duties, and Abraham greeted the *qibla* with *du'a,* saying, *"Lord, send them likewise an apostle from among them, who may declare thy signs unto them"* (2.129) (and God answered his prayer through Muhammad). Then he stood at a corner of the House and cried out, "O ye who worship God, make the pilgrimage to God's House and respond to him who calls for God." His voice reached the East and the West and was heard by those yet in the loins of men and the wombs of women; and whosoever replied was given the privilege of making the pilgrimage, and whosoever did not reply was not. Then Abraham returned to Syria.

It is said that Ishmael lived for one hundred and thirty-seven years and was buried in the rock where his mother Hagar had been buried.

53. *The Story of Lot*

Kaab al-Ahbar said: Then God spoke to Abraham, saying, "Send Lot as an apostle to the people of Sodom." Lot, son of Haran son of Terah, was Abraham's nephew and a prophet in the "Mu'tafikat", which were the greatest cities (that is, the greatest of that age), namely, Hann, Sodom, Hamud, Zoar, Gomorrah and Admah.[88] The largest of these cities was Sodom, the king of which was Shelach son of Haraq of the people of Nimrod. And the inhabitants of these cities were exceptional in their idolatry and abominations.

Therefore Abraham sent Lot as a prophet to the cities of the "Mu'tafikat". When Lot came to Sodom, he cried out at the top of his voice, "Fear God, obey Him, and eschew those evil deeds, which you did not use to commit!" As He hath said: *And remember Lot, when he said unto his people, "Do ye commit a wickedness, wherein no creature hath set you an example? Do ye approach lustfully unto men, leaving the women?"* (7.80f)

But the people said, *"Bring down the vengeance of God upon us, if thou speakest the truth!"* (29.29) Then they fell upon him from all sides and said, *"Unless thou desist, O Lot, thou shalt certainly be expelled our city"* (26.167).

But he said, *"O Lord, deliver me, and my family, from that which they act"* (26.169).

However, Lot dwelt among them for forty years, continually calling them to obey God and warning them of His punishment, but they did not believe.

* * *

Then God commanded four angels, Gabriel, Michael, Israfel and Azrael, to descend to Abraham in the guise of men to inform him that they had been sent to give him glad tidings of Isaac and of Jacob, who would come after Isaac.

Now as Abraham would eat only in the presence of guests and no guest had come to him for three days, he said, "Sarah, go prepare some food. I shall go out and find a guest." She did as she was told, and Abraham set out in search of a guest. When he saw the angels coming in their guise, they said, *"Peace!"*

He answered, *"Peace"; saying within himself, "These are unknown people"* (51.25). He went to Sarah and told her that four guests, comely in appearance and dress, had arrived and that she was to serve them. He then took a fatted calf and slew it, cut it in half and put it on a fire in a hole in the ground to roast. As he was offering it to them, Sarah was also standing by to serve them. Abraham ate without looking at them, *and when he saw that their hands did not touch the meat, he misliked them, and entertained a fear of them* (11.70).

"If I had known you were not going to eat," he said, "I would not have taken the calf from its mother." Gabriel stretched his hand to the calf and said, "Arise by your Lord's permission!" Immediately the calf got up and ran to its mother.

"Verily we are afraid of you," said Abraham.

They replied, "Fear not; we bring thee the promise of a wise son" (15.52ff).

He said, "Do ye bring me the promise of a son now old age hath overtaken me? what is it therefore that ye tell me?"

They said, "We have told thee the truth; be not therefore one of those who despair."

He answered, "And who despaireth of the mercy of God, except those who err?"

When Sarah, who was standing close by, heard this, she laughed and said, *"I am an old woman, and barren* (51.29). *This my husband also being advanced in years. Verily this would be a wonderful thing"* (11.72f).

The angels answered, "Dost thou wonder at the command of God?" And, although she was ninety years old, she immediately became fertile.

"Nay, Sarah," said Gabriel, *"thus saith thy Lord: verily he is the wise, the knowing"* (51.30).

"What is your errand, therefore, O messengers of God?" asked Abraham.

They answered, "Verily we are sent unto a wicked people: that we may send upon them stones of baked clay, (51.31ff) on each of which is written the name of a polytheist."

Grief-stricken out of compassion for Lot, Abraham said, *"Verily Lot dwelleth there"* (29.32).

They replied, "We well know who dwelleth therein: we will

surely deliver him and his family, except his wife; she shall be one of those who remain behind."

Then Gabriel returned to his true form, and Abraham recognized him, and Gabriel told him who was with him. When Abraham asked the number of believers in those cities, Gabriel said, "None save Lot and his two daughters."

The angels rode their steeds to the cities of Lot's people, arriving at dusk. Lot's daughter Rawaya saw them as she was drawing water and, approaching them, asked, "What brings you to the cities of such libertines, where none will receive you as guests? Go to that old man!" And they went to him.

When Lot saw them, he felt sorry for them because of his people's evil doings and asked, "From where have you come?"

"From far away," they answered. "Could you put us up as guests?"

"Certainly," said Lot, "but how can I do so with these abominators?"

"This is one testimony," said Gabriel to Israfel (for God had commanded them not to destroy Lot's people until they had heard four testimonies against them).

"Lot," they said, "night has drawn nigh while we have been in your courtyard."

"I told you before," said Lot, "that my people commit abominations against Him."

And Gabriel said, "This is the second testimony."

Then Lot said, "Descend from your beasts and stay here until the night is past lest anyone see you, for they are a people who abominate against Him."

"This is the third testimony," said Gabriel.

When night had fallen, Lot took the angels to his house, where he told his wife, "Woman! You have disobeyed God for forty years, and now God's angels have come to me. Keep them hidden." As He hath said: *God propoundeth as a similitude unto the unbelievers, the wife of Noah, and the wife of Lot.*[89] (66.10).

* * *

Noah's wife's treachery was that she told her people not to strike him because he was mad. Lot's wife's treachery was in grinding wheat if a guest came during the day and in kindling a fire if a guest came at night so that the people would know someone was there.

* * *

So she went out with a lighted lamp in her hand thus to inform her people that guests were there. Lot locked the doors, but the abominators came and dragged him out.

"O my people!" cried Lot, *"these my daughters are more lawful for you: therefore fear God, and put me not to shame by wronging my guests. Is there not a man of prudence among you* (11.78) to forbid you injustice and command you to do what is just?"

They answered, "Thou knowest that we have no need of thy daughters; and thou well knowest what we will have" (11.79). They broke down the gate and came inside; but Lot stood against the door of the house where his guests were, locked it and said, "I will not surrender my guests to you until my last breath is gone!" But one of the people slapped his face and pushed him away from the door, whereupon Lot said, "O my God, avenge me against them!"

Then Gabriel said, "This is the fourth testimony." Making a sign with his wing, he struck the attackers blind and turned their faces black. Gabriel said to Lot, "Arise and take your household away!"

Meanwhile, the people were wandering around the house, feeling the corners and walls and striking their heads and crying, "Lot has brought sorcerers who have cast spells over our eyes. Lot! You shall see what we will do to you!!"

Lot asked the angels, "For what purpose have you been sent, O angels of my Lord?" And when they told him, he asked when it would occur.

"Verily the prediction of their punishment shall be fulfilled in the morning: is not the morning near? Arise and go therefore, with thy family, in some part of the night, and let not any of you turn back, save thy wife" (11.81).

So Lot gathered together his daughters and all his possessions, and Gabriel sent him forth forty miles distant from the city. Lot's wife asked him where they were going. When he told her, she asked, "Does your Lord have the power to destroy all these cities?" Thereat a clay stone fell on her head and killed her.

* * *

It is said that she remained transformed into a black stone for twenty years, after which she was swallowed up into the bowels of the earth.

* * *

Then Gabriel spread out the Wing of Wrath; Israfel gathered up the corners of the cities; Michael placed his wing beneath the seven lower layers of the earth; and Azrael prepared himself to take their souls with fiery prongs.

When the first days of dawn broke, Gabriel uprooted the cities from one end to the other down to the black waters, then he lifted them up, together with the mountains, houses, trees, and rivers, to the sea which is in the air and turned it all upside down. The angels in the lower heavens, hearing the cocks crowing and dogs howling, asked, "Who are these upon whom God's wrath has fallen?" And they were told that they were Lot's people. Thereupon they set up a great clamor, praising God and blessing His name.

Then God cried out to Gabriel, "Strike the cities one against the other and rain down upon them stones of clay!"

As they were crumbling into the air, the people awoke and saw fire below and angels above, pelting them with marked stones. Then thick, black smoke, which no one could breathe, began to rise from beneath the cities. And the ruins were left to be a reminder to anyone who might see them.

* * *

Lot took his family to Abraham and told him what had befallen his people.

54. *The Story of Isaac*

Kaab al-Ahbar said: Sarah conceived Isaac on the very night Lot's people were destroyed, and when her months were accomplished she was delivered on a Friday eve, the *Ashura*.[90] From his forehead shone a light that lit up everything about him, and when he first touched the earth he fell down prostrate before God and raised his hands to heaven to proclaim the Divine Unity. Abraham too praised his Lord and, summoning the poor and unfortunate, gave them food and drink out of thanks to God.

When Isaac was in his seventh year, he went out one day with his father to the Sacred Temple, where Abraham went to sleep. Someone appeared to him in a dream and said, "Abraham, God commands you to make a sacrifice." When he awoke, he took a fat bull, slaughtered it and distributed it among the poor. The next night the voice again came to him and said, "Abraham, God commands you to make a greater sacrifice than a bull." When he awoke he slaughtered a camel and distributed it among the poor. The third night the voice came again and said, "God commands you to make a sacrifice greater even than a camel."

"What can be greater than a camel?" asked Abraham; and, when there was a motioning toward Isaac, he awoke in fright.

"My son," said Abraham to Isaac, "are you not obedient to me?"

"Yes, father," he answered, "even if you wanted to sacrifice me, I should not resist."

Then Abraham went into the temple, took a knife and rope and said to Isaac, "Son, come with me to the mountain."

When they had gone, Iblis came to Sarah and said, "Abraham has determined to sacrifice your son Isaac. Follow him and stop him!"

But Sarah, recognizing him, said, "Get thee hence, Accursed of God! He has set out to do it to please God."

Leaving Sarah, Iblis followed Isaac, saying to him, "Your father wants to sacrifice you."

But Abraham said to him, "Come, my son, and pay him no heed, for he is Iblis."

When they had come to the mountain, Abraham said, *"O my son, verily I saw in a dream that I should offer thee in sacrifice"* (37.102).

He said, "O my father, do what thou art commanded: thou shalt find me, if God please, a patient person." Then he added, "Father, since you are going to sacrifice me, take my shirt from my body lest, when my dear mother sees it, she weep long over me. Fasten also my shoulders lest I writhe before you and cause you pain. When you put the knife to my throat, turn away your face lest you be overcome by compassion and be not able to finish. Seek God's help in my loss. When you return, take my shirt to my mother that she may have some consolation for my loss; give her my greetings but do not tell her how you sacrificed me, neither how you took my shirt nor how you bound me with rope, lest she sorrow over me. Whenever you see a boy like me, do not look at him lest your heart grieve for me."

Then a voice cried out from heaven, "O Friend of God, how can you not have compassion on this small boy who speaks thus to you?"

Abraham thought it was the mountain speaking to him, however, and said, "O mountain, thus has God commanded me. Do not distract me with your words!" He took Isaac's shirt, tied him with the rope and said, "In the name of God the All-powerful, the Glorious," put the knife to his throat and raised his hand. But he paused and lowered his hand, whereupon the knife itself turned away and spoke, saying, "There is no might or power save with God the Sublime, the Magnificent." Then he whetted the blade on a stone until it was red-hot; but when he returned to Isaac, the knife again turned away and, speaking with God's permission, said, "Do not blame me, O prophet of God, for thus am I commanded to do!"

Then Abraham heard a voice crying, *"Now hast thou verified the vision." And we ransomed him with a noble victim* (37.105, 107) (that is, a tremendous ram). The voice then cried, "Abraham, take this ram and ransom your son. Offer it in sacrifice, for God has made this day a holy day for you and your children."[91]

The ram then spoke, saying, "O Friend of God, sacrifice me instead of your son, for it is more fitting for me to be sacrificed than him. I am the ram of Abel son of Adam, which he sacrificed to his Lord and which He accepted. I have grazed in the meadows of Paradise for forty autumns."

Abraham praised his Lord for ransoming Isaac. When he went to untie him, he found the bonds already loosed. "Who untied you, my son?" asked Abraham.

"He who brought the ram for sacrifice," answered Isaac. Then Abraham set upon the ram, slaughtered it and saw a white, smokeless fire come down from heaven and consume the ram whole, except the head, which he and Isaac took and returned home. When they told Sarah what had happened, she fell down prostrate in thanks to God.

* * *

Ibn Abbas said: Ishmael is the sacrificial lamb of God, according to Mujahid and al-Dahhak, as the Prophet said, "I am the son of the two sacrificial lambs."[92] Ibn Omar, Hasan, Husayn and Qatada said the sacrificial lamb was Isaac.

* * *

As the Canaanites claimed that Abraham and Sarah had found and adopted a foundling child, God caused Isaac to resemble his father.

* * *

Abraham saw that his hair and beard had turned white, and God said to him, "This is light and dignity."

"O Lord," said Abraham, "increase it for me." And all of his hair became white, whereby he was known to the people.

* * *

Then Sarah died and Abraham married a Canaanite woman named Zehorah, who gave birth to six children, Midian, Kishan, Aham, Sirhan, Naphish and Naphshan. Then she died and Abraham married her sister Keturah, who bore four children, Baladi, Shuhuh, Sheger and Zimram.

* * *

Abraham saw the Angel of Death come to him in a most beautiful guise. They exchanged greetings and Abraham asked, "Who are you, O noble man?"

"I am the Angel of Death," he said.

"Who could despise death when you are in such a guise?" asked Abraham.

"This is the form I assume for prophets."

"I ask you to show me the form in which you appear to infidels," said Abraham. When he changed his form and Abraham gazed upon him, he almost fainted and cried, "O Angel of Death, return to your first form!" So, returning to his first form, the angel was about to take Abraham's spirit, but could not bring himself to do it and departed.

Later he returned in the guise of an old man and said, "Do you have any food, O Friend of God?"

"Yes," he said and offered him some food on a tray. But the old man lifted the pieces of food to his chest, his ears and eyes, and said, "I have grown so old that I can no longer eat."

"How old are you?" asked Abraham.

"Two hundred," he replied.

"I myself lack six years to being two hundred," said Abraham, "and if I will be like this when I reach your age, then I wish to live no longer." And the angel took his spirit.

* * *

The people of learning have said that Abraham lived one hundred and seventy-five years and was buried in a field he had bought and in which Sarah had been interred.

55. *Jacob and Esau*

Isaac's wife was Rebecca, the daughter of Bethuel. Isaac dreamed of a great tree with many limbs and branches coming forth from his loins, and on each branch was a light. Then a voice spoke to him, saying, "These branches are your sons the prophets." When he awoke and told his wife of his dream, she said, "O prophet of God, I am bearing you two sons who are even now moving in my womb."

When her days were accomplished, she was delivered of twins, one following the other. The first was called Esau and the other Jacob. Isaac loved Esau while Rebecca loved Jacob.

One day Isaac said to Esau, "When a certain day comes, come to me that I may give you my blessing so that God may bring forth the prophets from your line."

The two brothers used to take turns grazing sheep. Esau's body was hairier, and he was the stronger and fiercer of the two.

Rebecca set upon a young kid, slaughtered it and placed its hide over Jacob's back and arms and said to him, "Go to your father. Perhaps he will give you his blessing." So Jacob came to his father; and Isaac touched him, felt his arms, found him hairy and said, "The speech is that of Jacob, but the skin is that of Esau."

Esau, meantime, was in the pasture; and, when Isaac called for him, he came after Jacob and sat before his father, saying, "O father, bless me as you promised."

"My son," said Isaac, "were you not with me today? I have already given you my blessing." But Esau said he had not been there before.

Isaac called for his wife and said, "Why have you done what you did?"

"I wanted your blessing for Jacob, for he loves both me and you, whereas Esau has never spoken kindly to me," she replied. Esau, resolving to kill Jacob, took all the money, leaving Jacob poor.

Then Esau married the daughter of the king of Abyssinia, who bore him two children, one called Asphar and the other Barman. Subsequently he married another woman who bore him one child called Rûm. When the king died, Esau took over his kingdom.

* * *

One day Jacob's mother said to him, "Your brother Esau has resolved to kill you. Go therefore to your uncle Laban son of Bethuel, whose home is in Harran."

In obedience to his mother, Jacob left for the city of Harran, where he found a well beside which was a bucket. He filled the bucket, drank, performed his ablutions and prayed two *rak'as.*

Laban's daughter saw him and said to her father, "There has come among us a man, whom I saw performing ablutions and praying as you do."

"Go to him," he said, "and bring him to me." She went to him and summoned him to her father's house.

When he stood before Laban, he asked, "Who are you, young man?"

"I am Jacob son of Isaac son of Abraham," he said.

"Then you are my sister's son," said Laban; and he asked him about his mother and father. Jacob told him all that had happened. Then Laban gave to him in marriage his eldest daughter, who was quite beautiful, except that she was bleary-eyed. Her name was Leah, and Jacob despised her.

"I want the girl who wears the veil," Jacob said.

"Jacob," said Laban, "don't you know that the younger daughter does not marry before the elder?" Then, to his daughter, he said, "Make a sacrifice. Perhaps God will cause your husband Jacob to be compassionate toward you." So she did, and God accepted her sacrifice and inclined Jacob's heart toward her, whereupon he lay with her. She bore him two male children, Reuben and Simeon, then two more, Levi and Judah. Then she died, and he married her sister, "the veiled one," who had veiled herself lest she tempt anyone with her beauty, and her name was Surriyya; she bore him Dan and Naphtali.[93] Then she died, and he married her sister Sherobah, who bore him two sons, Issachar and Zebulun, then two more, Gad and Asher. Then she bore him a daughter called Dinah. Sherobah died, and Jacob married her sister Rachel, the most beautiful of Laban's daughters, who was called Shamsun-nahâr because of her great beauty. All this was after forty years had passed, and Jacob's mother and father had died.

* * *

Inspiration came to Jacob from God, and he aproached Laban and thanked him for all he had given him, saying, "My Lord has sent me as a prophet to the land of Canaan, whither I must go."

When Laban heard this, he bowed down in thanks to God and said, "Jacob, since you first came amongst us, I have seen nothing but good from you: take what you will of my possessions."

"I want only sheep," Jacob said, so Laban gave him five hundred head of sheep and a like number of cattle, horses, mules and donkeys. And Jacob set forth for the land of Canaan with ten of his children.

* * *

News reached Jacob that his brother Esau had set out against him with his soldiers to take his possessions and kill him. When they came to a mountain, Jacob approached Esau with the power of prophethood, lifted him from the ground, flung him down and sat on his chest. Esau wept so that Jacob felt compassion for him and let him up. Embracing him, Esau said, "My brother, absolve me of what I have done to you, for God has set you above me by giving you prophethood and apostleship. Ask forgiveness for me!"

Jacob did pray for him and said, "Be of good cheer, for God will make prophets of your progeny, among them Job, a prophet, and also a king who will rule the East and West and who will be called Dhu'l-Qarnayn."[94]

Then they bid each other farewell, and Esau returned to his country.

* * *

There was in the land of Canaan a king named Sahim ibn Daran, who, when he heard of Jacob's approach to Canaan, set out with all his army to fend him off. When he came to Jacob, he asked, "Who are you and from where have you come?"

"I am Jacob son of Isaac son of Abraham, Friend of God," he said, "I have come to call you and your people to believe in God and to confess that I am His servant and messenger. If you believe in God, He will reward you with bounteous good things; otherwise, I shall truly, with the strength of God behind me, wage holy war against you!"

The king grew wrathful and said, "With whom will you fight me, as you have neither army nor soldiers?"

Jacob looked at his ten sons and said, "I will fight you with God, His angels and with these my sons." So saying, Jacob began battle.

When the battle had gone on a long time, they approached the king's fortress and said to Simeon, "Pull down this fortress with God's permission!" Simeon kicked the gate and said, "O God, conquer it for us, for thou art the best of all conquerors!" And the walls of the fort came tumbling down, and all who were inside perished.

When the news reached the people of Canaan, fear fell upon their hearts; and they came to Jacob and believed in him, all of them.

56. *The Story of Joseph*

Kaab al-Ahbar said: Then Rachel conceived and bore Joseph, and after him, Benjamin; and Rachel's beauty was inherited by Joseph.

When the boys were two years old, Rachel died, leaving them motherless. When the news of Rachel's death reached her father Laban, he equipped his younger daughter with great riches, betrothed her to Jacob and sent her to him.

On Joseph's fourth birthday his aunt Tumel, Isaac's daughter, gave him her father's girdle. Now God had given Abraham five things, all of which were passed down to Joseph: the Turban of Prophethood which God had given him when he was sent to Nimrod, the Coat of Friendship which He gave him when He took him as His friend, the Girdle of Victory and Contentment with which he girded himself the day he was thrown into the fire, the Ring of the Prophethood and the Staff of Light, which had five branches. On the first branch was written, "Abraham, Friend of God"; on the second, "Isaac, Sacrifice of God"; on the third, "Ishmael, Pure of God"; on the fourth, "Jacob, Israelite of God"; and on the fifth, "Joseph, Righteous of God."

While asleep, Joseph had a dream and, waking in alarm, said, "Father, I saw this staff planted in the ground. Its roots had taken hold and borne fruit, and its branches grown high into the sky. I saw the staffs of my brethren planted about it, but nothing was growing from them; and my staff was higher than theirs. Then mine plucked the others out and threw them aside."

"My son," said Jacob, "not every dream has an explanation or interpretation, so do not let it frighten you."

* * *

When Joseph had completed his tenth year, Jacob slaughtered a sheep. He and his children were seated before the food when a poor boy came and stood near the door. As none of the children gave him anything to eat, he went away.

"Did you give the poor boy anything?" Jacob asked.

"No," they said, "because you did not command us to."

Then God spoke to Jacob, saying, "Jacob, a poor boy, drawn by the aroma of your food, came to you; but you gave him nothing, thereby increasing his sorrow. So also shall I cause you great sorrow!" And Jacob was sorely afflicted.

* * *

That night he dreamed that ten wolves abducted Joseph and cast him into a wilderness. Then one of the wolves threw him into a pit, from which he did not emerge for three days. When Jacob awoke, he took Joseph and clutched him to his breast, kissed him on the forehead and wept. But no one learned of his dream.

* * *

During Joseph's twelfth year, he awoke suddenly one Friday night in alarm and said, "Father, I saw eleven stars, the light of which was like the sun and the moon, descending from their spheres, and with them the sun and the moon came down and fell prostrate before me."

"O my child," said Jacob, *"tell not thy vision to thy brethren, lest they devise some plot against thee* (12.5), for they will be jealous of what God has given you."

However, Joseph's brothers did hear of it and said, "Why shouldn't Joseph be like that, for his father has given him the Coat of Friendship, the Turban of Majesty, the Ring of Prophethood, the Girdle of Victory and Contentment and the Staff of Light. That is why he brings us these fabricated visions."

Then one of them said, *"Slay Joseph, or drive him into some distant or desert part of the earth, and the face of your father shall be cleared towards you"* (12.9).

But Judah said, *"Slay not Joseph, but throw him to the bottom of the well"* (12.10).

So they came to Joseph and played near him, and they even began to play with him.

"Joseph," said Simon, "in the pastures we have food, drink and games you cannot have at our father's house."

"O my brothers," said Joseph, "ask my father to send me with you." So they went to their father and said, *"O Father, why dost thou not intrust Joseph with us?"* (12.13).

Jacob replied, *"I fear lest the wolf devour him, while ye are negligent of him"* (12.13).

"Father," they said, *"surely if the wolf devour him, when there are so many of us, shall we be weak indeed"* (12.14).

Since he loved Joseph so much, Jacob decided, albeit reluctantly, to send him with them. He dressed him in his coat and trousers, annointed his head and gave him his staff. Then he said to them, "Feed him when he is hungry and give him to drink when he thirsts." And he made a pact with them to return him safe and watch over him, and they gave their word. Clutching Joseph to his bosom, he said, "My son, I entrust you to God, Lord of the Universe." And when they had disappeared from sight, he regretted what he had done and went down to his house, full of concern.

* * *

While Joseph's brothers were walking, he could follow them; but when they began to run ahead of him, he called out to them, saying, "My brethren, why have you not given me to drink, for I am terribly thirsty!" But they did not give him any water. Rather, Simeon broke the water jug and said, "Tell your lying dreams to quench your thirst!" Then Simeon came to him and slapped him on the face, and tears began to flow down his cheeks.

"How quickly have you forgotten your promise to your

father, my brethren!" cried Joseph. But they paid no heed to him and walked away, leaving him alone.

When at last he found them on a high mountain, they said among themselves, "Let us kill Joseph here on this mountain."

But Judah said, "Do not kill him, but throw him into the well." So they dragged Joseph to a deep, narrow, brackish well by the side of the road. (Shem, the son of Noah, had dug this very same well, and on it was written, "This is the Well of Sorrows.") They ripped his clothing from him, bound a rope tight around his waist and lowered him into the well. When he was almost halfway down, they let go of the rope so that he would fall and die, but Gabriel came to him and took him in his wings before he reached the bottom.

"Fear not! Joseph," said Gabriel, "for God is with you." Then Gabriel spread on the surface of the water a large rock that had been at the bottom of the well, sat Joseph upon it and brought him food and drink from Paradise. After Joseph had eaten and drunk, Gabriel clothed him with a shirt from Paradise.

Meanwhile, Joseph's brother set upon a young kid-goat, slaughtered it, ate its flesh and spattered its blood over the shirt that they were going to take to Jacob, their father.

When they returned weeping, Jacob said, "My sons, what has befallen you? And why do I not see my beloved with you?"

"Father," they cried, "the greatest calamity has befallen! *We went and ran races with one another, and we left Joseph with our baggage, and the wolf hath devoured him; but thou wilt not believe us, although we speak the truth*" (12.17). Then they added, "Father, this is his shirt." When Jacob saw the shirt, he cried out and fell down in a swoon.

After coming to, he said, "O Joseph, your dream about yourself was true, and all my precaution for you was in vain." Going up onto a high mountain, he called out as loud as he could, saying "O hateful and evil beasts, Jacob has lost his son Joseph and has forbidden himself laughter and joy. I had forbidden you to touch him. May you never rejoice!" Then he said, *"Nay, but ye yourselves have contrived the thing for your own sakes: however patience is most becoming, and God's assistance is to be implored to enable me to support the misfortune which ye relate"* (12.18).

Finally, he commanded the beasts, saying, "Bring me the wolf that devoured him!"

The beasts made obeisance and set out into the wilderness, where they hunted down a foreign wolf and brought him to Jacob, saying "This is the one who devoured him."

But God caused the wolf to speak, saying, "O prophet of God, I did not devour your child, for the flesh of the prophets is forbidden wild birds and beasts. I am but a foreign wolf who have lost my child and had come looking for him from the regions of Egypt when your creatures took me and lied before your very eyes about a crime I did not commit. By Him who caused me to speak, if you let me go, I shall bring you every wolf in your land, and they all will swear that they have not devoured your child." Therefore, Jacob set the wolf free.

* * *

Joseph remained in the well for three days, and on the fourth day the caravan of Malik ibn Dhu'r the Khazaite passed by, headed for the land of Egypt. Malik, searching for water from that very well and seeing a light gleaming from the pit, let down a bucket onto which Joseph hung so that Malik felt a weight. He looked at the man who was with him and said, *"Good news! this is a youth"* (12.19). He shouted to his companions to help him, and together they brought Joseph up out of the well in good health. While they were there, Jacob's sons approached and said, "This boy is our slave, who fled from us three days ago. Now you have found him. If you wish, we will sell him to you."

"Are you a slave?" asked Malik of Joseph.

"Yes," said Joseph (meaning that he was a "slave of God").

So they sold him for eighty dirhems. As they were dividing the money among themselves and Judah went to take his share, Joseph wept and said, "O my brother, do not take of my price, for God will ask you about it on the Day of Resurrection." Judah wept and took nothing.

Then they wrote a letter for Malik that neither he nor they would ever default on the transaction, and Malik took the letter and gave it to Joseph. (And the letter was still with him when his brothers later came to him.)

"This boy is a thief," they told Malik. "Bind him lest he attempt to escape." So he was bound and set on a camel, and the caravan moved until they reached the place where Joseph's mother Rachel was buried. Unable to restrain himself, Joseph fell on her grave, weeping and mentioning his brothers' deed. When Malik missed him, he returned in search of him and found him spread on the ground, weeping. He slapped his face and drove him harshly before him. On reaching the caravan, he put him on a mule and set out for Egypt.

Upon arrival, Malik said to Joseph, "Boy, get down here. Take off your shirt and wash in this river." When he had washed and performed ablutions with the water, the earth itself shone from his beauty, and the light of prophethood gleamed from his eyes and penetrated the very walls of Egypt, filling the entire country with light. The people were so astonished that they went out to Malik and asked him about the slave he had bought.

He dressed Joseph in finery, adorned him most magnificently and set him on a dais. Then he stood up and cried out as loudly as he could, "O people of Egypt, who will buy this Hebrew boy from me?"

Among the people were seven traders from Abyssinia, and each one had ten thousand dinars. They collected seventy thousand dinars among them and raised them up to Malik, but he would not accept. Then there came to him a woman called Qaria bint Tariq ibn al-Rawad ibn Awil ibn Shaddad ibn Ad the Great.

"O Malik," she said, "I will buy this boy from you for his weight in gold, silver and gems."

"I am asking more than that," he replied.

Then Zuleikha sent word to her husband, Potiphar, saying, "Buy him whatever the price, and let nothing deter you!" So he bought Joseph for a price beyond reckoning.

* * *

A man mounted on a camel stopped before Joseph, and the camel stretched out its head toward him as though saluting him.

"Who are you?" asked Joseph.

"I am from the land of Canaan," answered the man.

"In the land of Canaan do you know a tree whose roots are

firm in the ground and whose branches are in the sky?" asked Joseph. "It has twelve intertwined limbs, and the angels hover about it."

"This can only be a description of Jacob and his sons," said the bedouin.

"I am Joseph, son of Jacob," he said. "Do you know Jacob?"

"How could I not know him?" said the man. "He is one of my neighbors."

"How was he when you left him?" asked Joseph.

"Mourning for you," he said. "He has built for himself a house and called it the Abode of Sorrows."

Then Joseph said, "When you reach the Valley of Canaan, go to my father at the end of the day, for at that hour the gates of heaven are opened and the angels of mercy descend. Give him my greetings and tell him how I am, so that he may be comforted. And tell him that the mole which was on my right cheek has been washed away by my tears."

The bedouin left him, traveling in the direction of the land of Canaan, and God caused him to traverse the distance rapidly, until he reached the house of Jacob.

"Peace be with you, O prophet of God," he cried. "I have news from Joseph."

Jacob ran to him, and the bedouin told him what Joseph had said. When Jacob heard, he fell in a swoon. Upon waking, he said, "My God and Master, the lamps of mourning have been hung between the heavens and the earth. Extinguish them not until thou bring me together with my son Joseph, for thou art capable of all things."

Jacob asked the bedouin if he had any request to place before God. "My only request," he replied, "is that you pray for many children and much wealth for me."

Jacob prayed to his Lord, saying, "O God, make manifold his possessions and children and make him my companion in Paradise."

* * *

Ibn Abbas said: Then Potiphar brought Joseph to the palace of Zuleikha, the daughter of Akahirah, and said to her, *"Use him honourably; peradventure he may be serviceable to us, or we may adopt him for our son"* (12.21).

Zuleikha was so astounded by Joseph's beauty that she fell passionately in love with him.

"How lovely are your words, and how graceful you are!" she said.

* * *

Wahb said that Joseph's light shone in his eyes and also glowed beneath his skin, just as a wick shines in a crystal lamp.

* * *

"Zuleikha," said Joseph, "were you to see me after my death, you would not recognize me or have seen anything worse than me."

"O Joseph," she said, "I am passionately in love with you. I cannot but try to seduce you!"

"Zuleikha," he said, "having seen the signs of God, would you commit a sin?"

"How beautiful is your language," she replied, "but I do not understand it."

"It is the language of my grandfather Abraham," said Joseph. "Were it not forbidden to polytheists, I would teach it to you. I will speak to you in Qamarite if you wish."

"I prefer the Hauranite tongue," she said, "for that is the language of the people of Egypt."

She went to great pains to tempt him again: she built a beautiful bower, adorned with every sort of embellishment, and called it the House of Joy and Pleasure. She bedecked herself with finery, reclined on her couch and called for Joseph. She seated him on the couch and *shut the doors* (12.23) and pulled the curtains.

"O Joseph," she said, "I am yours!"

"But where is your husband Potiphar?" asked Joseph.

"I have nothing to do with him," she answered. "You are the only one for me. I am yours!"

"O Zuleikha, I fear this house will be a house of sorrow and a spot of hell."

"O Joseph, I love you with all my heart. Lift up your head and look at me in the fullness of my beauty!"

"Your master has more right to that than I do."

"Come close to me, Joseph!"

"But I fear lest my portion of Paradise be lost."

"I have discretely veiled my affair from the people, so come close to me!"

"But who will veil me from God, the Lord of the Universe?"

"If you do not do as I wish," she screamed, "I shall kill myself this very instant, and you will be put to death on my account!" And she put her hand on a knife as if to kill herself (but it was just a ruse on her part to trick Joseph). Hastening toward the knife, he snatched it from her hand and threw it aside. Then she threw herself upon him and untied seven of the knots in his trousers, one after the other. *She resolved within herself to enjoy him and he would have resolved to enjoy her* (12.24), had not just then Gabriel descended in the form of his father Jacob, biting his fingertips.[95] When Joseph saw the Proof, he hastened toward the door; but Zuleikha dashed after him, *and she rent his inner garment behind* (12.25) to shreds. And there, with Joseph in that state, they encountered the master.

"What is the matter with you, boy?" asked Potiphar.

"I have seen something forbidden in your palace. I am shamed to say that you wife has attempted to seduce me."

"Get back, slave! Or else I shall kill you," shouted Potiphar. And Joseph returned inside with the master.

When they entered the palace, Zuleikha ran to her husband weeping and saying, *"What shall be the reward of him who seeketh to commit evil in thy family, but imprisonment, and a painful punishment?"* (12.25).

"O master," said Joseph, "she tried to tempt me. I have been struggling with her ever since I entered this house."

Potiphar was about to strike Joseph with a sword he had with him, when God delivered him through one of the household who bore witness. There had been a six-month-old child of Zuleikha's sister sleeping in the palace, and it spoke by God's permission and said, "O Potiphar, be not hasty, for I heard the rending of clothing. *If his garment be rent before, she speaketh truth, and he is a liar: but if his garment be rent behind, she lieth, and he is a speaker of truth"* (12.26f).

And when he saw that his garment was torn behind, his anger with Joseph subsided. Approaching Zuleikha, he said, *"This is a cunning contrivance of your sex; for surely your cunning is great"* (12.28).

Then he said to Joseph, "Disclose not this event lest the people hear of it and blame me for it." Turning then to Zuleikha, he said, *"Ask pardon for thy crime for thou art a guilty person"* (12.29).

But the news spread quickly throughout the city that the wife of Potiphar had tried to seduce her slave-boy, and the women censured and blamed her, saying, *"We perceive her to be in manifest error." And when she heard of their subtile behavior, she sent unto them, and prepared a banquet for them* (12.30f), adorned the banquet hall and invited the wives of the chief scribe, the vizier, the exchequer, the chief of the secretariat and all the other wives of high office-holders.

When they came and were seated in their places, she offered them trays of citrons and honey, for such was their custom before partaking of a meal. *And she gave to each of them a knife.*

Having previously adorned Joseph in a most exquisite manner, she had said to him, "When you go out among the ladies, laugh and be cheerful. Hold your head aloft so that they can see your beauty and magnificence." Then she went to them and offered each a knife and a bowl of citron.

While they were busy slicing the citrons, Zuleikha sent for Joseph to come out among them. He entered, as she had ordered, smiling and showing his teeth, which were like strung pearls, and his face, which was like the full moon. When the women saw him, they lauded him and sullied themselves on the spot out of passion for him and cut their hands as they were slicing the citrons, saying "O Zuleikha! No one has ever seen the likes of this boy. He is a temptation to all who see him!"

"This is he, for whose sake ye blamed me," she said. *"I asked him to lie with me, but he constantly refused. But if he does not perform that which I command him, he shall surely be cast into prison, and he shall be made one of the contemptible"* (12.32).

Then Joseph said, *"O Lord, a prison is more eligible unto me than the crime to which they invite me"* (12.3).

Therefore Zuleikha sought permission from the master to have Joseph imprisoned. When he had given his permission, she had him incarcerated in a narrow cell, away from the people, where he remained so long as God willed.

* * *

And there entered into prison with him two of the king's servants, one called Abruha the Cupbearer, the other Ghalib the Baker. One day they came to Joseph, and the cupbearer said to him, "I dreamed the king released me from prison, and while I was in the palace I saw a limb of a tree, so I planted it in the earth and it bore a stalk of grapes, which I took and squeezed into a cup, which I then gave to the king."

"How excellent was what you saw!" said Joseph, "for you will be released tomorrow from prison and restored to your former position. *Remember me in the presence of thy Lord"* (12.42).

Then the other said, "I saw the king release me from prison and give me a plate of bread, which I carried on my head; and I saw birds pecking at my head and eating from the plate."

Joseph said, "The king will release you and will crucify you on an elevated place, and the birds will eat from your head."

When the morrow had come, the king released the two slaves, restoring the cupbearer to his former position and crucifying the baker, and the birds ate from his head.

* * *

When Joseph had remained in prison for a long time, Gabriel descended to him and asked, "Joseph, who fashioned you so beautifully?"

"God did," said Joseph.

"Why then have you forgotten God's favor toward you? and how could you have said to that cupbearer, 'Remember me in the presence of thy lord,' when he is an infidel?"

Joseph cried out and said: "Mercy, have mercy, O Most Merciful," and fell down prostrate.

* * *

For seven years he languished in prison. Then one Friday eve the king, Rayyan ibn al-Walid, had a strange vision of seven lean cows eating seven fat ones and seven green ears of grain and seven dry ears. Awaking in alarm, he called for his interpreters, to whom he related his dream.

"They are confused dreams," they said, *"neither are we skilled in the interpretation of such kind of dreams"* (12.44).

When the cupbearer heard this, he said, "Sire, there is a slave-boy named Joseph in prison who is learned in interpreting dreams. Would you permit me to go to him?" And he consented. Therefore the cupbearer came to Joseph in the prison and found that his condition had changed, but he informed him of the king's dream nonetheless.

Joseph said, "Return to the king and say to him, *'Ye shall sow seven years as usual: and the corn which ye shall reap, do ye leave in its ear, except a little whereof ye may eat. Then shall there come, after this, seven grievous years of famine, which shall consume what ye shall have laid up as a provision for the same, except a little which ye shall have kept. Then shall there come, after this, a year wherein men shall have plenty of rain, and wherein they shall press wine and oil'* " (12.47ff).

The slave returned to the king with the interpretation of the dream. "Who explained it to you?" asked the king.

"The one who is in prison, who is called Joseph the Hebrew," the slave-boy answered. "He explained a dream to me before, and it came true."

"Bring him unto me" (12.50), said the king, so the boy went to Joseph to give him the news of his release by order of the king.

"Return unto thy lord, and ask of him, what was the intent of the women who cut their hands (12.50) with knives the day they saw me," said Joseph.

When the cupbearer had conveyed this message, the king said, "He must be telling the truth, but I should ask the women."

Some of the women—others having died in the meantime—were summoned. When they stood before the king, and among them was Zuleikha, he asked, *"What was your design, when ye solicited Joseph to unlawful love?"* (12.51). They were all silent out of embarrassment before the king. So again he asked.

"God be praised!" they said, *"We know not any ill of him."*

And Zuleikha said "O king, *now is the truth become manifest: I solicited him to lie with me; and he is one of those who speak truth."*

Then the king said, "Bring him to me with honor," and

summoned his vizier and handed him the crown, sword and horse which were only used on state occasions. The vizier went to Joseph, mounted him on the king's horse and brought him before the king, who embraced him, sat him on the throne in the midst of the palace and said, "O Joseph, *thou art this day firmly established with us, and shall be entrusted with our affairs"* (12.54).

Joseph answered, "Set me over the storehouses of the land; for I will be a skilful keeper thereof" (12.55).

The king then proclaimed to the people of his kingdom, saying, "I hereby make Joseph governor over you, and he is my regent." And the people responded in obedience.

Then Joseph ordered them to sow grain, and they left not a single place unsown, even the bottoms of old riverbeds and the peaks of mountains. When they reaped the harvest, he ordered them to store it in the ear. And this they did for the seven fertile years, after which God held back from them the rain and nothing grew from the earth, neither seed nor green leaf.

The people therefore gathered around Joseph and said to him, "O Plenipotent, the food that was in our houses has gone, and we have sold what we possessed." In response to their plea, he sold them grain during the first year for dinars, the second for jewels, the third for mules and horses, the fourth for their houses, the fifth for their gardens and farms, the sixth for themselves (so they became his slaves), and then during the seventh year he fed them because they were his slaves.

Zuleikha, who was as afflicted with hardship and hunger as the other people, sold everything she possessed for food and became one of Joseph's slaves. One day she came to Joseph and said, "O Joseph, praise be to him who has turned slaves into kings and made them masters because of their obedience, and who has humbled former masters because of their disobedience. There is no god but God alone, who has no equal."

"Who are you, O woman?" asked Joseph.

"I am Zuleikha, the wife of Potiphar," she answered. When she mentioned her need for food, Joseph wept and said, "I shall send you all you require and shall restore to you all your former possessions and slaves, and you shall be a lady as you were." Then he married her, with the king Rayyan ibn al-Walid as witness and in the presence of the princes of Egypt. And God restored her beauty and youth.

When Joseph lay with her he found her a virgin, whereupon she said, "No man has ever touched me, and my husband Potiphar was impotent because he was prideful." She gave birth to two sons by Joseph, and he called one of them Ephraim and the other Manasseh.

57. *Joseph's Brethren in Egypt*

Wahb ibn Munabbih said: Then the famine spread to the land of Canaan, and Jacob and his sons were afflicted with hardship.

Jacob said, "Foreseeing hunger, go to Egypt and buy food for us from the Plenipotent; perhaps God will incline his heart toward you." So they equipped themselves, and the ten brothers traveled to Egypt.

Now Joseph had asked his Lord if he might see his brothers, but they knew nothing of this. And God answered his prayer. Joseph had stationed guards along the road to ask passers-by where they were coming from and where they were going; thus they could inform Joseph beforehand of any arrivals. When Jacob's sons came near the guards, they asked, "Where have you come from and where are you going?"

"We are the sons of Jacob son of Isaac son of Abraham," they said.

"Are all of you the sons of Jacob?" they asked. And they said they were. Then the guards said, "Stay here until we inform the Plenipotent."

"We have come to buy food from him," they said. But they had them wait in a certain place until Joseph had been informed and had given permission for them to proceed.

When they came to his gate, a chamberlain came out and said, "Who are you and where do you wish to go?"

"We are the sons of Jacob son of Issac son of Abraham," they said, "and we wish to see the Plenipotent to buy food for our people." The chamberlain held them for three days and nights, and every day Joseph sent them a table of fragrant foodstuffs and delicious wine. On the fourth day he ordered them shown into his presence. So they came into his court, *and he knew them, but they knew not him* (12.58), for it had been forty years since they had seen him. Turning his face away from them, he wept out of compassion.

"O people," he asked, "from where have you come?"

"O Plenipotent," they replied, "we have come from the land of Canaan, and we are the sons of Jacob."

"Are you all sons of one man?" he asked.

"Yes," they said, "but by different mothers."

"Have there been born to your father other children besides you?" Joseph asked.

"Yes," they answered, "two other sons were born by a woman named Rachel. One of them was called Joseph and the other Benjamin, whom we left at our father's side, for he never leaves him for an instant. Joseph was long ago devoured by a wolf." And they related the story of Joseph.

"How can I believe that you are really the sons of Jacob, as you say?" asked Joseph.

"O Plenipotent," said Reuben, "we will bring you the brother we left with our father, and he will confirm what we say."

Then Joseph told the corn-measurer to give them a measure and to return the wares they had given in barter to their caravan, but in such a way that they not know of it; and their names were written on their bags.

"Bring unto me your brother, the son of your father" (12.59), said Joseph, and they promised that they would.

They traveled back to their father, kissed him on the head and told him what had happened to them with the Plenipotent, saying, "O father, we saw more compassion and love from this prince than we have seen from anyone else." Then, going to their caravan and opening their baggage, they found that the wares had been returned to them; and they went to their father and said, "Father, we opened our baggage and found our wares inside, returned to us so we should not go in want."

"That food is unlawful for you if you did not give its price," said Jacob. "We are the clan of prophets, and it is our duty to be truthful."

"But father!" they cried, "how can we return to him, for we have guaranteed that we would bring our brother Benjamin to him?" And they told him that the Plenipotent had said, *"But if ye bring him not unto me, there shall be no corn measured unto you from me, neither shall ye approach my presence"* (12.60).

Jacob wept and said, *"Shall I trust him with you with any better success than I trusted your brother Joseph with you heretofore?"* (12.64).

"O father!" said Judah, *"What do we desire farther? this our money hath been returned unto us* (12.65), which we will return to him. Perhaps he will accept it from us. *We will take care of our brother; and we shall receive a camel's burden more than we did the last time. This is a small quantity"* (12.64ff).

Jacob said, "I will by no means send him with you, until ye give me a solemn promise, and swear by God that ye will certainly bring him back unto me, unless ye be encompassed by some inevitable impediment." And when they had given him their solemn promise, he said, "God is witness of what we say."

Then Jacob gave Joseph's shirt to Benjamin to wear, the one that had been brought to him spattered with blood.

"O my sons," said Jacob, "I entrust you to the might and power of God. Abandon envy and greed, lest the devil entice you. Guard your brother that you may return him safe to me. When you enter Egypt, let him go before you, and make him your spokesman. *My sons, enter not into the city by one and the same gate; but enter by different gates"* (12.67). They agreed and set out for Egypt.

When they reached the gate of Joseph's palace, they requested permission to enter, and were let in. As they were seated in his presence, he had them come closer and then looked at his brother Benjamin. Drawing him nearer, he said, "Benjamin, I see each of these with his brother. Why is it you have no brother among them?"

"O Plenipotent," said Benjamin, "I had a brother; but I do not know what happened to him—except that he went out to the pasture-land with these my brethren, and they said a wolf devoured him. They brought back his shirt, which I am now wearing, spattered with blood. My father Jacob's eyes have become dim from weeping over him."

"O sons of Jacob," said Joseph, "it is strange that a wolf could devour your brother, for among you I see one whose cry would cause a lion to fall down dead. One of you could take a wolf's leg and break it in two. The cry of one of you would cause the pregnant to miscarry. One of you could pluck out a tree by the roots, and one of you could outrun a horse."

"Yea, O Plenipotent," they said, "among us are those who could do even more than that. But when fate intervenes, sight is blinded and strength vanishes." Then Joseph wept out of longing for his father but controlled himself, fearing they would recognize him. He placed before them six tables and ordered each two sons of one mother to sit together at a table. Benjamin wept, and the prince asked why he was weeping.

"O Plenipotent," cried Benjamin, "my brethren are eating two by two, but I am alone. Were my brother Joseph alive, he would be eating with me." Joseph thereupon descended from his dais and ate with him. When his brothers saw this, they became envious and began to gaze upon Benjamin with the eye of hatred.

"Do you not see how all who see the sons of Rachel draw them near and love them?" they said among themselves. "By God, he will surely boast of this to our father, to our detriment!"

When they had finished eating and drinking, Joseph asked Benjamin if he had married, to which he replied, "Yes, and I have been blessed with three male children." Joseph asked their names. "The name of the eldest," he said, "is Dhib ["wolf"], because my brothers claim that a wolf devoured my brother Joseph. The second is called Dam ["blood"], because my brothers brought back Joseph's shirt spattered with blood. The name of the third is Joseph, like the name of my brother." Joseph could no longer refrain from weeping, nor could he remain seated, but rose and went into a bedchamber, and wept.

Afterwards he went out to his brethren and said to them, "You claim to have returned to your father."

"Yes," they replied, so Joseph told the corn-measurer to weigh them out a measure and be generous. Then he told his son Ephraim to take a cup and hide it in Benjamin's saddlebag without anyone knowing what he was doing. The boy did as he was told.

Jacob's sons joined the caravan as it departed. *Then a crier cried after them, saying, "O company of travelers, ye are surely thieves"* (12.70ff).

They said, (and turned back unto them,) "What is it that ye miss?"

They answered, "We miss the prince's cup. Return to him!"

"We hear and obey," they said, "for we will not disobey his order, even if he did prefer Benjamin to us."

When they had been shown in to Joseph, he said, "What provoked you to take the cup?"

"By God," they answered, *"ye do well know, that we come not to act corruptly in the land, neither are we thieves"* (12.73).

"What is the penalty for a thief in your land?" asked Joseph.

"O Plenipotent," they said, *"as to the reward of him, in whose sack it shall be found, let him become a bondman in satisfaction of the same: thus do we reward the unjust, who are guilty of theft"* (12.75).

"Then, with your leave," said Joseph, "we will search your saddlebags." And they agreed. The bags were inspected and nothing was found, but Benjamin's bag was not searched.

"O Plenipotent," they said, "search our brother Benjamin's bag so that he may not vaunt himself above us to our father."

"Do you know why I did not search his saddlebag?" asked Joseph.

"No," they said.

"Because," continued Joseph, "you gave your father a solemn promise that you would return him safe to him."

"Yes," they said, "that is true."

"You search yourselves!" he said. They opened his bag, searched through it and pulled out the cup, whereupon their complexions changed and they said to him in Hebrew, "Thief! Brother of a thief! You have disgraced us in the sight of the prince!"

Then they said, "O Plenipotent, *if Benjamin be guilty of theft, his brother Joseph hath been also guilty of theft heretofore"* (12.77).

* * *

Ibn Abbas said that when Joseph was at his father's house, he used to take crumbs from the table to give to the poor and unfortunate, and because of that they said that he had stolen heretofore.

* * *

They said, "Noble lord, verily this lad hath an aged father; wherefore take one of us in his stead; for we perceive that thou are a beneficent person" (12.78f).

Joseph answered, "God forbid that we should take any other than him with whom we found our goods; for then should we certainly be unjust." And he ordered his brother Benjamin to be taken away into the palace.

Judah said, *"Do ye not know that your father hath received a solemn promise from you, in the name of God, and how perfidiously ye behaved heretofore towards Joseph? Wherefore I will by no means depart the land of Egypt, until my father give me leave to return unto him, or God maketh known his will to me; for he is the best judge. Return ye to your father, and say, 'O father, verily thy son hath committed theft; we bear witness of no more than that what we know, and we could not guard against what we did not foresee* (12.80f). If your father asks you for proof, say to him that the camel will testify."

Thereupon the sons of Jacob set forth for the land of their father, but Judah went before the Plenipotent and said, "You have imprisoned my brother for his theft. Take me also with him that God judge for us." Joseph then treated them both extremely well.

In the meantime, Jacob's sons had reached their father and greeted him, but he immediately missed Benjamin and Judah.

"Where is Benjamin?" he cried.

"He stole the Plenipotent's cup," they said, "and was imprisoned for theft. We left Judah behind in the land of Egypt to seek his brother's release."

Jacob wept, his tears flowing like rain, and he cried, "Woe for Joseph and his two brothers!"

Then God spoke to him, saying, "By my Majesty and Awe, if thou mention Joseph's name I shall erase thine from the roll of prophets and shall write it in the register of the disobedient!" Jacob sobbed and fell down unconscious.

When he awoke, he said, "My God, my Lord, thou hast made a covenant with me that I not mention the name of Joseph unless thou give me permission."

"Cease thy weeping," said the Lord, "I shall unite thee and thy sons and shall restore thy sight." And Jacob was silent.

Then Jacob said, *"O my sons, go and make inquiry after Joseph and his brother"* (12.87).

"And where is Joseph?" they asked. "A wolf devoured him long ago. Nonetheless, we shall return to the Plenipotent of Egypt and tell him what has happened to you. Perhaps he will send back your son."

Again they equipped themselves for the journey to Egypt, and gathered before Joseph.

"Noble lord," they said, *"the famine is felt by us and our family; and we are come with a small sum of money: yet give unto us full measure, and bestow corn upon us as alms"* (12.88).

"You have committed a terrible crime against me," said Joseph. "I have a task for you. If you fulfill it, I shall pardon you your crime and free your brother."

"O Plenipotent," they asked "what is the task?"

"Can any of you read?" he asked.

"We can all read handwriting," they said, "but our brother Reuben can read even writing that has been obliterated."

"O Plenipotent," said Reuben, "I have read four hundred books in Hebrew and Syriac and have not left a single language unlearned." Then Joseph took out a writ and handed it to Reuben. When he opened it and read it, his countenance was altered and the writ fell from his hand.

Turning to his brethren in fright and shame, he said, "This is the paper we wrote the day we sold Joseph at the well."

Simeon came forth, picked up the writ, and read it and handed it to his brothers, who, recognizing their own writing, asked each other, "How did this writ fall into the hands of the Plenipotent? By Abraham's gray hair, if your father learns that you sold Joseph, his wrath shall be vented upon you for all eternity!"

"What is the matter, that you must consult so among yourselves?" asked Joseph. "What is keeping you from reading the writ?"

"O Plenipotent," said Simeon, "the letters of this writ have been obliterated through the long years, and we can make nothing of it."

"You lie" said Joseph. "And I shall now clarify the matter for you.

"Bring me my cup!" he said. "It will inform me." They brought him the cup, and he struck it. It rang out, and he said, "My cup tells me that you might testify by force and that you lie when you say the wolves devoured your brother Joseph."

He struck the cup again and it rang. "The cup says that you were jealous of your brother Joseph and took him away from his father's house in order to kill him; but instead you cast him into the depths of the well and sold him to Malik ibn Dhu'r. This is his writ!" Because of their fright and dismay, they could answer nothing.

A third time he struck the cup, and it rang out. "My cup tells me that among you is one whose hair bristles forth through his clothing when he becomes wrathful and that he does not become calm again until he sheds blood."

"It is true, O Plenipotent," said Judah. "It is I."

"Then why did you not defend your brother against such evil?" asked Joseph. But Judah was silent and did not speak.

Joseph then handed the writ to one of the patricians who could read Hebrew, and he read aloud:

> In the name of the Most Merciful God. Be it known that Malik ibn Dhu'r the Khazaite, owner of the Egyptian caravan, has purchased from the sons of Jacob an eloquent, comely Hebrew boy called Joseph. He has purchased him from Judah, Reuben and all of their brothers for twenty dirhems, the weight of which is eighteen drachmas. So be it.

"O people," said the brothers angrily, "this Plenipotent wishes only to do us evil. Yea, he has disgraced us in the sight of all creation!"

"Do you want me to let forth the scream of wrath to destroy them all?" asked Simeon.

"Yes!" they said.

Simeon began to protract his tongue in order to send forth his scream, when Joseph said to Ephraim, "My son, go to that man and take him by the hand." When the boy had done it, Simeon's wrath subsided.

"Which of you took me by the hand?" he asked. "My wrath has grown calm."

"It was none of us," they said. "It was that child who touched you."

"By God!" he cried, "a hand of the House of Jacob touched me!"

Then Joseph said to his aides, "Erect ten poles on the city gate so I may bind them there by the neck and crucify them as an example to those who come after!" And they trembled with fear.

"O people of Egypt," they cried, "may whoever of you go to the land of Canaan deliver our greetings to old Jacob and say to him, 'Long was thy sorrow over one: what will be thy sorrow over eleven sons?' " And they began to blame each other while awaiting their torment.

When Joseph saw them in that state, he sent for them. Taking his crown from his head, he showed them a mark which was exactly like the mark on Jacob's head. When they saw it, they knew him and asked, *"Art thou really Joseph?"* (12.90).

He replied, "I am Joseph; and this is my brother. Now hath God been gracious unto us. For whoso feareth God, and persevereth with patience, shall at length find relief; since God will not suffer the reward of the righteous to perish."

They said, "By God, now hath God chosen thee above us; and we have surely been sinners" (12.91).

Joseph answered, "Let there be no reproach cast on you this day. God forgiveth you; for he is the most merciful of those who show mercy" (12.92). He took off the shirt that God had given him in the well and gave it to Judah, saying, *"Depart ye with this my inner garment, and throw it on my father's face; and he shall recover his sight: and then come unto me with all your family."*

They all departed, and Judah went ahead with the shirt, the aroma of which was carried by the wind to Jacob while Judah was yet ten days' journey away. *"Verily,"* said Jacob, *"I perceive the smell of Joseph; although ye think that I dote"* (12.94f).

They answered, "By God, thou art in thy old mistake." But when Judah arrived and threw the shirt over Jacob's face, *he recovered his eyesight* (12.96)

"O prophet of God," said Judah, "we have kept Joseph from you. Forgive us!"

"I will surely ask pardon for you of my Lord; for he is gracious and merciful" (12.98), said Jacob.

Then Gabriel brought a camel from Paradise; and Jacob, mounted on the camel, along with his sons and their folk, went forth to the land of Egypt. And they were seventy-three people altogether.

Joseph came out with many people to receive Jacob. When they met, they embraced and wept. They entered Egypt on a Friday, and between the separation and reunion forty years had passed. *And he raised his parents* (that is, his father and maternal aunt) *to the seat of state, and they, together with his brethren, fell down, and did obeisance unto him. And he said, "O my father, this is the interpretation of my vision, which I saw heretofore: now hath my Lord rendered it true"* (12.100).

Jacob settled in Joseph's palace, and Joseph's children came to their grandfather, who rejoiced exceedingly over them. Zuleikha also came and kissed his head and hands. A bower, like the one he had had in Canaan, was constructed for him and a niche was made in it for each of his sons; and Jacob remained there in great joy and happiness.

58. *The Death of Jacob and Joseph*

Kaab al-Ahbar said: Then the king, Rayyan ibn al-Walid, asked Joseph to send his father to him. Joseph went to his father and told him of the king's request, and Jacob replied that he would do as his son wished. He came before the king, who seated him at his side and said, "Sir, how many years have passed over you?"

"One hundred and forty," replied Jacob.

Arim the Adite, however, said, "What you say, sir, is untrue." Jacob and his sons grew angry and called down a curse upon Arim, who collapsed on the spot, unable to speak, having been struck dumb.

The king was sorry for what had happened and said to Joseph, "You know that Arim knows all about the ancients, their battles and genealogies; and here your father has done with him as you see. Ask him to requite him."

"Sire," said Joseph, "he called my father a liar."

But Jacob prayed to God, and Arim's tongue was restored. "O prophet of God," said Arim, "by God, I meant not to call you a liar; rather I thought you were Isaac the son of Abraham."

* * *

Jacob dwelt peacefully and happily in the land of Egypt for forty years. Then God spoke to him, saying, "O Jacob, now hath thine end drawn nigh. Travel from the land of Egypt and go to the tombs of thy fathers that thy death may occur there." So Jacob called for Joseph and said, "O my son, God has informed me that my end draws nigh and has commanded me to go to the land of my fathers. Therefore I am leaving.

"O my son, when your end comes, let not Egypt be the resting place of your bones." Then he and his folk went to the land of Canaan.

When he had come to the tombs of Abraham and Isaac, he saw the angels gathered about a grave already excavated.

"For whom is this grave?" he asked the angels.

"For a servant who has served his Lord well," they answered. Then Jacob looked into the grave and saw beautiful people standing on high platforms. When he asked who they were, the angels replied, "These are the sons of Abraham." Jacob tried to enter into their midst and greet them, but the angels said to him, "No one may enter therein unless he drink from this cup." The Angel of Death handed him the cup, and when he had drunk from it he fell dead.

The angels washed him, wrapped him in shrouds from Paradise and, having prayed over his body, buried him beside his father Isaac. And there were four tombs in that one place, that of Abraham, Sarah, Isaac and Jacob.

* * *

Then Joseph's brethren returned to him and informed him of his father's death, which he mourned grievously.

It has been said that no one wished for death except Joseph, but God spoke to him, saying, "There remain yet sixty years of thy life. When thou shalt have accomplished these years, I shall take thee among the pious. So exhort the people of Egypt to believe."

Joseph ceased not to call the people of Egypt to be faithful until many of them did believe. Some others, however, complained to their king, Rayyan, who called Joseph and said, "O Plenipotent, you know that the people of Egypt have loved you greatly, but now they criticize you for calling them to Islam."

"What you say has reached my ears," said Joseph. "Therefore shall I depart your land for my own people."

Joseph left Egypt and went to the land where his father had settled, and there he excavated a branch of the Nile and called it the Faiyum. On the banks of the river he built edifices and constructed two cities, which he called al-Haramayn.

Joseph moved about among his people in the manner of a prophet until he grew old. Having made his bequest to Ephraim to govern his people righteously and to strive truly to make the people of Egypt walk in the path of God, he passed on.

* * *

It is said that Zuleikha died before Joseph and that Joseph was buried on the desert side of the Nile. God caused that side to flourish, and famine befell the other side in the land of Egypt. The king sent to Ephraim asking him to move his father's tomb to the Egyptian side so that they might benefit from the blessing of Joseph's body, which he did. Then that side grew fertile, leaving the other side barren. This was such a hardship that they moved his tomb to the middle of the river so that both sides would benefit. There it remained until God sent Moses and told him to bear away Joseph's sepulcre with him. However, he could not find the sepulcre until Sarah, the daughter of Bashir son of Jacob, directed him to it. He took away the sepulcre and bore it to Jacob's tomb, beside which it was interred.

* * *

Wahb said that whenever God sent a prophet He would tell him the story of Joseph, as He told it to our Prophet Muhammad.

Ibn Abbas said: "The people of the Torah used to conceal the story of Joseph. When God sent Muhammad as a prophet, the Jews came to him, among them Abdullah ibn Salam and many of the tribe of the Ahbar, and said to him, 'Muhammad, if you be a prophet, tell us the story of Joseph and his brethren.' And he began to recite it, sometimes raising his voice and sometimes lowering it. The Jews wept and said, 'Muhammad has been given more of the story of Joseph and his brethren than is in our Torah.' Then they asked him, 'Where did you learn this, Muhammad? for we conceal this chapter.' Muhammad said, 'My Lord has revealed it to me.' 'You speak the truth, Muhammad,' they said."

It is said that because of its greatness, the Jews used to write the story of Joseph with gold ink on silver sheets and suspend them in their tabernacles.

59. *The Prophet Job*

Kaab al-Ahbar and Wahb ibn Munabbih said: After Joseph there was no prophet until Job, the son of Amos son of Reuel son of Esau son of Isaac son of Abraham. Job was a wise, just and learned man, whose father possessed much property and livestock, camels, cattle, sheep, horses, mules and donkeys. And there was none like him in the land of Syria.

When Job had accomplished thirty years, his father died; and all his property passed to Job, who had married the daughter of Ephraim son of Joseph, and she was called Rahmah.[96] Of all people, she most resembled Joseph. She was a Muslim, and God had blessed them with twelve sons and daughters.

Then God sent Job as a messenger to his people, who were the inhabitants of the Hauran, and none among them denied him on account of the esteem in which they held him and his father. He had provisions which he placed before the poor and the unfortunate; he honored guests, and he was a compassionate father to the orphan, an affectionate husband to the widow and a devoted brother to the weak. Job had ordered his agents never to deny his bounty and his fruits to anyone. And the blessings of God increased upon Job morning and evening; and every year his livestock bore twins.

Iblis could find none of Job's property not sealed with the stamp of thanks or purified by alms, and he was jealous of him.

At that time Iblis used to ascend to the seven heavens and stand wherever he pleased, but when Jesus was raised up, four of the heavens were closed to him; when our Prophet Muhammad was sent, all the heavens were closed to him. In the time of Job, however, Iblis ascended and stood in his accustomed place, and there was jealousy and treachery in his heart toward Job. A voice cried to him, "O Accursed One, from where hast thou approached and what is in thy heart?"

"O my God, my Master," he said, "I have been traversing the earth to incite some of the sincere and pious to disobey thee."

"O Accursed One," said God, "hast thou considered my servant Job? Art thou able to tempt him?"

"O my God and Master," he said, "thou hast remembered him with graciousness and hast caused him to enjoy thy favor, so he must be thankful to thee; but, if thou givest me dominion over his property, thou wilt see how he will forget thee."

And God's voice said, "O Accursed One, go! for I give thee power over all he possesses."

Iblis swooped down, rejoicing, until he stood on the rock with which Cain had crushed his brother Abel's head, which was black and from which flowed putrid water. He gave out a cry that reverberated from the East to the West, and all the demons gathered before him.

"I am the master of the possessions of Job, and may do with them as I please," he said. "What power does each of you have?"

One of them said, "Give me dominion over his crops, and I shall transform myself into fire. No sooner will you give me the order than I shall burn them to ashes."

"Then that is your task!" said Iblis.

Then another said, "Give me dominion over his livestock, and I shall let out such a scream that their souls will depart their bodies."

"Then that is your task!" said Iblis.

Thereupon the first one changed himself into fire and scorched the trees and the bushes, and the other let out a scream at the sound of which the livestock fell down dead.

Coming to Job disguised as a shepherd, Iblis said, "Job, a fire has fallen from heaven and has burned up your possessions, and I heard a voice from heaven cry, 'This is retribution for him who is hypocritical in worshipping his Lord.' And I heard the fire say, 'I am the fire of wrath.' "

"They were not my possessions," said Job, "but the Lord's, and He may do with them as He pleases." And Iblis went away, disappointed, and ascended into heaven.

"O Accursed One," he was asked, "how didst thou find my servant Job and his patience over the loss of his property?"

"My God and Master," said Iblis, "thou hast blessed him with children. If thou give me dominion over them, thou wilt not find him so patient with what will be done to him!"

"O Accursed One," God called out, "go! for I give thee dominion over his family and children." So Iblis descended to Job's palace, where his children were, and gave forth such a great scream that the palace trembled and fell upon them; they all perished.

Then he approached Job and, finding him in worship of his Lord, cried out, "Job, how long would you go on praying were you to see that the palaces of your children have become their tombs, for I heard a voice say, 'This is retribution for your father, who is hypocritical in his deeds!' "

Job wept and, taking a handful of dirt, poured it on his head and fell down, prostrating himself before God. Then he said to Iblis, "Get thee from me unsuccessful, for my children were only entrusted to my custody by God." And Iblis departed and ascended into heaven.

The voice of God again came to him, saying, "O Accursed One, how didst thou find my servant Job?"

"My God and Master," said Iblis, "thou hast blessed him with soundness of body and limb, and in that is compensation enough for property and children; but wert thou to give me dominion over that, thou wouldst not find him among the patient."

"O Accursed One," said the voice of God, "go! for I give thee dominion over his body."

Iblis descended to earth and found Job in his council chamber, humbling himself before God. He breathed roaring flames into Job's nostrils, and his face was immediately scorched; as the fire spread throughout the rest of his body, his hair fell out and he became bald as though afflicted with smallpox. Such itching and vermin fell upon him that he scratched until his fingernails fell off, and he had to scratch himself with stones and pieces of wood. Whenever a worm fell from his body, he would pick it up and put it back, saying, "Eat my flesh until God release me from suffering."

Rahmah sometimes wept silently and sometimes cried out aloud, but Job forbade her, saying, "Am I not of the children of the prophets?" Then he said to her, "Rahmah, go and find me a place other than my place of prayer, and carry me thither." Therefore she went out and found a place for him and returned to carry him there. Along the way she saw a group of people to whom Job had formerly been kind and asked them to help her carry him from the prayer chamber, but they refused. She returned to Job and said, "Calamity has befallen you indeed when your own people, whom you used to feed and give drink, deny you."

"Rahmah," he said, "thus does God afflict prophets. Say that there is no might or power save through God, the Exalted and Mighty. Place your right hand under my head and your left under my side and carry me." She bore him, strengthened by God, until she had brought him out to the place where he used to store provisions for the poor and unfortunate. Then he said to her, "Rahmah, we still have charity left to us, so be diligent and proud in the service of the people."

He shed a tear, and Rahmah asked, "Why are you crying, O prophet of God?"

"Rahmah," he said, "you are a woman of great beauty, and there are many iniquitous people in the village. I fear you may fall prey to Iblis."

Rahmah cried out, saying, "O prophet of God, is my only retribution from you that you should accuse me, who am among the daughters of the prophets?" Then he gave her permission to enter service, and she carried water and swept houses and spent on Job what she earned from these labors.

One day Iblis approached the people of the village in the guise of a venerable old man and said to them, "How can you consider yourselves clean when you are served by this woman, who nurses that filthy, putrid husband of hers? She enters your houses and puts her hands into your food and drink!" When Rahmah came as usual, no one would take anything she served. Thereafter the people began to give her a little food without expecting any service in return, and she gave it to Job to eat but told him nothing lest his sorrow increase.

And Job's affliction grew so bad that no one from the village was able to remain at peace in his house because of the stench, so they sent dogs to lick him; but when they came near him even they turned back, wailing and weeping out of sorrow for the prophet of God, Job.

Finally the people of the village came to him and said, "Job, we can no longer endure your affliction. Either depart from among us, or we will stone you to death to be rid of you."

"Do not stone me," said Job, "but rather take me away from your village to one of the refuse heaps."

"We cannot endure you when you are far away," they said, "how can we come near enough to carry you?"

Then Job said to Rahmah, "My friend, go out into the highway. Perhaps you will find someone whom you can ask to help carry me." So Rahmah went out and found two passers-by.

"Who are you, woman?" they asked.

"I am Rahmah, the wife of Job," she replied.

"And where is our friend Job?" they asked. When she told them of his affliction and asked them to pray for his health, they said they would and asked her to give him their salutations.

Rahmah left them and told Job, who said, "They were the angels Gabriel and Michael who spoke to you." Then one of the angels came to Job and consoled him in his affliction, and they carried him to the hut that Rahmah had made and in which she had gathered ashes.

"Get up, Job," she said, "onto your carpet, now of ashes though once of silk, and onto your pillows, now of stone though once of embroidered cushions."

"Did I not forbid you to mention any of the finery of this world?" Job said. And so saying, he threw himself onto the ashes, praising God and blessing His name.

Rahmah went out to get food for him. As she approached the gate of a house, she said, "O people of this dwelling, I am the wife of Job the prophet. Do you have any task I might perform in return for some food?"

"Go away!" they said. "Your husband's Lord is displeased with him." On she passed to another gate, where she was told the same.

After going around the entire village and not obtaining anything, she returned to Job, weeping, and said to him, "The people have all turned me away and have closed their doors to us."

"God does not close His doors to us," said Job, "but, perhaps, Rahmah, you wish to be separated from me. Do what you must."

"God forbid!" replied Rahmah. "Nay, I shall carry you from this village to another, where perhaps they will be more compassionate." So she wrapped him in a mat and carried him to another village of the tribes of Israel and placed him on the outskirts. Then she entered the village and cried out, "If anyone wants his clothes washed, his house swept or water carried, I will do it in return for something to eat."

The women of the village came out to her and asked, "Who are you?"

"I am the wife of Job," she replied. They gave her much food and came to Job, and when they saw him they wept long. They took her in and treated her kindly.

Then she said to Job, "I have gotten so much food today that I can sit with you all day long and shall not leave you until it is finished."

It is said that Iblis then appeared to Rahmah in the guise of a physician with medical instruments and said to her, "When I heard the news of your husband, I came from Palestine to heal him; tomorrow I will visit him. Before I come, tell him to slaughter a bird and not speak the name of God over it. Have him then eat it and also drink with it a cup of wine. If he does this, I shall be able to heal him."

Rahmah came to Job and told him what had happened, but Job said, "Rahmah, when have you ever seen me eat anything over which the name of God has not been spoken, or yet drink wine? Rahmah, yesterday you were a messenger of Gabriel and Michael; today you are a messenger of Iblis." She apologized, and Job was again content with her.

Iblis appeared to her again, riding a donkey, and asked, "Are you not Rahmah?"

"Yes," she replied, "I am."

"Rahmah," said he, "I knew you when you had favor and wealth. What has changed your condition so?"

"God has afflicted us with the loss of our children and wealth," she said, "but the greatest affliction is what has befallen my master Job."

"What is the reason for these disasters?" asked Iblis.

"God willed to bestow upon us sufficient recompense," said Rahmah.

"Woe betide you for what you have said, Rahmah," said Iblis. "Rather, there is a god of the heavens and a god of the earth: as for the god of the heavens, he is God; as for the god of the earth, I am he. You abandoned worshipping me and worshipped the god of the heavens, so I stripped you of your children, livestock and property, all of which are now in my possession. If you like, follow me and gaze upon them." Rahmah followed him a short distance, and he cast a spell over her eyes so that she saw all her children and the possessions she had lost. Then he asked her, "Am I telling you the truth, or am I lying?"

"I cannot know until I return to Job and ask him," she said.

Thereupon she returned to Job and told him, but he said, "For shame, Rahmah! There is no other god but God, and he whom God causes to die cannot be brought back to life by anyone other than Him. The one who appeared to you was Iblis. I saved you from him once, and now this is the second time. I make a solemn vow to God that, if He heal me from the condition I am now in, I will whip you a hundred lashes!"

"O God," she said, "heal him, though he beat me two hundred lashes!"

* * *

Ibn Abbas said that Job remained afflicted for eighteen years, until nothing was left of him but his eyes turning in his head, his tongue with which to speak, though it was mere pulp like the rest of him, and his ears with which to hear. Then God spoke to him, saying, "Job, as thou wast patient in my favor, so hast thou been patient in my affliction."

* * *

Job had three students, one of whom was from the Yemen and was called Eliphaz; the second, from Palestine, was named Zadok; and the third, from Tarsus, was named Zophar.[97] They used to come to him and inquire about his condition: but when his affliction persisted, they rejected him and said, "Were Job sincere in his worship of the Lord, he would not have been stricken with such affliction." Then, gathered before him, they said, "Had you been full of good deeds, God would have rewarded you with the best compensation; but your plight shows that you did not act with good intention; otherwise, this torment would not have clung to you."

"I see you, O people," said Job, "rebuking me in ignorance; this is not what I had hoped for you, for God afflicts whichever of His servants He pleases that thereby His purpose may be known, for He has likewise afflicted other prophets and pious folk." Then Job raised his eyes to heaven and said, "My God and Master, let me taste the food of health, be it only for one moment of the day; turn not thy glorious face from me, for affliction has worn me out: my fingers have been cut off, my lips, my nose and tongue have rotted, my flesh has fallen away and my brains flow through my mouth. My color has changed, my face has become black; those who honored me now belittle me and he who was my friend now shuns me." And Job wept grievously.

Then a young boy found them and said, "Abide by me a while and know that you have abandoned the righteous opinion, for Job is among the best servants in the sight of God. You should have honored him. How can you rebuke him? Shame on you! Do you know whom you are rebuking? He is Job, the prophet, whom God has chosen for His message. God afflicts prophets, the pious and martyrs; it was not your part to heap misery upon misery."

Then Job said to the three, "I am astonished at you, for if you were to look inside yourselves you would find much shame; but I am now incapable of speaking of it. Praise be to Him who, if He willed, could relieve me of my affliction, which even the mountains and towering peaks could not have borne."

No sooner had he finished speaking than a black cloud, full of incessant peals of thunder and bolts of lightning, cast its shadow over him. Then, from the midst of the cloud, a voice cried out to him, saying, "Job, God speaks to thee. Here am I. I have drawn nigh unto thee, so speak to me of thine opinion.

"Rise up to the place of one omnipotent vying with another omnipotent! But thou wilt not be able unless thou canst measure rain and weigh fire, and bind up the sun and return today to yesterday.

"Where wast thou, Job, the day I created the earth and placed it on its foundation? Dost thou know its breadth, its length, its height, its depth? Dost thou know the springs which flow beneath it, the rivers above it? Or dost thou know with what the clouds are filled, and how many drops are therein? Dost thou know the dead that are quickened and the living that are caused to die? Or dost thou know the trees I have created, or the fruits that come from them? Dost thou know where heat and cold are stored, or where to find the storehouses of the souls of the dead? Dost thou know from what I created the intellect or how I fashioned it? Where wast thou, Job, the day I created the heavens to stand without support? Dost thou know where the treasures of my mercy and my torment are?

"Job, who taught the birds how to live and build their nests, and who inspired them to multiply and to care for themselves and their young? Job, who made the lions to know their purpose and gave them their strength? Who taught the eagle to hunt and to see its prey from afar?

"Job, wast thou with me the day I created the great serpent Tinnin in the sea and established him in the clouds? There is neither bone nor joint in him; his eyes burn fire and his nostrils belch forth smoke; his ears are like the breadth of the clouds and the screeching of his teeth is like peals of thunder; the gaze of his eyes is like a flash of lightning. Is thy might enough to take him and swaddle him with his own tongue, or to put a bridle in his jaws, or to command him to sing thy praise, or to fulfill thy pact, or to know the years which have passed over him, or how much remains of his life? Art thou capable of sustaining him? Job, who created the behemoth and the bull? Canst thou place thy hand on their heads, or muzzle their noses, or sit on their path? How long are they? How broad? What is below them? Above them?"

"My God and Master," said Job, "I am vile and am weak and have no strength. My tongue, my intelligence, my hearing, sight and understanding are too dull to speak with thee. My God, whenever thou mentionest the direction of thy wisdom, I know that thou art not incapable of anything. My God and Master, first affliction humbled me; then thou speakest, and I hoped nothing from thee for myself. Would that the earth swallow me up before I said anything to anger my Lord, and would that, before thou didst hand me over to torment, I were dust. O my God, here am I, humble and submissive before thee, seeking restitution from thee; forgive me and have mercy upon me."

Then the voice of God cried, "Job, be patient and mourn not!" And Job was patient.

His wife Rahmah, however, said, "Job, call upon your Lord to relieve you."

"I am too ashamed to call upon Him," he said. "If I perish, God will provide you with another mate."

Weeping out of compassion for him, Rahmah said, "By God, no one after you shall ever have me, Job." So saying, she went out to beg food for Job, but no one would give her anything. The wife of a baker, however, saw her and said that she would give her two loaves of bread in return for some locks of her hair. Rahmah, weeping at the thought, removed her scarf, and the baker's wife cut the tress on which Job supported himself when he rose to pray. She gave Rahmah two loaves, which she brought to Job, who had not eaten anything for three days.

Afterwards she told him what had happened and showed him where the tress had been severed. When he saw it he wept bitterly and said, *"Verily evil hath afflicted me: but thou art the most merciful of those who show mercy* (21.83). Yea, adversity afflicts me indeed when my wife sells her hair."

When it was Friday sunset, Gabriel descended and greeted him, saying, "I am Gabriel, who bring you glad tidings, Job, of God's forgiveness." Taking him by the right hand, he said, "Rise, with the permission of God!" And Job stood up.

The earth rushed at his feet, and suddenly from beneath him there flowed a spring, whiter than snow, sweeter than honey, more fragrant than camphor. When he drank from it, every single worm on his body fell off, and Job was amazed at the great number of worms. Then he washed in the spring and his beauty was restored. Gabriel brought him two vestments, and he put on first one and then the other. He gave him also a quince from Paradise, of which he ate half, leaving the other half for his wife Rahmah.

When Rahmah came and did not see Job in his usual place, she turned to the right and the left but could find no trace of him. Then Job asked her, "What are you looking for, woman?"

"Do you know anything of Job the afflicted?" she asked. "I left him right here, but now I do not see him."

Job smiled and said, "I am Job." And she rushed to him, and they embraced.

Then God restored their possessions, children, servants and livestock, as He hath said: *And we restored unto him his family and as many more with them, through our mercy* (21.84). And God showered down upon him locusts of gold which gathered on his robes; and God spoke to him, saying, "Job, art thou not satiated?"

"Who is ever sated of thy mercy, Lord?" asked Job. God gave him forty thousand camels, twenty thousand she-camels, four thousand head of sheep and a like number of goats, servants, and bondmaids. God blessed him with twelve sons and daughters, and gave him dominion over all the land of Syria. Job was then seventy-three, and God extended his life.

When he came to fulfill his vow to beat his wife, he took a bouquet from a delicate tree and with that carried out his oath. When his time had come, he commanded his children to treat the poor, the unfortunate, orphans and widows as they had seen him do. Then he died, and his wife Rahmah passed away a short time afterwards and was buried next to him.

* * *

Then a king called Lam ibn Duam conquered Syria and sent word to Hawmal, Job's son, saying, "You have constrained us in the land of Syria by the multitude of your livestock. My conditions are that you give me half of your possessions and marry your sister to me; otherwise I shall march upon you with my cavalry and shall seize all of your property."

Hawmal answered him, saying, "No one has a right to the possessions which are in our hands except orphans, the poor and widows. Thus our father Job commanded. As for our sister, if you want to marry her, enter into our religion; and as for your threatening us with your cavalry, we have put our trust in our Lord God, who is our Defender: how excellent is trust in Him!"

When the king received this message, he gathered his armies and set out to wage war against them. Hawmal too collected his army, and they met and fought a fierce battle. The army of Hawmal and his brothers retreated, and Lam ibn Duam took possession of all their property and livestock. He also captured Bashir, the son of Job, and was going to have him put to death. Hawmal collected a large amount of money with which he was about to ransom his brother when a man appeared to him in a dream and said, "Hawmal, do not give him this money, and fear not for your brother. God will free him from the king." In the morning Hawmal told his dream to his brothers, and they rejoiced; and he remained where he was.

Then the king ordered wood to be collected, and he struck fire to it and ordered Bashir to be cast in. When he was thrown into the fire, it did not harm him; and that fell upon the heart of the king, who submitted and believed in God. Then he sent a messenger to Job's children, and they gave him their sister in marriage.

God called Bashir, the son of Job, *Dhu'l-Kifl* because he had been a hostage of the king, and he was a messenger to the people of Syria until he died.[98] The king, Lam ibn Duam, fought against the infidels until he died, and the Amalekites conquered the land of Syria.

60. *The Prophet Shuayb*

Kaab al-Ahbar said: The scholars have differed over the interpretation of the letters of the alphabet.

Ibn Abbas said: As for *Alif, Be, Jim* and *Dal,* the explanation lies in the words *abâ* and *jadda*: Adam *refused* to obey and *was intent* on eating of the tree. As for *He, Waw* and *Zayn,* the explanation lies in the words *huwa* and *nazala*: *He* is God alone who hath no partner, and he *came down* from the heavens to the earth. As for *Ḥa, Ṭa* and *Ya,* the explanation is to be found in the word *ḥuṭiyat*: Adam's sins *were forgiven* through repentance. As for the letters *Kaf, Lam, Mim* and *Nun,* there are the words *akala* and *manna*: Adam *ate* from the tree, and his Lord *had clemency* on him. As for *Sin, 'Ayn, Fa* and *Sad,* the explanation lies in the word *'aṣâ*: He *disobeyed* his Lord and was expelled from grace. And finally *Qaf, Ra, Shin* and *Te,* the explanation of which is found in the word *aqarra*: He *confessed* his sin and was saved from torment.

Wahb ibn Munabbih said: The letters of the alphabet are the names of Shuayb's people, Abjad, Hawwaz, Huttiy, Kalaman, Sa'fas and Qurishat.

Qatada said: They are the names of the Lords of the Thicket.[99]

The astronomers have said that they are the numerically valued letters which they employ in their calculations.

It is also said that they are the names of the kings of the Amalekites, cousins of the Midianites, and have no connection or relation to Shuayb, he being the son of Zion son of Anka son of Midian son of Abraham.

The first that is known of Shuayb is that Midian, the son of Abraham, lived a long time and had an Amalekite wife, who bore him four sons, Nabeth, Japheth, Sahuh and Anka. Upon reaching maturity they all married, begat children and became a numerous folk. Then they built for themselves a fortified city and called it Midian after their grandfather, and hence the people were known as Midianites.

Then came the Lords of the Thicket, who took the city, built their own houses and mingled with the Midianites, who worshipped God while the Lords of the Thicket worshipped idols. Among the nobles of Midian was a man called Zion son of Anka, who married an Amalekite woman who bore him Shuayb, who was called Jethro.

* * *

The king of the Amalekites, Abu Jadd, had gained ascendancy over Midian and its people and had adopted idols for his people, thirty idols in all: ten for him and his children and twenty for the Lords of the Thicket. The Midianites were merchants and bought wheat, barley and other grainstuffs, which they kept in cellars in order to bring the highest price; they were the first speculators. They also had two different measures, one short and one long, the long for when they themselves bought, and short for when they sold; and thus were all their weights and measures.

Thus they remained for a long time, and among them was Shuayb, who neither associated nor socialized with them, but who was nonetheless highly respected among them. One day, while Shuayb was standing by the door of his house, a stranger approached, greeted him and said, "Shuayb, you are a pious man, but your people treat others unjustly. I have bought from them one hundred measures of food for a hundred dinars, yet it is deficient twenty measures. They tell me, 'It is our custom to buy long and sell short.' Therefore I have come to you for help."

Together they went to the market, and Shuayb made inquiries into the matter.

"Don't you know, Shuayb," they said, "that such is our custom and that of our fathers before us in our land?"

"O people," said Shuayb, "fear God and abandon this despicable custom. Give this man his due." But they cursed him and rebuked him.

Then Gabriel descended and said, "Your Lord informs you that He has made you an apostle to the Midianites and the Lords of the Thicket. Call them to obey Him and also to have true weights and measures!" And he ascended back into heaven.

Shuayb approached the Midianites and said, "O my people, worship God. He has sent me to you as a prophet, and I command you to obey Him with true weights and measures. I forbid you to worship idols. I fear God will wreak vengeance on you and yours if you go against me."

"Shuayb," they said, "how can you forbid us to worship the gods our fathers worshipped? You are one of us: we know you, we know your father. If we wanted to, we could exile you from our land and seize your property, but that we will not do until we have complained to your folk of what you have said and done."

Shuayb said, *"O my people, is my family more worthy in your opinion than God? and do ye cast him behind you with neglect? Verily my Lord comprehendeth that which ye do"* (11.92). As the people began to scoff at him, he withdrew to his house.

The next day the king and his retinue went to the market, took out their idols and put them on pedestals. The king took out his greatest idol, called Munis, which had a human face and a crown of gold, and cried out, "People of Midian and Lords of the Thicket, he who bows down to these our idols is of us; he who refuses will be severely punished!" When the people heard the proclamation, they bowed down in obeisance before the idols.

Shuayb, however, came forth from his house and said, "My people, these idols of yours can neither harm nor benefit you. Worship God and cease worshipping idols and using faulty weights and measures!"

"Shuayb," they said, "if you are telling the truth, then give us proof."

"My proof lies in these very idols of yours: if they speak in confirmation of what I say, then will you know that I am telling the truth?" he asked. The king accepted this condition and Shuayb continued, "Idols, who is your Lord, and who am I?"

God caused the idols to speak intelligibly, saying, "God is our Lord and the Lord of everything; you are Shuayb, His apostle." And that very day many men and women believed in Shuayb.

Then the king said, "Shuayb, if we are wrong, God would not have sustained us or caused us to multiply. Although we do not deny that God, to whom you call us, is the Provider, still we worship idols as a means to draw us nearer to God. I considered those who worship the sun, the moon and the stars, but I saw that they had no religion, as they worship things occupied with themselves. Then I considered those who worship fire and animals, but I saw that they had no religion because they worship things that die. We worship these idols because they are free of all defects; and besides, God has no need of the worship of creatures."

Thereupon Shuayb cried out against them, saying, *"O Lord, do thou judge between us and our nation with truth; for thou art the best judge!"* (7.89). And there arose a cold, black wind, in which were stones. Then God commanded Lahib and Sammum of Gehenna to scale over them until their bodies became emaciated and their faces black. Yet, in spite of that, they would not believe. Then God sent them a Shade that burned the infidels with its blaze and shielded the believers from the heat. It is said that the infidels heard a shout and fell dead, as He hath said: *Wherefore, when our decree came to be executed, we delivered Shuayb and those who believed with him, through our mercy: and a terrible noise from Heaven assailed those who had acted unjustly; and in the morning they were found in their houses lying dead and prostrate, as though they had never dwelt therein* (11.94).

One of the faithful sang:

Hast not thou heard what came to pass o'er Midian folk in ages past?

Th' advice of Shuayb came to them: they turned their backs without a plea.

Then came a Shadow, blowing o'er them, by stormy thunder borne aloft.

It left not one in Midian land, yea e'en the mighty, dead, decayed;
But Abjad, callèd Amr Dhu'l-Majawi, Akhu al-Hiffat,
And Hawwaz, Huttiy Dhu'l-Masawi, Sa'fas and too Qurishat.

Then came Ukht-Kalaman, who had believed in Shuayb, and saw the torment that had afflicted the people, whereupon she sang:

The punishment that has destroyed all the lords has also befallen the people:
Kalaman, then Huttiy, and Hawwaz also perished in the midst of the city-quarter;
Then Abjad was brought before the Wrath and the Blaze of the Dry Shade.
No trace remains of them save a fallen dwelling.

Shuayb and his friends, however, were delivered.

61. *Moses son of Manasseh son of Joseph*

Kaab al-Ahbar and Wahb ibn Munabbih said: To Joseph son of Jacob were born two sons. One was called Ephraim and was the grandfather of Joshua son of Nun; the other was called Manasseh.

Manasseh was blessed with a child whom he called Moses, and this was before the time of Moses son of Amram. The people of the Torah claim that it was Moses son of Manasseh who sought out al-Khidr, but Abdullah ibn Abbas related on the authority of the Prophet that Moses son of Amram was al-Khidr's companion.

It was Moses son of Manasseh to whom God said, "O Moses, tell thy people that I am absolved of anyone who practices sorcery or is enchanted; I am absolved of anyone who practices soothsaying or resorts to soothsayers; I am absolved of anyone who divines by omens or resorts to such. Whoso draweth nigh unto me, unto him shall I draw nigh; whoso draweth away from me, from him shall I draw away. Whoso hath confidence in anything other than me, so shall I entrust him to that upon which he relieth; whoso puteth his trust in other than me, let him prepare himself for affliction.

"O Moses, say to those who have drawn away from me, 'Remember the power of God over you and repent ye to your Lord, for that will be better for you,' for if I will, I can be merciful; and if I will, I can torment. The choice is theirs: if they hope for my mercy, so can my mercy extend to everything. Say to the king of the children of Israel that if they do as I command I shall send down to them the pastures of the earth and shall strengthen their kingdom and cause them to drink of the purest waters, and they shall be the inheritors. But if they do not as I command, then shall I cause them to enjoy the end of their appointed time and shall give dominion over them to those whom they now rule. I shall raise up what they put down and shall put down what they raise up; I shall give them foul water to drink and shall inflict them with the curse of those who call down curses. Tell my servants to remember me day and night and not to neglect to mention my name. Let them increase their remembrance of death, for verily that shall cause all passion to pass away."

Moses son of Manasseh recited all that to the children of Israel, and they responded to him. He remained amongst them for a long time before he died.

62. *The Story of Pharaoh*

Muqatil ibn Sulayman related on the authority of Kaab al-Ahbar, Wahb ibn Munabbih and Ibn Abbas: When God destroyed Rayyan ibn al-Walid, the king of Egypt, the Pharaohs inherited the kingdom. The first of them was Sanjab, who honored the children of Israel because they worshipped God publicly and privately and read the tablets aloud.

There were in Egypt a man named Musaab ibn Samir and his wife Rauba, both of whom were Amalekites. One hundred and seventy years passed and he had no children; but one day, while he was in the wilderness, a cow gave birth to a calf and cried, "O Musaab, be not in haste; God will grant you an unlucky child to be one of the pillars of Hell!" He returned to his wife and told her these words. He lay with her, and she conceived Pharaoh.

Musaab died before the birth. When the child was born, his mother called him Walid ibn Musaab and suckled and raised him. When he reached maturity, his mother turned him over to a carpenter. After learning all he could of that trade, he left carpentry and became fond of boasting and gambling. When his mother chastised him, he said, "Leave me alone, mother! I can take care of myself [*'awn nafsi*]." This nickname stuck to him, and he was known only as Awn-nafsih. One day while out gambling, he lost his shirt and had to flee naked; thus it was said, "Awn fled" [*farra 'Awn*] whence "Pharaoh" [*Far'awn*].

He came to a village called Tahla and presented himself to a grocer for employment at his establishment. But he did not hire him, so Awn-nafsih stood by the wayside beating the customers coming from the store; the grocer finally drove him away with the help of the people of the village. He traveled on, bought some greens and a melon for a dirhem and sat down on the roadside to sell them. The king, however, had a tax-collector who took a dirhem from everyone selling goods on the road. When the tax collector came and was not given anything, he confiscated everything Pharaoh had. Then Pharaoh began to roam about the city pilfering. They caught him and put him in jail, but after a time they turned him loose.

Later Pharaoh saw a man whose horse was shying. The man said, "Take the horse's reins, for I see that you possess great strength. If you stay and serve me, it will be more beneficial for you than the position you are now in." Pharaoh did as he said and, following him to his house, remained in his service until the man died. As the man had left no heirs, Pharaoh inherited all the man's wealth and gave it to his mother. Yet, Pharaoh kept squandering and gambling until he had run through his fortune. Thereafter the idea came to him to sit at the gate of the graveyard of Egypt to ask a pittance from those in funeral processions. He spread out a carpet, sat down, and charged everyone who came with the dead a voluntary amount, until at length he had amassed a large quantity of money.

When the king's daughter died and was carried to the cemetery, Pharaoh prevented them from burying her. For this offense the king was determined to have him killed, but Pharaoh ransomed himself with the money that he had collected, so the king set him free and allowed him to resume his activity.

Pharaoh returned to the gates of the graveyard and assessed a king's funeral with a payment of one thousand dirhems, a prince's funeral one hundred dirhems, an ordinary funeral ten dirhems, and that of a poor man one dirhem. When this had gone on long enough, the people of the city complained to the king and said, "The news has spread to the kings of the earth that you collect a tax on the dead: this is a loathsome affair!" Therefore the king called for Pharaoh, prohibited him from presenting himself to the people at the cemeteries, and set up a guard against him.

Pharaoh then built himself a dome in the middle of the town and stationed henchmen and thugs around. Anyone they came across at night they would kill, whoever he be.

One night Sanjab, the king, had a terrifying dream and awoke in fright. He called for the dream-interpreters and said to them, "In my dream I saw myself seated on my throne, when suddenly a scorpion with four stingers, the brilliance of which encompassed all Egypt, came and opened its mouth. I saw that it had four sharp fangs, and it said to me, 'Sanjab, your end is near. Choose for yourself among three alternatives: either I swallow you, or I kill you, or I sting you. I chose the latter and it stung me, threw me on the ground, sat on my throne and said, 'O people of Egypt, be my slaves until the end of time!' Then I saw issue from the loins of Amram, the son of Musaab, a black snake bearing a golden horn and a silver horn, a brass horn and an iron horn. This is what I saw."

The dream-interpreters said, "Sire, this dream has great importance. Give us a month's time." The king granted it, and they withdrew, saying, "Surely a man of no origin will seize his kingdom, for the scorpion is of the dirt. From the seed of Amram will emerge a child by whose hand the kingdom of Sanjab will be destroyed."

When they told this interpretation to the king, he was grief-stricken and refused to eat or drink. One night as he was going without his servants to seek consolation from his vizier, Pharaoh's henchmen seized him and took him to their master. All the while he kept telling them that he was the king, but they paid no heed and thought he was trying to trick them. When they came to Pharaoh they killed him. Afterwards, recognizing him as the king, they took him and hid him in the ground. Then Pharaoh entered the king's palace, sat on his throne and put the crown on his own head. Thus all kingdom on earth became his, though he was no more than an Egyptian slave.

The first to bow before him was Iblis, who called him "lord." After him Haman and all the viziers, sorcerers and soothsayers bowed down. Then he called for the elders of the children of Israel, who came and fell down prostrate before him (by which they meant to prostrate themselves to God).

Pharaoh had crafted a bull of gold with silver legs, ruby eyes, emerald ears and an ivory nose. He built a temple for it, and set it on a silver throne. Pharaoh worshipped the bull, the Egyptians worshipped other idols, and the children of Israel worshipped God. Knowing this, Pharaoh called for the priests of Israel and said to them, "It has reached me that outwardly you obey me but that inwardly you disobey me. Bow down to me or I will punish you with all sorts of torture!"

"Pharaoh's punishment is but for the hour and passes away," they said amongst themselves, "but not so God's punishment. We will not bow before any but God, the creator of heaven and earth and all that is in between." And Pharaoh executed them to the last.

After the massacre Pharaoh saw a man coming out of the walls of his palace biting his nails and saying, "O Accursed One, do you think that your Lord is blind to your evil deeds against the people or to the fact that they bow before you, they who were slaves of the Lord of the Universe!" Pharaoh was terrified and moved to another palace, but the same man came to him and said, "O Accursed One, you will be destroyed to the end of time if you do not believe in God!" So Pharaoh moved to yet another palace.

He continued to move from one palace to another until he had built forty palaces, but always he saw the man. The last he built on a magnificent scale and called it Heliopolis on account of its beauty.

One day while riding his horse, Pharaoh passed by a building that Joseph had built and saw two old women coming out. They said, "O Accursed One, who are your people? Ad and Shaddad and all the obstinate! Pharaoh of many palaces will perish!" And Pharaoh ordered them to be killed.

To Haman he said, "I think my destruction will not come but from the hand of the Israelites; but bring me Amram, the son of Musaab, who is their chief." So Amram came to him and was made grand vizier, so that Haman and the rest of the viziers were under him.

63. *The Story of Asiya, Daughter of Muzahim*[100]

Kaab al-Ahbar said: When God created the most beautiful dark-eyed houris, the angels said, "Our God and Master, hast thou created anything more beautiful than the dark-eyed houris?"

"O hosts of angels," came the cry in response, " I have created among the women of the world four girls who excel the houris as the sun excels the moon and the other constellations. They are Asiya daughter of Muzahim, Mary daughter of Amram, Khadija daughter of Khuwaylid, and Fatima daughter of Muhammad."

It is said that Muzahim, the father of Asiya, married a woman on the same day that Joseph married Zuleikha and that he went into her and begat Asiya on the same night that Zuleikha conceived Manasseh.

When Asiya had reached her twentieth year, a white bird in the form of a dove appeared to her with a white pearl in its mouth.

"Asiya," it said, "take this white pearl, for when it turns green it will be time for you to marry; when it turns red God will cause you to suffer martyrdom." Then the bird flew away. Asiya took the pearl and fastened it to her necklace.

When Pharaoh heard of her beauty, he wanted to marry her and sent to her father Muzahim to dispatch his daughter. When Muzahim told Asiya the news, she wept bitterly and said, "How can a woman who believes be the wife of an infidel?"

"My daughter," he said, "you are right; but if I do not do as he says, he will destroy us and all our people." Therefore she complied with his wish.

As a bride-price the king gave her thousands of okes of gold and ordered so many thousands of sheep slaughtered that there was not a soul in Egypt who was not invited to partake of the feast he had prepared.

When she entered under his roof, Pharaoh came in intent upon her; however, God kept him from her and made him impotent. Then he heard a voice saying, "Woe unto you, O Pharaoh! Verily the end of your kingdom draws nigh at the hand of a man from the children of Israel called Moses."

"Who is that talking?" asked Pharaoh.

"I do not know," answered Asiya.

* * *

One day while asleep on his throne, Pharaoh dreamed that a man approached him, a staff raised in his hand, and struck him on the head. Then the man took him by the feet and cast him into the Nile. Pharaoh awoke terrified and called for the dream-interpreters, who, when told of his dream, said to each other, "This dream indicates the destruction of Pharaoh and the end of his kingdom." But they told the king, "This is an obscure dream which certainly should not cause you any anxiety." And they went away from him to their own houses.

The next night Pharaoh dreamed of the same man with a

staff in his hand who struck him on the head. Then he saw Asiya, winged, flying into heaven. The earth convulsed and swallowed him up. Awaking in fright, he called for the dream-interpreters and told them the dream.

"This dream indicates a child at whose hand will be your destruction and that of your people," they said. Next Pharaoh consulted his viziers and the grandees of his realm, who said, "The prevalent opinion is that you should guard all pregnant women. If they give birth to males, kill them; if they give birth to females, leave them." Following this advice, he had twelve thousand women and seventy thousand babies killed.

* * *

It was Amram's custom to sit at the head of Pharaoh's bed while he slept, never leaving him. While thus seated, suddenly one night Amram saw his own wife on the wing of a bird. God cast desire into his heart so that he arose and lay with her on Pharaoh's rug, and thus she conceived Moses. Afterwards the bird carried her back to her own house, unseen by the thousand guards and watchmen at Pharaoh's gate.

The next morning when Pharaoh arose, the astrologers came to him and said, "Sire, the child you feared has this night been conceived by his mother, for his star has ascended and is brilliant in the extreme." Pharoah called for old women and midwives and ordered them to go to the Israelite women and seek out those who were pregnant. As they were performing this task, they did not enter Amram's house because they knew he never left the king at night.

When Moses' nine months were accomplished, his mother delivered him in the middle of the night with no one to help but her daughter. Upon birth, Moses shone with a bright light, and Pharaoh heard a voice saying, "Moses is born and you are destroyed, Pharaoh!"

Pharaoh ordered a more intense effort in seeking out newborn babes, and Moses' mother nursed him in constant fear of discovery by Pharaoh, lest he be killed. Whenever she went out of the house, she concealed him in the oven. One day, however, when she went out, having as usual hidden him in the oven, her daughter lit the stove; and the fire blazed inside without her knowing that Moses was there. Haman and his aides came and, entering Amram's house, said, "There is not a newborn babe here, is there?"

"How could there be a baby here," asked Moses' sister, "when Amram is imprisoned by you?" Haman searched every corner of the house until he came to the oven. But as it was blazing, he left, certain that there could be no baby inside the fire.

As Moses' mother was returning, she met the aides coming from her house and almost fainted with anxiety. Entering the house and rushing toward the stove, she asked her daughter if Haman had found her child. When she saw the oven ablaze, she slapped her face and cried, "What use is caution against fate? You have burned up my child in the fire!"

But Moses cried out from inside the oven, "Fear not, mother, for God has delivered me from the fire and kept it from me. Put your hand into the oven and draw me out: God will keep the heat from you." She stretched forth her hand and pulled him from the oven, and the fire did not touch her; she put Moses into his cradle.

She went to a carpenter named Saayam ibn Jaafar and said, "Make me an ark of such length and width, and make it secure against water."

"What are you going to do with it?" asked the carpenter.

"I have given birth to a child whom I fear Pharaoh will kill." she said. "I am going to cast him into the river."

The carpenter thought the ark was for Aaron, as there were only three years difference between him and Moses. When she had gone away, the carpenter was going to inform Haman, but the earth swallowed him up to his ankles and said, "If you return and make her the ark as she wishes, I shall let you go; otherwise I shall swallow you until you die!" The carpenter swore that he would build the ark, and the earth set him free. He did make the ark, which he took by night to Amram's house and delivered to Moses' mother. She took the child, nursed him, and placed him in the ark; stealing forth to the riverbank, she cast it upon the water.

Kaab said the ark remained on the Nile for forty days; Ibn Abbas said three days, whereas Wahb said one night, and that

Amram died before Moses was forty days old, the age at which he was cast onto the river.

* * *

Pharaoh had seven daughters, not one of whom was free of disease. As treatment the physicians had advised them to bathe in the water of the Nile, so Pharaoh had a large pool constructed in his house, and filled it with Nile water. God commanded the breeze to carry the ark and leave it in that stream. The eldest daughter discovered the ark, opened it and saw Moses inside, shining with the brilliance of the sun. When she took him up, all her diseases left her; and no sooner had all the girls taken him up in their arms than they too were cured of their afflictions by the blessing of Moses.

Then Asiya took him, not knowing that he was the son of her uncle Amram, and carried him to Pharaoh, who said when he saw him, "Asiya, I fear that this may be my enemy. I must therefore kill him."

"This child is a delight of the eye to me, and to thee," said Asiya. *"Kill him not, peradventure it may happen that he may be serviceable unto us; or we may adopt him for our son* (28.9). Sire, if he be your enemy, you can have him destroyed whenever you wish. But keep him until such time."

As Moses was hungry, wet-nurses were brought from every corner of the kingdom; but he would not take the breast of any of them, as He hath said: *And we suffered him not to take the breasts of the nurses who were provided* (28.12), lest he suckle at the breast of any but his mother.

Moses' mother longed to see him and said to her daughter, "Go seek news of your brother." When the girl came to the palace, which was not closed that day to women capable of nursing, she saw Moses on Asiya's lap and said, *"Shall I direct you unto some of his nation, who may nurse him for you, and will be careful of him?"* (28.12).

"Go and bring them to me," said Pharaoh.

She therefore returned to her mother and told her what had happened. Straightaway Jochebed, Moses' mother, went to Pharaoh.

"Take this boy," said Asiya, "and give him your breast. Perhaps he will take it." She did as she was told, and Moses accepted her to nurse him. Jochebed lived three years in Pharaoh's house.

* * *

One day while Moses sat playing in Pharaoh's lap, he grabbed his beard and held onto it; with his right hand he slapped Pharaoh's face so hard that his eyes became red and his crown fell from his head.

"This child is my enemy," said Pharaoh, ready to kill the child.

"This boy is young,' said Asiya, "and does not know what he is doing. I will give you proof." She ordered a silver salver, placed in it a glowing ember and a pearl and said to Moses, "Take whichever one you want." Moses put his hand out for the pearl, but Gabriel caused his hand to swerve toward the ember, which he picked up and put to his mouth, burning his tongue. He threw it from his hand and began to cry.

"If Moses had reason," said Asiya, "he would not have chosen the ember over the pearl." And thus was Pharaoh's anger abated.

* * *

When Moses was five years old, a cock in the palace flapped its wings and crowed.

"You are right," said Moses to the cock.

"What did the cock say?" Pharaoh asked.

"It says it is glorifying the Lord by saying, 'Praise be to him who has graced a shepherd's son with long kingship!' "

"What do you mean, the cock said these words?!" said Pharaoh. "It is you who are saying them."

Moses said to the cock, "Say what you said before in an intelligible tongue."

"On condition that if they kill me you will ask your Lord to restore me to life," said the cock. Moses promised, and the cock repeated intelligibly what it had said to Pharaoh, who ordered it killed. God restored its spirit, and it was not seen afterwards.

* * *

When Moses was nine, he kicked the legs of the chair Pharaoh was sitting on and it broke. Pharaoh fell and broke his nose, and the blood flowed over his beard. He wanted to kill Moses, but

Asiya said, "Sire, it would do you no harm to have a son of such strength who could drive away your enemies."

* * *

When Moses was twelve he saw on a table a stuffed camel about to be carved and eaten. When the meal was over, Moses said, "Rise up with your Lord's permission!" And the camel rose up on the table. Pharaoh was terrified, but Asiya said, "Would it not make you content to have a child who could perform such miracles?"

* * *

When Moses was thirteen, he went out to the banks of the Nile to perform ablutions and pray. Just then a man passed by and asked, "Do you not worship your father Pharaoh?"

"God's curse upon Pharaoh and upon you too!" said Moses.

"I shall certainly tell Pharaoh," said the man.

"O Earth," cried Moses, "take him!" And the earth swallowed him up to his waist. When he swore that he would not tell anyone and would believe in him, Moses said, "O earth, set him free!" And he was loosed.

Pharaoh was informed, however. He called Moses and asked, "To whom were you praying?"

"To my Master who has fed, raised and clothed me," said Moses.

"You have spoken well," said Pharaoh, "for it is I who have done all that for you." And he ordered the man who had informed him to have his hands and feet cut off and to be burned in the fire.

* * *

Moses then began to sit with the elders of the children of Israel.

"How long have you been in Pharaoh's land?" he asked them.

"For a long time," they answered.

"In your books do you find deliverance from Pharaoh?"

"Yes," they replied, "at the hand of a man of our own seed."

"What will you do if God delivers you?"

"We will increase our worship of God and feeding of the poor. We will obey our Lord and never disobey Him."

"O children of Israel," said Moses, "I have heard that there was an idolatrous nation to whom God sent a prophet to call them to the Lord. They kindled a great fire to burn him, but God made the fire cool and safe for him."

"That was our father Abraham," they said. "O Moses, we do not doubt that you are the man at whose hands we hope for deliverance."

"Children of Israel," said Moses, "by the God of Abraham, Ishmael, Isaac and Jacob, I love you as a brother!" So when Moses was at the peak of his strength and maturity, he commanded the children of Israel to do justice and to eschew evil; and word spread throughout the city that he had gone against Pharaoh.

* * *

One day one of Pharaoh's cooks, who had bought some firewood, attempted to force a follower of Moses to carry the wood to Pharaoh's palace. The follower of Moses would not obey, and Pharaoh's man angrily assaulted him. The abused man sought help from Moses, who said, "Let him go!" When the cook refused, Moses struck him on the chest and he died. Moses regretted his action and said, *"O Lord, verily I have injured my own soul: wherefore forgive me"* (28.16).

God said to him, "Had the man you killed worshipped me for one instant, I would cause you to taste a painful punishment!"

* * *

It is related on the authority of the Prophet, that "The end of the world is easier for God to bear than the killing of one believer. Whosoever kills a believer will be turned by God on his face into Hell on the Day of Resurrection.

"Whoever slays a Muslim will be caused to stand before God; the one who has been murdered will be brought; his jugular vein will stream with blood and he will say, 'O Lord, this one killed me injustly.' And God will say, 'I am the doer of what I will.' The murdered man will be taken to Paradise and the murderer to Hell.

"Whosoever aids in killing a believer without right will find on the Day of Resurrection the following written before his eyes: 'Despair of the mercy of God.'

"On the Day of Resurrection the slain will be given the insrument by which he was killed, and with it he will strike the one who killed him in this world; for he shall know the same pain as the other knew in this world. Then God will judge between them."

* * *

The next day Moses went out and saw that one of the Egyptians had seized the youth he had championed the day before.

"Moses," he cried, "this Egyptian wants to take me before Pharaoh."

"Dost thou intend to kill me, as thou killedst a man yesterday?" (28.19) asked the Egyptian, who then went to Pharaoh and told him that Moses had killed a man. Pharaoh gave the friends of the dead man permission to kill Moses whenever they found him.

Harbel the Believer came to Moses and said, *"Verily the magistrates are deliberating concerning thee, to put thee to death: depart therefore; I certainly advise thee well"*[101] (28.20).

Moses left the city, headed for Midian, but did not know the way. Nonetheless, he put his trust in God and traveled, guided by the stars at night and by a huge lion in the daytime. Along the way he chanced upon a shepherd grazing his flocks; when the sheep saw Moses, they bowed down to God and said intelligibly, "Our God and Master, this is thy servant Moses, who has come out of the city afraid, hungry and thirsty. Preserve him wherever he may go, for thou art capable of everything." And the shepherd too became one of his followers.

Moses traveled night and day until, on the seventh day, he came to Midian, where he found a group of Midianites watering their flocks with a large bucket. Among them were two women, whom he asked, *"What is the matter with you?"*

They answered, "We shall not water our flock, until the shepherds shall have driven away theirs; for our father is an old man, stricken in years" (28.33).

"Is this water their private property?" asked Moses.

"No," they said, "it is for all the people."

When the shepherds finished drawing water, they took a large rock and closed the top of the well so that no one could draw water from it. When they had withdrawn, Moses told the two women to bring their sheep to the pool. Then he advanced to the well, kicked the rock away and watered their sheep, whereupon he sought the shade of a tree. The two women went to their father Shuayb and told him about Moses. Shuayb told the more bashful of his daughters, Zipporah, to summon Moses.

When she came to Moses, she said, *"My father calleth thee, that he may recompense thee for the trouble which thou hast taken in watering our sheep for us"* (28.25). So he followed her; but while she was walking before him, the wind revealed her thigh.

"Walk behind me and direct me by throwing stones before me, and beware lest you speak to me!" said Moses. She did as he told her, and whenever he departed from the right way she would throw a stone. When they reached Midian and came to Shuayb's house, they exchanged greetings, and Moses told Shuayb his tale. Shuayb called for food; and after he had blessed it with God's name, they ate. When finished, he praised God; and Zipporah said to her father, *"My father, hire him for certain wages: the best servant thou canst hire is an able and trusty person"* (28.26).

He said, "Verily I will give thee one of my daughters in marriage, on condition that thou servest me for eight years and if thou fulfil ten years, it is in thine own breast; for I seek not to impose a hardship on thee." Moses accepted these terms, and Shuayb called Zipporah and betrothed her to Moses.

Moses asked for a staff for shepherding, and Zipporah said, "Go into that house; there are many staffs in it." Moses entered, prayed two *rak'as*, and took a red staff from the bundle. Shuayb took the one he had chosen, placed it beneath the house under the others and said to Moses, "Enter and take a staff from among these." He went in and took the one from the top, and it was the same one.

"Moses," said Shuayb, "this staff is from the trees of Paradise and was given to Adam the day he left there. After him, it supported Abel, Seth, Enoch, Noah, Hud, Salih, Abraham, Ishmael, Isaac and Jacob. Never put it from your hand, for no prophet has ever held it but God gave him victory over his enemies.

"Now," continued Shuayb, "here is a valley which has very good pasture, but for a large serpent that devours all sheep that pass by." So Moses took out Shuayb's flock, which then numbered forty head, and set out for that valley. When the serpent perceived the sheep, it went out in search of them; but Moses struck it with his staff, cutting it in two. When he returned to Shuayb and told him of the serpent's death, the old man rejoiced. Then the flock increased in number to eighty, then one hundred and fifty; and every year his flock increased until it numbered four hundred head. Now none of the shepherds of Midian dared approach the water before Shuayb's flocks.

* * *

Waqidi said: A man asked our Prophet which of the two terms (i.e. eight or ten years) Moses fulfilled, but he did not know; so he asked Gabriel, who said he would ask Michael. Michael was asked and said that he did not know either. Then Michael asked Israfel, who said he would ask his Lord. And God told Israfel, "Tell Gabriel to tell my beloved Muhammad that Moses fulfilled the better of the two terms and fulfilled it ten times over."

* * *

When Moses decided to leave, Shuayb wept and said, "Moses, how can you go? I have grown old and weak, and you will leave my flocks with no shepherd."

But Moses said, "Your flocks do not need a shepherd, for I have made a pact with the wolves and lions that they cause no harm; and I have made this ram with the horns the shepherd."

"If you were to pray to God to restore my sight, I could see you," said Shuayb.

"You pray yourself," said Moses, "and I will guarantee your prayer."

Shuayb therefore prayed, "O Lord, restore my vision and vigor." And Moses guaranteed his prayer. Gabriel descended with some of the nectar of Paradise and gave it to Shuayb. When he drank of it, his sight and strength were restored by God. Rushing to Moses and embracing him, he said, "Moses, be as a compassionate father to my daughter Zipporah." Then to his daughter he said, "Go with Moses and never leave him. How excellent is your master!" He gave them his blessing and escorted them part of the way.

Thus Moses departed Midian and set out for Egypt, but when night fell, the sky was filled with lightning; a heavy rain began to fall and the wind blew. Moses pitched a tent in the valley and kept his wife inside. At that time Zipporah was with child and birth pains were beginning, so Moses gathered dry kindling and tried to light a fire. He took two pieces of flint and struck them together, but nothing ignited, whereupon he grew angry and went out of the tent, full of woe. Suddenly he saw the light of a fire in the distance and *said unto his family, "Tarry ye here; for I see fire: peradventure I may bring you thence some tidings of the way, or at least a brand out of the fire, that ye may be warmed"* (28.29f).

And when he was come thereto, a voice cried unto him from the right side of the valley, in the blessed bottom, from the tree, saying, "O Moses, verily I am thy Lord: wherefore put off thy shoes; for thou art in the sacred valley of Towa. And I have chosen thee; therefore hearken with attention unto that which is revealed unto thee. Verily I am God; there is no god besides me; wherefore worship me, and perform thy prayer in remembrance of me." Then God said, *"Now what is that in thy right hand, O Moses?"* (20.17).

He answered, "It is my rod whereon I lean, and with which I beat down leaves for my flock; and I have other uses for it" (20.18) (as he used to stick it in the ground and hang his cloak on it to provide shade from the sun).

Then he was told, *"Cast it down, O Moses!" And he cast it down, and behold, it became a serpent, which ran about* (20.19f).

As Moses drew back from it, Gabriel said, "Do you flee from your Lord?"

"I do not flee from my Lord," said Moses, "but from death!"

"Is there life or death except with God's permission?" asked Gabriel.

Therefore Moses returned to his place, and God spoke to him, saying, *"Take hold on it, and fear not: we will reduce it to its former condition"* (20.21). Moses stretched out his hand and took it, and suddenly it was again a dry staff.

Then God said to him, *"And put thy right hand under thy left arm: it shall come forth white, without any hurt"* (20.22).

Thereupon Moses' fear was dispelled, and God cried, "O Moses, I have chosen thee to be mine apostle; I will send thee to Pharaoh, for he hath been ungrateful of my bounty. Deliver my message to him and call him to worship me."

Moses said, "Lord, enlarge my breast, and make what thou hast commanded me easy unto me: and loose the knot of my tongue" (20.25ff) (that is, the glowing ember that had burned his tongue). *"And give me a counsellor of my family"* (which God granted in the person of Aaron) (20.29).

Then Moses mentioned the Egyptian's death, saying, *"O Lord, verily I have slain one of them; and I fear they will put me to death"* (28.33).

"Fear not, Moses," said God, "for mine apostles have no need to fear." And He made mention of His grace upon Moses, saying, *"Go ye unto Pharaoh and say, 'Verily we are the messengers of thy Lord: wherefore send the children of Israel with us, and do not afflict them* with construction labor, moving stones, carrying wood, and the like' " (20.43, 47).

"My brother Aaron is of a more eloquent tongue than I am," said Moses, *"wherefore send him with me for an assistant, that he may gain me credit"* (28.34). And Moses was granted all he asked.

Meanwhile, Zipporah, his wife, was in such great pain with labor that the inhabitants of the valley heard her cries. In that place were many genii, the chief of whom at that time was Shamakh ibn Sumaydi ibn Amr ibn Affan. They gathered in the valley, lit a fire and sat around her, turning her until she gave birth. When Moses returned, an angel brought him the newborn babe and said, "Moses, this is your son. Circumcise him and name him, and go forth in your Lord's business." So Moses took two sharp rocks, circumcised him and spoke God's name over him until the flow of blood stopped.

An angel took Zipporah and her son back to her father, where they remained until Moses had finished his mission to Pharaoh and had gone into the wilderness. Then Shuayb sent Moses' wife back to him.

64. *Moses and Aaron*

Kaab al-Ahbar said: At that time Aaron was one of Pharaoh's viziers who, like his father Amram, never left him day or night. One night someone came to him in a dream bearing a ruby cup and said, "Aaron, drink this, for it is a marvel of glad tidings concerning your brother, who has set out from the land of Midian as an apostle to Pharaoh; and you are his partner." The angel bore him up and cast him on the upper part of the road; Gabriel descended on his horse Harqum and bore him to the left bank of the Nile, opposite which stood Moses.[102] Moses crossed the Nile and approached Aaron; they embraced, exchanged vows of fidelity and apostleship, and went to see their mother.

When they came to the door, Aaron tore it off, and they found her standing in an attitude of prayer. She saw them, screamed and fainted. When she came to, Moses told her all that had happened to him, and she fell down prostrate in thanks to God. Later Gabriel bore Aaron back to Pharaoh's palace, and Moses spent the night in his mother's house.

The next day Moses went to Pharaoh's gate and struck it with his staff. As it opened, he entered upon Pharaoh. The people stared at him, some recognizing him while others did not. One of the viziers entered and said, "Sire, I saw a man at your gate whom I did not recognize. I inquired about him and was told that he is Moses son of Amram." The king was terrified and ordered Haman to go out and see the man. Haman at once recognized him, ordered him to be seized and imprisoned, then returned to the king and told him that he had ordered Moses imprisoned.

The king sent for Moses, who was brought into his presence. Pharaoh recognized him, yet asked, "Who are you?"

"I am God's servant and apostle," he answered.

"Why have you come here?"

"I am a messenger to you and all the people of Egypt."

"Why were you sent?"

"In order that you might profess that there is no god but God alone who has no partner, and that I am Moses, His servant and messenger."

Aaron had been seated on his chair, but now he stepped down and said, "Pharaoh, we both are messengers of your Lord, who commands you to send the children of Israel forth with us and not to torment them with exploitation."

"Who is your Lord, O Moses?" asked Pharaoh.

He answered, "Our Lord is he who giveth all things: he hath created them, and directeth them by his providence" (20.49f).

Whenever Moses said anything to Pharaoh, Aaron would say, "You have spoken the truth, O Moses."

Pharaoh grew annoyed at Aaron and said, "Haman, tear off his clothing so he may taste humiliation and disgrace." Haman stripped him down to his underclothing, whereupon Moses took off his *midraa* and covered Aaron with it; and Gabriel descended, bringing a shirt from Paradise with which he covered Aaron. The shirt was of pearl and gave off a light and brilliance which amazed Pharaoh. All the merchants of the land gathered to establish its worth, which they fixed at the land-tax of Egypt for ten years. (At that time the tax amounted to one hundred and seventy houses of gold and silver per annum.)

Then Pharaoh said to Moses: *"Have we not brought thee up among us, when a child; and hast thou not dwelt among us for several years of thy life? Yet hast thou done thy deed which thou hast done and thou art an ungrateful person"* (26.18f).

Moses replied, "I did it indeed, and I was one of those who erred; wherefore I fled from you, because I feared you: but my Lord hath bestowed on me wisdom, and hath appointed me one of his apostles (26.20f). And you, Pharaoh, you mention your goodness towards me, but you forget the evil that you have done to the children of Israel by enslaving them, slaughtering their fathers and outraging their women, who are servants of the Lord of the Universe."

"Moses," said Pharaoh, *"verily if thou take any god besides me, I will make thee one of those who are imprisoned"* (26.29).

"Although I come unto you with a convincing miracle?" (26.30) asked Moses.

Pharaoh replied, "Produce it therefore, if thou speakest the truth" (26.31). While he was speaking, the rod trembled in Moses' hand. As he threw it down, it became a writhing serpent the size of a camel, which began to crush the blocks of stone in

Pharaoh's palace and swallow up everything in its path. It approached Pharaoh and said loudly, "Witness that there is no god but God and that Moses is His apostle!" When Pharaoh, who was lame, started to flee, the serpent caught the train of his robe and threw him behind the throne.

"Moses!" cried Pharaoh, "for Asiya's sake, save me from this serpent!" When he heard Asiya's name, Moses cried to the serpent, which came to him as a tame dog comes to its master. Moses put his hand in its mouth and caught its tongue, whereupon it was again a staff.

"Moses," said Pharaoh, "you are indeed a sorcerer. Do you have any more tricks?"

"Yes," said Moses, putting his hand into his pocket. When he drew it out, it shone as brilliantly as the sun.

Pharaoh was determined to have Moses killed, but Harbel the Believer said, *"Will ye put a man to death because he saith, 'God is my Lord'; seeing he is come unto you with evident signs from your Lord? If he be a liar, on him will the punishment of his falsehood light; but if he speaketh the truth, some of those judgments with which he threateneth you will fall upon you"* (40.28). Pharaoh was frightened by these words, and Harbel said, "Are you frightened of me for showing you what I see and leading you on the way of the rightly guided?"

Then memory of the torments experienced by the ancient nations caused them fear, and Pharaoh said, "It appears, Harbel, that you are one who believes in this sorcerer. Renounce him, or I shall punish you with all manner of torture."

"O my people," said Harbel, *"as for me, I invite you to salvation; but ye invite me to hell fire"* (40.41). So saying, he left Pharaoh and joined Moses and Aaron.

Pharaoh then sent for all the magicians in his realm; and seventy thousand magicians gathered, from whom he chose seventy. To Moses he said, *"Verily we will meet thee with the like enchantments; wherefore fix an appointment between us and thee; we will not fail it, neither shalt thou, in an equal place"* (20.58f).

Moses answered, "Let your appointment be on the day of your solemn feast; and let the people be assembled in open day."

People came from all corners of Egypt; and when the magicians had gathered, they asked, *"Shall we certainly receive a reward, if we do get the victory?"* (26.41).

Pharaoh answered, *"Yea; and ye shall surely be of those who approach my person."*

Then Moses and Aaron came and saw the valley filled with crowds of people. In the middle they had placed ropes and staffs, between every two white ropes a black staff and between every two black staffs a white rope. Among all the magicians were two great ones, called Razzam and Rabbab, who advanced and said, *"O Moses, whether wilt thou cast down thy rod first, or shall we be the first who cast down our rods?"* (20.65f).

He answered, "Do ye cast down your rods first." So the magicians came forward and cast their cords and staffs and said, "By the might of Pharaoh, verily we are the victors!" And they enchanted the eyes of the people *and behold, their cords and their rods appeared unto him by their enchantment, to run about like serpents.*

"The enchantment which ye have performed," said Moses, *"shall God surely render vain"* (10.82). He threw his staff into the midst of the valley, and, bursting into flame, it consumed all that the magicians had enchanted. Then it became a serpent with seven heads, each of which was as large as a camel, and swallowed their cords and staffs.

The magicians all fell down prostrate and said, *"We believe in the Lord of Aaron and of Moses"* (20.70). Pharaoh was furious when he realized that the victory was Moses' and ordered the magicians crucified, their hands and feet cut off.

* * *

Ibn Abbas said: These magicians were of Pharaoh's party at the beginning of the day, but by the end of the day their souls had gone to Paradise.

* * *

And Pharaoh said, "O Haman, build me a tower, that I may reach the tracts, the tracts of heaven, and may view the God of Moses; for verily I think him to be a liar" (40.36f).

Haman assembled fifty thousand builders and masons, some of whom moved stones and carried plaster, and some of whom beat iron into nails. They built ceaselessly day and night and raised a tower into the air higher than anyone had ever done. God commanded Gabriel to destroy the tower, and he toppled it completely. He also sent upon them a flood, which remained for eight days and nights, during which time no one saw the sun, the moon, the sky, or the earth. Fearing they would be drowned, they took refuge with Pharaoh, who said, "Go away! I will lift it from you." When they left, he asked Moses to pray to his Lord to lift the flood from them, whereupon he would believe in him and would release the children of Israel. Moses prayed and the flood receded. God hath said: *But when we took the plague from off them, behold, they brake their promise* (43.50) .

God sent them locusts that devoured their crops, fruits, and trees. This plague lasted eight days, and again they complained to Pharaoh, who promised to relieve them. So he called for Moses and assured him that if he would relieve them of the locusts he would believe in him. Moses prayed to his Lord, and God sent a cold wind that killed all the locusts; but they broke their word again and would not believe.

Then God sent them a pestilence of lice that ate everything remaining on the face of the earth and got into their clothing, making them itch. Again they complained to Pharaoh, who called for Moses and promised to believe; so Moses prayed to his Lord, and they were relieved of the pestilence.

Next God sent frogs; and when they complained, Pharaoh again called Moses and promised to believe. Moses prayed, and God killed the frogs.

Then God told Moses to strike the Nile with his staff, and it was transformed into blood. When a Pharaonite and an Israelite came to the same place at the same time, they both would find the water changed to blood; yet when the Israelite drew from it, he drew cold water, and when the Egyptian drew from it, he drew blood.

When they could no longer endure the thirst, they resorted to Pharaoh; and God lifted that plague also from them by virtue of Moses' prayer, after Pharaoh had guaranteed him that he would believe in him.

* * *

Husayn said: Between each sign were forty-two days.

* * *

Then Moses said, "O Lord, *verily thou hast given unto Pharaoh and his people pompous ornaments, and riches in this present life, O Lord, that they may be seduced from thy way: O Lord, bring their riches to nought, and harden their hearts; that they may not believe, until they see their grievous punishment*" (10.89). God answered his prayer by turning them all into stone: men, women, children and possessions—even couples in embrace turned to stone, and the baker at work beside his oven. God hath said: *We heretofore gave unto Moses the power of working nine evident signs* (17.101).

* * *

Omar ibn Abdul-Aziz said: The nine were the staff, the hand, the deluge, the locusts, the lice, the frogs, the transformation, the turning of the sea into blood, and the parting of the sea.

* * *

Kaab al-Ahbar said: The wife of Harbel the Believer was a lady's maid for Pharaoh's daughters and was also a believer. One day the comb fell from her hand and she said, "Wretched be he who is ungrateful to the Lord of the Universe."

"You mean my father," said Pharaoh's daughter.

"God's curse upon your father and upon anyone who is ungrateful to God!" said she. And Pharaoh's daughter hastened to tell her father what her maid had said.

Pharaoh grew angry and ordered her brought before him. "What is this that has reached me concerning you?" asked Pharaoh.

"Your daughter has told the truth," she said. "I am a believer in Moses' Lord."

Pharaoh's anger waxed, and he ordered iron stakes to be driven into the earth. They cast the maid onto the ground among the stakes, to which they fastened her hands and feet. Her children were brought, and they said to her, "Recant or we will kill you and your children."

"You have neither charity nor honor, O enemy of God!" she said. And they slaughtered one of her children over her breast, and then another, whereupon she said, "Praise be to God who hath hastened my children to Paradise." Then they brought the third child, who was only twelve months old, and laid him across her breast. He took her breast and began to nurse.

"Recant what you have said and we will honor you," they said. She was silent for a moment out of pity for her child, so that he could nurse and have nourishment for departing this world. Then God caused the child to speak intelligibly, and it said, "My mother, be patient and do not recant from Moses' community."

They slaughtered the child on her breast and cast her and her children into fire, wherein they were consumed.

* * *

When Asiya, Pharaoh's wife, heard what had happened, she was stricken with grief and said to Pharaoh, "O accursed one, how long must I endure you while you kill God's friends? O accursed one, how long will you consume God's provisions and be ungrateful to Him?" As she spoke, she picked up an iron rod that lay before her to strike Pharaoh on the head, but he screamed for Haman and his companions.

When he told them what had happened, they said, "Sire, she is your enemy. You must destroy her so that the people will know that, despite your love for her, you had no mercy on her. Then the élite and common people alike must tremble before you."

Pharaoh ordered iron stakes to be driven into her breast until she collapsed, whereat Gabriel descended and gave her the glad tidings of Paradise, telling her that God would join her with Muhammad. Then he handed her a cup of the nectar of Paradise to drink, and took her soul; and she experienced no pain from Pharaoh's torture.

65. *The Parting of the Sea*

Kaab al-Ahbar said: And God sent darkness over the people of Egypt for three days, during which time they could not distinguish day from night. The source of the Nile was cut off, and people died of hunger and thirst. Pharaoh gathered his armies and took them out to the banks of the Nile, whereupon he drew himself aside to a place where he could not be seen. Raising his hands to heaven, he said, "My God and Master, I know that thou are the God of the heavens and the earth and that there is no god but thee. O God, all creation is thine, all people are thy slaves, and thou suppliest their daily bread. For their sakes cause the waters of the Nile to flow." Pharaoh mounted his steed, and as he rode the Nile flowed with him; when he halted, so also did the waters cease to flow. When the people saw this, they fell down before him and said, "Who is like Pharaoh? The Nile itself obeys him!"

Now Gabriel descended to Pharaoh in human guise and said, "I am a slave of the king, come to you seeking requital of another slave who availed himself of my beneficence and good offices. Afterwards, he grew haughty, denied me my right and called himself by my name. What do you deem his retribution?"

"I deem his retribution to be drowning in this river," said Pharaoh.

"Write that for me in your own hand," said Gabriel, and Pharaoh gave him an affidavit to that effect. Gabriel took the paper and went to Moses.

"Moses," said Gabriel, "God commands you to quit this place." So Moses sent word to the children of Israel to ready themselves for travel. They set out, six hundred thousand in number, all progeny of Jacob. Pharaoh, too, gathered his armies and marched close behind the children of Israel.

"Moses!" cried the people, "Pharaoh and his armies have caught up with us!"

"Nay," said Moses, "my Lord is with me to lead me aright."

"But they are near," they said. "Before us is the sea and behind us the sword. Truly we are lost!"

But God spoke to Moses, saying *"Smite the sea with thy rod."*

He struck, and *it became divided, and every part was like a vast mountain* (26.63). There appeared twelve paths, one for each of the tribes, so that they would not mingle together. They passed through, able to talk to and see each other, with Moses in the lead and behind him Aaron, until they had crossed the sea and stood looking at the waters.

Then came Pharaoh and his armies. He gazed at the dry sea and at the paths opened through the water and, hesitating to cross, held his steed in check. Just then Gabriel descended, mounted on a mare, and rode in front. Pharaoh's horse, smelling the mare, followed her; and the armies followed him. Then Gabriel said, "O king, be not in such haste!" And Michael drove the Egyptians forward until not one of Pharaoh's soldiers remained on the shore. Then Gabriel took out the affidavit and gave it to Pharaoh, who, when he opened it, recognized it and knew that he was about to perish.

"I believe that there is no God but he, on whom the children of Israel believe; and I am one of the resigned" (10.91), said Pharaoh.

"Now dost thou believe," answered Gabriel, *"when thou hast been hitherto rebellious, and one of the wicked doers?"* (10.92).

All the Egyptians were drowned, and the children of Israel stood watching them as they went down. Some of them, however, claimed that Pharaoh had not drowned, so God commanded the sea to cast him up on the shore for the children of Israel to see; and they knew that he had indeed perished.

Moses and the Israelites set out for Sinai, where they found a people who had built idols and were adamant in their idolatry. The Israelites said, *"O Moses, make us a god in the manner of these people"* (7.138).

Mose answered, "Verily ye are an ignorant people. My people, seek God's forgiveness for what you have said." The people departed, but in their hearts was a love for idols.

* * *

After Moses had come to Sinai and appointed his brother Aaron to rule over the Israelites, he went up to the mountain. When Moses had gone to the appointed place, the Samaritan[102a] said to the children of Israel, "My people, all this jewelry is of no use to you. Give it to me that I may make you a calf to worship." They consented, and he fashioned them a calf. He also had with him a handful of sand which he had taken from the spot on the shore touched by the hoof of Gabriel's mare. This he cast into the hollow inside of the calf, and it began to bleat. Then he said to the children of Israel, *"This is your god, and the god of Moses; but he hath forgotten him"* (20.88).

Many sided with the Samaritan, but others refused and went to Aaron to inform him. "O children of Israel," said Aaron, *"your Lord is the Merciful: wherefore, follow me, and obey my command"* (20.90).

They answered, "We will by no means cease to be devoted to its worship until Moses return unto us" (20.91). Aaron was grieved by their actions but feigned patience with them, as he feared they would kill him.

* * *

Gabriel descended to Moses and said, "Arise and mount my pearl- and coral-studded wing, which no one has ever mounted before." And Gabriel bore Moses to the place where God had spoken to him. There Moses heard the rush of the Pen across the Tablet and the emerald slates.

God said to the Pen, "Write!"

"What should I write?" asked the Pen.

"Write: 'O Moses, I am God. There is no god but I. Worship me and associate not anything with me. Anyone who associates another with me shall I cause to enter Hell.' "

Ibn Abbas said: The equivalent of this in the Koran is: *Be grateful unto me, and to thy parents. Unto me shall all come to be judged* (31.14).

* * *

"O Moses, kill not an inviolate soul except rightfully, for if you do then the earth will deny you comfort eternally."

The equivalent of this in the Koran is: *Whoso killeth a believer designedly, his reward shall be hell; he shall remain therein forever* (4.93).

* * *

"O Moses, steal not that which belongs to another, for my torment will befall you in this world and in the next."

The equivalent of this in the Koran is: *If a man or a woman steal, cut off their hands, in retribution for that which they have committed* (5.38).

* * *

"O Moses, commit not fornication with your neighbor's wife."

The Koranic equivalent is: *Whoso among you hath not means sufficient that he may marry free women, who are believers, let him marry with such of your maid-servants whom your right hand possess, as are true believers* (4.28).

* * *

"O Moses, do unto others as you would have them do unto you."

The equivalent of this in the Koran is: *Verily the true believers are brethren; wherefore reconcile your brethren* (49.10).

* * *

"O Moses, eat not that over which my name has not been spoken."

The equivalent of this in the Koran is: *Eat not therefore of that whereon the name of God hath not been commemorated* (6.122).

* * *

"O Moses, give thyself leisure to worship me on the sabbath day; give leisure to all the people of thy household, for it is noble in my sight so to do."

The Koranic equivalent of this is: *Moreover ye know what befell those of your nation who transgressed on the sabbath day* (2.65).

* * *

Then Moses said, *"O Lord, show me thy glory, that I may behold thee* (7.143), for thou art the Merciful and the Benefactor."

"O son of Amram," God said, "thou hast asked something no one before thee has ever asked. No one has seen me who did not perish utterly of awe."

"My God and Master," said Moses, "I long to see thy face and die, for I prefer that to not seeing thee and remaining alive."

"O Moses," said God, *"thou shalt in no wise behold me; but look towards the mountain, and if it stand firm in its place, then thou shalt see me." But when his Lord appeared with glory in the mount, he reduced it to dust. And Moses fell down in a swoon* (7.143).

God commanded the angels of heaven to present themselves to Moses, and they passed before him in ranks. As he witnessed their different forms and the magnificence of their shapes, fear and trembling overcame him; and Gabriel passed his wing over Moses' heart to quieten his fear. Then Gabriel stood on the summit of the mountain and ascended into heaven.

"O Lord," said Moses, "I find in the tablets which thou hast revealed to me that thou wilt create a community of people who will command justice and forbid injustice, and that thou wilt make them thy nation."

"O Moses," cried the Lord, "that is the community of Muhammad."

"I find a nation whose gospels are in their hearts, who read their book literally, whereas before they read esoterically. I shall make them my nation," said Moses.

"That is Muhammad's nation," he was told.

"I find a nation who fight those in error, hypocrites and the defective, and to this nation the taking of booty is permitted. If one of this nation intends a good deed and does it, thou writest for him ten good deeds; and even if he does it not, thou writest for him one. If he intends an evil deed and does it not, thou writest nothing against him; if he does it, thou writest against him one evil deed. I shall make them my community."

"That is Muhammad's community," cried the Lord. "O Moses, I have decreed for Muhammad deliverance from Hell and have made for him a place in Paradise. Among all the progeny of Adam, I have created no one nobler in my sight than Muhammad. All the apostles before thee have believed in him and longed for him, and likewise shall those who come after thee, for he is the best prophet and his nation is the best nation: his name is MUHAMMAD and I am the MAHMUD: his name is derived from mine own.

"O Moses, no prophet will emerge from the grave until

Muhammad come forth from his, he and his nation. No one will enter Paradise until Muhammad and his nation enter.

"O Moses, if a man of Muhammad's nation pray two *rak'as* before sunrise, I will forgive him the sins he has committed during the day and night; if he pray four *rak'as* at sunset, I will open all the gates of heaven to receive his prayer. I will grant him forgiveness, tip the balance in his favor and charge the angels to intercede on his behalf; and the dark-eyed houris will watch over him.

"O Moses, if he pray four *rak'as* in the afternoon before sunset, there will not be an angel in heaven or earth that will not ask forgiveness for him, nor will I punish him in Hell. If he pray three *rak'as* after sunset, that is better in my sight than a year of worship. And if he pray four *rak'as* when night has fallen, I will open the gates of Paradise to him and will forgive him.

"O Moses, if he perform his ablutions with water, for every drop I shall give him a degree in Paradise and will erase a like number of evil deeds from his register.

"O Moses, if he fast the month of Ramadan,[103] I will give him the wages of thirty martyrs."

* * *

Then God said to Moses, *"We have already made a trial of thy people, since thy departure; and the Samaritan hath seduced them to idolatry* through worship of the calf" (20.85). *Wherefore Moses returned unto his people in great wrath, and exceedingly afflicted* (20.86).

When he saw the children of Israel, his anger increased and he said, "O children of Israel, *an evil thing is it that ye have committed after my departure; have ye hastened the command of your Lord?" And he threw down the tablets, and took his brother* Aaron *by the hair of his head, and dragged him unto him* (7.150). He kindled a fire and burned the calf to ashes; then he took the tablets, some of which had been broken, picked up part of them and said, "O children of Israel, you have wronged yourselves by adopting the calf after having worshipped God and after having been delivered by Him from Pharaoh!"

"O Moses," they said, "ask your Lord to forgive us."

But God said to Moses, "I shall not forgive them so long as there remain in their hearts anything of the calf." Therefore Moses collected the ashes of the calf and threw them into the sea, after which he told them to drink of the water to purify their hearts. When they had drunk it, there remained no more sorrow or grief in their hearts; but those in whose hearts something of the calf did remain turned yellow and their stomachs swelled. The condition persisted, and they knew for certain that they would perish.

"Moses," they said, "the only means of redemption we have is sincere repentance, and we are sincerely penitent. Even if you were to order us to kill ourselves, we would do so."

God said to Moses, "Verily shall I be content with their judgment of themselves if they be truthful in their hearts, for if they do not act as they say they will, I shall prolong their affliction."

"O people," said Moses, "let those who did not worship the calf find those who did and slay them." Thereupon God cast a darkness over them so that they could not see each other. Brothers slew their own brothers, fathers and cousins, without knowing who they were because it was so dark. The massacre of those who had worshipped the calf continued until those who were left waded in blood up to their thighs. The women and children cried out to Moses, saying, "Have mercy!" Moses wept and prayed to God to pardon them; He did, and their weapons did them no further harm. God accepted their repentance and lifted the darkness.

* * *

It is related on the authority of Ibn Abbas that the number of those who worshipped the calf was two hundred thousand, of whom seventy thousand were slain and the rest were pardoned by God.

* * *

Moses then brought to the children of Israel the Torah and said, "This is a book from your Lord in which are written that which is allowed and that which is forbidden, restrictions and codes, customs and duties, stoning for the fornicator, the severing of the thief's hand, and the retribution for every sin."

They raised a great clamor and said, "We have no use for these restrictions. Worshipping the calf was easier, for there was no stoning, severing or retribution whatsoever."

"Lord," said Moses, "thou knowest that they have rejected thy book and denied thy signs." Then God commanded the angels to lift Mount Sinai into the air until the heavens were obscured, whereupon a voice cried to them, "Accept the book! Otherwise God will hurl this mountain down upon you."

"We hear and obey not!"[104] they said, and the mountain came slowly down over them until they thought it would crush them. Some of them were resigned while others were indignant, but they fell down prostrate and turned their heads sideways so they could see the mountain (which is why the Jews usually prostrate themselves with their heads turned). When they accepted the book, God took the mountain away.

Moses read to them every sabbath day and delivered the law until they led righteous lives and their wealth increased.

* * *

When the children of Israel bathed, they exposed themselves; but they saw that when Moses bathed he covered himself, wherefore they thought that Moses had a blemish on his body.

To bathe himself Moses always put his clothes on a rock and covered himself with his robe. Then he beat the rock with his staff until water came out, and he would wash himself. When he finished he would put on his clothing and return to the children of Israel. One day, however, the rock slipped from its place and began to roll along the ground with his clothes. Moses ran after it, covering himself with his hands and yelling, "Ai rock! my clothes!" He ran after it until it came to rest in the midst of a group of Israelites, who looked at Moses and saw that his body was without blemish, as God hath said: *God cleared him from the scandal which they had spoken concerning him* (33.69).

* * *

The children of Israel then said to Moses, *"Show us God visibly."*

God said to Moses, "Choose from among them seventy men and go with them to Mount Sinai. Take with thee thy brother Aaron and leave behind in thy stead Joshua son of Nun." Moses took them, as he had been told, to Mount Sinai, over which a mist fell, casting it into darkness. Mose and Aaron stood below the cloud with the seventy, and God said to Moses, "Tell these who desired to see me to steel their hearts."

When Moses told them, they said, "We are strong, Moses. Show us your Lord!"

God commanded the angels to descend to the mountain in their finery and in their most awesome forms. When the children of Israel looked upon them, they were thunderstruck and died, whereupon Moses said, *"O Lord, if thou hadst pleased, thou hadst destroyed them before, and me also; wilt thou destroy us for that which the foolish men among us have committed?"* (7.155).

God restored to them their spirits, and they said, "O Moses, we now know that we are not able to endure the sight of Him or to hear His word. Therefore, you be our mediator."

And God said to Moses, "Recite to them until they memorize my commandments, fulfill the covenant and recollect my favor towards them when I delievered them from Pharaoh's torment and from his land." And Moses did as he was told.

* * *

They altered the Torah, however, by adding to and deleting from it. What they liked they left; what they disliked they erased.

Moses then said, "O people, our Lord says for us to go to the Hitta Gate in the Holy Land and to enter therein bowing down in thanks to Him. Afterwards you are to fight the giants who occupy the Holy Land and who practice idolatry in the domain of the prophets."[105]

"Moses," they replied, "the day you took us out of the land of Egypt you promised us that God had sent you to deliver us from Pharaoh's torment, but now you are obliging us to do that which is more difficult to bear than that torment. How can we, encumbered with women, children, and old men, cross the canyons and wild lands that lie between us and the Holy Land? We have neither provisions nor clothing."

"He who delivered you from Pharaoh and parted the sea will provide you with what you need," said Moses. "Praise Him and trust in Him!"

"Moses," said God, "tell them that I shall cause manna and quail to rain down upon them, for thus have I commanded the heavens to do. The winds have I commanded to bring the quail; the rocks have I commanded to gush forth with sweet water. I have commanded the clouds to move when the people move and to stop when they stop. I have compelled their clothes and sandals neither to get wet nor to become soiled and to fit them all, young and old alike." When the people heard this, they set out for the Holy Land in acquiescence.

When the children of Israel marched, the clouds shaded them; when they camped, there would rain down upon them manna sweet as honey and quail like water fowl. They were provided everything they needed, even fat and honey. At night columns of light would shine so that they had no need of lamps, and at dawn the winds would bring them quail like young doves, which they slaughtered and ate. Moses would strike the rocks, and twelve springs would flow forth.

* * *

Moses chose twelve men and said to them, "I am going to send you into the city of the giants to gather information, but conceal what you learn from the children of Israel." They departed, among them Joshua son of Nun and Caleb son of Jephunneh. When they reached the city, they encountered one of the giants,[106] who seized them and locked them in a room. Later he brought them to the city, where the giants assembled and mocked their small bodies, saying, "Are these they who claim they will drive us from our city?!" They determined to kill them, but one of them said, "No, do not kill them. Let them be our slaves." And they spared their lives.

Under the cover of darkness, however, they escaped to a wooded vale called Wadi al-Anqud, where they saw marvelous fruit. They picked a pomegranate and a bunch of grapes and carried them by turns until they came to their people, whom they told of the wonders they had seen.

"We have come from a people," they related, "each of whom is this tall!" When they showed them the pomegranate and the grapes, the children of Israel trembled with fright.

"Did not I tell you *not* to tell them what you saw?" cried

Moses. "Why have you frightened them unnecessarily?" And the ten of them who had spoken died, leaving only Joshua son of Nun and Caleb son of Jephunneh, who only of the twelve had concealed what they had learned.

Fear of the giants overcame the Israelites, and they said, *"O Moses, we will never enter the land, while they remain therein: go therefore thou, and thy Lord, and fight; for we will sit here* (5.24). Moses, we desire another commander: we have no further use for you."

Joshua and Caleb said, "O people, *enter ye upon them suddenly by the gate of the city; and when ye shall have entered the same, ye shall surely be victorious"* (5.23). But they paid no attention to what they said.

Then Moses said, *"O Lord, make a distinction between us and the ungodly people!"* (5.25).

And God answered him, saying, *"Verily the land shall be forbidden them forty years; during which time they shall wander like men astonished on the earth"* (5.26).

No one who was born in Egypt entered the Holy Land, for God caused them to wander until all those who had gone against the others had died. Then Moses went to the Hitta Gate, over which was written the Great Name of God, which, whenever invoked, is answered and which is composed of certain Hebrew letters.

* * *

Wahb said that *hitta* means "pardon" in their language and that when the believers bowed down they said, "Our Lord, we have heard and obeyed," but the abominators entered the Hitta Gate backwards and said, *"Samqa hitta,"* which means "red wheat." God hath said: *But they who were ungodly among them changed the expression into another, which had not been spoken unto them* (7.162), so God afflicted them with the plague until the last of them died.

66. *Balaam son of Beor, and Korah*

Then Moses and the children of Israel marched to the city of Balqa; there ruled a king called Balak son of Zippor, who consulted the people of his realm.

"Send for Balaam son of Beor," they said. "His prayers are always answered. Ask him to curse Moses and his people." So the king sent messengers to Balaam son of Beor asking him to come into his presence.

"Wait while I ask my Lord," said Balaam, who went to his oratory, prayed two *rak'as* and asked his Lord's permission to go to the king.

"O Balaam," said God, "dost thou not know that the troops thou desirest to go out against are the children of Israel? This king is seeking thy aid to curse them. Go not to him!"

"My Lord has forbidden me to go," said Balaam to the messengers, who returned to the king and told him what had happened.

"Sire," said the viziers, "you can get him to come if you give his wife a present on condition she persuade him to come to you."

The king therefore sent her a silver tray filled with gold and handsome objects and asked her to persuade her husband to go to the king. She accepted the gift and kept nagging and urging her husband until he finally asked his Lord's permission again.

"I forbade thee to go to them," God said, "but now the choice is thine." When he heard this, he was relieved.

Wearing a woolen cloak, he mounted himself on a she-ass and set off in the direction of the king.

The ass brought him to a place where part of a mountain jutted out into the road. As the ass squeezed through the defile, it crushed Balaam's legs, for which he beat the creature; but God caused it to speak, saying, "Balaam, do not beat me, for I am commanded to do thus. Look before you!" Balaam looked and saw an angel blocking the East and the West with its wings. Overcome with fright, he fell down prostrate before God; and the angel departed.

Balaam was about to return home when Iblis appeared and said, "Balaam, were God not resigned to your proceeding, He would not have caused the angel to go away." So Balaam went to the king, who seated him in the assembly and took counsel with him concerning Moses and his people.

"Sire," said Balaam, "God has told me not to curse Moses and his people, but I can tell you that the children of Israel read a certain book. If they go against its precepts, calamity will befall them. Therefore, when they descend into your plain, adorn your women and send them out to Moses' soldiers that they may commit abominations with them, for when they disobey God He will set you up in their stead." And this plan was executed.

Among the women was an especially beautiful one upon whom a man of the tribe of Simeon gazed. He threw her down amidst her baggage to commit adultery with her; but one of the tribe of Judah, realizing what was happening, took his spear, attacked the two of them as the man was lying on her, and impaled them both. Then he carried them on his spear among the soldiers. And the children of Israel realized that this was Balaam's plan.

A great massacre was carried out in which many were killed, including Balak and Balaam; and the rest were routed. Then said the children of Israel, *"O Moses, pray unto thy Lord therefore for us, that he would produce for us of that which the earth bringeth forth, herbs and cucumbers, and garlick, and lentils and onions"* (2.61).

* * *

They marched, more than forty thousand in number, to the cities of Syria, where they occupied themselves with plowing, reaping, winnowing, and grazing livestock.

Moses had a nephew called Korah son of Ebiasaph son of Musaab son of Kohath son of Levi son of Jacob; and Korah was poverty-stricken.

God said to Moses, "O Moses, I command thee to decorate the ark of the Torah with gold. Teach Korah also the art of alchemy." So Moses gave him all the gold he needed to cover the ark in which the Torah was kept.

Moses' sister was Korah's wife, and she had learned the art of alchemy from her brother. Korah learned it from her and practiced it. As his wealth increased, he built palace after palace with walls of gold and silver.

It is said that it took forty mules just to carry the keys to his treasure-stores, and every sabbath day he used to ride out in such finery as no one had ever before possessed.

Korah conspired against Moses and said, "Moses, in what respect are you better than I? I read the Torah just as well as you do, and I am of the children of Levi, as are you."

"It is as you say," Moses replied, "except that I am God's apostle."

Wahb said Korah conspired against Moses by sending for an ungodly woman, to whom he said, "If you perform a task for me, I will make you rich: when the children of Israel are assembled, I will be there. You come among the people and say, 'Moses summoned me and propositioned me, but I would not submit to him.' "

The next day, however, God cast repentance into her heart, so she stood at Korah's gate and said, "O children of Israel, Korah sent for me yesterday and said thus and so to me."

When Moses heard this, he was furious and said, "Lord, give me victory over Korah!"

"O Moses," said God, "I command the earth to obey thee, and I give thee dominion over him."

Moses came to Korah and said, "Enemy of God, you enticed the woman to scandalize me before the people, but God prevented it." Then he said, "O earth, seize him!" Korah's palace sank a cubit into the earth, and it swallowed him up to his knees.

"Moses," cried Korah, "do not do it!"

"O earth," said Moses, "take him!" The earth swallowed him up to his navel, and he was unable to speak. It is said that if he had once sought God's aid, He would have delivered him. Then his palace and everything in it sank into the earth, which rattled with him inside, as He hath said: *And we caused the ground to cleave in sunder, and to swallow up him and his palace* (28.81).

67. *al-Khidr*

Wahb ibn Munabbih said: When God revealed the Torah to Moses and bestowed wisdom upon him, Moses asked, "O Lord, hast thou given anyone what thou hast given me?"

"I have a servant to whom I have given knowledge which I have not given to thee," said God. "His name is al-Khidr son of Malkan son of Peleg son of Eber son of Shelah son of Arphaxad son of Shem son of Noah."

Then Moses requested his Lord's permission to seek out this person, and God granted it, saying, "O Moses, know thou that I have servants to whom I do not give the devil access, and know also that al-Khidr resides on one of the islands in the sea."

Moses and his servant Joshua son of Nun set out toward the sea, taking along as provision a loaf of barley-bread and a roasted fish. Then God spoke to him, saying, "O Moses, when thou seest the fish thou hast with thee come to life, then thou wilt have reached the place."

Moses traveled until he reached a great dome, under which there were men prostrating themselves and performing rites of prayer. He asked them about themselves and about al-Khidr, and they said, "We are angels of our Lord, who have been worshipping Him since the creation of this sea. As for al-Khidr, go straight ahead and you will pass by many domed structures; but when you reach the last of them, you will find the one you are seeking."

Therefore Moses traveled until he reached a huge rock, from which a spring flowed. He sat down at the base of the rock to rest and fell asleep. Joshua sat down beside Moses and threw the remains of the fish into the spring, and it came to life. When Moses awoke, Joshua forgot to tell him what had happened, so they walked on until they reached a river that flowed into the sea.

"Bring us our dinner," said Moses, *"for now we are fatigued with this our journey"* (18.61).

Joshua took out the bread for him and told him what had happened to the fish. *"This is what we sought after!"* said Moses (18.63). *And they both went back returning by the way they came,* until they had come to the rock. Moses looked and there was al-Khidr standing in an attitude of prayer.

"I have found my companion," said Moses to Joshua. "You return to the children of Israel and stay with Aaron until I return to you." Joshua departed, and Moses approached and greeted al-Khidr, who responded.

"Shall I follow thee, that thou mayest teach me of that which thou has been taught, for a direction?" asked Moses (18.67).

He answered, "Verily thou canst not bear with me: for how canst thou patiently suffer those things inasmuch as I act on inner meaning and you act on external form?" (18.68f).

He replied, "Thou shalt find me patient, if God please" (18.70).

al-Khidr said, *"Ask me not concerning any thing,* even though you disapprove." And Moses agreed.

* * *

While they were walking along the shore, suddenly a bird drew near, plunged its beak into the sea and flew away toward the East. Then it returned and plunged again, but this time flew toward the West. Again it returned and cried out.

"Do you know what this bird is saying?" al-Khidr asked Moses.

"No," he replied.

"He says," continued al-Khidr, "that the knowledge which has been given the children of Adam is analogous to the amount of water he has taken in his beak from the sea." And Moses was astonished.

* * *

Then they came to a village and began to examine the skulls and bones of those dead for centuries. In one place there were seven skulls.

"Moses," said al-Khidr, "these are the heads of the mighty of this village, who were seven brothers." Then he told him about each one of them, his name and what he had done.

* * *

They left the village and found a ship which sailed the sea; they said, "Take us with you," and were accordingly taken on board. But, when they had come to the middle of the sea, al-Khidr took a plank from the side of the ship, tore it out and stuffed his cloak into the hole.

Moses asked, *"Hast thou made a hole therein, that thou mightest drown those who are on board?* This is no recompense for such as have taken us on their ship" (18.72).

"Did I not tell thee that thou couldst not bear with me?" said al-Khidr.

He said, "Rebuke me not because I did forget" (18.74).

They traveled a little further, where they encountered the ship of the king of the realm and were told, "The king wants your ship if it has no defect." When the king's men boarded and found the ship damaged, they departed without confiscating it. Then al-Khidr put the plank back where it had been. When they reached the shore, Moses and al-Khidr disembarked.

* * *

They walked until they found a boy playing. al-Khidr struck him on the head with a rock and killed him.

"What!" cried Moses, *"Hast thou slain an innocent person?"* (18.75f).

He answered, "Did I not tell thee that thou couldst not bear with me?"

Moses said, "If I ask thee concerning any thing hereafter, suffer me not to accompany thee" (18.77).

* * *

Then they walked along until *they came to the inhabitants of a certain city: and they asked for food of the inhabitants thereof; but they refused to receive them hospitably*, saying, "This is a time when we do not receive guests." *And they found therein a wall, which was ready to fall down; and so* al-Khidr *set it upright* with his own hands (18.78).

Moses asked, "Why do you trouble yourself for a people who will not give you anything to eat when you ask for food?"

al-Khidr smiled and said, *"This shall be a separation between me and thee; but I will first declare unto thee the signification of that which thou couldst not bear with patience* (18.79).

"The vessel I damaged because it belonged to ten orphan brothers, and a king in Jordan was confiscating every ship which had no defect. I tore out the plank so that he would not take the ship. Then I put it back in its place, as you saw.

"As to the youth I killed, if he had grown, he would have become a highwayman. His parents are pious, and I killed him lest he nullify their piety."

* * *

It is said that God blessed them with a maiden who later gave birth to seventy prophets, and the murdered boy went to Paradise.

* * *

"And the wall belonged to two orphan youths in the city, and under it was a treasure hidden which belonged to them (18.83). Had the wall fallen, the treasure would have been lost, *and thy Lord was pleased that they should attain their full age, and take forth their treasure, through the mercy of thy Lord,* because their parents had been pious."

* * *

Ibn Abbas said that Moses then walked along the shore, where he found tablets of gold, on which was written:

In the name of God the Compassionate the Merciful
There is no god but God
Muhammad is the Apostle of God
How strange it is that one who believes in fate and destiny could be angry or frivolous.
How strange it is that one who knows he will die could rejoice.
How strange it is that one who is certain of the transitoriness of this world and sees the vicissitudes amongst its people could be tranquil at heart.

Moses put down the tablets and returned to the children of Israel.

68. *Og son of Anak*

Kaab al-Ahbar said: When Cain killed his brother Abel, Adam drove him out of his house and, commanding his children not to associate with him, proclaimed him outlaw. Cain took his sister Anak, and together they went to the Yemen, the most fertile of God's lands, where he honored her greatly and married her.[107] God had created her with twenty fingers, each of which had two nails, with which she dug the earth and cut trees. She bore many children, who engendered tribes.

She bore Og and named him Daniel. When he was twenty years old his father died, and his mother said to him, "Daniel, I am going to sleep: catch some animals for me to eat when I awake." And she slept. Og was so distracted with his play, however, that he gathered nothing for her. When she awoke, she grew angry and beat him. Just then Iblis appeared with a rock to strike Anak and kill her; but when Og saw the rock falling on his mother, he pulled his hand from hers and knocked the rock with his head. When Anak saw her son protecting her life with his own, she drew him to her breast and prayed for strength and long life for him. And God granted her prayer.

When two hundred years of his life had passed, his mother died and Og was left an orphan. He was three hundred and three thousand cubits tall. When he bathed, the deepest of the seas reached only to his knees; when he walked, the earth quaked and trembled beneath his feet. When he wept, floods poured forth from his tears; when he hungered, he could eat two enormous elephants. When he was by the sea, he would reach his hand to the bottom and take how ever many fish he wanted; then he would raise his hand to the sun itself to roast them. He ate once a day and slept twice a year, once in winter and once in summer, when he would sleep for a day and a night. When he thirsted, he would lean over a flowing river, put his mouth to it and drink; and the river would cease to flow. God had made him unaware of lust except with women who could bear him.

When Noah came, Og helped him build the ark by carrying

boards and planks. During the flood the waters reached only to his knees.

* * *

Og saw kingdoms and nations come and go, until there came Nimrod, whom he saw ascending in the ark borne on the backs of eagles. Then Og became tyrannical, magnified himself and turned infidel. He stretched his hand to the sky, passing the clouds, and said, "If I desired to arrange the heavens, I would not be incapable of doing so!" And God commanded the angel of light, who turns over day and night, to cause the light to pass away from him; and darkness filled his eyes so that he could not see. Fear and hunger overcame him, and he knew that God was indeed capable of everything. Falling down before Him, he said, "My God, I repent. Make this darkness pass away from me, O thou who art not pleased with obedience and whom disobedience does not harm!" God had compassion on him and illuminated the darkness.

His age increased until he reached the time of Moses, who sent Joshua to Khayshum, the king in the land of Egypt, to call him to worship God. When Joshua came before the king, Og son of Anak was present at the assembly on account of the king's beautiful daughter, who was as large as he was.

"Who are you?" asked the king.

"I am Joshua," he said, "the messenger of Moses son of Amram, sent to you that you might believe in the one God, who has no partner."

But the king said, "Return to your master, for I am about to march forth to meet him in battle." Joshua accordingly went back to Moses and told him what had happened.

Moses set out with the children of Israel to wage war against the city of the king. The king said to Og son of Anak, "Do you wish to marry my daughter?"

"Yes," he replied. "What do you want from me as her bride-price?"

"I want you to help me against Moses himself, for I can destroy his army with my own soldiers." Og agreed and went to see Moses' army. He saw that it was two parsangs in width and breadth, so he went to the mountain, where he cut out a huge rock in the same proportions as the army, and carried it on his head to throw over the tribes of Israel that they might all perish thereby. But God sent the hoopoe-bird, which began to peck at the stone that was on Og's head. When it had made a hole in it, it fell down around Og's neck and he was unable to throw it off. The hoopoe pecked at his head until it reached his brain. Then Moses, who was twenty cubits tall, came forth with his staff, lept up twenty cubits from the ground and struck him on the knee; and Og fell dead.

69. *The Story of the Cow*

It has been said that during the time of Moses there was a pious servant of God who died leaving his wife with child. After his death she gave birth to a son whom she called Manasseh. As he grew, he was always courteous and obedient to his mother, for whom he gathered firewood and spent what he earned on her and himself. He also kept house for her and served her.

One day his mother said, "My son, when your father died, he left me a calf. When you were born I gave it out to a shepherd in a certain village. Go now and reclaim it, for it should have become a full-grown cow." So he left his mother and went to the shepherd, whom he reminded of the calf.

"Take your cow," said he; and he took it. When he was half-way home, God caused the cow to speak, saying, "O you who are courteous to your mother, ride me, for the way is long."

But the youth said, "My mother did not command me to do so."

Then Iblis appeared to him in the guise of a weak, old man and said, "I ask you for God's sake to let me ride on the back of your cow, as I am a weak old man."

But the youth replied, "My mother did not command me to do so."

When he had come to his mother, she said, "My son, take the cow to market and sell it."

"For how much?" he asked.

"For three dinars," she said, "but do not sell it without consulting me."

The boy took the cow to market, where an angel appeared to him and asked, "For how much will you sell your cow, Manasseh?"

"For three dinars," said he, "after I consult with my mother, as she commanded me."

"I have five dinars I will give you," he said, "but do not ask permission from your mother." But he would not accept it.

When he had returned to his mother and told her what had happened, she said, "Sell it, but do not seal the bargain until you have my permission."

He went to the market and said to the angel, "I will sell the cow for five dinars, but not until I consult my mother, as she has commanded me to do."

"I have ten dinars I will give you," he said, "on condition that you do not ask your mother's permission." But he refused, returned to his mother and told her.

"My son," she said, "the one who has appeared to you is an angel of the Lord, sent to see how courteous and obedient you are to your mother. Tomorrow when he appears to you, say to him, 'O Angel, for how much should I sell the cow?' and do whatever he says."

The next day he took the cow to market and the angel appeared to him, saying, "How much will you sell the cow for?"

"For however much you say," he answered.

"Take your cow back home," said the angel, "for one of the children of Israel is to be killed by an unknown assailant. Moses will buy your cow to bring the murdered man back to life, and you may sell it for what you think it worth."

Manasseh returned to his mother and told her what the angel had said. A short time afterwards, one of the children of Israel, called Ammiel, was killed and his body cast off by a gateway. The heirs of the murdered man said, "The owner of the house by the gate of which the body was found must have killed him." And they sought Moses' mediation. The householder swore he had not killed the man and produced forty pious people to bear witness to his character.

Then God said to Moses, "Tell the friends of the slain man to slaughter a cow and to strike the murdered man with it: he will be raised from the dead and will tell who slew him."

Moses told them this, but they said, "O Moses, *dost thou make a jest of us?*" (2.67f).

Moses said, "God forbid that I should be one of the foolish."

They said, "Pray for us unto thy Lord, that he would show us what cow it is."

Moses answered, "He saith, 'She is a red cow, intensely red, her colour rejoiceth the beholders.' "

They said, "Pray for us unto thy Lord, that he would further show us what cow it is, for several cows with us are like one another, and we, if God please, be directed" (2.69).

Moses answered, "He saith, 'She is a cow not broken to plough the earth, or water the field, a sound one, there is no blemish in her' " (2.70).

The only cow of such a description they could find was Manasseh's. When they came to him, he would not sell the cow for less than its skin full of gold. They bought it, slaughtered it, cut off its ears and struck the slain man with it, whereupon he stood up.

"Who killed you?" they asked.

"So-and-so son of So-and-so," he said and fell down again dead. They put to death the one he had named, skinned the cow, filled its hide with gold and gave it to Manasseh.

70. *The Death of Aaron and Moses*

After that, Aaron saw in the desert a huge mountain, a fertile garden at its base. Together with Moses he went to explore the mountain, which they discovered to have an abundant supply of water, as well as herbage and caves. From the mouth of one particularly wide cave light was streaming. They went inside and found a golden throne, covered with tapestry, over which was written in Hebrew:

† This throne is for him who is the right height †

Moses sat down on it, but his legs were too long. Then Aaron mounted the throne and found that he was the right size. The Angel of Death appeared and greeted them saying, "I am the Angel of Death, sent to take Aaron's spirit."

Aaron wept and said, "My brother, I leave my children in your care. Convey my greetings to the children of Israel." The Angel of Death took his spirit, and Aaron was one hundred and twenty-seven years old.

When the angels had washed him, Moses prayed over him and departed; and the angels sealed the entrance to the cave.

* * *

When Moses returned to his army, the children of Israel asked where Aaron was. Moses told them that he had died, but they said that Moses had killed him. Moses therefore asked his Lord to cause Aaron to appear to them. God commanded the angels to bring him forth, and they bore his throne from the cave into the air so that the children of Israel could see it. "O children of Israel," cried the angels, "accuse not Moses for the murder of Aaron! Here is his dead brother, who has passed away. We love him, and you shall follow in his footsteps." They mourned him greatly, for he had been beloved of them because of his compassion towards them.

Thereafter God raised up Kedar, Aaron's son, and endowed him with gravity and leniency; and he read to them from the Torah in place of his father.

* * *

Wahb said: "I have heard that Moses turned his face toward heaven and said, 'My God and Master, if thou didst desire all the people to worship thee, they would obey thee, for thou lovest to be obeyed and loveth not to be disobeyed. Why dost thou not torment them with fire?'

" 'O Moses,' God said, 'sow seed and water it, then harvest it when it is ripe. Winnow it and keep it for when it is needed.'

"Moses did this; and when it was done, his Lord called to him, saying, 'What hast thou done with the crop?'

" 'Lord,' he replied, 'I did as thou didst command.'

" 'O Moses, hast thou left anything?'

" 'Only that which was not fit.'

" 'And thus is he who doth not worship me: he is not fit.' "

* * *

Moses threatened and warned the children of Israel; he cautioned them and preached to them. He caused them to believe in themselves and in God and His angels by means of his communications with them. "Be faithful in your covenant with God," he told them, "and do not abandon the faith. Do not eat carrion or blood or pork. Do not confound the good with the abominable; eat not that over which God's name has not been spoken. Fear God insofar as you can both secretly and openly, and discharge your duties of prayer and alms. Be a father to the orphan, a husband to the widow and an amicable source of strength to Muslims. Alter not the Torah. Give brotherly advice to the oppressed. If you follow my commandment, then you shall have mercy from above, and you shall be with me and I with you. Remember my commandment, and be wise and learned in religion."

* * *

God spoke to Moses, saying, "I shall now fulfill my promise to take thee, O Moses." But Moses was saddened to be parted from the world.

"Moses," said God, "who safeguarded thee on the mountain for forty days without food or water when thou didst not leave thy place until that protection was concluded? Then did I not reveal my word to thee? And who kept thee in the ark when thy mother cast thee off? Who saved thee from the sea? Who cast love of thee into thine enemies' hearts? Who delivered the children of Israel from Pharaoh's torment? Who caused them to inherit the land, and who gave them victory over the giants?"

"My God and Master," said Moses, "thou hast bestowed all that of thy bounty, and for all of that thou deservest praise."

"Moses," said God, "I have ordained that all my creatures die."

"My God and Master," said Moses, "I fear the bitter taste of death."

The Angel of Death descended to Moses, who was seated reading the Torah. "Peace be with you, Moses," said the angel.

"And with you peace," replied Moses. "Who are you?"

"I am the Angel of Death, come to take your spirit."

"From where will you take it?" asked Moses.

"From your mouth."

"It was through my mouth that I spoke to God," said Moses.

"Then from your hands."

"In my hands I held the tablets," Moses replied.

"Then from your ears."

"Through my ears I heard my Lord address me and heard also the rush of the Pen across the Preserved Tablets."

"Then from your eyes."

"With my eyes I saw the Light of my Lord."

"Then from your feet," said the angel.

"I stood barefoot on Mount Sinai when I conversed with my Lord," said Moses.

"Moses," said the Angel of Death, "I see you are speaking to me after the manner of one who has drunk an intoxicant."

With that, Moses' mind became confused, and he said, "I have never drunk wine!" but the Angel of Death drew nigh and took his spirit.

* * *

It is said that when Moses did not want to die, God said, "Put thy hand on the hide of a bull, and thou shalt be granted a year for every hair covered by thy hand."

"And after that what?" asked Moses.

"Death," said God.

"Lord," said Moses, "death is preferable now." So God took his spirit.

* * *

It is related that Moses said, "Lord, if thou takest my spirit, then who will remain to care for my two sons?" Thereupon God commanded him to smite the sea with his staff. When he smote it, it was cloven asunder, revealing a huge rock. Then God commanded him to strike the rock with his staff; when he struck it, it split apart and a red worm emerged with a green leaf in its mouth, saying, "Praise be to Him who does not forget me even in my distant place."

"O Moses," said God, "I forget not this worm at the bottom of the sea and in the middle of a rock. How then could I forget thy sons, who are believers?"

"My God and Master," Moses replied, "inform me when thou wilt take my spirit that I may prepare myself to meet thee."

"Moses," answered God, "I have never informed anyone thus before, but I shall take thy spirit on a Friday." Thereafter Moses put on new white garments every Friday and prayed, waiting for death. When the Angel of Death did come, Moses left Joshua son of Nun as his successor to rule the children of Israel and died at the age of one hundred and sixty.

71. *Joshua son of Nun*

Kaab al-Ahbar said: Joshua was so earnest in waging war for God that He gave him victory over more than thirty of the cities of the infidels in Syria and Arabia. Their children he took prisoner, their property he confiscated, their warriors he killed.

Afterwards Joshua assembled the children of Israel and addressed them, saying, "You know that Moses pledged us to wage holy war; he conquered the city of Jericho and forbade it to giants. Now they have returned: therefore equip yourselves for battle, and God will grant you victory over them!"

The Israelite warriors marched of one accord under Joshua until they reached the battlefield of the giants, where they fought until many on each side had been killed. The giants retreated and withdrew into their city on a Friday eve. Joshua feared the sun would set before he had gained his objective (being the eve of the sabbath, fighting would then be forbidden). Yet there remained about one hour of daylight, or one "lance." (Wahb ibn Munabbih said that one "lance" is a forty-year distance traveled by the sun and is equivalent to one hour of the day, since each day the sun travels from east to west the distance of six hundred years.)

Then Joshua stretched forth his hand to the heavens and called upon his Lord, saying, "O Lord, the children of Israel are the children of thy friend Abraham; and they have become like a mole on a black bull—nay even less and weaker than that! O God, thou knowest our condition. Imprison the sun for us for the remainder of this battle that we may fight the people of Jericho." And God commanded the angel who was entrusted with the sun to keep it in its sphere so that Joshua could finish the battle. They fought on until they had extinguished the giants from the face of the earth, and then the sun set. From that day forth the regulation of the stars has been confused.

Joshua divided the booty and entered the city of Jericho.

Kaab said that before our Prophet, booty had not been lawful to anyone except Joshua.

* * *

God had given Aaron a shirt with twelve markers on it, the number of the tribes of Israel. Whenever anyone of the tribes cheated, the marker would change color and would stay that way until what was owed the booty-house had been returned. If it were not restored, rout would eventually befall that tribe.

The day after the battle of Jericho, Joshua realized that one of the markers on his shirt had changed color; and he knew thereby that dishonesty had beset that tribe and that they would be routed. When they were routed, Joshua called to them, saying, "You have held back booty! What has made you do this?" (One of them had held back a piece of velvet; they brought it to Joshua, who burned it.)

Joshua and his company went to Canaan and waged war there until they had killed more than thirty kings and conquered more than thirty fortresses. And he slew a man called Jadim ibn Hadim, who was an Amalekite.

Joshua and the tribes of Israel traveled until they came to the river Jordan, which they found to be a great, fast-flowing river. They camped beside it for forty days, during which time they were unable to cross. Then Joshua said "O children of Israel, this river is not greater than the sea that God split asunder for us when we were with Moses. God will make it of service to you just as He has given you victory over the giants. Verily He is capable of all things."

When the morrow had come, Joshua and the children of Israel

went to the river. There, on the banks of the river, were two great mountains, which inclined toward each other until they became a bridge; and they all crossed over.

Then Joshua and those with him settled in the land of Syria, where a number of bedouins came to him seeking amnesty, saying, "We have come to you before you come to us with your cavalry and men."

Joshua gave them amnesty and leave to go to their own country, which was the region of Askelon. But when Joshua found that they were from that region, he had them brought back and said, "You have no amnesty with me, for you are enemies of the children of Israel!"

"O prophet of God," they said, "you gave us amnesty. One like you does not go back on his word."

And God spoke, saying, "Joshua, these people have surrendered themselves to thee, and thou hast been hasty in retracting thine amnesty. Now break not thy pact." So Joshua gave them leave to their land in safety along with their families, property and folk.

Joshua remained among the children of Israel until God took his spirit, and he was then one hundred and twenty years old and had ruled for forty years after Moses.

72. *Josephus son of Caleb son of Jephunneh*

Kaab al-Ahbar said: When death took Joshua, he left Caleb son of Jephunneh son of Isa son of Judah son of Jacob as ruler over the children of Israel, and Caleb acted well among the Israelites and they obeyed him until his death. He left his son Josephus as ruler.

Everyone who saw Josephus thought that he was Joseph on account of his beauty. In fact, he was so handsome that women were aroused by him. Because of this, he asked his Lord to change his appearance; God afflicted him with pox so that his hair fell from his head and eyelids, his nose became leprous, and his aspect was so completely altered that the people did not recognize him. Yet they gathered around him out of compassion and asked him what had happened. But they annoyed him—for they disturbed his worship of God—so he asked God to increase what He had done before; his face became so flabby and his teeth so long that no one could bear to look at him.

The people nevertheless knew his earnestness and striving and made him their lord, listening to him and obeying. He remained thus for forty years, and then God took him up unto Himself.

73. *Eleazar son of Aaron and Elijah son of Asasiah*

Wahb ibn Munabbih said: When Josephus was taken away, the rule passed to Eleazar, the son of Aaron, who was advanced in years and had no children. A certain group among the children of Israel began to say that he was childless because of some sin he must have committed, but they feared to break the line of succession from Aaron. So grieved was Eleazar when he heard this that he would not go out among the Israelites for several days.

Turning his face to heaven, he said, "My God and Master, I have reached this advanced age, and thou hast not granted me a child. Now the ignorant among the children of Israel believe it to be on account of some sin I have committed. I promised Moses I would keep the office of the high priest in Aaron's line. O Lord, give me a son that the high priesthood may be his."

God cried out, saying, "I am the answerer of prayers, and I have granted thy request."

The next morning Eleazar went to his house and found that God had restored his wife's youth, so he lay with her and she conceived. When her months were accomplished, she went into labor and was delivered of a beautiful male child, whom she called Asasiah; and he most resembled his grandfather Aaron.

When a period of Asasiah's life had passed, his father took him to the temple and stood him on the pulpit. Even then, despite his youth, he delivered such an eloquent sermon and read so beautifully from the Torah that the people were amazed at his knowledge.

"Would you be content to have him as your leader and my successor?" asked Eleazar.

"Yes," they replied.

"Then I appoint him as my successor over you, and I give you tidings of a child yet to come from my son's seed, who will be a human, yet angelic prophet. When you see him, obey him. You will know him by his large head, expansive chest, lank belly, narrow thighs, hooked nose and sharp gaze. On his chest will be a white mole. Master of the wilderness and mountains will he be and many miracles will he manifest." So saying, Eleazar departed to his house, where he found a handsome and pleasant man.

"Who are you, and who let you into my house?" Eleazar asked.

"I entered only with the permission of its owner," he said. And Eleazar knew him to be the Angel of Death.

"O Angel of Death," said Eleazar, "do what you have been commanded to do!" The angel drew near him and took his soul. His son Asasiah washed his body, wrapped him in shrouds, prayed over him and buried him.

* * *

Asasiah married a woman called Zipporah, who bore him Elijah, who resembled Moses in stature as well as in temper and irascibility. By the time he was seven years old he had committed the Torah to memory without anyone having taught him, despite his extreme youth.

One day he said, "O children of Israel, I shall show you something amazing about myself." And he gave out such a loud cry that their hearts beat swiftly with fear. The king was about to have him destroyed, but he fled to a mountain where he remained in retreat—but they set out in search of him. The mountain opened up as they approached, and he entered into its bowels. The mountain spoke to him, saying, "Elijah, in me shall be your dwelling and your refuge." And he walked with the wild beasts.

When he reached the age of forty, Gabriel descended to him. They exchanged greetings, and Gabriel said, "I am Gabriel, and I bear you tidings of prophecy. Verily God has sent you as an apostle to the idolatrous kings. Go to them and call them to obey God and worship Him!"

"How can I go out against them?" asked Elijah. "For they have recourse to weapons, while I am alone and but a single man."

"Elijah," said Gabriel, "strength lies not in horses and soldiers but is derived from God, who has given you signs that have not been given to anyone else. He has commanded the mountains to obey you and has given you the strength of seventy prophets."

Elijah went out to face the tyrant who reigned over seventy villages, in each of which there ruled a petty tyrant. They worshipped an idol called Baal, which was in the shape of a woman.

* * *

Approaching one of the villages, where there was a king called Ahab, Elijah stopped near the palace and began to recite the Torah with a beauty and grace that attracted the attention of the king and his wife Jezebel.

Jezebel looked out over the palace wall at Elijah, who was standing in prayer wearing a woolen cloak.

"Who are you, sir?" Jezebel asked. "And where do you come from?"

When he finished his prayers, he told her his name and that of his father, and his mission to them as God's apostle: that they might proclaim God's unity, worship Him, and abandon idolatry and disobedience of God's will.

"What proof have you?" asked the queen.

"Among the proofs of my prophecy is that I can call fire, and it will answer me through the might of God," said Elijah. She brought fire and placed it before him. "Answer me through God's might!" said Elijah, and the fire flew into the air and landed again before him.

It spoke and said, "There is no god but God; Elijah is the apostle of God." The woman was amazed and hastened to her husband to tell him what had happened, and they both believed in Elijah.

* * *

On Fridays it was their custom to go out in finery and set the idol Baal on its throne. Elijah watched their practices and sacrifices. Then, raising his voice, he said, "O dissolute people! Do you not fear the punishment of God? *Do ye invoke Baal, and forsake the most excellent Creator? God is your Lord, and the Lord of your forefathers"* (37.125f).

"Who are you, O slave?" they asked.

"Do you call me a slave?" said Elijah, "when I am Elijah son of Asasiah son of Eleazar son of Aaron son of Amram!"

They threw dirt in his face and stoned him from all sides.

* * *

The greatest of their kings was Ammiel, who ordered Elijah to be seized and brought before him, and called for a brass cauldron full of oil and pitch. To Elijah he said, "Recant, or I shall cast you into the boiling oil!"

"O fire," said Elijah, "sing praise, with God's permission!" And the oil ceased boiling, to the people's amazement.

"Elijah," said Ammiel, "you have given us some proof. Be patient for a day so that we may investigate this affair of yours."

Assembling the kings and wise men of the area, he asked, "What say you of Elijah?"

"We have seen this man described in the Torah," said the wise men. "He is sent to us as an apostle, and God gives him dominion over fire, beasts and the mountains. No one can hear his voice without becoming humble and obedient."

But one of the wise men said, "Sire, these men have lied in what they have told you of him. He is a sorcerer and should not frighten you. The fact is that he wants to set free those wretches who are in prison in order that he may thereby gain additional strength against you." So they only increased torment of the prisoners.

When Elijah heard this, he was grieved. As night was falling, he approached the tyrants' gates and said, "Do you sleep on soft mattresses while you torment the children of Israel in prison? Woe unto you! Come and believe in your Lord. Release the prisoners and torment not those who are without sin! Do not play games with God's prophets, and be of those who shall perish!"

When King Ammiel awoke, he sent for Elijah and said, "Be not hasty with us, for we must investigate your affair."

"I have been commanded to be lenient toward you, and I am in no haste. Investigate my case at your leisure." Then Elijah returned to King Ahab and informed him of what had happened.

"Elijah," said Ahab, "I have been taken in by you, for you promised me that whoever believed in you would be powerful, yet I see that those of your people who are with you have neither power nor honor. You have made me refrain from pleasurable things. Be gone! I have no need of your religion."

"Ahab," said his wife, "even if you revert to your old religion after having converted to Islam, I shall never renounce my Islam!" And she joined Elijah and became one of the pious.[108]

* * *

Ammiel had a wife named Muzina, who saw one night a shaft of light over Elijah's bower reaching up to the heavens. "O Elijah," she cried, "I believe in you, and I confess that there is no god but God and that you, Elijah, are His servant and apostle." She left her husband to join Elijah. The king, however, had her cast into a fiery pit. Elijah prayed to God, and the fire did not harm her. Astonished, the king said, "This is some of your magic, Elijah!"

Later the king's son grew gravely ill. Elijah went to King Ammiel to inform him of his son's death. The king, seeing his son dead, fell down in a swoon. When he came to, Elijah said to him, "Sire, if your god Baal be true, then ask him to restore his spirit and return him to life." Ammiel went before the idol and prostrated himself for his son to be restored; but it was to no avail, and he came away angered and disappointed.

Approaching Elijah, he said, "I prayed to Baal to bring back my son to life, but he did not respond. If you can restore him, then you are truly the prophet of God."

"That is simple for my Lord," said Elijah, who then prayed

to Him. God, by His omnipotence, brought the lad back to life. He lept up and said at the top of his voice, "There is no god but God alone, who has no partner; Elijah is His servant and apostle." When Ammiel saw that, he gave all his possessions as an offering, abdicated the throne, put on a woolen garment and followed Elijah in his religion.

* * *

Ammiel, his wife and son then died, and Elijah was left alone. When he complained, God said, "Death is the path of everyone. Grieve not over their deaths, for I am close to thee and responsive. Call then upon me."

Elijah dived into a flowing river, bathed and prayed two *rak'as,* saying, "My God and Master, I ask thee not to take me from this world until I have gained victory over these people. I also ask thee to give me mastery over their daily bread and to afflict them with hunger and famine if they do not repent and believe in thee and thine apostle; otherwise, destroy them!" And God granted his request.

Elijah went out among the people and said, "My people, God has put the decision as to your torment into my hands. If you do not believe in God and confirm my apostleship, I shall afflict you with sorrow and bring famine into your land."

"We will never believe in you or your Lord, do what you will!" they said. So God held back the rain from them, the earth gave no yield, the springs dried up, and the trees withered. After they had eaten all the sheep and cattle they had, they had to resort to eating dogs and cats—even the bones, carcasses, and skin. When their hunger and thirst increased, some of them went out in search of Elijah but could not find him.

God spoke to Elijah, saying, "Heaven and earth have wept for them, but you have made no response to them. Be just, Elijah, with my creation, and be compassionate toward my servants, for they disobeyed me and yet did I sustain them. I do not hold back their sustenance even though they be ungrateful."

Elijah was terrified and said, "My Lord and Master, I was angry with them only for thy sake. Thou knowest best what is good for thy servants."

"Go then to them," said God, "and call them to me. If they

believe, their respite will be in thy hands; if they disbelieve, I will still have more compassion on them than hast thou." So Elijah set out, and coming into a village, saw an old woman crying over the lack of food.

"Why are you weeping, old woman?" asked Elijah.

"I am crying from hunger," said the woman, "and, by my god Baal, it has been a long time since I tasted bread. I also have a son who follows Elijah's religion, and he is as hungry as I am."

"What is your son's name?" he asked.

"His name is Elisha son of Ahitub, of the offspring of Aaron," she answered.[109]

"If God were to fill your house with bread," said Elijah, "would you believe in Elijah's God, who has no partner?"

"Yes," said the woman. Then, to her son Elisha she said, "Would you like to eat bread?"

"And how can I obtain bread?" he cried, whereupon he convulsed in a swoon and died.

The woman came to Elijah and said, "If God will bring my son back to life, I will believe in him and in your apostleship."

Elijah arose, prayed two *rak'as* and asked God to restore her son's life. As God brought him back to life, he said, "There is no god but God; Elijah is the apostle of God!" And he added, "God has made me your successor, Elijah, and your vizier." Suddenly, as they were standing thus, a dish filled with foodstuffs and meat descended to them. The old woman believed in Elijah, and she and her son ate.

She went out to her people and told them what God had wrought. They gathered around her and strangled her to death. Elisha was grief-stricken, but Elijah said to him, "Grieve not, for God will grant you both salvation."

Elijah then went to his people, who said to him, "Are you really Elijah?"

"Yes," he said.

"Do you not see the hardship, hunger and famine we have endured for seven years?" they asked.

"Why do you not call on your idol Baal to relieve you?" said Elijah.

"We have called on him," they replied, "but to no avail.

Elijah, call now upon your Lord to deliver us from this hardship, and we will believe in you."

Elijah prayed to his Lord; and the skies poured down rain, the earth gave forth its fruit, and God brought to life all the fathers, children, and mothers who had died. Yet, when they saw it, they only became more obstinate in their disbelief.

"Thou hast delivered thy message," said God to Elijah. "Now appoint Elisha as thy successor and leave the region of thy people. Mount whatever steed thou findest, for thou art my servant and among those who are close to me."

Coming to Elisha, Elijah said, "You are my successor in command of the faithful, with God's permission." He bade him farewell, and departed on a Friday.

Suddenly Elijah came upon a steed with multicolored wings enveloped in flame. When the steed saw Elijah, it called out to him, "Approach me, O prophet of God. I have been created for you." Elijah took the reins and mounted in obedience.

Gabriel came to him and said, "Elijah, fly with the angels wherever you wish, for God has clothed you with feathers and has caused you to cease reliance upon food and drink. He has made you at once human and angelic, heavenly and earthly." The mare spread her wings and took to flight over the East, the West, all regions, directions, seas, and into the true heavens.

Then God commanded Gabriel to order Malik, the warden of Hell, out of Gehenna to cast his thunder and lightning bolts over the region of Elijah's people. Malik hurled forth into the air a spark that the myrmidons drove forward until it was directly above that region. Then such torment was rained down upon the people that they all perished.

Afterward the region was uncovered, and there they lay, scorched. Nothing remained, neither that which walked on the ground nor that which flew in the air.

* * *

Elisha established faith and right conduct among the people and remained one of their leaders until the inevitable came to him.

74. *Samuel, Saul, David and Goliath*

Kaab al-Ahbar said: When God had taken up Elisha, the children of Israel differed among themselves; and sin and corruption increased among them. So God sent them Samuel son of Nal son of Ham son of Aven son of Vaphad son of Aaron; who called them to obey God; but they denied him and did not believe. Therefore, God gave Goliath dominion over them, and Goliath ruled the shores of the Mediterranean from Egypt to Palestine. He raided them, killed a great number of them and took away the Ark from them.

Now the children of Israel used to derive victory and sustenance through the blessing of the Ark, so they were greatly afflicted by its loss. "The Ark would be taken from us only because of some great sin," they said amongst themselves. "Let us assemble before Samuel and believe in the message he has been preaching to us. Perhaps then God will restore the Ark to us and send us a king under whom we may fight our enemy Goliath." Therefore they came to Samuel and believed in him, as He hath said: *Hast thou not considered the assembly of the children of Israel, after the time of Moses; when they said unto their prophet Samuel, "Set a king over us, that we may fight for the religion of God"* (2.246).

Samuel humbled himself before God in order that a king might be appointed from among them. God spoke to him, saying, "I have answered thy prayer and have established the kingship in a man. The sign shall be that when he entereth into thy house thou shalt see the oil boiling. Anoint his head with the oil, and this shall be the sign of his kingship over the children of Israel."

Among the Israelites was a man who sowed the earth and tanned hides, and his name was Saul son of Bashir son of Genub son of Benjamin son of Jacob. One day he went out in search of a strayed animal. When he came to Samuel's house, he entered and asked if Samuel had any knowledge of the beast. Samuel told him that the animal was at a certain house and that he should go and take it back. Just then Samuel saw the oil boiling. Taking a bit of the oil, he annointed Saul's head and said,

"God has made you king over the children of Israel." Then, to the children of Israel, he said, *"Verily God hath set Saul, king over you"* (2.247).

They answered, "How shall he reign over us, seeing we are more worthy of the kingdom than he, neither is he possessed of great riches."

But Samuel said to them, *"Verily, God hath chosen him before you, and hath caused him to increase in knowledge and stature, for God giveth his kingdom unto whom he pleaseth."*

"O prophet of God," they said, "show us a sign in him that we may not doubt that God has made him king."

And their prophet said unto them, "Verily the sign of his kingdom shall be, that the ark shall come unto you: therein shall be tranquillity from your Lord" (2.248). And they were content.

* * *

When the Ark had been seized, Goliath had ordered it placed in a village in Palestine called Jordan; and there it was put in a synagogue. Later it was buried beside an orchard, where the people used to perform certain necessary functions. For this, God struck them with hemorrhoids.

When they realized that their affliction was due to the Ark, they removed it and put it back inside the synagogue as it had been. Then one of the pharaohs raided them and killed a large number of them. Upon entering the synagogue, he found the Ark and took it away. He tried to open it but could not, so he carried it from village to village and finally loaded it on a calf and sent it to the land of the children of Israel. When the calf reached the middle of the plain, the angels, with God's permission, bore it to the land of the Israelites; and when the children of Israel saw the Ark on the calf, they confirmed Saul as their king and asked him to raid Goliath.

He rode out with seventy thousand Israelites, who said, "O king, water is so scarce along the way, ask God to cause a river to flow for us."

"I shall do it if God wills," Saul answered.

* * *

They marched into the desert until their water supply was exhausted, whereupon they became extremely thirsty. Saul called upon his Lord to cause a river to flow, and God spoke to him, saying, *"Verily God will prove you by the river"* (that is, the river Jordan). And God caused a river to flow before their very eyes, as He hath said: *For he who drinketh thereof shall not be on my side (but he who shall not taste thereof, he shall be on my side), except he who drinketh a draught out of his hand* (2.249). When the river appeared before them, however, they persisted in drinking from it and in filling their waterskins, except for three hundred and thirteen men who did not exceed the handful permitted, using that amount for both themselves and their animals.

To those who had disobeyed his order, Saul said, "Go back, for I have no need of you!" They departed, and Saul was left with three hundred and thirteen men.

* * *

It is related from the Prophet that on the day of the Battle of Badr he said to his companions: "Today you are the same number as the companions of Saul."

* * *

Saul and his men crossed the river, and they said, *"We have no strength to-day, against Goliath and his forces"* (2.249) (Goliath had three hundred thousand men).

God said, *"How often hath a small army discomfited a great one, by the will of God!"*

With Saul that day were seven of David's brothers; but, as he was the youngest, David had been left behind with his father at home. He was comely of appearance, of light complexion, with loose lank hair and long eyelashes. On that day his father said to him, "David, news of your brothers is slow in coming. Take them some food, and tell me how they and the army are faring."

David set out carrying a bag containing the food for his brothers, and around his waist was fastened his sling. As he was walking, a stone cried out to him saying, "David, take me! I am a stone that belonged to your father Abraham." David picked up the stone and put it in his bag.

A little further on, another stone cried out, "David, take me!

I am a stone of your father Isaac." He took this one too and put it in his bag.

When he had gone a little further, yet another stone cried out, "David, take me! I am a stone that belonged to your father Jacob." This one too he took and put in his bag. He walked on until he reached Saul's camp, where he went to his brothers and gave them the food. While he was there, he began to hear something of the might of Goliath and the great strength of his army.

The next day Saul came among his soldiers and said, "My people, if anyone can stand up to Goliath for me, I will give him my daughter in marriage. I will also make him my partner in ruling the kingdom and my successor after me." But no one answered.

David said to his brothers, "Did not you hear what Saul said?"

"Yes," they said, "we heard."

"Then why do you not volunteer?" he asked.

"No," they said, "we are not strong enough to contend with Goliath."

"Then I shall kill him with my sling!" said David. They all scoffed at him, for he was the youngest and weakest of them all. Yet he repeated what he had said and added, "Inform the king!" So they went before Saul and told him.

"Do you know that he has such strength?" Saul asked.

"Yes," they said, "he does. He takes on the wolves that attack his sheep and breaks them in two. When he casts a stone with his sling, he invariably hits his mark." And so Saul ordered David to be brought before him.

When he stood there, Saul questioned him concerning his talk about Goliath. David answered, "I shall kill him with God's permission. And the conditions are to be as you said."

"So be it," said Saul; and David was paraded around the camp, mounted on Saul's own horse.

Then Goliath appeared with a great army, himself mounted on an elephant, and adorned with every sort of caparison and wearing five hundred rotls of armor (according to what is mentioned in the book). Goliath was eighteen spans tall—while David was only ten—and so he could be seen towering over the ranks of his army.

"Who will come forth to meet me?" cried Goliath. David came out with his slingshot. When Goliath saw him, he became apprehensive and said, "Who are you, boy? You are little and puny—no helmet and no armor. Have you come to do battle with me with your slingshot?"

"I am David, the son of Jesse," he replied. "I have come forth to fight you."

Then Goliath said, "You may be able to strike wolves and dogs with your slingshot . . ."

"And I can strike you too," said David, "for you have disobeyed God and His apostle." Goliath grew angry at these words.

David put his hand into his bag and took the three stones, and hurled them. The first went to the right flank of the army and it was routed; the second fell among the left flank, and they too were routed; the third flew towards Goliath and struck the nosepiece of his helmet, and he fell dead to the ground. His companions too were completely routed.

When the news reached the prophet Samuel, he was overjoyed and praised God. Saul, however, became envious of the might given to David and determined to betray him.

David came to him, saying, "Sire, you made a pact with me to give me your daughter in marriage and to make me a partner in the kingdom and your successor, so do what you promised!"

Saul answered, "David, it is as you say; but my daughter must have a dowry, and you do not have enough money for a proper dowry. However, if you want to marry her, then go to the giants. If you kill them, you will not have to pay a bride-price for my daughter." (That was a ruse on Saul's part to have David killed.)

"How many do you want me to kill?" asked David.

"Two hundred," said Saul.

"Then you shall have them!" David said.

David mounted his horse and headed for the land of the giants, whom he set about killing. When he had killed more than two hundred, he cried out, "I am David the Goliath-killer!" And they were completely routed. He took everything they had brought with them as booty and returned to Saul with the spoils. Therefore Saul married him to his daughter and gave him a third of his kingdom.

From that time on, Saul heard so much talk of David and of how excellent and mighty he was that he grew envious of him.

Saul used to carry a stick to lean on, a spear-point at one end and an iron claw at the other. One day he came into his daughter's apartment and threw the stick at David, who dodged clear of it so that it stuck into the wall.

"Do you want to kill me?" asked David.

"No," answered Saul, "but I wanted to test how you would react if someone tried to stab you."

David walked over to the stick, pulled it from the wall and said to Saul, "Now prove to me as I have proven to you!" Saul grew pale with fright and made David swear by his relation as son-in-law that he would not do it, but David said, "Evil should be recompensed with like evil, as is written in the Torah."

Saul replied, "Do you not know what He has said? *If thou stretchest forth thy hand against me, to slay me, I will not stretch forth my hand against thee, to slay thee*" (5.28). And David threw the spear from his hand.

The news spread among the children of Israel that Saul's plan had been foiled, and still he did not know how to get rid of David. Later, he approached his daughter and said, "You know, daughter, that David is not of your station. I want you to help me kill him; later you can repent before God."

"You speak of helping you to kill him and then repenting," she answered. "What makes you think that God will forgive us? I am astonished at you, father, that the murder of a Muslim should lie so easily upon your conscience, especially when you know that he has helped you against your enemies. Rid your heart of the desire to kill him! Furthermore, David is so strong that neither you nor I could possibly overpower him, for he can beard a lion and pull out its teeth with his bare hands, and can seize a man with the strength of a wolf and break him in half."

Saul grew angry and said, "I hear the words of a woman infatuated with her husband. I had resolved to break off the relationship between myself and him, but now I shall have to kill either him or you. Chose what you will!" And he left her.

When David came and saw her upset, he asked what had happened; and she told him the truth of all that Saul had said.

"Make him think he can take me by surprise," said David.

"There is no might or power save with God!" So she went to her father.

David took a piece of hide, got into bed and put the hide on his belly between himself and the blanket. Saul came in during the night and asked his daughter where David was. Following the motion of her head, he struck David across the belly with a sword and thought he had cut him in two. The sword, however, only grazed the hide. David immediately lept from beneath the blanket and fell on Saul, threw him down and took the sword from his hand. As he was about to kill him, Saul said, "You are nobler than that, David. You have frightened me enough with what you have done." David let him go, and Saul returned to his own house in a state of fright. And this news too spread among the children of Israel.

After this event, David came to his wife and said, "I have seen much hatred and envy from your father, and I know that he is determined to kill me. Therefore, I am going away from Jerusalem to dwell in the mountain."

When he had gone from his house, as he said he would, the news reached the best people, who followed him; and along with them went a great number of the children of Israel. To these David said, "You all know that Saul promised a third of his kingdom to me the day I killed Goliath. He also promised me the contents of his treasuries, which he still owes me." David took therefore a third of what was in Saul's treasury and distributed it among his companions, ordering them to equip themselves with provisions. They bought supplies, joined David, and went up to one of the mountain surrounding Jerusalem in open rebellion against Saul, who assembled his clients, his relatives and their children to set out in search of David to wage war with him. When he learned what was missing from his storehouses and treasury and that David had had them opened, he asked his companions, "Why did you let him do it?"

"Inasmuch as he was your partner in the kingdom," they said, "it was right for us to do so." But Saul led them out of the treasury and ordered them to be executed. Then he set out to search for David, who had fortified himself along with his companions on one of the mountains.

David went down by himself, sword in hand, and found Saul

asleep in a rocky place, his seal-ring on his hand and his armor lying by his side. David took the ring from his finger and bore away the armor. Returning to his people, he told them what he had done. They thought he had killed Saul, but David said, "I should be ashamed before my Lord were I to kill Saul, who is a Muslim, in this world."

When Saul awoke and found his ring and armor missing, he thought that one of his soldiers had taken them and was about to put a group of men to death, when David cried out from the top of the mountain, saying, "Saul, it was I who carried off your ring and armor. Do not accuse any of your own soldiers!" And he held up the pieces of armor one after the other for Saul to see.

Saul was ashamed of himself before his companions and sent a message to David, saying, "I acted tyrannically toward you, and you were all the while closer to the truth than I was. Had you wanted to kill me when you found me asleep, you could have; yet you stayed your sword. Now I ask your pardon for the evil that I have done you. As God is my witness, I shall never bear you evil again. Come to me, safe of person and easy of mind." David went down, and Saul clasped him to his breast and asked his pardon.

The two remained where they were for three days and then returned to their homes to find that Samuel the prophet had died, and they wept long over him.

Then the children of Israel left Saul and joined David. Now during this time Saul's enemies had surrounded him; as he could find no course of action against them, he went to an Israelite woman known for having her prayers answered, and asked her to pray God to bring Samuel to life. The woman, however, said, "Saul, I have no such station before my Lord as to bring the dead to life with my prayer, but I will pray God that you may see Samuel in a dream. Go to his grave and worship the Lord all night long." Saul did as she had said; and, when the dawn appeared, sleep came over him.

In his dream he saw Samuel saying to him, "What is your purpose in consulting me, Saul?" And Saul told him of the dispersal of the children of Israel from him and the appearance of his enemies.

"Indicate to me, O prophet of God," said Saul, "what you think I should do."

"Woe unto you, Saul!" answered Samuel, 'for God had guided you aright and had given you kingdom and power. Why have you disobeyed Him to the point that you rely upon yourself? He made your enemies appear when I was alive, and I always told you what was inspired to me by God, yet you never acted upon it. Now, after my death, you come to me and want to turn my words to your own advantage." Then Samuel disappeared from his sight, and Saul awoke, frightened.

Approaching David, he said, "David, help the children of Israel against their enemies." In response, David gathered his people to march out against the enemy, who numbered eighty thousand. They fought hard from sunrise to sunset and killed a great number of them. After that Saul became humble and submissive to David, into whose hands the kingdom passed.

75. *David's Mission*

Ibn Abbas said: Then the children of Israel became divided and occupied themselves with amusements of the devil: there were those who played lutes and those who played drums, pipes, castanets and the like—until God sent David as a prophet and revealed sixty lines of the Psalms to him. He also gave him such a voice he could recite correctly and sedately in more than seventy melodies, the likes of which no one had ever heard for sonority and volume. Through his pipes he could cause the thunder to speak and could reproduce the song of birds and the dulcet tones of wild beasts; and from his pipes came every pleasant sound in the world. The children of Israel left their diversion and amusements and came to David's Tower to hear his music.

When he sang praise, so also did the mountains, the birds and the beasts along with him, as God hath said: *We compelled the mountains to celebrate our praise with him, in the evening and at sunrise, and also the birds, which gathered themselves together unto him* (38.19f).

David was so enamoured of women that he married ninety-nine wives. He divided his time into three: a day for worship, a day for his wives, and a day for sitting in judgment. On the day for worship the ascetics would come down from the mountains and caves, and the birds and beasts would come from the air and the valleys and stand in rows around his Tower, which was like a lofty mountain. He had had it made of carved stone, raised twenty cubits from the ground; the base was sixteen cubits high and made of colored glass. It had twelve doors, one for each of the tribes; and no one could enter by other than his own tribe's door. At each door was stationed a priest to read the Torah, the Psalms and other holy writ. Atop the Tower was a small temple with four doors, facing each of the four winds.

On his day of worship, David ascended to this small temple, prayed from the leaves of the Psalms and repeated his melodies; but he would not play anything on his pipes unless the birds and beasts came to him when he repeated his melodies.

On the day set aside for his wives, none of the children of Israel ever saw him.

On the day he sat in judgment, they would gather before him to be instructed in legal decisions and cases, as God hath said: *And we gave him wisdom and eloquence of speech* (38.21). Even the angels sought God's permission to visit David, and they descended and surrounded his Tower. As they repeated his hymns of praise, the birds flapped their wings, the mountains sang praise along with him, and the beasts glorified the Lord.

David was loved by the children of Israel as a mother by her child, for no one saw him who was not made to feel intimate with him. Some even said, "David is better in God's sight than Abraham, Ishmael, Isaac, Jacob, Joseph, the patriarchs, Moses, Aaron, Elijah or Elisha."

When David heard this, he assembled them and said, "Children of Israel, it has reached me that you have set me over the past prophets. Nay! God took Abraham as His friend, revealed to him the Book of Seth, singled him out as a devout Muslim, gave him victory over Nimrod and made the fire cool and safe for him. As for Ishmael, God named him Sadiq al-Wa'd; and from his seed shall come the best of the universe, Muhammad.[110] Isaac was purified by God and was tried with slaughter, from which He ransomed him with a great sacrificial lamb from Paradise, the day of which he made a feast for the faithful and especially for his son Jacob.

"Jacob was purified by God and was named Israel; his eyesight and his son Joseph were restored to him. As for Joseph, God called him Siddiq and gave him dominion over the land of Egypt.

"God conversed with Moses and drew him close and caused him to hear the rush of the Pen; to him He gave the tablets with the knowledge of the first and last things. As for Aaron, God made him his brother's vizier and placed the priesthood in his line. Elijah was sent to the tyrants of the world, against whom he struggled long, after which He took him to Himself, cloaked him in feathers and robed him in light, relieved him of the necessity for food and drink, and made him eternal that he might fly with the angels over all the regions of the earth until the Last Day.

"As for Elisha, he was Elijah's successor to the children of Israel and guided them as Elijah had done for a number of years.

"How then can you claim that I am better than these?"

"We would like you to tell us how God has exalted you," said the children of Israel.

"God singled me out as a prophet from among my brothers; He used me as an instrument to kill Goliath and the giants with my bare hands; He revealed the Psalms to me as a book of poetry." Then something came over David; and, entering into his Tower, he said, "Lord, thou hast favored Abraham with friendship and made the fire cool and safe for him; thou hast favored Ishmael with fidelity to the promise, Isaac with ransom, Jacob with the tribes and with a name from thine own self Joseph has thou favored over his brothers; Moses hast thou made thy prophet and confidant; Aaron hast thou favored with the priesthood forever in his line; to Elijah hast thou given victory over his people, then thou didst clothe him in feathers and enable him to fly eternally throughout the world; after him thou madest Elisha his successor.

"I ask thee, God, to single me out with a measure of ennoblement as thou hast ennobled them."

"David," replied God, "I have favored thee with an excellent voice, the likes of which no one except thy father Adam has had. I have commanded the mountains to walk with thee and to reply to thee in thy melodies. I have softened iron for thee and have taught thee to make chain-mail.[111] I have commanded the birds to assemble above thy head and to sing hymns of praise along with thee; I have commanded sand and stone to glorify with thee. I have made thee judge over all the earth.

"David, I tried Abraham with fire, and he was patient; I tried his son with slaughter and resignation to his fate, and I ransomed him with the ram; I tried Jacob with grief over Joseph, and he was patient; I tried Joseph with acts of devotion, and he was patient; I tried Moses, despite his youth, with the ark, and he was patient; I tried Job mightily, and he was patient and even gave thanks; I tried Elijah and Elisha with the pharaohs, and they were patient. But thou, O David, thou hast been exempt from all trial, so do not ask me to afflict thee!"

David fell down prostrate, then raised his face and said, "Lord, thou didst call me David because thou desirest all creatures to love me, but I ask thee to make me like the other prophets. Try me as thou hast tried them that thou mayest remember me as thou rememberest them."

Then God said, "David, prepare thyself for temptation and bear with it patiently!"

76. *The Bird of Temptation*

Wahb ibn Munabbih said: God gave David respite for a period of his life until he had forgotten.

One sabbath day, while he was in his Tower worshipping his Lord and reading the Psalms behind closed doors, suddenly there appeared a bird of such beauty, colors and marvelous shape as had never before been seen. David left his reading of the Psalms and said, "If this bird were to appear to the people of these times, they would forego food and drink and would devote themselves to looking at it."

* * *

Ibn Abbas was asked if the Devil had any part in this. "No," he answered, "because the prophets are too noble in God's sight for Iblis to be able to tempt them. Rather it was a temptation for David because he had so cursed transgressors at every opportunity. Whenever he came across a verse in the Psalms in which transgressors were mentioned, he would say, 'Lord, do not forgive the transgressors!' "

* * *

David gazed upon the beauty of this bird and saw the ineffable. He said to himself, "This is surely one of the birds of Paradise, attracted to my voice." He stretched out his hand to seize it, but it flew away. He followed it until it had flown to a tree next to a pool behind his Tower, where it disappeared from sight. While he was searching for it, he saw the bird perched on a tree beside a pool where the Israelite women used to bathe. As David came out, he heard the women splashing water about; and, seeing a woman bathing in the pool, he averted his gaze. But she was one of the most beautiful of women and her name was Bath-Sheba. Wife of Uriah son of Hannan, and daughter of Jeshua, she had married that very year but had not yet conceived. Her husband was away with the army under David's nephew Nabal son of Zeruiah, and he was killed there. (It was said that David sent a message to his nephew Nabal to advance Uriah to the front lines, which he did. When he was killed, David married his wife, Bath-Sheba.)

God then commanded Gabriel and Michael to descend to the earth in beautiful shapes, to inform David of his transgression. As David was saying, "Lord, forgive not the trespassers, and defend the oppressed against the oppressors," the two angels descended through the roof of the Tower in human form—in the guise of two litigants, one strong and the other weak—and stood before him. David was so startled by them that he dropped the book of Psalms and grew pale with fright.

"Fear not, O you who are so harsh on transgressors," they said, "and hear what we have to say, as we have come to you from a far-distant place," as He hath said: *Hath the story of the two adversaries come to thy knowledge; when they ascended over the wall into the upper apartment, when they went in unto David, and he was afraid of them?* (38.22f) David returned to his judgment-seat and said, "Tell me what has happened to you."[112]

"O prophet of God," began Gabriel, *"this my brother had ninety and nine sheep,* all white and fat and having given birth several times; *and I had only one ewe: and he said, 'Give her me to keep'; and he prevailed against me in the discourse* (38.24). I complained of this to my Lord, who sent me to you because you are His viceroy on earth."

David grew angry and said, "*Verily he hath wronged thee in demanding thine ewe as an addition to his own sheep: and many of them who are concerned together in business wrong one another,* as your brother has wronged you" (38.25).

"O prophet of God," said Michael, "you have not given a just decision, for he may do wrong who is in no partnership."

David grew furious at these words and, taking a rod in his hand, said, "I shall lash you with this rod!"

But the rod cried out from David's hand, saying, "If this be your sentence upon a transgressor, then you are a transgressor, O David!"

Michael smiled and said, "You deserve the rod more than I do, O David, for you decide for the plaintiff before you hear the defendant." So saying, the two of them lept up, and crashing through the roof, departed as they had entered. *And David perceived that we had tried him by this parable, and he asked pardon of his Lord: and he fell down and bowed himself, and repented* (38.25). He remained prostrate, agitated and humiliated for forty days, until the flesh on his face sagged, and greenery grew from his tears. The angels set up a clamor and said, "Our God, this thy prophet and thy viceroy on earth has caused our eyes to weep: overlook his transgresssion and pardon his backsliding as thou hast pardoned his father Adam."

"Keep silent!" said God. "I am the most merciful of the merciful; my gate is open to those who worship me and I accept the repentance of the penitent."

77. *Absalom, David's Son*

The foolish among the children of Israel regarded David as having committed an unlawful act. "David shall never escape his transgression," they said; and they called for him to be deposed. Approaching his eldest son, Absalom—a more handsome person was not to be found—they said, "Absalom, your father has grown too old and senile to lead the children of Israel: he has fallen into evil ways and is preoccupied with weeping over his transgression. As you are the eldest of his sons, the prevalent opinion is that you should call the people to yourself. If your father David is displeased by this, then tell him that you have acted lest any of his enemies have designs on the kingdom." Thus they deposed David and made preparations for crowning his son, Absalom.

When the news reached David and he realized that it was in propitiation for his transgression, he fled from his dwelling, taking with him two men: Jesse, who had been his vizier, and Nabal son of Zeruiah, the general of his armies—and among the children of Israel there was none more courageous than him, nor of more worthy opinion. So David departed with these two to one of the mountains of Jerusalem, there to remain until God should relieve him of his burden. On the way, he chanced upon one of the foolish Israelites, who cursed him and said, "Praise be to God, who has brought you down, humbled you, and taken your kingdom away from you." Nabal drew his sword and was about to overwhelm the man, when David intervened and said, "He has not cursed me, rather it is a result of my transgression." They hastened to the mountain, in fear of being killed.

Absalom sent to one of the foolish Israelites named Tuphel,

whom David had rejected from his army because of a transgression he had committed; but Absalom summoned him, drew him aside and said, "I have known you long through my father. What do you think I should do?"

"You will not be safe as king while your father is alive," said Tuphel. "You must kill him, but no one must know what you are about. Go now and plunder his kingdom while God is displeased with him." So Absalom determined to wage war against his father David; when the news reached David, he came to his vizier Jesse and said, "My son has decided to fight me. Go to him and dissuade him from doing such a thing."

The vizier went to Absalom and said, "I have come to you from your father David that you might not go against him, for God will surely forgive him. Do not be deceived by what the foolish say."

"Will He restore him?" Absalom asked.

"Have you ever heard of a prophet who had transgressed grievously whose repentance God did not accept?" asked Jesse. "Or a son who killed his father and was not then forsaken? What will you say to your Lord on the Day of Judgment, when he who has seduced you to evil will be of no avail? I have also heard that there are those who have advised you to marry your father's wives. If you do that, then not even repentance will be available to you!"

"Then I shall sit here," said Absalom, "until my father comes to me. If he forgives me, then it will be a blessing from God. If he fights me, I shall strive to preserve my life."

Thus the vizier returned to David and informed him that his son would again do him obeisance. David's skin had, in the meantime, dried up on his bones from grief, hunger, thirst and weeping. While prostrate in prayer he would say, "My God, thou knowest that I have been cowardly out of fear of thee. Forgive me my transgression, for if thou dost not pardon me, I shall be among the lost."

"David," said God, "go to Uriah's tomb and ask him to absolve thee. If thou do this, then I will forgive thee." David rejoiced at the prospect of forgiveness and went to Uriah's tomb, where he prayed two *rak'as* and cried out, "O brother Uriah, speak to me, with God's permission."

A voice answered him from the grave, saying, "Who is that who has disturbed me?"

"It is I, David."

"What do you wish, O prophet of God?" asked the voice.

"I want you to absolve me of my debt to you," David said.

"Then you are absolved."

David returned to the mountain and said, "My God, thou knowest what he said."

But God said, "Go to him once more and tell him that thou didst send him to battle in order that he be killed prematurely, and that thou then didst marry his wife."

David returned to Uriah, weeping, and told him all this. "God is the best of all judges," said Uriah. And David returned to the mountain, incessantly weeping and humbling himself before God.

* * *

Wahb said: Uriah went to Paradise. While he was walking in the different levels of Paradise, he chanced upon a mansion which seemed to him more beautiful than a luminescent pearl, such that the inside could be seen from the outside and in which was a houri so beautiful that one glimpse of her would infatuate the world.

"Lord," he said, "for whom is this mansion?"

"It is for him who relinquished in the world what by right was his, and who has pardoned his brother Muslim."

Then Uriah said, "O Lord, bear thou witness that I forgive David and absolve him of his debt to me."

Thereupon God pardoned and forgave David, restored his comeliness and his beautiful voice, and restored him to the throne as he had been.

When the news reached Tuphel, he feared for his life; he strung a rope around his neck and hanged himself until he was dead.

* * *

Then God spoke to David, saying, "In the hollow of the Tower hang a chain of iron between yourself and the people, and fasten thereto a bell: for some people give false testimony, and the chain will decide between the true and the false. Order litigants to pull the chain; it will descend for the truthful to take hold of it. It will draw back, however, from the false, who will not be able to pull it." Thus, whenever two opposing parties came and pulled the chain to ring the bell, David would hear it and go out to them from an opening in the Tower to sit in judgment.

One day two men came to him quarreling, and one of them said, "O prophet of God, I entrusted to this friend some jewels—pearls and rubies—and then he denied me what was mine and proved treacherous towards me."

"What say you?" David asked the other.

"It is true that he entrusted me with some jewels," he began, "but I returned them to him."

"Take the chain!" David said to the plaintiff. He reached, and was able to take it. (His opponent had stashed the jewels in the hollow of his staff, on which he was leaning at the time.) However, when David told the defendant to take the chain as his friend had done, he gave the stick to his friend and asked him to hold it while he took the chain. The plaintiff took the staff with his jewels inside. When the defendant stretched his hand toward the chain, it came so close to his grasp that he could almost touch it; but, as he was about to take hold of it, it went up out of his reach.

"Your case is truly strange," said David. "Since the chain has hung here, I have not seen it do such a thing as it has today. I have examined your case, and I see from the chain that one of you has told the truth and the other has lied; one of you gave a trust and the other proved treacherous; one of you is innocent in his oath and the other has committed a crime, yet the chain acts in such a way!" Then David said to the plaintiff, "Go home and search your belongings. Perhaps this man has sent the trust and left it in your house."

He went home and searched his belongings and, having found nothing, returned to David. (All the while the staff in which the jewels were hidden was propped beside the Tower, its owner not having picked it up.)

Then David asked the owner of the jewels, "Do you have anything that belongs to this man in which he might have hidden your belongings in order to be innocent when he took the test?"

"I have nothing of his," he began, ". . . except that he handed me his staff when he was about to take the chain."

"Where is the staff?" asked David.

"It is propped up beside the Tower," he said.

"Tell me the truth," David said to the owner of the staff. "Is your staff hollow or solid?" The man answered that he did not know, so David ordered the staff be split open. When the jewels poured out, he gave them to their rightful owner and caused the traitor's name and description to be known among all the tribes so that henceforth he was not to be believed, nor was evidence given by him to be accepted.

It is said that on that very day the chain went up and never again returned.

78. *The Birth of Solomon*

Wahb ibn Munabbih said: When David had been confirmed king and prophet, he raised his eyes to heaven and said, "My God and Master, thou hast given me of thy kingdom, and thou hast blessed me with thy grace. I now ask thee to give me a pious son to inherit these and to succeed me."

"O David," said God in response, "I will answer thy prayer and fulfill thy desire."

David heard the good news and rejoiced, for at that time his children were Absalom son of Saul's daughter, Amnon, Ibhar, Adonijah, Shepatiah, Ithream, Elishua, Shobab, Nathan and Daniel. Then he rose and bathed, went to his wife Bath-Sheba, the daughter of Jeshua, and lay with her, whereby she conceived Solomon. And a voice cried out to Iblis, saying, "O Iblis, on this night has a child been conceived at whose hands will be your sorrow, and your children will be his slaves!"

Iblis grew wrathful, and gathered together the evil spirits and demons from the East and the West, whom he told what he had heard. "Keep you here in this place until I come to you with news!". he told them.

Approaching David, he saw the angels' banners hung round David's Tower and heard a mysterious voice say, "Bath-Sheba has conceived Solomon, who will reign over the kings of mankind."

"Who is this Solomon?" Iblis asked the angels.

"David's son," they answered, "at whose hands will be your destruction and that of your seed."

Iblis returned to his troops, melting from grief as lead melts in fire.

* * *

When her days were accomplished, Bath-Sheba gave birth to Solomon and saw that he was of fair complexion, with a round face, well-delineated eyebrows, and black eyes; from his countenance radiated a dazzling light. The demons lost their senses and became as dead, not to wake again for seventy days. Iblis sank into the Great Sea, where he remained for seventy days. Then he came to the shore and saw the earth laughing and the beasts bowing down in David's direction.

David hastened to his house and saw the angels arranged in ranks, saying, "O David, since our Lord has created us, we have come down to the earth only for the birth of Abraham and for this the birth of your son Solomon." David fell down prostrate, rendered thanks to his Lord and made a great sacrifice.

* * *

Kaab said: The earth laughed on the day Adam first walked upon it and it laughed until Cain killed his brother Abel, from which time it wept until Abraham was born. It laughed until he was cast into the fire, and then it wept until Solomon was born.

* * *

David called Nabal son of Zeruiah and said, "My son Absalom has withdrawn from me out of fear for his life, but I am not one who would kill his own son. Therefore, I want you to go to him along with a company of your friends, and if you can persuade him, bring him to me honorably. But woe unto you if you bring him ignobly or kill him, for if you slay him I will slay you in his stead."

Nabal went out in search of Absalom and found him in a

certain place in the land of Syria, where many of the foolish Israelites had joined him and had been incorporated into his army. There they fought a pitched battle, and Absalom was routed. As he was fleeing on his horse, he passed under a tree and a branch caught him by the head and pulled him off his horse, leaving him hanging by the branch. Nabal caught up with him and stabbed him in the stomach, killing him, and left him hanging at the top of the tree. When he returned to David and told him what had happened, David grew wrathful and said, "I sent you to bring him here, and you killed him. Now I will kill you without delay," and he lunged at Nabal and killed him.

* * *

When Solomon reached three years of age, David ordered him to break his fast, and called him to read the writings of the children of Israel. Solomon would memorize instantly whatever David read to him from the Psalms or the Torah. Thus he committed to memory the whole of the Torah in less than a year. When he was no more than four years old, he prayed one hundred *rak'as* every day along with a verse from the Psalms and one from the Torah. When he walked, he would hear voices from all sides saying, "Blessed be thou, O son of David, for thou has been given a kingdom in stewardship that your father Adam was not given." David sought his counsel in all matters and ruled according to what he said.

* * *

It is said that one day his mother saw an ant on his clothing and said to him, "Kill it!"

Solomon, however, picked it off his clothing and said to his mother, "Every animal will have a tongue on the Day of Resurrection. I would not like this ant to say, 'Solomon, the son of David, killed me.' "

* * *

Kaab said: One day when Solomon was with his father, a dove appeared, perched before Solomon and said, "O son of David, I am one of the doves of this house, but I have not been given any offspring to hatch." So Solomon stretched out his hand to her womb and said, "Go, and may God cause seventy chicks to issue from your womb. May your offspring increase in number until the Day of Resurrection."

It was a turtle dove, and all the turtle doves that have been and will be born until the Day of Resurrection are from the issue of that one dove.

* * *

Kaab said: One day when David was standing by the gate of his house with Solomon, a cow came to them, saying, "O David, I belong to one of the tribes of Israel, and they so overloaded me with work that I could not bear it. I calved twenty times, and they slaughtered all my young. Now that I have grown old, they are going to slaughter me."

"You were created to be slaughtered," said David.

Solomon took her home, and she guided him along the way to the door of her owner, who, when he opened the door for them, said "What do you desire, O son of David?"

"I desire you to sell me this cow," said Solomon, "and not to slaughter her."

"Who told you we intended to slaughter her?" he asked.

"She told me herself," answered Solomon.

"We will give her to you," they said, "for we are all about to die anyway."

"How do you know that?" asked Solomon.

"Yesterday there came a voice, crying, 'When you see a boy of a certain description at your door, then your terms will have expired,' and you are without doubt that selfsame boy."

And the very next day Solomon was informed of the destruction of that tribe. The cow was turned loose to graze until she died.

* * *

One day Solomon passed by one field that was ready for harvesting and another field in which there was not a single grain or stalk, and in between the two was only a wall.

Solomon was amazed at this situation and asked the first field about it. The field spoke, saying, "My owners took God's portion from me at harvest time; therefore, I am as you see me."

Then he questioned the other field and heard it say, "When

my owners harvested me they did not reap God's portion, and I am therefore as you see me."

* * *

One day as Solomon was with his father, two men came before them. One of them said, "O prophet of God, I purchased from this man a plot of land of such-and-such dimensions, and I found some money in one corner of it. I told him about it, but he refuses to accept the money and says that it does not belong to him."

"What say you?" David asked the second man.

"O prophet of God," he said, "I bought that land from a tribe that has since perished. It is not my money."

"Then divide the money between yourselves," said David.

"But we have no need of it," they said. And David did not know what to say.

"My father," said Solomon, "if you will permit me, I will speak."

"Speak, my son," said David.

To the first man he said, "Have you a son?"

"Yes, I do," he answered. "And he has reached maturity."

"And have you a daughter?" he asked the other, who said that he did.

"Then go and marry your daughter to this man's son and give them the money to have in common," said Solomon.

The two men went away and did as he had said.

* * *

Wahb ibn Munabbih said: While Solomon was with his father, who was seated in judgment, a tribe came to David and said, "O prophet of God, we plowed a field, sowed and watered it until the harvest time had come. Then these people sent their sheep into our field in the middle of the night, and they ate all that was there, leaving nothing for us."

"What say you?" David asked the owners of the sheep.

"They speak the truth," they answered, "except that we know not how the sheep came to graze there."

To the tillers David said, "What was the worth of the crop?" And they named a price.

"And how much are the sheep worth?" he asked the shepherds, and they stipulated their worth. Then, to the owners of the sheep, he said, "Either give your sheep for these people's crop, or give them of your money in recompense."

"O prophet of God," said Solomon, "if you give me permission, I will speak."

"Speak out, my son," said David, "with your opinion."

"Tell the owners of the sheep to give their sheep to the owners of the field to profit from the wool and milk. Tell also the owners of the field to give their land to the others to tend until the crop is harvested, when they will turn over the field along with its crop and take back their sheep." And both parties were satisfied with this solution, as God hath said: *And on all of them we bestowed wisdom, and knowledge* (21.79).

* * *

God said to David, "Wisdom is in ninety parts, seventy of which are in Solomon and the other twenty in all the rest of the people."

* * *

Solomon divided his days: an hour for his mother and an hour for his father, an hour for worshipping God and an hour for reading the Psalms, an hour for the ancient traditions of the children of Israel, and the rest of the day for meditation upon death, the stricture of the grave, eschatology, the final reckoning, and God's judgment.

With the passage of time, Solomon increased in humility and asceticism. One day during the week he would go out to the mountains and say, "Praise be to Him who knows every iota of the mountains," and the mountains would reply, "Praise be to Him, who hath adorned the heavens and the earth with His radiance."

* * *

The chiefs of the Israelites saw Solomon sitting with his father and were jealous of him. Therefore, God told David to raise Solomon up as a preacher that they might hear the wisdom that was bestowed upon him and know thereby his excellence over them.

David assembled the ascetics, the hermits and monks from the wilderness and clothed Solomon—who was at that time twelve years old—in the garb of the prophets, white wool, and permitted him to mount the pulpit. He praised God and mentioned His greatness and power, after which he told a parable and recited the Book of Adam as well as the Books of Seth, Enoch, Abraham and Moses. Afterwards he began to comment on the Torah and the Psalms so that the people were astonished at his eloquence and wisdom. He then bowed down in thanks to God and said, "Praise be to Him who bestoweth wisdom on whomsoever He willeth."

The people came to David and said, "Truly it is for one such as him to sit at your right hand in judgment, and for you to accept his opinion, since he speaks with wisdom." Thereafter they looked kindly upon Solomon.

* * *

Wahb ibn Munabbih said: Solomon reminded the children of Israel of Adam's transgression, the murder of Abel, Seth's legacy, Idris' translation, Noah's ark, Hud's apostleship, Salih's slain camel, Abraham's friendship with God, Ishmael's purity, Isaac's sacrifice and his fortitude in the face of affliction, the patience of Job, the trustworthiness of Shuayb, Moses' conversations with God, the ministry of Aaron, Elijah's troops, the regency of Elisha, and the wisdom of Luqman,[113] who had been given a thousand chapters of wisdom, each chapter of which was divided into a thousand sections, each section of which was subdivided into a thousand branches, each of which comprised a thousand of the different types of knowledge.

* * *

Solomon had been given all the languages of mankind, the birds and the beasts. When he was seventeen years old, Gabriel came down to David with a page of gold and said to him, "O David, God sends you greetings and tells you to assemble your children and to read them the problems contained on this page. Whoever answers them will be your successor."

David told his children what Gabriel had said and read the problems to them; but, since none of them knew the answers, they had to declare their inability. Then David said to Solomon, "My son, I will ask you these questions. What is your opinion?"

"Ask, father," said Solomon, "and I pray God guide me to answer them correctly."

"My son," David began, "what is something?"

"The believer."

"You are correct," he said. "What is the least thing?"

"The incapable."

"What is nothing?"

"The infidel."

"From what is everything?"

"Water," said Solomon, "for everything is made of it."

"What is the greatest thing?"

"Gratitude to God."

"What is the sweetest thing?"

"Property, children and good health."

"What is the bitterest thing?"

"Poverty after riches."

"What is the most odious thing?"

"Apostacy after faith."

"What is the most beautiful thing?"

"The soul in the body."

"What is the most dreadful thing?"

"The body without the soul."

"What is the closest thing?"

"The next world to this world."

"What is the farthest thing?"

"This world from the next."

"What is the most evil thing?"

"An evil woman."

"What is the best thing?"

"A pious woman."

"What is the purest thing?"

"The earth."

"What is the vilest thing?"

"The dog and the pig."

David proclaimed him correct on every question. When the questioning was finished, David asked the learned men, "Do you reject anything my child Solomon has said?"

"We reject nothing," they answered.

"Then I am content," said David, "that Solomon be my successor to rule over you. What say you?"

"Yes," they acclaimed. "We are content with him."

79. *The Story of Those Who Did Not Keep the Sabbath*

There was in the time of David a tribe of Israel, sons of the kings who had been with Moses; and they lived in a village by the sea called Eloth. Now God had forbidden the children of Israel to labor on the sabbath day, which was Saturday, and had commanded them to occupy themselves with worship and glorification of Him. Moses had ordered them to worship on Friday, but they had refused, saying "It is not meant for us to worship except on Saturday, for that is the day on which our Lord finished creation." And once they had chosen Saturday, God made it difficult for them.

The Christians chose Sunday, as He hath said: *The sabbath was only appointed unto those who differed concerning it* (16.124). And thus they remained for a long time.

On the shore were two large white rocks to which, on the sabbath eve and sabbath day, the fish came out of the sea; but the Israelites did not catch them. Sunday eve, however, they would go down to the sea, as He hath said: *When their fish came unto them on their sabbath day, appearing openly on the water; but on the day whereon they celebrated no sabbath, they came not unto them* (7.163).

Then the ungodly of Eloth began to say, "God forbade our fathers to fish on the sabbath, but not us! And these fish come out on the sabbath and sabbath eve. It is impossible not to go after them." So they agreed to catch them; and on the sabbath they caught, roasted, and ate the fish. The true believers smelled the fish and warned them of retribution; but they paid no attention.

When they did not cease, but actually increased their activity, the faithful threatened them with weapons. The ungodly, however, said, "Do not enter our village!"

"This village belongs to us as well as to you," said the faithful. "It is not lawful for you to drive us from our own village. Either do as we do, or we will divide the village. You will have a sector and we a sector." Therefore, the faithful divided the village with the others, and they built a high wall between, with gates, each faction having a gate of its own.

From the sea to the door of his house, each of the ungodly dug a canal, into which the fish swam on the sabbath eve. Then, when the sun had set and the fish were about to return to the sea, they sealed off the canals and took all the fish they wanted. But the faithful still warned them of God's punishment.

When this had gone on for some time, the faithful said one to another, "How long must we advise them, since they only increase in tyranny and lawlessness?"

Then David heard of the situation and cursed them: while they were drinking and at play, the ground trembled under them and God transformed them into apes, as He hath said: *And when they proudly refused to desist from what had been forbidden them, we said unto them, "Be ye transformed into apes, driven away from the society of men"* (7.166).

God related this story to our Prophet Muhammad in order that he not make the forbidden lawful, and not forbid what God had made lawful.

* * *

God hath said: *Those among the children of Israel who believed not were cursed by the tongue of David, and of Jesus the son of Mary. This befell them because they were rebellious and transgressed* (5.78).

Those who were cursed by Jesus son of Mary were those who asked for the table to descend and, when it had descended, disbelieved, wherefore God transformed them into pigs at Jesus' request.

* * *

One of the men who had been changed into an ape came to one of the faithful, who said, "You are So-and-So."

The other nodded his head as if to say yes.

"When we warned you, you would not accept our advice, so now this has befallen you."

* * *

All the apes in the world are descended from those very apes, who were those who did not keep the sabbath, just as all swine are descended from those who asked for the table.

* * *

David then asked his Lord to show him his companion in Paradise; and God said to him, "O David, I have willed it so. Go toward the sea until thou see him. Girt thyself with a woolen girdle and put on sandals."

David took his staff and walked until he came to a village. Upon entering the village, he saw the people buying and selling in the market. There he saw a man with a bundle of firewood on his head, saying, "Who will buy good with good?" A man came and bought the bundle for a loaf of bread, a lawful trade. The first man took the loaf, broke it and gave half to the needy. Taking the other half, he set out for the mountain.

To himself David said, "Doubtless this man is my companion in Paradise." And he followed him to the top of the mountain.

There, beside a spring, the man performed his ablutions and prayed until the sun had set, when he said, "My God, I ask thee to insure that I will be awed by the horrors of the Day of Resurrection!" Then he prostrated himself, saying, "My God, would that I were one of the wild beasts of the mountains or one of the birds, who do not know the horrors of the Day of Resurrection." He wept and prayed the evening prayer, after which he took the rest of his loaf, ate it, and drank from the spring. He praised God and prayed two *rak'as*.

David came forth and greeted him. Returning the greeting, the man asked, "Who are you and who brought you here where only al-Khidr ibn Malkan and I, Matthew son of Hanun, companion to David in Paradise, come?"

"I am David, he said, "come in search of you." The man embraced him and kissed him.

"I want to ask you about something," said David.

"Ask, O David," said the man, "and if you wish I will tell you even before you ask." David asked him to tell him.

"You want to ask me what I meant while selling the firewood when I said, 'Who will buy good with good?' "

"You speak truly," said David.

"O David," he said, "There are on this mountain trees that are deemed lawful to cut; but lest I cut of that which bears fruit that someone before me may have gathered and profited from, I take the branches scattered in the valleys and wasteland, which I gather and sell so that thereby there be lawful from the lawful."

David said to him, "You could end this weariness for yourself by coming with me to my kingdom and enjoying my bounty."

"I have fled the world," he said. "Nor would I care to return to it. However, you could be like me and keep me company, could you not, in this place of mine?"

"I return to the children of Israel to conduct their affairs," said David, taking leave of him. Then he returned, and God shortened the distance for him.

80. *The Death of David*

Wahb said: David was exceedingly jealous of his women, and whenever he went out he would lock them in and take the keys with him.

One day he went out, and upon his return, saw a handsome man in the middle of the hall. Angrily he said, "Who are you, and who let you into my hall among my women?"

"He let me in who is the Master of the hall and who gave you dominion and authority. I am he who fears not kings. I am the Angel of Death, come to take your spirit."

David trembled and said, "O Angel of Death, let me go to my people and my children to bid them farewell."

"I cannot do that, O David," said the angel. "Have you not heard that *when their term therefore is expired, they shall not have respite for an hour, neither shall their punishment be anticipated?"* (10.50).

David wept and said, "O Angel of Death, I have wept much over my sins and transgressions. Will my tears avail me or not?"

"Yes, David," he said, "every tear that falls from a penitent sinner's eye weighs more in His scales than the earth and the mountains."

"O Angel of Death," said David, "who will the children of Israel have after me?"

"Your successor is Solomon," said the angel.

"Then now is my spirit ready for death," David said. "Take that which God has commanded you to take." And the angel took his spirit.

* * *

It is related on the authority of the Prophet that David lived for one hundred years and died on a Saturday. It is also said that his spirit was taken while he was preaching from the pulpit.

* * *

Then Solomon undertook the annointing of his father's body, and his brothers helped him. He wound him in a winding sheet that had descended from Paradise, and he and his children and the Israelites prayed over David and bore him to Abraham's grotto, where he was buried. And the birds hovered in mourning over his grave for forty days.

81. *The Story of Solomon*

When David died, Gabriel descended to Solomon and said, "God gives you the choice of dominion or knowledge."

Solomon bowed down before God and said, "O Lord, knowledge is more precious to me than any possession."

Then God said to Solomon, "I have given thee dominion and knowledge, reason and perfect temper."

The four winds came and stood before him and said, "O prophet of God, God has subdued us for you, so ride us to any place you desire."

Then the birds and beasts came and said, "God has commanded us to obey you so that you may do with us as you please." Gabriel brought from Paradise the seal of vicegerency, which shone and glistened like the Milky Way. It had four points, on the first of which was written,

THERE IS NO GOD BUT GOD

On the second was written:

EVERYTHING WILL PERISH EXCEPT HIS FACE

On the third was written:

HIS IS THE KINGDOM AND THE POWER AND THE GLORY

And on the fourth was written:

BLESSED BE GOD THE BEST CREATOR

Every point of the ring was for one kind of creature: the first for the rebellious genii, the second for the birds and beasts, the third for the kings of the earth, and the fourth for those that inhabit the seas and the mountains. Gabriel gave the ring to Solomon, saying, "This is the gift of dominion, the adornment of the prophets and the symbol of obedience of mankind, the genii, the beasts and all the rest of creation." This took place on a Friday, the third day from the end of the month of Ramadan.

When the ring fell into Solomon's palm, he was unable to look upon it because of its brilliance until he had said, "There is no god but God," whereupon he looked and found that God had given him the power to gaze upon it and had also increased the light of his sight.

This seal was Adam's while he was in Paradise; but, when he was expelled, the ring flew from his finger and returned to Paradise, where it remained until Gabriel brought it down to Solomon.

* * *

Solomon commanded the Israelites to take up arms, and he brought out the twelve thousand breastplates which his father David had made. Gabriel then spread one of his wings to the

East and the other to the West, and the genii and demons swarmed from every direction, Gabriel driving them as a shepherd drives his flocks. They came to stand before Solomon, numbering that day four hundred and twenty bands, each band representing a different sect. Solomon gazed upon their different sorts: among them were yellow, blond, white and black; among them were those like horses, mules, donkeys and other beasts of burden; among them were those like the beasts of the wilds: lions, hyenas, dogs and other predatory beasts; among them were those with trunks, long tails, ears and hooves, and bodiless heads and headless bodies.

Solomon asked them about their tribes and their names, their kindred and their dwelling-places. Then he said, "I see that you are of different shapes and sizes, but yet you all spring from Jann."

"O prophet of God," they answered, "that is because of the multitude of our sins and because Iblis has mingled his blood with ours. Thus we are of different sects: among us are those who worship fire and those who worship the trees, the sun and the moon; and each one says that he is right."

Solomon then placed his seal on each of their necks and dismissed them to their abodes; and not one of them disobeyed him except Sakhr the Rebellious,[114] who hid himself on an island in the sea. As for Iblis, he remained without aides and fled until Solomon found him and said, "What makes you think you can escape me?"

"I did not humble myself to your father Adam," said Iblis. "How therefore could I humble myself to his progeny? I have been made immortal until the first blow of the trumpet, and I have been given mastery over the sons of Adam and the daughters of Eve, save those whom God protect against me."

* * *

Solomon discharged the rebellious genii to perform various works in iron, brass, wood and stone, and to build villages, cities and fortresses. Their women he ordered to spin silk, cotton, linen and wool, and to weave carpets. He ordered them to make clay pots and bowls, from each of which a thousand men could eat. He put one group to work diving in the seas for coral and pearl; he ordered some of them to dig wells and to extract treasure from the bowels of the earth. Then he organized the learned genii into four castes: the warrior caste wore green turbans and red belts, the caste of servants to the army wore pure, multi-colored robes; there was a servant caste to the children of Israel, and a caste for all other tasks.

* * *

Solomon's tables stretched for one mile, and he had a thousand cooks, each of whom had a demon to help him slaughter cows and sheep, break up firewood and wash pots and pans. He had a thousand bakers, and in his kitchens were slaughtered every day thirty thousand head of camel, cattle and sheep. The ascetics were seated on cushions of green silk, the genii on iron benches and the demons on benches of brass. The latter consumed nothing but aromas; and the birds ate wheat, barley, rice, beans, corn, millet and lentils.

Then said Solomon, "O Lord, I ask thee to put into my hands the feeding of all thy creatures for one day."

"O son of David," came the answer, "of that thou art not capable."

"O Lord," said Solomon, "just for one hour."

God answered him, saying, "Then I shall give thee this thing, but begin with the inhabitants of the seas."

Therefore Solomon gathered grain and ordered the winds to transport him to the sea. When he had come to the shore, he called out, "O inhabitants of the sea, come and take your sustenance!"

As the fish, frogs and beasts of the sea were assembling, suddenly a whale raised its head (which was as large as a mountain) out of the water and said, "Give *me* enough to eat, Solomon."

"Is there anything else in the sea like you?" asked Solomon.

"O prophet of God," it said, "in the sea there are fish so big that were I to go into the mouth of the smallest of them I would be like a mustard-seed in the desert."

And the creatures of the sea cried out, "Son of David, feed us, for we are hungry."

Now the sea became turbulent, and out came the head of a fish larger than a mountain.

"O God," said Solomon, "is there anything in the sea larger than *this?*"

"O Solomon," came a voice, "there are in the sea those that can eat seventy like this one and still not be satisfied." Solomon realized that his kingdom was as nothing before God, and departed.

* * *

God commanded Solomon to build a temple at the Ascension Rock, so he assembled the rebellious genii, the spirits, and the wise among men and dispersed the demons to cut stone, lay marble and perform other tasks. He ordered the foundations to be dug until they reached water; and he ordered the foundations to be laid, but the water corroded the foundations. Therefore the genii made domes of brass and lead and wrote on them, "There is no god but God." Thus the foundations became firm; and the building was raised.

The people, however, complained of the noise made by the rock-cutting; so Solomon asked the rebellious genii if they knew how to cut stone without making a din.

"We have no such knowledge," they said, "but Sakhr the Rebellious knows how to do it." Solomon told the demons to bring Sakhr to him; but they said, "We have no power over him. We can, however, waylay him when he comes, as is his monthly custom, to drink from a certain spring. We think the spring should be filled with wine so that when he drinks he will become intoxicated. Then we can seize him and bring him to you." Solomon gave them permission to carry out this scheme.

They filled the spring with wine; and when Sakhr thirsted and came there, he found it full of wine. "O good wine!" he cried. "You dull the mind and make the wise ignorant. By God! I shall not drink anything from you." So saying, he left and went on his way.

The next day, however, as his thirst had become unbearable, he came and found the spring as it had been the day before. "What is the use of precaution against predestination," he said as he gazed at the spring, burning with thirst. And he drank it all.

The demons came, bound him with iron and took him to

Solomon. Tongues of flame lept from his nostrils; but when he looked upon Solomon's ring, he bowed down humbly and said, "O prophet of God, may your kingdom be magnified. Yet, in the end, it will pass away from you."

"You speak truly," said Solomon, "but tell me of the strangest thing you have seen mankind do."

"O prophet of God," he began, "one day I passed by a man pulling on a rotten rope nearly eaten through by locusts, and I realized that he was feeble-minded. And I passed by another man who claimed knowledge of the occult; and, since only God knows the occult, I was astonished at his foolishness."

Solomon laughed and told him of the people's complaint about the noise made by the genii stone-cutters.

"O prophet of God," he said, "I know how to deal with that." Then he added, "I need an eagle's nest and eggs." When these had been brought, he called for a glass dome, which he placed over the eagle's nest. When the eagle came and saw that she could not reach her nest, she flew away to the East and the West. The next day she brought a piece of diamond, which she dropped on the glass, shattering the dome. She took her nest and departed, leaving the rock. Sakhr took it to Solomon, who said, "Where did you get this rock?"

"O prophet of God," said Sakhr, "it is from a high mountain at the utter extreme of the West, which is called Mount Samur, and which no one can reach." Solomon sent the demons there to gather what they needed to cut the stone, and from that time on no one heard any noise.

Solomon made the temple lofty and covered it with onyx and all kinds of jewels. In it he had built a thousand pillars of marble. On each of these was a lamp of gold. After forty days, during which time he put to work every day a thousand demons, a thousand spirits and a thousand human masons, the building was finished. Inside he hung golden lamps from silver chains, and afterwards made a great sacrifice saying, "My God and Master, thou hast clad me with the garments of prophethood and hast given me great dominion. I ask thee to give me in building thy holy house what thou gavest Abraham thy friend in building the Kaaba."

Even the angels sought their Lord's permission which he

granted to visit the temple. It is said that they visit it every year, every month and every Friday, and that it will be a place of blessing until the Day of Resurrection.

Solomon selected servants for the temple from among the devout of the children of Israel. The kings of the surrounding regions heard of the temple and came to visit it; they were astounded by its beauty and magnificence.

Then Solomon had twelve thousand seats built of ivory and aloe-wood, one for every scholar; and none of these was higher than any other. For Solomon, Sakhr made a throne of ivory with pedestals of gold, and on it he put statues of the birds and beasts. It was also studded with pearls the size of ostrich eggs. On the first step was a grapevine wrought of gold, with leaves of emerald and bunches of gems to look like grapes; to the right and left of the seat he fixed a palm tree of gold, on each of which were peacocks, birds and hawks that were hollow and studded with jewels. When the wind blew through the hollow cavities, they would sing songs, the likes of which no one had ever heard. On the second step he installed two great lions, and on the third, birds, peacocks and eagles. When Solomon ascended the first step, the eagles and birds flapped their wings and scattered musk over him. When he ascended the second step, the beasts roared and voices could be heard from behind, saying, "O son of David, thank God for the great dominion which He has given you!" When he ascended the fifth step he heard a cry saying, *"God seeth that which ye do."* At the seventh step the throne itself revolved with all that was upon it and came to rest for Solomon to seat himself. And the birds perfumed him with musk and ambergris.

Whenever litigants came for Solomon's judgment, the lions would stare at them as though speaking, the birds would rustle and the genii would murmur. The litigants would be struck with such unbearable awe that they could not utter a word other than the truth.

* * *

Kaab al-Ahbar said: One day as Solomon was headed toward Damascus, he saw swarms of ants like dark clouds and said to his companions, "I see something black." And the winds caused him to hear what one of the ants was saying in warning to its kinfolk, as God hath said: *"O ants, enter ye into your habitations, lest Solomon and his army tread you under foot, and perceive it not."*

And Solomon smiled, laughing at her words, and said, "O Lord, excite me that I may be thankful for thy favour, wherewith thou hast favoured me, and my parents; and that I may do that which is right, and well-pleasing unto thee: and introduce me, through thy mercy, among thy servants the righteous" (27.18f).

Solomon dismounted as the ants, line after line, were entering their dwellings, cried out to them and showed them the ring, whereupon they came humbly before him with their queen, who was larger than a bear. She bowed down to him and said, "O prophet of God, when I saw you on your steed with your army, I called to the ants to go to their dwellings out of fear of your armies and soldiers. I saw before you more than twenty thousand angels, but not one of them was like you."

"What is your name?" asked Solomon.

"I am called Watkam," she said.

"How many are you in number, and when were you created?" he asked.

"O prophet of God," she began, "there is not a mountain or a valley anywhere that has not thousands of the warriors of the ants, and God created us two thousand years before your father Adam."

Solomon then cried out to the ants, and they approached to make obeisance to him and his soldiers, row after row of varying colors; and the queen said, "O prophet of God, know that not a single ant dies before producing swarms of her like." And Solomon was astonished.

"My God," he said, raising his gaze to heaven, "hast thou created anything more numerous than the ants?"

"Yes, Solomon," answered God, "and I shall show thee." Thereupon God commanded the king of the mosquitoes to have his folk assemble before Solomon; and they approached, swarm after swarm, like clouds. Then their king came before Solomon and said, "Peace be with you, O prophet of God. We were in this valley two thousand years before your father Adam was created."

"How many are you and where are your abodes?" asked Solomon.

"O prophet of God," said the king, "there are under my dominion seventy swarms, each of which could veil the light of the sun. Among us are those who take refuge in the mountains, those who dwell in the sea, and those whose dwellings are in trees." All the mosquitoes bowed down before Solomon.

* * *

When Solomon wished to ride the wind, he would call for the four winds. He would spread his carpet, one side of which was red and the other green; no one except God knows how long or how wide it was, but it is said that it was six hundred and sixty cubits long. Then he would sit on his throne, borne aloft on a carpet from Paradise. The learned men also rode with him, borne by the winds and shaded by the birds. Solomon held the reins of the winds in his hands as one holds the reins of a horse. He would lunch after crossing a distance that would normally have taken a month and would dine after another month's journey.

One day as he was traveling in the air, he passed over Medina, the city of our Prophet Muhammad, and said to those who were with him, "This is the abode, after migration, of a prophet who will be the lord of all apostles. Blessed be he who sees him and believes in him." Then he passed over Mecca and said, "This is the birthplace of that prophet. The excellence of this city over all others is as the excellence of Muhammad over all other prophets." And Solomon passed over no city or island that did not obey him.

82. *The City of Sheba*

Kaab al-Ahbar said: The first king of the Yemen was Abdul-Shams ibn Qahtan ibn Yashjub ibn Ya'rab, but he was called Sheba [*Sabá*] because he was the first to take captive [*sabá*] the Arabs, and he was a tyrant. He built a city and called it Sheba after his own name. He laid its foundations strong and built palaces with iron gates, and he planted orchards which became sanctuaries for wild beasts and birds, as He hath said: *The descendants of Saba had heretofore a sign in their dwelling; namely, the two gardens on the right hand and on the left* (34.15). And Sheba had built for himself a hundred palaces of marble and stone with roofs of ivory and aloe-wood.

He had seven sons, each of whom had a kingdom; and their names were Himyar ibn Saba, the eldest, Amr, Damra, al-Askar, al-Anmar, Kalan and Nujayla. They all spoke Arabic and were disobedient and tyrannical. God sent to them thirteen prophets who summoned them to God, but they denied them and put them to death.

Among them was a man called Amr ibn Umayra, who had a frightening dream. When he awoke, he said to his son, "My son, in my dream I saw the city of Sheba and all the surrounding cities inundated. My son, it is certain to happen. Tomorrow, when I am seated among my people, speaking of what is to be, you must contend with me. When I call out to you, rise and slap me in the face."

And so the boy did as his father had ordered; but the old man attacked his son and was about to kill him, when his people intervened and said, "By God, had anyone other than your son done that, we would have given him his due."

"By God," he said, "I shall not dwell with him in this city." So he sold all he possessed and set out for another town. Then he wrote to his cousins telling them what had happened; and they informed the king, who sent to the soothsayers asking about the man's dream.

"We have found in our books," they replied, "that the city will be destroyed by red mice, which will make holes in the dam. The people will also be dispersed." Thereupon the king grew furious and went to the dam, reinforced it and tied to it many cats. Thus they tried to thwart their Lord.

When God willed their destruction, the red mice came to the dam and the cats ran toward the mice, but to no avail: The mice made holes in the dam until they reached the water, thereby causing it to collapse. A flood rushed over the people from a place called al-Gharam, while they were unaware; Sheba and his people were utterly destroyed. The water did not subside until the people ceased to be recalcitrant. Then, in place of the orchards, there grew bitter herbs, tamarisk and the lote-tree.

* * *

After them came a tribe descended from the son of Himyar ibn Saba, who settled there and said, "This is the land of our forefathers." The first to be king among them was called Amr ibn Amra ibn Saba ibn Shaddad, from the progeny of Himyar. After him ruled Ibrahim al-Rakis, who is called Dhu'l-Minar because he instituted fire and was the first to define boundaries. He was of the offspring of Qahtan and dwelt there for a time before dying an infidel. Then there ruled Sharakh ibn Sharahil the Himyarite. He levied one maiden a week from his subjects; he ravished each maiden, and would return her to her people only to receive another the following week. He had a vizier called Dhu-Sharkh ibn Hudad, who was of a comely appearance and was an avid hunter. It happened one day that, as he was passing by a place with many trees, he heard voices singing poetry; and he realized that they were genii.

He called out to them at the top of his voice, saying, "O assemblies of the genii, I have come to stay the night with you. Do let me hear your songs." So they sang him a verse of their poetry; during the verse Umayra, the daughter of the king of the genii, appeared. When he saw her, he was enamoured of her beauty, but she disappeared from his sight. Nonetheless, he loved her in his heart.

"Who is this maiden?" he asked.

"She is the daughter of our king," they said.

"Please take me to your king," he said, "in order that I may see him."

When he was brought into the king's presence, the vizier said, "Greetings to you, O most gracious king."

"And our greetings to you," answered the king. "Who are you?"

"I am the vizier of the prince of the city of Sheba," he said. "May it please your majesty to marry me to your daughter." The king approved of him because of his beauty and gave her to him in marriage. He knew her and she conceived Bilqis.

* * *

Wahb ibn Munabbih said: When her months were accomplished, she gave birth to a girl, radiant as the sun, and called her Bilqis.[115] The mother then died, and she was raised by the daughters of the genii and grew to such beauty that she was called the Venus of the Yemen.

When she had reached maturity, she said to her father, "Father, I despise living among the genii. Take me to the land of humans."

"My daughter," he said, "the humans have a tyrannical king who ravishes his people's virgins out of wrath. I fear for you."

"My father," she said, "build me a palace outside his city and install me therein. Then you will see what I shall do to him."

When he had built the palace and had a throne of ivory made for her, he installed her there, where she dwelt for a long time. Her reputation spread to the king, so he mounted his horse and approached the palace. He sent in his stewardess, who, when she had entered the palace and seen how beautiful and lovely Bilqis was, quickly returned to the king and told him what she had seen.

He called for the vizier and said to him, "You built this palace and did not tell me."

"Sire," said he, "I built this palace but a short while ago when this girl was born of the daughter of the king of the genii. Her mother was dead, and she hated living among the genii, so I installed her in this palace."

"I want you to marry her to me," said the king.

"Your wish is my command," said he. "But first I must ask her consent."

The vizier went to his daughter and said, "My daughter, what I feared has indeed befallen, for the king has asked me for your hand."

"Marry me to him," she said, "for I shall kill him before he touches me." So her father returned to the king and informed him of her consent.

The king rejoiced at what he heard and wrote her a letter, in which he said, "I have fallen in love with you because of your renown, without having set eyes on you. When you have read my letter, hasten to me."

But Bilqis wrote in answer, "I long the more for your countenance, but this palace is constructed by the genii; and I have had herein installed devices that are suitable for the likes of you."

When her letter was brought to him, he arose and had his finest garments lain out. He put them on and rode out in the company of the nobility until he came to the palace, whereupon Bilqis ordered her father to go out to the king and tell him to enter the palace alone.

There were seven doors to the palace, and at each door was stationed a daughter of the genii as radiant as the sun. In their hands were plates of gold, filled with dirhems and dinars, with which Bilqis had commanded them to shower the king when they saw him. As the king entered, they poured the coins over him; and he asked each of them, "Are you my beloved?"

"No," they replied, "I am only her servant. She is yet before you." He proceeded until he finally reached the last door. When Bilqis came out and he saw her great beauty, he almost went mad.

She set before him a table of gold, upon which was a variety of foodstuffs; but he said, "I have no need of these." Therefore she had wine brought and began to pour for him. He drank and moaned. She then offered him a heavy wine; and, when he had become intoxicated, he fell down on the ground, as immobile as a piece of wood.

Bilqis arose, cut off his head and said to her serving girls, "Take this infidel and hide his body in the sea." They tied him to a rock so that he would not float up to the surface of the water.

She then sent to the king's treasurers to bring her all the money and riches that were in the storehouses; when the letter reached the treasurers, they gathered together all that was there and sent it off to Bilqis' palace. Thereupon she invited the viziers and offered them wine, which they drank.

"The king says for you to send him your wives and daughters," she said.

They became furious and said, "Is he not satisfied with what he has already had?"

When she realized that anger had taken control of them, she said, "I shall return and acquaint him with your wrath." And she left them alone for a time. Upon her return she said, "I have told him what you said, but he says he must have it so." And they increased in rage, whereupon she said, "Would you like me to kill him and rid you of his evil, in which case I would reign over you?" They agreed to this and swore fealty to her. Then she left them for a time and returned with the king's head. They rejoiced exceedingly and made her queen, and she dwelt there for seventeen years.

* * *

Wahb ibn Munabbih said: One day as Solomon was riding about on his carpet with the hoopoe as his guide, the hoopoe said to himself, "It is time for Solomon to descend to the earth and ask me to find water." Therefore he flew high into the sky to locate a place with water. Suddenly he came upon a hoopoe from the Yemen and asked him where he was from.

"I am from the region called the Yemen," came the answer.

"I am from Syria," said Solomon's hoopoe, "of the legions of Solomon, the king of men and genii."

"In my country," said the Yemenite hoopoe, "we have a mighty queen who commands ten thousand leaders, and under each leader are ten thousand soldiers. Can you come with me to the Yemen and see what is there?" Solomon's hoopoe accepted and went with the other to the Yemen, where he saw Bilqis' palace and observed what she was like.

In the meantime, Solomon had missed the hoopoe and could not locate him anywhere, so he sent the raven to summon him. The raven flew east and west and finally found the hoopoe hastening in his flight, and brought him before Solomon, who was about to pluck out his feathers when the hoopoe said, "O prophet of God, remember that tomorrow you will stand between Paradise and Hell!" And Solomon let him go.

The hoopoe said, *"I came unto thee from Sheba, with a certain piece of news. I found a woman to reign over them, who is provided with every thing requisite for a prince, and hath a magnificent throne. I found her and her people to worship the sun, besides God."*

Solomon said, "We shall see whether thou hast spoken the truth, or whether thou art a liar" (27.22ff).

Then Solomon asked about the water, and the hoopoe said, "O prophet of God, there is water beneath the pillar of the throne." Solomon commanded the throne to be moved, and the hoopoe came forward and pecked at the earth with his beak, whereupon water gushed out. Solomon and those with him performed their ablutions and prayed.

When he had finished his prayer, he said to the hoopoe, *"Go with this my letter, and cast it down unto them; then turn aside from them, and wait to know what answer they will return"* (27.28).

Then he called for a leaf of gold and said to Asaph ben-Berachiah, "Write this: *'It is from Solomon, and is: In the name of the most merciful God, Rise not up against me: but come, and surrender yourselves unto me'* " (27.30f). Sealing the letter with musk, he gave it to the hoopoe, who flew to Bilqis' palace.

There he found her asleep on her couch, so he threw the letter on her breast and flew up to perch in the window. (It is also said that she awoke from her slumber and saw the hoopoe with the letter in his beak, whereupon he threw it to her.)

She summoned her people and read them the letter. Then she said, "My people, what is your opinion, for we have been commanded to submit?"

The nobles answered, "We are endued with strength, and are endued with great prowess in war; but the command appertaineth unto thee: see therefore what thou wilt command" (27.33ff).

She said, "Verily kings, when they enter a city by force, waste the same, and abase the most powerful of the inhabitants thereof: and so will these do with us. But I will send gifts unto them; and will wait for what further information those who shall be sent shall bring back. If he is one of those impious, worldly prophets, we will satisfy him with money and rid ourselves of him. If, on the other hand, he is a pious prophet, he will not be satisfied with anything less than submission to himself." As she ordered gifts to be made ready, the hoopoe was watching all that she did.

When the hoopoe returned to Solomon and told him all that had happened, Solomon summoned the genii and said to them, "This queen is going to send me a present of gold and silver. I want you to cover the courtyard with bricks of gold and silver." Now Bilqis had made ready one hundred bricks of gold and an equal amount of silver, one hundred beardless slaveboys dressed as girls, one hundred serving-girls clad in boys' clothing, and one hundred horses with magnificent trappings and harnesses of brocade and silk. Then she placed an unpierced pearl in a golden globe and a hollowed out piece of onyx on a stand of ivory; along with the tribute she sent one of her ministers, whom she had ordered to hold his tongue when he went before Solomon. Then she wrote a letter in which she said, "I have sent to you slave boys and serving girls for you to distinguish the male from the female without uncovering their private parts; also an unpierced pearl I want you to bore and string without using any implement; also an onyx vial for you to fill with water that has neither fallen from the sky nor come up from the ground."

When the minister came and saw Solomon's courtyard, the treasure that was laid out there and the horses that were tied around, his heart sank. He went before Solomon and handed him the letter, but Solomon told him the contents without reading it. He then ordered a golden ewer of water to be brought and commanded the slave boys and serving girls to wash their hands: as the boys poured the water over the backs of their hands and turned them to the side, while the girls poured water down the underside of their arms, in this manner he was able to distinguish the boys from the girls. Next he commanded a worm to pierce the pearl and string it. Finally, he ordered the horses to be run until they sweated, and he collected their sweat into the vial.

He then told the minister, "Return to your mistress with the gifts you have brought and tell her, *'Will ye present me with riches? Verily that which God hath given me is better than what he hath given you: but ye do glory in your gifts'* " (27.36). Therefore the minister took the tribute back to Bilqis and told her what he had seen of Solomon.

To her people she said; "Now you see that my opinion was more correct than yours; for, by God, he is a prophet and we have no strength to resist him." She then gathered her retainers and her treasury, loaded them up—all except her throne, which she locked behind seven doors—and set off in Solomon's direction to enter into his dominion.

When the news reached Solomon, he said to those who were with him, *"Which of you will bring unto me her throne, before they come and surrender themselves unto me?"* (27.38f).

A terrible genii answered, "I will bring it unto thee, before thou canst arise from thy place."

"I want it faster than that," said Solomon. *And one with whom was the knowledge of the scriptures,* who was Asaph ben-Berachiah, *said, "I will bring it unto thee, in the twinkling of an eye."*

And when Solomon saw the throne placed before him, he said, "This is a favour of my Lord, that he may make trial of me, whether I will be grateful. Alter her throne, that she may not know it, to the end we may see whether she be rightly directed, or whether she be one of those who are not rightly directed" (27.40f).

The genii said to him, "O prophet of God, I shall build you such a palace of glass that whosoever sees it will imagine it to be water with fish." So Solomon permitted him to build it. (Now it had been mentioned to him that Bilqis had hairy legs.)

When the genii had finished his labor, Bilqis arrived and, coming near the palace, saw her throne and was astonished.

"Is thy throne like this?" asked Solomon (27.42).

She answered, "As though it were the same." And she realized that it was her throne indeed, and coming near the hall, *she imagined it to be a great water; and she discovered her legs. Whereupon Solomon said unto her, "Verily this is a palace evenly floored with glass."*

Then said the queen, "O Lord, verily I have dealt unjustly with my own soul; and I resign myself, together with Solomon, unto God, the Lord of all creatures" (27.44).

Then she married Solomon and bore him a son called Rehoboam, whose arms reached down to his knees, which is a sign of chieftainship.

* * *

Wahb said: Bilqis dwelt with Solomon for seven years and seven months before she died, and Solomon buried her beneath the walls of Palmyra in Syria.[116]

83. *Sedition and the Loss of the Ring*

It was reported to Solomon that the king of an island, who was named Nuriah, had taken on a troupe of genii and demons. This was grievous to Solomon, so he set forth with his armies upon his carpet until he looked down upon the island of King Nuriah. He killed the king, took his daughter Segubah and returned to Syria.

Segubah was fantastically beautiful and, when the religion of Islam was offered her, she became Muslim. Solomon married her and built her a palace in which to dwell by herself. She asked Solomon to command the demons to make her an image of her father and mother so that she might be comforted and feel less lonely. Therefore Solomon commanded Sakhr the Rebellious to make her the images in her palace. When Asaph son of Berachiah learned that she bowed down before these images, he asked Solomon's permission to go among the children of Israel and preach to them. Asaph therefore mounted the pulpit, praised God and prayed for every prophet except Solomon. When he came to Solomon's name, he fell silent and did not praise him but descended from the pulpit. Solomon reproached him, but he said, "How could I eulogize you when you have married a woman who worships idols in your own house?" Solomon grew angry, divorced Segubah and broke the idols.

* * *

Sakhr the Rebellious built Solomon a palace on the sea-coast and dwelt there with him. Now Sakhr the Rebellious knew that the secret of Solomon's mastery lay in his ring, and he therefore determined to take it away from him. Solomon had a handmaid named Amina, who never left his side. When he withdrew to be alone with his women, he would entrust his ring to her safekeeping.

One time, however, when Solomon went into the harem and gave the maid his ring as usual, Sakhr represented himself to her as Solomon and asked her for the ring. She, believing him to be Solomon, handed it over to him. Sakhr then went and sat on the throne of Solomon.

When Solomon himself came out of the harem, changed by God into Sakhr's form, and asked the girl for his ring, she said, "I seek refuge in God from you, O Sakhr. Solomon has already taken his ring. Go away!" Solomon perceived that he had been seduced and tried; therefore, he fled.

* * *

Ibn Abbas said that Sakhr was not able to deal with Solomon's wives or his treasury, and the birds and beasts departed from him. The people also began to hear things they had never before heard about Solomon.

* * *

Hungry, Solomon came to a village and said, "I am Solomon; my kingdom has been taken from me because of a transgression. I am hungry. Give me something to eat and God will return my kingdom to me. I will reward anyone who feeds me." Then he said, "O my God, thou hast afflicted the prophets, but thou hast never deprived them of their sustenance. My God, have mercy upon me, for I am repentant unto thee."

But Solomon remained as he was for forty days, eating nothing. He found a piece of dry bread which he took to the river bank to moisten, but a wave snatched it from his hand and it was lost to him.

Later he came across some fishermen from whom he begged fish, but they drove him away, saying, "We have never seen anyone more hideous than you!"

"My people," he cried, "I am Solomon." But one of the men came over and struck him on the head with his staff and said, "You lie about Solomon."

At this, the angels wept out of compassion, but God told them, "Be ye silent, for this is a misfortune of mercy and not a misfortune of torment." Thereupon God cast compassion into the hearts of the fishermen, who gave him a fish. When Solomon cut open the fish's belly, he found his ring inside. Washing it and placing it on his finger, his beauty was immediately restored.

Setting out for his palace, he passed by nothing that did not bow down to him. Sakhr the Rebellious did likewise and then fled.

Solomon sat upon his throne, and the genii, men, beasts and fowl all gathered before him as they had before. He had Sakhr the Rebellious bound in iron and covered with two boulders, which he sealed with his ring. Then Solomon commanded him to be cast into a lake, where it is said that he is still and so shall be until the end of time.

84. *The Death of Solomon*

Kaab al-Ahbar said: One day, while Solomon was seated on his throne, suddenly there appeared a figure with sword in hand, destroying everything in its path.

"Who are you?" Solomon queried.

"I am a destroyer of palaces and a leveler of mountains," he answered. "I am the Angel of Death."

Solomon was so alarmed that he turned pale. Going into his household, he said, "The Angel of Death has appeared to me and gone away, but he will most certainly return. This is my son, Rehoboam, whom I leave as regent over you. Listen to him and obey his command."

"Obedience be to you and to him, O prophet of God," replied the children of Israel.

Solomon then prayed and fasted so much that he would get up at night, delirious and unable to sleep because of an incessant voice crying, "Rise up, O prophet of God, in the service of the Lord!"

In his place of prayer Solomon had a garden, where one day

he saw a plant that he did not recognize. "What plant are you?" he asked.

It answered, "I am the locust, which only grows in a place that has been destroyed."

Solomon continued to fast and pray until his strength diminished and he had to lean on his staff for support. Then the Angel of Death came to him and gave him an aroma. When he smelled it, it took his spirit.

He remained leaning on his staff for a year, until worms infested it and he tumbled to the earth. This is as He hath said: *Nothing discovered his death unto them, except the creeping thing of the earth, which gnawed his staff. And when his body fell down, the genii plainly perceived that if they had known that which is secret, they had not continued in a vile punishment* (34.14).

* * *

Ibn Abbas said that when the demon Sakhr sat on Solomon's throne, he realized that he could not remain there forever, so he wrote a magic formula and placed it beneath the throne. Then, when Solomon died, the demons said that Solomon had been a sorcerer and that his magic was under the throne. The learned told them it was not the work of Solomon; nonetheless, when God sent our Prophet Muhammad and revealed to him concerning Solomon, the Jews of Medina said, "Are not you amazed that Muhammad claims that Solomon was a prophet, when he was only a sorcerer?" Then God revealed to him the verse, *Solomon was not an unbeliever* (2.102).

* * *

Solomon lived for sixty years, and after him the children of Israel split into three groups: one group apostatized and followed magic; another group withdrew and said, "We will not obey anyone after him"; and the third group followed Rehoboam, who was a king but not a prophet. When he died his son Abijam, who was an obstinate tyrant, became king. God sent him a prophet named Daniel (not Daniel the Wise, who was at the time of Nebuchadnezzar), because Abijam had begun to call the people to idolatry. Abijam's son Asa was a believer but kept his faith concealed for fear of his father. When Daniel heard this, he clothed himself in a woolen garment and set out for Abijam's palace, but he found that the king had died during the night.

"Praise be to Him who has exiled him far from His mercy," said Daniel. Then, to Abijam's son Asa, he said, "Reestablish the religion of your fathers." Asa accepted, and Daniel rejoiced.

Asa commanded his people to do justice and to eschew evil; but they neither listened to him nor obeyed, even until he died.

85. *Jonah son of Matthew*

Kaab al-Ahbar said: Matthew, the father of Jonah, was a pious man who lived in Jerusalem and was of the lineage of the prophets. His wife Sadaqa had dwelt with him for a long time but had not produced a child. At the age of seventy, however, he lay with her on the eve of the *Ashura,*[117] and she conceived. When her months were accomplished, she bore a son and called him Jonah. Then her husband Matthew died, and she was left with nothing but a wooden bowl. She would go to sleep at night, and upon awakening in the morning, would find the bowl full of food and meat, provided by God. As she was not given milk to suckle her son, however, she went out among the shepherds and asked them to give him some sheep's milk to drink. Some would let him suckle from the sheep and some would not. When he was hungry he would suck his fingers, and God would force a ewe to leave the flock and give him to drink.

When he had reached the age of seven, his mother bought him a garment of wool and took him to the ascetics and scholars; and he remained with them, worshipping with them until he was twenty-five years old. Then, in a dream, he saw his father Matthew saying to him, "Jonah, go to Ramla, for there is a saint named Zacharias son of Johanna, who has a pious daughter called Anak.[118] Engage yourself to her and marry her!"

When he awoke he went to that village and found Zacharias

son of Johanna seated in the marketplace on a mat, wearing expensive clothing and buying and selling herbs. He smiled and laughed a great deal. Jonah was astonished and said to himself, "These are not the characteristics of a prophet!"

Zacharias turned to him, rose and embraced him in greeting and said, "Jonah, I saw you yesterday in a dream, and you have come to ask for my daughter in marriage. I have been commanded to give her to you." Then he took him to his house and set food before him, and Jonah told him his dream.

"Zacharias," he said, "I was astonished at your mingling with the people and at how much you smile in their presence."

"Jonah," said Zacharias, "know that merchants are liars, except the merchant who takes only what is due and gives in return what is due, performs his prayers and pays his alms. I am of that kind. As for my merriment, it is to attract the hearts of the poor and unfortunate."

Jonah married his daughter and remained at Zacharias' house for three days. Afterward he took his wife and his possessions and returned to his people in Jerusalem.

* * *

There was in the city of Nineveh a king called Thaalab ibn Sharid, a haughty tyrant who had raided the Israelites, killing many of them and taking captive a group of them.

God spoke to Jonah, saying, "I have chosen thee as a prophet to the city of Nineveh."

"Send someone else," said Jonah.

"Jonah!" cried God, "Go and do what thou hast been commanded to do and disobey not my command!"

Jonah took his household and children, and having reached the bank of the Tigris, took his elder son across the river and placed him on the bank. Then, while returning to take his younger son, all the possessions that he had with him sank. A wolf came to his elder son and carried him off. Jonah began to run after the wolf, but it turned to him and said intelligibly, "Jonah, turn back from me, for I am commanded so to do." Jonah returned sorrowfully to the bank of the Tigris, but could not find his wife.

God spoke to him, saying, "Thou didst complain of the

burden of family, so I have relieved thee of that. Now go and do what thou hast been commanded to do, and then I shall restore thy family and belongings to thee."

Jonah walked to Nineveh, where, in the midst of the city, he cried out in a loud voice, "Confess that there is no god but God and that I, Jonah, am His servant and messenger!" But the people beat him and cursed him, and they only increased in their disbelief and pride. Jonah preached to them for forty days, and they declared him mad.

Then God spoke to him, saying, "Go out from among them, for they will not believe until they experience torment." So he went away from them and sat on a high hill to watch the descent of the punishment upon them. And God spoke to Gabriel, saying, "Descend to Malik, the Warden of Hell, and command him to cause sparks to issue forth from Hutama to Jonah's people." Gabriel did as God had commanded, and Malik sent forth sparks the size of thunderclouds.

With that, the king arose and rent his fine robes, ordering his people to do likewise. This they did, weeping and crying out in loud voices, "O God of Jonah, forgive us! We repent to thee, O Most Merciful!"

God accepted their repentance and lifted the punishment from them, but Jonah grew angry and said, "O God, they have denied me, and thou hast pardoned them. Why should I return to them?"

* * *

He saw a ship about to set sail and said, "Take me with you." When they took him on board with them, the winds churned up the sea about them and they almost sank. They began to pray, but Jonah kept silent. The people on the ship asked him, "Why do you not pray with us?"

"Because I have lost my wife and children," he answered.

"Then," they said, "there is no doubt that this is because of you, Jonah." They cast lots, and they fell against him; but they said, "The lots fall and may be mistaken. Let us cast names upon the sea." So each one wrote his name on a lead ball and threw it into the sea. The ball of each except Jonah sank, but his name appeared on the surface of the water.

Then a great fish appeared with its mouth open and cried

out, "Jonah, I have come from India in search of you." Jonah threw himself into the sea, and the fish swallowed him up and took him first to the Mediterranean and then to the Coral Castle.

* * *

The length of time he was in the fish's belly has been disputed: some have said forty days, but Muhammad ibn Jaafar al-Sadiq said only three days.

* * *

Then God commanded the fish to cast him out onto the bank of the Tigris, where it cast him out; and he emerged from the fish's belly like a featherless chick, for he was no more than skin and bones and had no strength to stand or to sit, and his vision had gone.

God caused a gourd plant with four branches to grow over him; and Gabriel came to him and rubbed his hand over Jonah's body, causing his skin and flesh to grow again. His sight too was restored. Then God sent a gazelle to give him milk as a mother does to her child. Under the plant was also a spring in which he made his ablutions and the water of which he drank. He remained thus for forty days.

When he awoke from his sleep and saw that the tree had dried up and the gazelle had departed, he wept.

God spoke to him, saying, "Jonah, thou weepest over a gourd and a gazelle, but thou dost not weep over a hundred thousand of my servants!"

Then Jonah traveled back among his people and entered a village with many trees and fruits, which the people were uprooting and casting onto the ground.

"Good people," said Jonah, "why are you destroying these fruits?"

God spoke to him, saying, "Jonah, thou feelest sorry for fruit tree, but thou dost not feel sorry for my people!"

Then he went to another village, where a potter took him into his house. God spoke to him saying, "Jonah, order him to break his pottery!"

When Jonah told the man to do this, he said, "I received you as a guest tonight because I thought you were a pious man, but you are a fool with no intelligence to order me to break the pottery that I have made. Go away from me!" And the man turned him out of his house in the middle of the night.

God then spoke to him, saying, "Thou didst tell the potter what thou didst tell him, and he put thee out of his house, yet thou wishest the destruction of a hundred thousand and more!"

Rising the next morning and setting out on his way, he found a man sowing, who said to Jonah, "Pray to God that my crop be blessed." He prayed and the crop at once grew up waisthigh. The man took Jonah to his house and honored him as a guest. And God spoke to him, saying, "I shall send locusts upon this man's crops to eat them up."

"My God," said Jonah, "thou didst answer my prayer for the crops and now thou wishest to destroy them?"

And God spoke to him saying, "O Jonah, thou feelest sorry for crops thou hast not sown, but thou dost not feel sorry for my faithful people!"

"My Lord and Master," he said, "I shall not do it again!"

He came to another village, where he found a man crying out, "Whoever will take this woman to the city of Nineveh to her husband, Jonah son of Matthew, will have a hundred dinars." Jonah at once recognized his wife and said, "Tell me about this woman."

"She was seated on the bank of the Tigris. The lord of this village noticed her and took her off to his castle, where he attempted to entice her to sin, but his hands withered. He asked her to pray God that he be comforted and he would never again approach her; so she prayed and God pardoned him. Then he asked her about her husband, and she said that she was the wife of Jonah son of Matthew. He sent her to me and gave me this gold for her and for the expense of transporting her to her husband."

"I will take her," said Jonah; and the man gave him the woman and the gold.

They walked on together and entered another village, where there was a man selling fish. Jonah bought one and, when he cut open its belly, found all his wealth inside.

Then he saw a man riding an ox, and behind him was a young boy, whom Jonah recognized as his younger son.

"I am Jonah son of Matthew," he said to the man. As the boy greeted his father, Jonah asked what had happened to him.

"I am a fisherman," said the man. "I cast my net into the sea, and this boy fell into it. I found him still alive, and he told me he was the son of Jonah son of Matthew."

Then they went along until they came upon a shepherd watching his flocks. Jonah recognized him as his elder son, and the boy recognized him.

"Father," said the boy, "these sheep belong to a man from this village; come with me so that I can take them back to him." They all went to the owner of the sheep, who, when he heard that the shepherd-boy had found his father Jonah, rejoiced for him and said, "One day I was grazing my sheep when suddenly a wolf approached with this boy and spoke to me in an eloquent tongue, saying, 'This boy is given in trust to you by God.' I took him with devotion: now receive your son safe and sound."

They all went to Jonah's own city, and when the people there saw him they rejoiced. He remained among them, exhorting them to do justice and chastising them for evil, until he died.

86. *Jesus son of Mary*[119]

Wahb ibn Munabbih and Kaab al-Ahbar said: Zacharias and Amram were the children of Solomon. Zacharias' wife was named Elizabeth, and Amram's wife was named Anna. Zacharias was a carpenter before being sent as a prophet, and he was very devout. While he was in his oratory, Gabriel descended to him and greeted him, saying, "Your Lord sends you as a prophet to Israel that you may call them to worship Him." Zacharias fell to the ground prostrate. Arising, he went out to the children of Israel and called them to worship God. Some of them believed in him while others denied him, yet he remained among them.

Neither Zacharias nor Amram had been blessed with children.

One day, while Amram's wife was sitting in the house, she saw a dove brooding over her young. Anna wept and said to her husband, "Pray to God to bless us with a child."

"Rise up," he said, "perform the ablutions and pray. We will ask our Lord."

When they had prayed, they fell asleep. Amram dreamed of someone saying to him, "O Amram, God has answered your prayer. Rise up and lie with your wife, and she will conceive." So he awoke and lay with her, and she conceived a child.

"If we are blessed with a male child," said Anna, "I shall consecrate him to the temple."

"That which is in your womb is female," said her husband.

"Lord," she said, *"verily I have vowed unto thee that which is in my womb, to be dedicated to thy service: accept it therefore of me* even if it be female" (3.35). And when her time was accomplished, she gave birth to a girl and named her Mary.

When the girl was weaned, Anna took her to the temple, where she found Zacharias and one of the priests. "This is my daughter Mary," she said, "whom I have consecrated to God, and He has accepted her from me."

"This girl is small and must have someone to provide for her until she reaches maturity, when she may be a servant in the temple," said Zacharias. Then he added, "Since I am married to her aunt, I will provide for her."

The priest, however, said, "No, we will cast lots for her." They wrote their names on reed stalks, which they took and cast into the well of Seloam. As Zacharias' reed appeared on the surface of the water and the others sank, Zacharias took her and provided for her. And her father Amram died.

* * *

God caused Mary to flower into a beautiful young girl; Zacharias and Joseph, her aunt's son, used to gaze upon her. *Whenever Zacharias went into the chamber to her, he found provisions with her,* summer produce in winter and winter fruits in summer (3.37).

He said, "O Mary, whence hadst thou this?"

She answered, "This is from God."

Then he raised his hands to heaven and said, *"Lord, give me from thee a good offspring"* (3.38). Mary offered him a stalk of grapes and some dates and figs, which he ate.

Gabriel descended to him and said, "God has answered your prayer."

"Were the child with which you have made me happy to inherit the earth, I would have no need of it," he answered.

"He shall desire only the next world," said Gabriel.

Zacharias said, *"Lord, give me a sign"* (3.41).

The angel said, "Thy sign shall be, that thou shalt speak unto no man for three days, otherwise than by gesture with your lips and eyes."

* * *

When Mary reached the age of womanhood, Zacharias came in to her; and she said to him, "I have seen a horrible thing" (that is, she had begun to menstruate). So he ordered her to remain in her aunt's house until she was again pure. Then she returned to her chamber in the temple, as He hath said: *And remember in the book the story of Mary; when she retired from her family to a place towards the east, and took a veil to conceal herself from them; and we sent out spirit Gabriel unto her, and he appeared unto her in the shape of a perfect man* (19.16ff).

She said, "I fly for refuge unto the merciful God, that he may defend me from thee: if thou fearest him, thou wilt not approach me."

He answered, "Verily I am the messenger of thy Lord, and am sent to give thee a holy son."

She said, "How shall I have a son, seeing a man hath not touched me, and I am no harlot?"

Gabriel stretched out his hand toward her and breathed into her: the breath reached her womb, and she conceived Jesus. Zacharias had lain with his wife at the same time, and she conceived John. When Mary's pregnancy became evident, she feared for herself; but Gabriel descended to her and said, "Mary, God gives thee glad tidings, and thy son shall be called Christ Jesus." From that time forth she was comforted.

* * *

When Joseph the carpenter learned of her pregnancy, he said to her, "Mary, does anything grow without seed?"

"No," she answered.

"Can there be a child without a father?" he asked.

"Yes," she said, "Adam was without father or mother."

"How did you come to have the child you are carrying?" he asked.

"He is a gift from God," she said. "And he is like Adam, whom He shaped from dust and to whom He said, 'Be' and he was."

God caused Jesus to speak from his mother's womb and say, "O Joseph, what are these words that you speak?"

* * *

Zacharias went to his wife and told her of Mary's pregnancy, saying, "I fear lest the Israelites accuse her with Joseph."

"Only good shall come of it," she said.

But news of Mary's pregnancy reached even the king of Israel, whose name was Herod. To the children of Israel he said, "What is this woman of whose pregnancy I have heard from you?"

"Sire," they said, "she is possessed." And the king was quiet.

* * *

When her days were accomplished, she went out into the wilderness by night and sat under a dry tree, which became verdant for her time. God also brought forth for her a spring of clear, running water. Yet when her pains became great, she said, *"Would to God I had died before this and had become a thing forgotten, and lost in oblivion"* (19.23f).

And he who was beneath her called to her, saying, "Be not grieved: now hath God provided a rivulet under thee."

* * *

al-Dahhak said that it was Gabriel who cried out to her; Hasan said that it was her child Jesus.

* * *

She was told, "If thou see any man and he question thee, say, 'Verily I have vowed a fast unto the Merciful: wherefore I will by no means speak to a man this day'" (19.26).

Zacharias' wife gave birth that very night to a male child, and Zacharias rejoiced over him.

He went to Mary but could not find her, wherefore he called

for Joseph, and together they set out in search of her. They found her seated beneath a tree. He spoke to her, but she did not speak to him. Jesus, however, spoke and said, "O Joseph, I bring glad tidings that I have emerged from the darkness of the womb into the light of the world. I have come to the children of Israel as a messenger." Mary carried her child on her breast and looked down on the children of Israel.

Aaron, a brother from her father, called her and said, "*Thy father was not a bad man, neither was thy mother a harlot.* Where did you get this child?" (19.28).

Jesus spoke to him from the cradle and said, *"Verily I am the servant of God; he hath given me the book of the gospel, and hath appointed me a prophet. And peace be on me the day whereon I was born, and the day whereon I shall die, and the day whereon I shall be raised to life"* (19.30).

* * *

News of this reached the king, who made it clear that Mary and her son should be killed. Zacharias, fearing for them, ordered Joseph to take them to Egypt, where God might protect them from the evil of that tyrant king. So he put her on a donkey and placed her child in her lap; Zacharias gave her provisions and sent them out by night from Jerusalem on their journey.

* * *

While they were on their way, suddenly they came upon a huge lion in the middle of the road; and they were alarmed. But Jesus said to them, "Put me before him." When they sat him in front of the lion, he took hold of the lion's ear and said, "What made you sit here?"

The lion said, "O Spirit of God, I am waiting for an ox to come to me so that I can eat it."

"The ox might belong to poor people," said Jesus. "Go to such-and-such a place, where you will find a camel. Eat it and leave the ox to its owners." So the lion went off in the direction of the mountain.

* * *

They traveled until they came to a village where they found a group of people gathered about a house. "O people," said

Jesus, "you have said to yourselves that you would come to this house by night and take the property of its owner by force. Do not do it, for therein is a man who believes in God. I shall direct you to a treasure whose owner has been dead for a long time and left no heir. Take from it what will satisfy you." They agreed to this and went with him. He showed them a place and said to them, "Dig here and you will find enough treasure."

* * *

Then Jesus and his mother traveled and entered a village in which was a great king, and the people had gathered at the gate of his palace, prostrating themselves before an idol of stone. Jesus heard that the wife of the king was having great difficulty in giving birth, as half of the child had emerged and half remained. So Jesus said, "O people, go to the king and inform him that I will place my hand on her womb and she shall be delievered in haste." They went off to the king and told him.

"Bring him to me," said the king.

They brought Jesus, who said, "In your wife's womb is a beautiful boy: one of his ears is longer than the other, on his chest is a black mole, and on his stomach is a white birthmark." Jesus placed his right hand on her abdomen and said, "Come forth sound!" And she gave birth to a boy of the exact description Jesus had given.

* * *

They then traveled until they entered Egypt, where they remained for a time. One day, while Jesus was sitting with some boys who were playing, one of them, who resembled Jesus, jumped on another boy and killed him. The judge came to the boys, among whom was Jesus, and said, "Jesus, I saw you kill this boy."

"You are judging in ignorance if you say I killed him," said Jesus. "You should rather ask, 'Who killed him?' " Then Jesus drew near the slain boy and said, "Arise!" And the boy stood up.

"Who killed you?" asked Jesus.

"So-and-so son of So-and-so," he said. "You are innocent of

my blood." Thus saying, he fell down dead. They then killed his murderer.

* * *

Mary took Jesus to a teacher. The teacher asked, "What is your name?"

"Jesus," he said.

"Say the alphabet," said the teacher.

"What is the alphabet?" asked Jesus.

"I do not know," he replied.

Then said Jesus, "Get up from your place so I may sit there, and I shall teach you the explanation of the alphabet." The teacher got up, and Jesus sat down and said, "The alphabet begins with four letters, *alif, be, jim,* and *dal:*

Alif: Alláh, "God";

Be: Bahá' Alláh, "God's splendor";

Jim: Jalál Alláh, "God's awesomeness";

Dal: Dín Alláh, "God's religion";

He: Huwa Alláh, "He is God";

Waw: Waylat Alláh, "God's woe";

Zayn: Zabániyat al-káfirin, "the myrmidons of infidels";

Ḥa: Ḥiṭṭa li'l-kháṭi'in, "forgiveness for those in error";

Ṭa: shajarat Ṭúbá li'l-mu'minín, "the Tuba tree for believers";

Ya: Yad Alláh 'alá khalqihi ajma'ín, "God's hand over all of His creation";

Kaf: Kalám Alláh, "God's word";

Lam: Liqá' Alláh, "meeting God";

Mim: Málik yawm al-dín, "the king on the Day of Resurrection";

Nun: Núr Alláh, "God's light";

Sin: Sunnat Alláh, "God's path";

'Ayn: 'Ilm Alláh, "God's knowledge";

Fa: Fi'l Alláh, "God's action";

Ṣad: Ṣidq Alláh fí wa'dih, "God's sincerity in His promise";

Qaf: Qudrat Alláh, "God's might";

Ra: Rabúbiyyat Alláh, "God's divinity";

Shin: Mashí'at Alláh, "God's will";

Te: Ta'allá Alláh 'ammá yashkurún, "God is more exalted than that for which He is thanked."

Then the teacher said to him, "You have done well, Jesus." He took him to his mother and said, "Your child did not need a teacher."

* * *

Then Mary said to Jesus, "My child, I want you to go with me to the dyer so that he can teach you a trade by which you may profit."

She took him to the dyer, and the master said, "Jesus, fill this jug with water, dye these clothes and hang them on the line." However, he did not explain to him anything about the colors. So Jesus set to work dyeing the clothes, which he put into the jug and then hung on the line. When the master came and saw what Jesus had done, he said, "You have ruined me, boy, and have spoiled the people's clothes!"

"You ordered me to dye them, but you did not tell me what colors," Jesus said. Then he asked, "What is your religion?" The man said that he was a Jew. "Say there is no god but God and that I, Jesus, am His messenger, and you will take out each garment in whatever color you want," said Jesus. The dyer did this and indeed pulled out every robe in the color its owner had wanted.

* * *

The king of Israel died; and Zacharias sent to Mary and Jesus to return to Jerusalem, so they set out from Egypt, headed for Jerusalem. They went down into Nazareth (from when derives the Nazarene), and Jesus called the people to the faith.

"What proof have you of your prophecy?" they asked.

He said, *"I will make before you, of clay, as it were the figure of a bird; then I will breathe thereon, and it shall become a bird, by the permission of God; and I will heal him that hath been blind from his birth; and the leper: and I will raise the dead by the permission of God"* (3.49).

"Here is the tomb of Shem, the son of Noah," they said. "Revive him for us." (Shem was in a sarcophagus of stone.)

Jesus approached the tomb, prayed, took a vessel of water, sprinkled it on the tomb and said, "Arise, Shem, through the might of God!" And the tomb was split asunder, and Shem lept out, his hair and beard white.

"How long have you been dead?" Jesus asked.

"For four thousand years," he said. Then he added, "And when I heard the cry of Jesus, I thought that it was the Cry of Resurrection. My hair and beard turned white out of terror." Then Shem returned to his tomb, and they said, "O Jesus, you have done a marvelous thing. Tell us what we eat and what we drink." And Jesus informed each one of them what he ate and drank and what he had stored in his house and that however much it increased they became more recalcitrant.

Thereupon Jesus cursed them, and God transformed them into apes and pigs, whereafter they lived for three days and then died. The people who believed in him remained, and Jesus stayed among them until God raised him up to Himself.

* * *

He remains alive in heaven until God will give him permission to descend to wage war against the Antichrist, whom he will slay. Then he will fill the earth with justice, as it has been filled with tyranny and oppression. Then he will marry a woman from among the Arabs, and she will give birth to a child who will perform the pilgrimage and will live a long life before dying.

Then the Gog and Magog will emerge and will produce progeny in all directions, and the earth will be so filled with them that the beasts and reptiles will no longer have any place to settle. Then the children of Gog and Magog will head for Jerusalem to wage war against Jesus. And on that day they will be of three kinds, the first of which will be like towering date-palms because of their length and breadth, and they will eat the trees and fruits. The second kind will be a cubit long and a cubit wide, and they will eat the plants from the valleys. The third kind will be a span long and its ears a cubit, and they will spread one ear beneath and the other above, and they will drink all the waters. Thereupon Jesus will cry out against them, and God will send forth the demons of the genii, who will destroy them to the last.

When Jesus' forty years on the earth are accomplished, God will send to him the Angel of Death to tell him that God has not created a single creature but that it must die and that he will lay him into the tomb wherein he is to be buried. Then the Angel of Death will descend to him and will find him in the temple at Jerusalem reading the Torah, the Gospel and the Psalter. He will appear to him in the form of a man of radiant countenance and will say to him, "I have come to thee to traverse the earth with thee." Jesus will answer him and together they will set out and will walk until they see a great funeral.

"Jesus," the angel will say, "revive for us someone from this funeral so that he might inform us concerning the taste and bitterness of death."

Jesus will ask his Lord, and three men will rise up, one of whom will have a face like the moon, the second a face the color of saffron and the third a face like a black rat. Jesus will ask them concerning their circumstances in this world, and the first will say, "I was poor but grateful, and when my spirit was taken, my Lord made me enter Paradise."

The second will say, "I was very rich and thought that grace would not pass away, until I tasted the cup of death, and I am tormented in my grave until now."

The third will say, "I did not believe in one God and did not worship Him, until death came to me, and then my spirit was seized by grapples of blazing fire and I was given a draught of hot water."

Then Jesus will say to them, "Return to where you were, your Lord is all-knowing concerning him who follows His way."

Then they will come to the tomb of Muhammad, whom they will greet. He will return their salutation from the tomb.

The Angel of Death will say, "Jesus, I am the Angel of Death, come to thee to take thy spirit, for every created thing must die." Then Gabriel will come to him, bringing musk from Paradise, and will hand it to Jesus, who will take it and smell it. And his spirit will be taken up in the musk. Then the angels will descend to him and will wash and prepare him for burial. Then they will bury him beside Muhammad's tomb.

And when God shall say unto Jesus, at the last day, "O Jesus son of Mary, hast thou said unto men, 'Take me and my mother for two gods, besides God?'" He shall answer, "Praise be unto thee, it is not for me to say that which I ought not" (5.116f). Then God will send an aromatic fragrance by which the Angel of Death will take the spirits of the believers, and the Koran and the banner will be raised up.

Then, at sunrise on Friday, shall the Last Hour begin.

Notes to the Text

1. ʿAbdullāh ibn ʿAbbās (d. 687), known as the "father of Koranic exegesis," is credited with the first philologically oriented Koranic interpretation. It will be seen throughout this work that almost all citations made by Kisāʾī that do not quote Wahb ibn Munabbih or Kaʿb al-Aḥbār directly refer either to Ibn ʿAbbās or to one of his students, Mujāhid, ʿIkrima, Saʿīd ibn Jubayr, Qatāda or Ḍaḥḥāk. See *EI*[2], I, 40f; Sezgin, *GAS*, I, 26.

2. Kaʿb al-Aḥbār ibn Mātiʿ, Abū Isḥāq (d. ca. 652), originally a Yemenite Jew converted to Islam in the early days of the orthodox caliphate, was the oldest authority for Jewish traditions among the Muslims and teacher of Ibn ʿAbbās (n. 1) and Abū Hurayra (see n. 10). His title, "aḥbār" (< Aramaic *ḥaber*), denoted a scholar of somewhat lower rank than "rabbi" among Babylonian Jews. See *EI*[1], II, 582f; Sezgin, *GAS*, I, 304f.

3. The "Canopy" (*ʿarsh*) and "Throne" (*kursī*) of God are sometimes translated as "throne" and "footstool" respectively. It is clear from this passage, as well as from what is known of the structure of oriental thrones, that two distinct parts are meant: the *kursī* is a raised platform on which the king sits, the *ʿarsh* a vaulted canopy that covers the *kursī,* hence the reference to the *ʿarsh* as covering the *kursī* and the heavens as a roof over the earth. The "Throne-verse" (Koran 2:255) is held in particular reverence by Muslims and is often inscribed as a charm on jewelry: "God! there is no God but he; the living, the self-subsisting: neither slumber nor sleep seizeth him; to him belongeth whatsoever is in heaven, and on earth. Who is he that can intercede with him, but through his good pleasure? He knoweth that which is past, and that which is to come unto them, and they shall not comprehend any thing of his knowledge, but so far as he pleaseth. His throne is extended over heaven and earth, and the preservation of both is no burden unto him. He is the high, the mighty." See also p. 31 below.

4. Wahb ibn Munabbih, Abū ʿAbdullāh (ca. 656–ca. 730), a celebrated authority on the traditions of the Himyarite kingdom of South Arabia, ancient Israel and Christianity, was born near Sanaa, Yemen. His mother was a descendant of the Himyarite kings and

his father was of the *abnā'*, the descendants of the Persian soldiers sent to the Yemen by Chosroës Anushirvan. Works attributed to Ibn Munabbih include a *Kitāb al-mubtada'* (Book of Creation) on biblical legend from which the *Qiṣaṣ al-anbiyā'* attributed to him was probably later extracted, *Kitāb al-mulūk al-mutawwaja min Ḥimyar &c.* on the South Arabian kings, a translation of the Psalms of David into Arabic, and *Ḥikmat Wahb,* a collection of wisdom literature related by Wahb's nephew. See *EI*[1], IV, 1084f; R. G. Khoury, *Wahb.*

5. Abū Dharr al-Ghifārī, famous traditionist (*muḥaddith*) and Companion to the Prophet Muhammad noted for humility and asceticism. See *EI*[2], I, 144.

6. Mount Qāf. The name of this mountain is often connected with the first verse of Koran 50 "Qāf wa'l-Qur'āni l-majīd" as well as being the name of the twentieth letter of the alphabet, "*q.*" When Dhū'l-Qarnayn/Alexander reached the limit of the earth, he queried Mount Qāf on the smaller mountains that surround it and was told that they are Qāf's "veins" and that when one of these veins is moved it causes earthquakes in that region of the earth connected to it (Tha'labī, *Qiṣaṣ,* p. 4).

7. Tha'labī (*Qiṣaṣ,* p. 6) gives the following schemata of the seven earths from Ibn Munabbih: (1) Adīma, (2) Basīṭa, (3) Thaqīla, (4) Baṭīḥa, (5) Mutathāqila, (6) Māsika, (7) Tharā (< Koran 20.6). Of the names given by Kisā'ī, several accord with names from Jewish legend, such as Ḥeled-Khalada, Arḳa-Arqa, Ḥarabah-Ḥaraba (see Ginzberg, *Legends,* I, 10f).

8. The configuration of the world resting on the bull, which in turn rests on the fish, is admirably illustrated in an allegorical painting of the Mughal Emperor Jahangir by Abū'l-Ḥasan, ca. 1620 (Chester Beatty Library, Dublin, MS. 7, No. 15) reproduced in Bamber Gascoigne, *The Great Moghuls* (New York: Harper & Row, 1971), p. 153.

9. The "name" of the Behemoth is Lawatyā (= Leviathan, see Job 41:1), and it is known (*kunya*) as Balhūt and Bahamūt (= Behemoth, see Job 40:15); see Tha'labī, *Qiṣaṣ,* p. 4. The Behemoth is also known as the "Nūn" (< Syriac *nūnā,* "fish"), whence it is often connected to the opening verse of Koran 48, "Nūn wa'l-qalam" (Tha'labī, *Qiṣaṣ,* p. 5; Ṭabarī, *Tārīkh,* I, 52). As "*nūn*" is also the name of the letter "n," the Behemoth is sometimes connected with the saying "Bayna kāf wa-nūn" ("between 'K' and 'N' = *kun!* "Be!", the divine creative fiat); see Maqdisī, *Bad',* I, 147. It is told that the Leviathan was almost seduced by Iblīs to throw the world off its

back and thus rid itself of such a burden when God sent an insect into its nostril and, by threatening it with a return of the insect, extracted a promise from the beast that it would contemplate no further disobedience (Tha'labī, *Qiṣaṣ*, p. 4; Maqdisī, *Bad'*, II, 49).

10. Abū Hurayra al-Dawsī al-Yamanī, Companion to the Prophet and prolific narrator of tradition especially from 'Abdullāh ibn Salām (see n. 12), died ca. 678. See *EI*², I, 129.

11. The names and properties of the seven heavens are given variously: as here by Kisā'ī they are (1) Birqi', emerald (*zumurruda khaḍrā'*); (2) Faydūm, ruby (*yāqūta ḥamrā'*); (3) 'Awn, topaz (*yāqūta ṣafrā*); (4) Arqalūn, silver (*fiḍḍa*); (5) Ratqā (< Koran 21:30), red gold (*dhahab aḥmar*); (6) Rafqā (< Koran 21:30), white pearl (*durra bayḍā'*); (7) Gharibyā, shimmering light (*nūr yatala'la'*). The tradition given by Tha'labī (*Qiṣaṣ*, 11) from Ibn Munabbih is as follows (1) Dīnāḥ, (2) Dīqā, (3) Raqī', (4) Fīlūn, (5) Ṭifṭāf, (6) Simsāq, (7) Isḥāqā'īl; the tradition given from Ḍaḥḥāk and Muqātil is: (1) Birqi'ā, iron; (2) Qīdūm, copper; (3) al-Mā'ūn, brass (? *ka-lawni l-shabah*); (4) Fīlūn, white silver; (5) al-Lāḥqūq, gold; (6) 'Ārūs, red ruby; (7) al-Raqī', white pearl, above which is a region called Marhūthā inhabited by the archangels.

12. 'Abdullāh ibn Salām (d. 664), originally a Jew from Medina, converted to Islam after the Hegira. He related biblical narratives later incorporated by Ṭabarī into his *Tārīkh*. Among his pupils was Abū Hurayra (see n. 10). See *EI*², I, 54.

13. 'Ā'isha bint Abī Bakr, daughter of Abū Bakr the first "orthodox" Caliph, third and favorite wife of the Prophet, was born at Mecca ca. 614 and died at Medina in 678. She related tradition and was noted for her knowledge of poetry and Arab history and for her eloquence. See *EI*², I, 307f.

14. The "Visited House" (*al-bayt al-ma'mūr*) is the heavenly prototype of the Kaaba. Ibn 'Arabī gives the following report (*Muḥāḍarat al-abrār*, I, 400f): "Some say it is in the sixth heaven, others in the seventh. Ibn 'Abbās said: 'There are fourteen houses such that if the topmost one were to fall it would fall on the one beneath it, and likewise all the houses down through the seven heavens and seven earths. God has made there creatures to circumambulate after our own likeness (*'alā ṣuwarinā*); there is even an Ibn 'Abbās there like me. Every day seventy thousand angels enter the Visited House, but they never again return to it.'" A separate tradition (*ibid.*, 401) on these angels is quoted from Abū Zayd al-Suhaylī's *al-Rawḍ al-ānif*: "Every day Gabriel plunges once into the River of Life; and when he shakes himself dry, seventy thousand drops of water fall

from him. From these drops God creates angels who enter the Visited House." On the origin of the custom of circumambulating the Kaaba, the following tradition is given (*ibid.*, 401f) from 'Alī ibn Abī Ṭālib: "When God said to the angels, '*I am going to place a substitute on earth*'; *they said, 'Wilt thou place there one who will do evil therein, and shed blood?* [Koran 2:30] O Lord, make that substitute from among us, for we will do no evil, neither will we shed blood or indulge in hatred, envy or sedition. *But we celebrate thy praise and sanctify thee* [Koran 2:30] and will obey thee always.' God answered: '*Verily I know that which ye know not* [Koran 2:30].' Therefore the angels suspected that they might have spoken in contradiction of God and that He was angry with them, so they sought refuge at the foot of the Throne, raised their heads and held out their hands, humbly weeping for forgiveness. They circumambulated the Throne for three hours, after which God gazed mercifully upon them: He placed beneath the Throne a house on four emerald pillars covered with ruby and called the house "al-Ḍirāḥ." Then God said to the angels, "Circumambulate this house and leave the Throne." The angels therefore began to circumambulate that house instead of the Throne and found that it was easier, and this is the Visited House of which it is said that every day and night seventy thousand angels enter it but never return." See also p. 62 below.

15. The *dhikr* is a pious "recollection" or "remembrance" practice during which one or a number of the Names of God (see note 46) are recited, either silently or aloud, by those present. Among mystics the *dhikr* is considered a means of inducing a mystical state of ecstasy.

16. 'Illiyyīn, Sijjīn. Both words are Koranic: see 83:18f. and 83.7f.

17. The *'Īd al-Fiṭra* marks the end of the month of fasting, Ramaḍān (see note 58). This feast is observed on the first day of Shawwāl. *Yawm al-Aḍḥā*, the "Day of Sacrifice," is one of the concluding acts of the pilgrimage to Mecca, during which the pilgrims sacrifice a lamb in commemoration of the sacrifice of the ram by Abraham in place of his son Isaac (story found in §54); it is observed on the tenth of the month of Dhū'l-Ḥijja and is also called *Yawm al-naḥr*.

18. Of the seven words used for the gates of Hell, Gehenna (Arabic *jahannam*) is the only one taken from Hebrew/Aramaic sources (see Ginzberg, *Legends*, I, 15); the rest are words meaning "flame" and are taken from the Koran. *Jaḥīm* as the special abode of the Jews, Christians and Magians, the so-called "people of the book" or those who had previously received divine revelations, is probably taken from Koranic references to those who deny the divine origin

of the Koran (see, e.g., 5:10, 5:86, 22:51, 57:19). These words have been studied by T. O'Shaughnessy, "The Seven Names."

19. Mārij: taken from a misunderstanding of Koran 55:15, "wa-khalaqa l-jānna min mārijin min nār" ("he created the genii of fire clear from smoke"), where "*al-jānn*" ("the genii") and "*mārij*" ("smokeless fire") were both taken to be proper names, thus rendering the meaning of the passage 'he created al-Jann from Marij out of fire."

20. See note 23 below.

21. Such anatomical descriptions are fairly representative of the type of literature generally included in the "wonders of creation" genre. It is on the basis of such references that the author of this *Qiṣaṣ al-anbiyā'* has been identified with the author of *'Ajā'ib al-makhlūqāt*. See Introduction, p. xxxiii, n. 29.

22. Ja'far ibn Muḥammad al-Ṣādiq, Abū 'Abdullāh (700–765), Fifth Imam of the Ismailis, Sixth Imam of the Twelver Shia and teacher of Jurisprudence par excellence, whence his epithet "Ṣādiq" ("the truthful"). An authority on Tradition, he lived quietly in Medina. Like Pope Sylvester, however, later tradition has attributed him with occult knowledge, and he figures prominently in the Hermetic tradition. See *EI*², II, 374f.

23. It is of significance that Iblis is not, as is his Christian counterpart Satan, originally an angel who placed himself in opposition to God and consequently fell from grace. The Islamic view of angels holds that they possess no will of their own but, according to the doctrine of angelic impeccability, are able merely to execute God's bidding; they are, therefore, incapable of such a willful act of disobdience to God's command as that of Iblis. By maintaining his absolute but mistaken devotion and fidelity to God alone, Iblis refused to obey God's command, although, as his act has been interpreted, he was involuntarily obedient to God's eternal will and knowledge, inasmuch as He had willed before all time that Iblis *not* bow down to Adam, in contradistinction to His command that he do obeisance. "God can *command* a thing and yet *will* that it not be, and He can *will* a thing be and *command* it not to be: He *commanded* Iblis to bow down to Adam but *willed* that he not bow down; had He willed it, he would have necessarily obeyed. He *forbade* Adam to eat of the tree but *willed* that he eat; had He willed that he not eat, he would not have eaten" (Kulaynī, *al-Uṣūl*, I, 151). As expressed by the martyr-mystic Ḥusayn ibn Manṣūr al-Ḥallāj, executed in Baghdad in 922, Iblis was like a man bound hand and foot and cast into the sea while being admonished not to get wet! Because Iblis was incapable of recognizing the divine part of man

to which he was bade prostrate himself, the later mystics dubbed him "the absolute monotheist" and "the one-eyed." For a comparative study, see Jung, *Fallen Angels*.

24. See note 52.

25. Adam, who was shaped and fashioned by God's own hand, was unlike any other creature, for the rest of creation had been brought into existence by God's creative word, "Kun!" (Be!). See note 9 and Introduction, p. xx.

26. ʿAlī ibn Abī Ṭālib, cousin and son-in-law of the Prophet, fourth orthodox caliph of Islam, First Imam of the Shia. See *EI*[2], I, 381ff.

27. In every instance the Arabic *awḥā Allāh ilā* has been translated as "God spoke to" or "God said to," although it should be noted that throughout this work the verb proper for "to say" or "to speak" ("*qāl*") is employed with reference to God only to introduce a quotation from the Koran, which is, according to Muslim belief, the direct and unaltered Word of God, communicated to the Prophet Muhammad through the intermediacy of the Archangel Gabriel. God does not "speak" to human beings or even to angels; He "causes an inspiration" (*awḥā*) to them.

28. The Burāq is a fabled animal, generally depicted from late medieval times on with the body of a winged horse and a human head, on which the Prophet Muhammad ascended into heaven on his Night Journey (*miʿrāj*).

29. Riḍwān. The word occurs in the Koran (e.g. 9:21, 72) generally in connection with Paradise, where the normal interpretation is that it means "acceptance (into God's Paradise)." Here, however, it has been interpreted as the name of the "gatekeeper of heaven." See below p. 38f.

30. Maymūn, literally "felicitous," is the name given to Adam's horse.

31. The Ṭūbā tree. The name derives from Koran 13:29: "They who believe and do that which is right shall enjoy blessedness [*ṭūbā*], and partake of a happy resurrection," where the word "*ṭūbā*" has been interpreted by many of the commentators as the name of a tree in Paradise. See below p. 91.

32. The names of these two angels, Hārūt and Mārūt, derive from the Harvotat and Amurtat of the Avesta, although their function is identical to that of Shemhazi and Azael in Jewish legend. See Horovitz, *KU*, 146ff; Margoliouth, "Harut and Marut."

33. For the story of Idrīs see §38 and note 72, below.

34. *Rakʿa* is a cycle of Muslim prayer, consisting of (1) a statement of intention, (2) ritual sanctification, (3) standing in the pos-

ture of prayer, (4) recitation from the Koran, (5) bowing, (6) prostration, and (7) pronouncement of peace. This type of liturgical prayer, to be accomplished five times daily, is called *ṣalāt* and is to be distinguished from *du'ā'*, extemporaneous or intercessory prayer (see note 36).

35. All the things and places mentioned here in connection with Iblis are either expressly forbidden in the Koran or highly disapproved by Islamic mores.

36. Essentially the same three aspects of man's relationship to God are found in a report in Ibn Qutayba's *'Uyūn al-Akhbār* (II, 277f.), "The Prophet of God said, 'Your Lord said, "Three: one for me, one for you, O son of Adam, and one between you and me. As for the one that is for me, you will be sincere to me and associate nothing with me. As for the one that is for you, I shall recompense you for your deeds. As for the one that is between you and me, you make invocation (*du'ā'*) and I am obliged to respond." '" Note here that God's obligation to respond to an invocation is stressed (*minka l-du'ā'u wa-'alayya l-ijābatu*).

37. *al-Mu'awwidhatayn*, chapters 113 and 114 of the Koran, called the "two cries for refuge and protection" and considered to have talismanic effect: "[113] Say, I fly for refuge unto the Lord of the daybreak, * that he may deliver me from the mischief of those things which he hath created; * and from the mischief of the night, when it cometh on; * and from the mischief of women blowing on knots; * and from the mischief of the envious, when he envieth. [114] Say, I fly for refuge unto the Lord of men, * the king of men, * the God of men, * that he may deliver me from the mischief of the whisperer who slyly withdraweth, * who whispereth evil suggestions into the breasts of men; * from genii and men."

38. *al-Ikhlās,* chapter 112 of the Koran, held in particular veneration by Muslims: "Say, God is one God; * the eternal God: * he begetteth not, neither is he begotten * and there is not any one like unto him."

39. 'Amr ibn al-'Āṣ (d. ca. 42/663), one of the wiliest of early Muslim politicians, led the conquering forces of Islam into Egypt. Because of his involvement in the political issues of early Islam, he is quoted as an authority in the *ḥadīth* literature. See *EI*², I, 451.

40. Adam is also said to have descended to a place in India called Dahnā, or variously to a mountain called Bawdh (Ṭabarī, *Tārīkh*, I, 121f). Maysān, where Iblis fell, is a district between Basra and Wasit (Yāqūt, *Mu'jam al-buldān*, VIII, 224). The Pico de Adam,

(Adam's Footprint) atop a mountain in Ceylon (= Serendip) is described by travelers (see Sale, *The Alcoran,* p. 5, note f).

41. "When God said to Adam, 'O Adam, thy Lord has mercy upon thee,' Adam put his hand on top of his head and moaned. 'What is the matter, Adam?' asked God. 'I have committed a sin,' replied Adam. 'Why do you think that?' asked God. 'Because,' said Adam, 'mercy is for sinners.' And thus it became a practice (*sunna*) among Adam's children that, whenever any of them is afflicted with misfortune or tribulation, they put their hands on their head and moan" (Tha'labī, *Qiṣaṣ*, p. 24).

42. Qatāda ibn Di'āma ibn Qatāda al-Sadūsī, Abū'l-Khaṭṭāb (679–736), Koranic comentator, jurisprudent and authority on poetry. genealogy and ancient Arabian history, student of Ibn 'Abbās. See Sezgin, *GAS,* I, 31f.

43. Sa'īd ibn al-Musayyib, Abū Muḥammad (634–713), authority on genealogy, history and tradition; see Sezgin, *GAS*, I, 276.

44. Makḥūl ibn Abī Muslim Shuhrāb al-Dimashqī (d. between 730 and 737) transmitted tradition from 'Ā'isha (see note 13) and Abū Hurayra (see note 10) and was a source for Muḥammad ibn Isḥāq. 'Ikrima (d. 723) was a student of Ibn 'Abbās. Muḥammad ibn al-Ḥanafiyya (638–700) was a son of 'Alī ibn Abī Ṭālib (see note 26) and Khawla; see *EI*[1], III, 671.

45. Mujāhid ibn Jabr al-Makkī, Abū'l-Ḥajjāj (d. 722), was a student of Ibn 'Abbās who consulted Jews and Christians for information on the biblical legends.

46. Beautiful Names (*al-asmā' al-ḥusnā*), the ninety-nine names, or attributes, of God found in the Koran. The hundredth is the secret Great Name, the Tetragrammaton of the Hebraic Cabalistic tradition, for which in Islam see p. 243 below, and G. Anawati, "Nom suprême."

47. 'Abdullāh ibn 'Umar, teacher of Sa'īd ibn Jubayr and Mujāhid; see Sezgin, *GAS*, I, 28f.

48. The stoning of the devil (*rajm al-shayṭān*) forms part of the pilgrimage ritual. Pilgrims gather stones at Arafat and bring them to Mina, where pillars set up to represent Satan are pelted. From this comes Satan's epithet "al-Rajīm" ("the stoned one").

49. *Qibla*, the direction of the Kaaba in Mecca, towards which all Muslims in all parts of the world turn in prayer.

50. The "people of the left" (*aṣḥāb al-shimāl*): the reference to the "people of the left" as the damned is Koranic, see Koran 56:41, as opposed to the elect, the "people on the right" (*aṣḥāb al-yamīn*), see Koran 56:27 &c.

51. The depiction of all the as yet uncreated souls of human kind marshalled forth to bear witness to their acknowledgment of God as their unqualified lord made a tremendous impact on all Islamic literary expressions that derived inspiration from the writings of the great masters of mysticism, who called this "day" in preeternity when this event took place "*rūz-i alast*" ("the day of *alast*") or "*bazm-i alast*" ("the banquet of *alast,*" after the initial word of God's question, "Am I not your Lord? [*alastu bi-rabbikum*]").

52. The major prophets in Islam have fixed epithets that refer to their primary function or some aspect of their relationship to God: Adam is known as *Ṣafwatullāh* ("chosen by God"); Moses as *Kalīmullāh* ("conversant with God," < Koran 4:164), referring to the conversation Moses had with God on Mount Sinai; Abraham as *Khalīlullāh* ("friend to God," < Koran 4:125), cf. 2 Ch. 20:7, "*Abraham ohebak*", and Jas. 2:23, "*philos*"; Ishmael as *Sādiqul-wa'd* ("he who is true to his promise," <Koran 19:54), Isaac as *Dhabīḥullāh* ("sacrificed to God"); Jacob as *Isrā'īliyyullāh* ("Israelite of God," see Gen. 32:28, "Thy name shall be called no more Jacob, but Israel"), Joseph as *Ṣiddīqullāh* ("true friend of" or "devoted to God") because of his sincerity in worshipping God; Jesus as *Wajīhullāh* ("respected by God") and also *Ḥabībullāh* ("beloved of God'); Muhammad is generally simply *al-Muṣṭafā* ("the chosen") although he too is called *Ḥabībullāh.*

53. The words given are: "Labbayka, labbayka, lā sharīka laka, labbayka. Inna laka l-ḥamdu wa'l-ni'matu wa'l-mulku. Lā sharīka laka, labbayka." For variants see Muḥammad ibn Ḥabīb, *Kitāb al-muḥabbar,* 311f.

54. Sa'īd ibn Jubayr (665–714), one of the earliest commentators on the Koran and student of Ibn 'Abbās and 'Abdullāh ibn 'Umar.

55. Presumably the meaning is that the cock's feet, like a bull's, are small in relation to the size of its body.

56. "al-Ḥārith" ("the tiller of the soil"). The concept reflects the antiagricultural prejudice of presedentary nomads; cf. the hostility between Cain, the "tiller of the ground [*'obed adamah*]," and Abel, the "keeper of sheep" (Gen. 4:2). In Islam, this epithet of Iblīs is difficult to reconcile with the prophetic *ḥadīth,* "Aṣdaqu l-asmā'i l-ḥārithu li'anna l-ḥāritha huwa l-kāsib" ("The truest name is al-Ḥārith because the tiller of the soil is one who works to gain his livelihood," see Ibn Manẓūr, *Lisān al-'arab,* s.v. ḤRTH). Another tradition is interpolated by Nuwayrī, who gives the name of the child as 'Abd Shams ("Slave of Sun"), as Iblīs had promised that the child would live so long as the sun continued to rise and set

(Nuwayrī, *Nihāyat al-arab,* XIII, 30); cf. Abraham's search for the deity, p. 138 below.

57. The name here read as Siboë (Sībawayh) is a variant reading of the "Shabūba" given in Ṭabarī, *Tārīkh,* I, 145f., where the known names of Adam and Eve's sons are listed as Qayyin (Cain, note that the name follows the Hebrew Kayin and not the normal Arabic Qābīl), Hābīl (Abel), Shīth (Seth), Abād, Bālagh, Athathī, Tawba, Bannān, Shabūba, Hayyān, Darābīs, Hadhar, Yaḥūr, Sandal, and Bāraq; their daughters' names, insofar as are known, are Hazūra, Labūdhā, and Ashūth, to which we might add Kelimath (see note 60).

58. Ramaḍān, the ninth month of the Islamic lunar calendar during which Muslims fast from sun-up to sun-down and during which supererogatory acts of piety are considered especially efficatious. According to tradition, on the first day of Ramaḍān the gates of heaven are opened and the gates of Hell are shut; on the third, scripture was revealed to Abraham; on the fourth, the Koran was revealed to Muhammad; on the seventh, the Torah was revealed to Moses; on the eighth, the Gospel was revealed to Jesus (Qazwīnī, *'Ajā'ib al-makhlūqāt,* I, 117).

59. As in Psalm 119, each phrase or epithet begins with the letter of the alphabet, e.g. *alif – anā Allāh, bā' – badī' al-samawāt, tā' – tawaḥḥada, thā' – thābit,* &c. Such acrostics or "Golden Alphabets" are common in the Semitic tradition and spread throughout the Islamic world; they were particularly popular in the regional languages of Muslim India, where they are known as *"sī-ḥarfī."* See also p. 204 & 332.

60. The reason for this contest by sacrifice between the two brothers is given by many extrabiblical sources as follows: Cain and his twin sister, Lebuda, were conceived in Paradise before the Fall of Adam and Eve and were therefore the most beautiful of all their children, while Abel and his sister, Kelimath, were conceived on earth. Likewise, all the children of Adam and Eve were born in male and female pairs. The sons could marry any of their sisters except their twins. When Adam proposed to marry Cain, who considered himself superior to Abel, to Kelimath, who was not favored with any beauty, and Abel to the beautiful Lebuda, Cain refused to have any but his own twin in marriage. This was the bone of contention Adam suggested they let God resolve by means of burnt offerings. *Cherchez la femme!* The names of the twin sisters are sometimes reversed, but the legend remains the same in all sources; see e.g., Rappoport, *Myth and Legend*, I, 193ff; the Syriac *Me'ārath*

gazzē, text pp. 34–37, Budge trs. p. 69; Ṭabarī, *Tārīkh*, I, 145; Tha'-labī, *Qiṣaṣ*, 37; Grünbaum, *Neue Beiträge*, 69f; Lidzbarski, *Legenda*, 11.

61. The first two *bayts* are also found in Ṭabarī, *Tārīkh*, I, 145.

62. Hibatullāh, literally "gift of God" = Theodore, Deusdedit, &c.

63. *Sidrat al-muntahā*, the "heavenly lote-tree," Koran 53:14, 16. This tree, said to stand in the seventh heaven on the right hand of the Throne of God, is called *al-muntahā*, "of the limit," because it is the boundary beyond which even the angels do not pass. "Pearl" (*jawhar*) can also be rendered "substance, essence (*ousía*)."

64. Dark mole, a foreshadowing of the sign of prophecy detected in the Prophet Muhammad by the Syrian monk Baḥīrā.

65. The tradition does not seem to be "canonical."

66. For similar descriptions of the believer dying with sweat on his brow see Wensinck, *Handbook*, 53.

67. For 'Illiyyīn and Sijjīn see note 16.

68. "Firm handhold" (*al-'urwa al-wuthqā*), see Koran 2:256 and 31.22.

69. In Christian legendary material such as the *Me'ārath gazzē*, Adam requests Seth to bury his body in the Cave of Treasures (*me'ārath gazzē*), where it is to remain until such time as the sons of Seth leave the sacred land. Accordingly, it was taken from the cave by Moses and subsequently reinterred on Golgotha, the "centre of the world," "for in that place shall redemption be effected for me and for all my children," in the words of Adam's testament. As this could have little significance for a Muslim audience, Adam's sepulchre is taken away by Noah, who later replaces it "where he found it." The word used for the "Ark" of the Covenant (*tābūt*) later in the tales is also used for Adam's sepulchre and for the ark in which Moses was set afloat in the Nile, thus providing a basis for continuity throughout the tales that cannot be reproduced in English.

70. Imām, the leader of the Muslim communal prayer. For the Friday midday prayer, males congregate in the mosque and are led in prayer by the imam.

71. The Great Exaltation (*takbīr*), the pronouncement of *Allāhu akbar* ("God is great"). The *takbīr* is normally pronounced four times over the dead.

72. In Jewish lore Enoch underwent a change that transformed him into Metatron, the recording angel and Prince of the World (*sar ha-'olam*) see Rappoport, *Myth and Legend*, I, 44ff. In Islamic lore as Idrīs (the name seems to be derived from the Greek form of Ezra, Esdras, or from Andreas, Alexander the Great's cook who

gained immortality by accidentally falling into the Fountain of Eternal Youth) the figure incorporates attributes both of Enoch and of Hermes Trismegistos. See Horovitz, *KU*, 88f.

73. Cf. Gen. 6:4, "There were giants in the earth in those days; and also after that, when the sons of God [*benai ha-elohim*] came in unto the daughters of men [*banot ha-adam*], and they bare children to them, the same became mighty men which were of old, men of renown." See also Grünbaum, *Neue Beiträge*, 74.

74. Wadd . . . Nasr] The names of these five idols are mentioned in Koran 71:23 as the idols of Noah's people, although the commentators say that they were worshipped by the ancient Arabs after the Deluge. See also p. 93 below.

75. Ibn al-Azhari] Not identifiable in available sources.

76. The three kings, Darmesel, Julian and Tophredius, none of whom is mentioned in the Noah legend by Ṭabarī or Tha'labī, seem to have been interpolated by Kisā'ī. The description of Darmesel as "the first to drink wine, gamble, sit on thrones, commission work in iron, brass and lead, and to adopt clothing spun with gold" accords with the descriptions of Jabal, Jubal and Tubalcain (Gen. 4:20–22). "Lamel" may be Lamech son of Methusael (Gen. 4:18), [great-grand] son of Enoch son of Cain; Darmesel is in any case of the offspring of the iniquitous Cainites, known for their godlessness, particularly for playing on musical instruments, devices of the devil. In the *Me'ārath gazzē* (pp. 60ff.) there is detailed description of the "lascivious frenzy" to which men and women were stirred up by "the devilish playing of the reeds which emitted musical sounds, and by the harps which the men played through the operation of the power of the devils" (trs. Budge, p. 87f.). The name Darmesel (**DRMSYL*) is probably a corruption of the Hebrew *Darmesheki* ("Damascene"); it is found in a genealogy of Japheth's wife in Ṭabarī, *Tārīkh*, I, 202; Huart (*Le Livre de la création*, III, 13 and 28) renders the name "Aldermasila." "Julian" (*Yūlīn*) could be a mistranscription of any number of names; Julian the Apostate is generally called Yūlyānūs and was known to Muslims as a godless, tyrannical king, as was Diocletian (normally Diqliṭyānūs, whom "Tophredius" [**ṬFRDYWS*] may represent).

77. The wives of Noah and Lot are mentioned in the Koran (66:10): "God propoundeth as a similitude unto the unbelievers, the wife of Noah, and the wife of Lot: they were under two of our righteous servants, and they deceived them both; wherefore their husbands were of no advantage unto them at all, in the sight of God: and it shall be said unto them at the last day, Enter ye into

hell fire, with those who enter therein." The commentators generally give the name of Noah's wife as Wā'ila and that of Lot's wife as Wāhila, although sometimes reversed. See p. 157f.

78. The "Eighty" in Arabic (*thamānūn*) derives from a miscomprehension of the Syriac *qrīth tmānōn* ("village of the eight") after the eight people in the ark. Cf. *Me'ārath gazzē* (text, p. 102): "Bnaw qrīthā wa-qraw shmāh Tmānōn 'al shem tmānā naphshīn da-npaqw men qābūthā" ("They built a village and called its name Tmanon after the eight people who came out of the ark"). Tha'labī (*Qiṣaṣ*, 51) says that the place was called Sūq Thamānīn ("Market of the Eighty") after the eighty persons who had believed in Noah and were taken on the ark.

79. Tubba' was the title of a powerful Himyarite king, usually identified as Abū Karb As'ad, the first to introduce Judaism into the Yemen, about seven hundred years prior to the time of Muhammad (see Sale, *Alcoran*, p. 403, note "m"). The name is mentioned in Koran 44:37 and 50:14.

80. Cf. the "Barren Wind" with the "Wind Flood" in Budge, *Cave of Treasures*, pp. 139ff.

81. Kānūh ibn 'Ubayd is not the name usually given for Ṣāliḥ's father. As in Tha'labī (*Qiṣaṣ*, p. 58), the father of Ṣāliḥ is named 'Ubayd b. Āsif b. Māsiḥ b. Ḥādhir b. Thamūd, whence the prophet is normally called Ṣāliḥ ibn 'Ubayd.

82. The "Lords of al-Rass" (*aṣḥāb al-rass*) are mentioned twice in the Koran, 25:38 and 50:12. The commentators give various vague accounts of this tribe; see Sale, *Alcoran*, p. 299, note "a."

83. Ṭabarī (*Tārīkh*, I, 233) mentions "al-Hāṣir" as one of the names of Nebuchadnezzar. The genealogy established here is highly confused (cf. 1 Ch. 1:8–10), and the episode seems to have been interpolated by al-Kisā'ī.

84. The original name, perhaps even Apollo (cf. the legend of St. George in Tha'labī, *Qiṣaṣ*, pp. 386ff.), has been garbled beyond recognition through successive mistranscriptions.

85. As Abraham figures as the prototype of the monotheist, the first to establish truly monotheistic worship, neither Jew nor Christian, and hence "the first Muslim," Gabriel is said to have given him the "nectar of Unity (*tawḥīd*)."

86. "Ūshā" is probably a mistranscription: Ṭabarī (*Tārīkh*, I, 310) gives the name of Abraham's mother variously as Tūtā bint Karīnā (read Karnabā) ibn Kūthī of the offspring of Arphaxad, Anmūtā of the offspring of Ephraim son of Reu son of Peleg son of Eber,

and Anmutalī bint Yakfūr or Nakfūr (= Emtelai daughter of Carnebo, see Rappoport, *Myth and Legend,* I, 226).

87. Hāla: Ṭabarī (*Tārīkh,* I, 314) gives her name as al-Sayyida bint Muḍāḍ ibn 'Amr al-Jurhumī and the names of the children as in Gen. 25:13.

88. "Al-Mu'tafikāt," literally "the overturned ones," is the name given ex post facto to Sodom and Gomorrah in accordance with their fate. The term occurs in Koran 9:70 and 69:9.

89. See note 77.

90. *'Āshūrā'* is the tenth day of the month of Muḥarram, first month of the lunar year, the day whereon the martyrdom of the Prophet Muhammad's grandson Ḥusayn ibn 'Alī at Kerbala is commemorated. The Shiite sect have adopted this day as a special day of mourning for the redemptive suffering of Ḥusayn. Other events said to have taken place on the tenth of Muḥarram are that God bestowed repentance upon Adam; Noah's ark came to rest on Mount Judi; Abraham, Moses, and Jesus were born; Abraham was saved from the fire; Jonah's people were released from torment; Job's affliction was ended; Jacob's sight was restored; Joseph was rescued from the well; Solomon was given his kingdom; Zacharias' prayer for a son was answered; and Moses gained victory over the magicians (Qazwīnī, *'Ajā'ib al-makhlūqāt,* I, 114).

91. See note 17.

92. The two "sacrificial lambs" are Ishmael, in Isaac's stead, and 'Abdullāh, father of the Prophet Muhammad, who died during the Prophet's infancy, according to Fārābī, *Kitāb al-milla,* p. 100 and Maqdisī, *al-Bad' wa'l-Tārīkh,* IV, 114. There has been a dispute in Islamic sources from the beginning over *which* of Abraham's sons, Ishmael or Isaac, was to be sacrificed. The Koranic account of this episode (37:102–107), wherein the name of the son is not given, is followed (112f.) by the birth of Isaac. Many have claimed that the "sacrificial lamb" (*dhabīḥ*) was Ishmael, who, as progenitor of the Arabs, is given precedence over Isaac, progenitor of the Jews.

93. In Ṭabarī (*Tārīkh,* i, 317), in agreement with the Biblical narrative (Gen. 30), after marrying the two sisters Leah and Rachel, Jacob took their two slave-girls, Zilpah and Bilhah, as concubines (Arabic, *surriyya,* understood by Kisā'ī as a proper name). Kisā'ī may also have taken *surriyya* to be *sirriyya* ("mysterious one"), upon which reading he elaborated the episode of the mysterious "veiled lady" whom Jacob first wanted to marry.

94. Dhū'l-Qarnayn ("the two-horned") is most often identified in Islamic sources with Alexander the Great, although this identifica-

tion is not without dispute and many go to great lengths to make two Dhū'l-Qarnayns, one of whom they say was a prophet and the other Alexander. His exploits are normally part and parcel of any version of the prophetic tales, although they do not appear here. On account of Dhū'l-Qarnayn/Alexander's wanderings in search of the Water of Life, he is always closely associated with al-Khiḍr (see §67). Dhū'l-Qarnayn is mentioned in Koran 18:33ff.

95. As Sale gives the interpretations of al-Bayḍāwī, al-Zamakhsharī, and Jalāl al-Dīn al-Suyūṭī, it was the "apparition of his father Jacob, who bit his fingers' ends, or, as some write, struck him on the breast, whereupon his lubricity passed out at the ends of his fingers" (*Alcoran*, p. 190, note "g").

96. According to two versions given by Ṭabarī (*Tārīkh*, I, 322) Job's wife was either Leah, daughter of Jacob, or Raḥmah, daughter of Ephraim son of Joseph (as here), who held the region of Bethany as her dower. Job is placed into the prophetic line as the son of Lot's daughter.

97. Job's comforters are elsewhere spoken of, as in the Biblical narrative (Job 42:9), as Bildad, Eliphaz and Zophar (see Tabarī, *Tārīkh*, I, 324).

98. Dhū'l-Kifl ("he of the double requital"), mentioned twice in the Koran (21:85, 38:48), is said variously to be Elijah, Zacharias (Tha'labī, *Qiṣaṣ*, 232), or a pious man charged by Elisha to fast by day, maintain vigil by night and never to wax angry (Tha'labī, *Qiṣaṣ*, 144f. and 231); though tempted by Iblīs, he remained steadfast to his vow. Job's son is elsewhere called Bishr, not Bashīr.

99. The "Lords of the Thicket" (*aṣḥāb al-ayka*) are mentioned in Koran 15:78, 26:176, 38:13 and 50.14.

100. It has been suggested (Walker, "Asiya," 48) that Āsiya is a scribal error for Āsina (= Asenath, the daughter of Poti-pherah and wife of Joseph, see Gen 41:45, 41:50 and 46:20), although there is little justification for this interpretation since Āsiya is in all sources named as the daughter of Muzāḥim and has no connection whatsoever with Joseph, in whose legend the roles of both Asenath and of the wife of Potiphar have been combined in the figure of Zuleikha. Walker connects Āsiya's legend, especially her martyrdom at the hand of Pharaoh, with that of St. Catherine of Alexandria, who shares a number of attributes with Āsiya, including a connection with Moses in that Catherine's supposed tomb is at Jebel Ekaterina in Sinai near the Jebel Musa, where the Decalogue is said to have been revealed. St. Catherine was of royal lineage; Ibn Kathīr (*Qiṣaṣ al-anbiyā'*, II, 8) gives Āsiya's name as Āsiya bint Muzāḥim ibn

'Ubayd ibn al-Rayyān ibn al-Walīd, thus establishing her to be of royal lineage also. Of striking similarity to Pharaoh's torture of Āsiya is the account of the martyrdom of St. Catherine: Āsiya is tortured to death with iron stakes, after which the angels bear her off into heaven in a dome of light (see Nīsābūrī, *Qiṣaṣ al-anbiyā'*, p. 187), a standard topos in martyrologies; cf. the old woman put to death by Nimrod (p. 141 above) and the martyrdom of Queen Alexandra in the St. George legend (Tha'labī, *Qiṣaṣ*, p. 392 and also in the Syriac version in *Acta martyrum et sanctorum*, ed. Bedjan, I, 295ff.). Āsiya's last words are given in Koran 66:11: "Lord, build me a house with thee in paradise; and deliver me from Pharaoh and his doings, and deliver me from the unjust people."

As Āsiya is Pharaoh's wife and not his daughter (called Thermutis in Midrashic literature), she is placed in relation to Haman the Vizier as was Esther, from whose legend Haman (chief minister to Ahasuerus) was lifted. There may possibly be some connection between Esther's name, Haddasah ("myrtle"), and the Arabic *ās* (also "myrtle") and *Āsiya*. The Arab lexicographers derive Āsiya's name from the verb *asā* (from which, by pseudo-etymology, Mūsā, "Moses," may also be derived), meaning "healing" and "solace" (cf. the Syriac *āsiyā*, "physician"), which latter function she performs with respect to both Moses and Pharaoh. The possibility of Mūsā as "source/instrument of healing" was recognized and employed in the legend when, as a babe, his presence heals the diseased daughters of Pharaoh.

There are some unmistakably alchemical elements in the Moses legend, particularly the "nonburning" of the Moses-infant amidst the raging fire (this has its parallel too in the Abraham legend) and the subsequent casting of the child into the waters for a certain period of time (all of the variant lengths of time recorded would be of significance), after which the infant effects miraculous cures. The connection of Moses with alchemy is carried further in his relation to Korah (see p. 245). Moses is known to figure prominently in the alchemical literature of late antiquity and in the Greco-Arabic tradition also (see E. J. Holmyard, ed., *The Arabic Works of Jābir ibn Ḥayyān*, I, p. 86).

101. Tha'labī (*Qiṣaṣ*, p. 166) mentions that there were three persons who were faithful believers but who, on account of their circumstances, had to conceal their faith. The first was Ḥabīb the Carpenter, referred to as "Ṣāḥib Āl Yāsīn" and variously identified as Ḥabīb ibn Marī or Ḥabīb ibn Isrā'īl, a pious and charitable man of Antioch but horribly disfigured by the pox, who openly declared

his faith in the apostles of Jesus of Nazareth and called upon his people to convert, whereupon they fell upon him and killed him. The second, Ḥiziqīl (Ezekiel, but here called Ḥarbēl) of Pharaoh's people is identified on the one hand with the carpenter who made the ark for Moses' mother (a confusion with the above-mentioned Ḥabīb the Carpenter of Antioch) and on the other as the believer mentioned in the Koranic narrative (40:28) and said to be Pharaoh's treasurer. The faithful maidservant who was tortured to death along with her children is made his wife. The third was ʿAlī ibn Abī Ṭālib of Muhammad's people.

102. Gabriel's horse, Ḥarqūm, is more generally known as Ḥayzūm (see Ṭabarī, *Tārīkh,* I, 453).

102[a]. For al-Sāmirī, the "Samaritan," see Horovitz, *KU,* p. 114.

103. See note 58.

104. The Hebrew formula "we hear and obey" (Deut. 5:27, *shamaʿnu we-ʿasinu,* "and we will hear it and do it") was heard by the Arabs as the Arabic formula of revolt, *samiʿnā wa-ʿaṣaynā* ("we hear and disobey"). See Margoliouth, "Harut and Marut," p. 78 on the distortion of certain Hebraic formulae.

105. The Holy Land is said to be Syria, which was at that time occupied by the giant Canaanites, who were Amalekites, descendants of Amalek son of Eliphaz son of Shem [!] (Thaʿlabī, *Qiṣaṣ,* p. 213). Other opinions on the location of the Holy Land are 1. Sinai and environs, 2. Elath and Jerusalem, 3. Jericho, 4. Damascus, Palestine and part of Jordan, 5. Ramla, Jordan and Palestine, and 6. all of Syria (Thaʿlabī, *Qiṣaṣ,* p. 209).

106. Thaʿlabī (*Qiṣaṣ,* 163) identifies this giant/tyrant with Og son of Anak, see §68.

107. Anak, the Biblical son of Arba and progenitor of the giant race, the Anakim (see Num. 13:22–23 and Deut. 9:2, Josh. 15:13f., 21:11, Judg. 1:20), has been transformed into a woman and made the mother of the giant Og (Hebrew ʿŌg, Arabic ʿŪj, like ʿAnāḳ = "long-necked, giant"), the Biblical king of Bashan defeated at Adrei (see Deut. 3:1–13 and Psa. 135:11).

108. The story of Ahab and particularly of Jezebel has been confused with the legend of some pious, probably Christian queen. In other Islamic renderings Jezebel meets the same end as in the Biblical account of her (1 Ki. 21, 2 Ki. 9).

109. If the identification of the Arabic Yakhṭūb = Aḥīṭūb be correct, the "misidentification" of Elisha's father must have arisen from a confusion of Ahitub's father, Phinehas son of Eli (1 Sa. 14:3), with Phinehas son of Eleazar b. Aaron (1 Ch. 6:4). Elisha is clearly

spoken of as son of Shaphat of Abel-meholah in 2 Ki. 3:11; nonetheless, he is consistently spoken of in Islamic sources as Elisha son of Ahitub (see Tha'labī, *Qiṣaṣ*, 229).

110. See note 52. Ishmael, as progenitor of the Arabs, was thus the ancestor of Muhammad.

111. David is known in Islamic lore as a maker of chain mail and armor. See p. 301 below.

112. The litigation of the two angels is essentially the same as Nathan's parable to David in 2 Sam. 12.

113. Luqmān is the sage par excellence in Arabic lore. The maxims of Luqmān the Wise form part of the Arabic genre of wisdom literature, and he is often included in Tales of the Prophets (see, e.g., Tha'labī, *Qiṣaṣ*, 313–315).

114. Sakhr's counterpart in Jewish legend is Asmodæus. For parallels on the capture of Asmodæus by Solomon's servant Benaiah son of Jehoiada (the Islamic Asaph son of Berachiah [see 1 Ch. 6:39]), see Rappoport, *Myth and Legend*, I, 79ff.

115. In Tha'labī (*Qiṣaṣ*, 278) the Queen of Sheba is variously named Bilqīs bint al-BSHRKH who is "al-Hadhhādh" and Bal'ama bint Sarāḥīl b. Dhū-Jadan b. al-BSHRKH b. al-Ḥārith b. Qays b. San'ā' b. Yashjub b. Ya'rab b. Qaḥṭān.

116. The Queen of Sheba has here been confused with Zenobia, Queen of Palmyra.

117. See note 90.

118. The word *walī* is generally loosely translated as "saint" although its true meaning is one who is "close to" or "friend of" God. In later Islamic times the word connotes something quite similar to the Christian notion of a "saint" or a holy person capable of intercession with God on behalf of man. The Zacharias mentioned in Luke 1 *passim* as father of John the Baptist was likely confused with the prophet in Judah, Zechariah, whose book remains as part of the Old Testament.

119. The legends surrounding the birth of Mary and Jesus and of His boyhood, few of which as given by al-Kisā'ī agree with or are indeed even to be found in the canonical Gospels, are almost all from the apocryphal gospels. These gospels, with extrabiblical roots in older oriental parallels (for Indian, Egyptian and Persian parallels see Hennecke, *NTA*, I, 364; van den Bergh van Eysinga, *Indische Einflüsse*; Norden, *Die Geburt*; Cheyne, *Bible Problems*), are presumed to have been written down between the second and fourth centuries before being condemned as noncanonical by Bishop Gelasius and the Council in Rome of 494 (see Budge, *History of the B.V.M.*,

p. xi). As the monophysitic churches had been ruled against at the Council of Chalcedon in 451, however, it is unlikely that much of oriental Christianity would have heeded the ban of 494. These works survived the Gelasian condemnation, therefore, and were especially popular with oriental Christians and enjoyed widespread popularity even in Europe during the Middle Ages, influencing Christian art perhaps more than the Bible itself (see Cullmann, "Infancy Gospels," p. 368).

Among the apocryphal works centering around the birth of Mary, the birth of Jesus, and His boyhood miracles which closely parallel the versions given by al-Kisā'ī, there are:

(1) *The Protevangelium of James.* A Syriac version dates from the V–VIth centuries in *Studia Sinaitica XI*, *Apocrypha syriaca* (1902). The Armenian redaction of this same work is found in Conybeare; the Georgian version appears in Garitte in *Le Muséon.* Also extant are Ethiopic (Chaine, *Corpus scriptorum*) and Sahidic texts (Leipoldt, *ZNWKUC*). For Greek text see Tischendorf, *Ea,* 1–50; for English see Hennecke, *NTA*, I, 374–388.

(2) *The Arabic Infancy Gospel.* This group of tales of Jesus' birth and boyhood miracles is thought by Tischendorf to be of Syriac origin (Arabic text in Thilo, *Codex,* 66–131; Latin in Tischendorf, *Ea,* 181–209; English in Walker, *AGAR,* 100–125).

(3) *The Infancy Story of Thomas* gives many of the boyhood miracles found herein and closely parallels the *Arabic Infancy Gospel.* The Syriac rescension may be found in Wright, *Contributions* and also in Budge, *History of the B.V.M.*, I, 217–222. A Georgian fragment also exists, see Garitte, "Le fragment."

(4) *The Pseudo-Matthew Gospel.*

(5) *The Nativity of Mary.*

(6) *The Transitus Mariæ.* Syriac text in *Studia sinaitica XI*: *Apocrypha syriaca* (1902); Arabic text in Enger, *Akhbār Yūḥannā.*

The Syriac *History of the Blessed Virgin Mary* (edited by Budge), of which similar Arabic versions may have existed and may have been known to al-Kisā'ī or at least to oriental Christians in Baghdad at al-Kisā'ī's time, is "a careful selection of the most important of the stories concerning the Virgin and Child which were current in Syria and Palestine as early as the end of the IVth century of our era, as well as some which were incorporated with them at a later date" (Budge, *History,* viii). Also extant are Ethiopic versions which would reflect stories current among the Coptic Christians of Egypt, from whom Muslim story-gatherers could have culled information. Of these, especially "The Conception and Birth of our

Lady Mary, the Bearer of God" (see Budge, *Legends,* 122–142) accords with the version of the present work and is based on Coptic and Arabic versions of the *Protevangelium of James* and the *Nativity of Mary* (Budge, *Legends,* lxxii). The entire corpus of apocrypha may be found in the Greek and Latin, along with a discussion of same, in de Tischendorf, *Evangelia apocrypha.* English translations are available in A. Walker, *Apocryphal Gospels, Acts, and Revelations.* A more recent discussion and evaluation of the infancy gospel group is in O. Cullmann, "Infancy Gospels."

The existence of these stories in languages as far afield as Ethiopic/Coptic and Armenian/Georgian, as well as the centrally located Syriac/Arabic versions, indicates how widely these legends were known. There would have been no lack of availability to al-Kisā'ī and his predecessors or contemporaries.

Bibliography of Relevant Literature and Works Cited

Note: Asterisks indicate printed versions of the *Tales of the Prophets.*

'Abd al-Karīm [b. Ibrāhīm] al-Jīlānī. *al-Insān al-kāmil fī ma'rifat al-awākhir wa'l-awā'il.* Cairo: Maṭba'at Muḥammad-'Alī Ṣabīḥ, 1383/1963.

Abdel-Maguid, Abdel-Aziz. *The Modern Arabic Short Story: Its Emergence, Development and Form.* Cairo: al-Maaref, 1946.

Ahlwardt, Wilhelm, *Verzeichnis der arabischen Handschriften der Königlichen Bibliothek zu Berlin.* 10 vols. Berlin, 1887–1889.

Ahrens, Karl. "Christliches im Koran." *Zeitschrift der deutschen morgenländischen Gesellschaft* 84 (1930): 15–73, 148–190.

Aichele, Walther. "Biblische Legenden der Schī'iten aus dem Prophetenbuch des Ḥosainī." *Mitteilungen des Seminar für orientalische Sprachen zu Berlin* 18/2 (1915): 27–57.

Aigrain, René. *L'Hagiographie: Ses sources, ses méthodes, son histoire.* Paris: Bloud & Gay, 1953.

'Alī, Fu'ād Ḥanīn. *Qaṣaṣunā al-sha'bī.* Cairo: Dār al-Fikr al-'Arabī, 1947.

*al-'Āmilī, 'Abd al-Ṣāḥib al-Ḥasanī. *al-Anbiyā: Ḥayātuhum, qiṣaṣuhum.* Beirut: al-A'lamī, 1391/1971.

Anawati, Georges C. "Le Nom suprême de Dieu (*ism Allāh al-a'ẓam*)." *Atti 3 Cong. studi arabi e islamici,* pp. 7–58. Ravello, 1966.

'Aṭṭār Nīshāpūrī, Farīd al-Dīn Muḥammad. *Manṭiq al-ṭayr.* Edited by Sayyid Ṣādiq Gawharīn. Majmū'a-i Mutūn-i Fārsī, 15. Intishārāt-i Bungāh-i Tarjuma wa-Nashr-i Kitāb, 164. Teheran, 1342.

'Azīz al-Dīn Nasafī. *Majmū'a-i rasā'il-i mashhūr bi-Kitāb al-Insān al-kāmil.* Edited by Marijan Molé. Bibliothèque Iranienne, 11. Teheran: Dept. d'Iranologie de l'Institut Franco-Iranien, 1962.

al-Balkhī, Abū Zayd Aḥmad. See Maqdisī, al Muṭahhar b. Ṭāhir.

Basset, René. *Mille et un Contes, récits et légendes arabes.* Volume 3: Légendes réligieuses. Paris: Librairie orientale et américaine Maisonneuve Frères, 1926.

Baumstark, A. "Eine altarabische Evangelienübersetzung aus dem

Christlich-Palästinensischen." *Zeitschrift für Semitistik* 8 (1932): 201–209.

——. *Geschichte der syrischen Literatur mit Ausschluß der christlich-palästinensischen Texte.* Bonn, 1922.

——. "Das Problem eines vorislamischen christlichkirchlichen Schriftums in arabischer Sprache." *Islamica* 4 (1929–31): 562–575.

Bedjan, ed. *Acta martyrum et sanctorum; Sharbê d'sâhdê wad'-qaddîshê.* Volume One. Paris & Leipzig: Otto Harrassowitz, 1890.

van den Bergh van Eysinga, G. A. *Indische Einflüsse auf evangelische Erzählungen.* Göttingen: Vandenhoeck und Ruprecht, 1904.

Bezold, Carl, ed. and trs. *Die Schatzhöhle.* German translation. Leipzig: J. C. Hinrichs'sche Buchhandlung, 1883. Syriac and Arabic texts. Leipzig, 1888.

Bishai, Wilson. "A Possible Coptic Source for a Qur'ānic Text." *Journal of the American Oriental Society* 911/1 (1971): 125–128.

Blochet, E. *Catalogue des manuscrits persans de la Bibliothèque Nationale.* Paris, 1905–12.

Boyd, C. O. "Sin and Grace in the Biblical Narratives Rehearsed in the Koran." *Moslem World* 13 (1923): 139–159.

Budge, E. A. Wallis, trans. *Book of the Bee.* Oxford: Clarendon Press, 1886.

——, trans. *The Book of the Cave of Treasures.* London: Religious Tract Society, 1927.

——, ed. & tr. *The History of the Blessed Virgin Mary, and The History of the Likeness of Christ Which the Jews of Tiberias Made to Mock at.* London: Luzac, 1899.

——, ed. & tr. *Legends of Our Lady Mary the Perpetual Virgin and Her Mother Hannâ, Translated from the Ethiopic Manuscripts Collected by King Theodore at Makdalâ & Now in the British Museum.* London: Medici Society, 1922.

——, ed. & tr. *Miscellaneous Coptic Texts in the Dialect of Upper Egypt.* London: British Museum, 1915.

Canaan, Taufik. *Mohammedan Saints and Sanctuaries in Palestine.* Luzac's Oriental Religions Series, 5. London: Luzac's, 1927.

Chaine, Marius. *Apocrypha de B. Maria Virgine.* Corpus Scriptorum Christianorum Orientalium (Scriptures Aethiopici), series 1, vol. 7 (1909), pp. 3–19.

Charles, R. H. *The Apocrypha and Pseudepigrapha of the Old Testament.* Oxford, 1963.

——, trans. *The Book of Jubilees.* London, 1917.

Chauvin, Victor. *Bibliographie des ouvrages arabes ou relatifs aux Arabes.* 12 vols. Liège: H. Vaillant-Carmanne, 1892–1922.

——. *La Recension égyptienne des Mille et une Nuits.* Brussels: Société Belge de Librairie, 1899.

Cheikho, L. "Quelques légendes islamiques apocryphes." *Mélanges de la Faculté Orientale de l'Université St. Joseph de Beyrouth* 4 (1910): 33–56.

Cheyne, T. K. *Bible Problems and the New Material for Their Solution.* New York: G. P. Putnam, 1904.

Conybeare, F. C. "Protevangelium Jacobi." *American Journal of Theology* 1 (1897): 424–442.

Crooke, William. *The Popular Religion and Folklore of Northern India.* 2 vols. Westminster: Archibald Constable, 1896. 2nd edn. Oxford: Oxford University Press, 1926.

Cullmann, Oscar. "Infancy Gospels." Translated by A. J. B. Higgins. In Hennecke, *NTA*, I, 363–417.

Dames, M. Longworth. *Popular Poetry of the Baloches.* London: Folk-lore Society, 1907.

Delehaye, Hippolyte. *The Legends of the Saints: An Introduction to Hagiography.* Translated by Mrs. V. M. Crawford. New York: Longmans, Green, 1907.

Denis, Albert Marie. *Introduction aux pseudoépigraphes grecs d'Ancien Testament.* Leiden: E. J. Brill, 1970.

Desparmet, Joseph. *Coutumes, institutions, croyances des indigènes de l'Algérie.* Translated and edited by Henri Pérès and G.-H. Bousquet. Algiers: Imp. "La Typo-litho" et J. Carbonel, 1939.

Doutté, Edmond. *Magie et religion dans l'Afrique du Nord.* Algiers: A. Jourdan, 1909.

EI[1] *Encyclopaedia of Islam.* 1st edition. 4 vols. Leiden: Brill, 1913–42.

EI[2] *Encyclopaedia of Islam.* 2nd edition. Leiden: Brill, 1954–.

Eichler, P. A. *Die Dschinn, Teufel und Engel im Koran.* Leipzig, 1928.

Eickmann, W. *Die Angelologie und Dämonologie des Korans.* New York & Leipzig, 1908.

Eisenberg, Isaac. *Die Prophetenlegenden des Muḥammad ben 'Abdallāh al-Kisā'ī.* Bern, 1898.

Enger, Maximilian, ed. *Akhbār Yuḥannā al-salīḥ fī naqlat Umm al-Masīḥ, id est Johannis Apostoli de Transitu Beatae Mariae Virginis Liber.* Elberfeld: Friederich, 1854.

Finkel, Joshua, "Jewish, Christian and Samaritan Influences on Arabia." In *Macdonald Presentation Volume*, pp. 147–166. Princeton U. P., 1933.

———. "Old Israelitish Tradition in the Koran." *Proceedings of the American Academy for Jewish Research* (1930–31): 7–21.

Frazer, James G. *The Golden Bough.* Edited by Theodor H. Gaster. New York: Criterion, 1959.

Fück, J. "Zum Problem der Koranischen Erzählungen." *Orientalistische Literaturzeitung* (1934): 73–77.

Furūzānfar, Badī' al-Zamān. *Ma'ākhidh-i qiṣaṣ wa-tamthīlāt-i Mathnawī.* Teheran: Dānishgāh, 1333/1954.

Garitte, G. "Le fragment géorgien de l'Evangile de Thomas." *Revue d'Histoire Ecclésiastique* 51 (1956): 513–520.

———. "Le 'Protévangile de Jacques' en géorgien." *Le Muséon* 70 (1957): 233–265.

Gaster, Theodor H. *Thespis: Ritual, Myth and Drama in the Ancient Near East.* 2nd edition. Garden City: Doubleday, 1961.

Geiger, Abraham. *Was hat Mohammed aus dem Judenthume aufgenommen?* 2nd edn. Leipzig: M. W. Kaufmann, 1902.

Ginzberg, Louis. *The Legends of the Jews.* Translated by H. Szold. 7 vols. Philadelphia: Jewish Publication Society of America, 1909–1938.

Goldziher, Ignaz. "The Influence of Buddhism upon Islam." English summary of his *A Buddhismus hatása az Iszlamra* (1903), by T. Duka. In *Journal of the Royal Asiatic Society* (1904): 125–141.

———. *Muslim Studies (Muhammedanische Studien).* Edited by S. M. Stern. Translated by C. R. Barber and S. M. Stern. Volume 2. Aldine: Geo. Allen & Unwin, 1971.

Graf, Georg. *Geschichte der christlichen arabischen Literatur.* 4 vols. The Vatican, 1944–51.

Grünbaum, Max. *Neue Beiträge zur semitischen Sagenkunde.* Leiden: E. J. Brill, 1893.

Guidi, Ignazio. *Testi orientali inediti sopra i sette dormienti di Efeso.* Rome. Academia dei Lincei, 1885.

———. *Le Traduzioni degli Evangelii in arabo e in etiopico.* Rome, 1888.

Ḥājjī Khalīfa "Kâtib Çelebi." *Kashf al-ẓunūn.* 2 vols. Istanbul: Maârif Matbaası, 1941.

Heller, Bernard. "Egyptian Elements in the Haggadah." In *Ignace Goldziher Memorial Volume,* edited by S. Löwinger & J. Somogyi, pp. 412–418. Budapest, 1948.

———. "La Légende biblique dans l'Islam." *Revue des Études Juives* 98 (1934): 1–18.

———. "Rẹcits et personnages bibliques dans la légende mahométane." *Revue des Études Juives* 85 (1928): 113–136.

Hennecke, Edgar. *New Testament Apocrypha*. Edited by Wilhelm Schneemelcher. Translated by R. McL. Wilson. 2 vols. Philadelphia, 1963.

Holmyard, E. J., ed. *The Arabic Works of Jābir ibn Hayyān*. Volume 1. Paris: Paul Geuthner, 1928.

Horovitz, Josef. *Koranische Untersuchungen*. Studien zur Geschichte und Kultur des islamischen Orients, 4. Berlin & Leipzig: Walter de Gruyter, 1926.

Horst, H. "Studien zur Ueberlieferungsgeschichte des Korankommentars aṭ-Ṭabarīs." *Zeitschrift der deutschen morgenländischen Gesellschaft* 103, new series 28 (1953): 290–307.

Huart, Claude. "Wahb b. Monabbih et la tradition judéo-chrétienne au Yémen." *Journal Asiatique* 10/4 (1904): 331–350.

———, trans. *Le Livre de la création et de l'histoire d'Abou-Zéïd Aḥmed ben Sahl el-Balkhî*. 3 volumes. Paris: Ernest Leroux, 1899–1903.

*al-Ḥusaynī, 'Abd Allāh ibn Muḥammad. *Qiṣaṣ al-anbiyā*. See W. Aichele.

Ibn al-Jawzī, Abū'l-Faraj 'Abd al-Raḥmān. *Kitāb al-quṣṣāṣ wa'l-mudhakkirīn*. Edited & translated by Merlin L. Swartz. Beirut: Dar el-Machreq, n. d.

———. *al-Mudhish*. Beirut: al-Mu'assasa al 'Ālamiyya, 1973.

Ibn al-Nadīm. *al-Fihrist*. Edited by Gustav Flügel. Beirut: Khayyāṭ, 1964 (reprint). Edited & translated by Bayard Dodge. 2 vols. New York & London: Columbia U. P., 1970.

Ibn 'Arabī, Muḥyī al-Dīn. *Muḥāḍarat al-abrār wa-musāmarat al-akhyār fī al-adabiyyāt wa'l-nawādir wa'l-akhbār*. 2 vols. Beirut: Dār al-Yaqẓa al-'Arabiyya, 1388/1968.

———. *Tafsīr al-Qur'ān al-karīm*. 2 vols. Beirut: Dār al-Yaqẓa al-'Arabiyya, 1387/1968.

*Ibn Kathīr, Ismā'īl ibn 'Umar. *Qiṣaṣ al-anbiyā'*. Edited by Muṣṭafā 'Abd al-Wāḥid. 2 vols. Cairo: Dār al-Kutub al-Ḥadītha, 1968.

*Ibn Khalaf al-Nīsābūrī, Abū Isḥāq Ibrāhīm ibn Manṣūr. *Qiṣaṣ al-anbiyā*. Edited by Ḥabīb Yaghmā'ī. Majmū'a-i Mutūn-i Fārsī, 6. Intishārāt-i Bungāh-i Tarjuma wa-Nashr-i Kitāb, 119. Teheran, 1340/1961.

Ibn Khallikān. *Wafayāt al-a'yān wa-anbā' abnā' al-zamān*. Edited by Iḥsān 'Abbās. Beirut: Dār al-Thaqāfa, n. d.

Ibn Qutayba, 'Abd Allāh ibn Muslim. *Kitāb al-ma'ārif*. Edited by Tharwa 'Ukāsha. Dhakhā'ir al-'Arab, 44. Cairo: Dār al-Ma'arif, 1969.

———. *'Uyūn al-akhbār*. 4 vols. Cairo, 1964.

Ibn Sa'd Muḥammad. *al-Ṭabaqāt al-kubrā*. 9 vols. Beirut: Dār Ṣādir, 1957–1968.

*al-Jazā'irī, al-Sayyid Ni'mat Allāh. *al-Nūr al-mubīn fī qiṣaṣ al-anbiyā' wa'l-mursalīn*. 2 vols. Najaf, 1374.

Jensen, P. "Das Leben Muhammeds und die David-Sage." *Der Islam* 12 (1922): 84–97.

Jung, Leo. *Fallen Angels in Jewish, Christian and Mohammedan Literature*. Philadelphia: Dropsie College, 1926.

*Juwayrī, Muḥammad. *Qiṣaṣ al-anbiyā'*. Edited by Ḥājj Sayyid Aḥmad Kitābchī. Teheran, n. d.

Kaḥḥāla, 'Umar Riḍā. *A'lām al-nisā' fī 'ālamay al-'arab wa'l-islām*. 5 vols. in 3. 2nd edn. Damascus: al-Maṭba'a al-Hāshimiyya, 1959.

Khoury, Raif Georges. *Wahb b. Munabbih*. 2 pts. Codices arabici antiqui, 1. Wiesbaden: Otto Harrassowitz, 1972.

Khūrshīd, Fārūq. *Fī al-riwāya al-'arabiyya: 'Aṣr al-tajmī'*. Alexandria: al-Dār al-Miṣriyya li'l-Ṭibā'a wa'l-Nashr, n. d.

*al-Kisā'ī, Muḥammad ibn 'Abd Allāh. *Qiṣaṣ al-anbiyā'*. Edited by Isaac Eisenberg. 2 parts. Leiden. E. J. Brill, 1922–23.

Köbert, R. "Die älteste arabische Genesis-Übersetzung." In *Die Araber in der Alten Welt*, edited by F. Altheim & R. Stiehl, vol. 2, pp. 333–343. Berlin: de Gruyter, 1964–69.

Koran. *The Alcoran of Mohammad*. Translated by George Sale. 9th edn. Philadelphia & London: J. B. Lippincott, 1923.

Krauss, S. "A Moses Legend." The *Jewish Quarterly Review*, new series 2 (1911–12): 339–364.

Krenkow, F. "The Two Oldest Books on Arabic Folklore." *Islamic Culture* 2 (1928): 55–89, 204–236.

Künstlinger, David. "Christliche Herkunft der Kuranischen Lot-Legende." *Rocznik Orjentalistyczny* 7 (1929–30): 281–295.

———. "Die 'Frau Pharaos' im Koran." *Rocznik Orjentalistyczny* 9 (1933): 132–135.

al-Kulaynī al-Rāzī, Abū Ja'far Muḥammad ibn Ya'qūb. *al-Uṣūl min al-kāfī*. Edited by 'Alī-Akbar al-Ghifārī. 2 vols. Teheran: Dār al-Kutub al-Islāmiyya, 1388, 3rd edn.

Leipoldt, J. "Ein saïdisches Bruchstück des Jacobus-Protevangeliums" *Zeitschrift für die neutestamentliche Wissenschaft und die Kunde des Urchristentums* 6 (1905): 106–107.

Leszynsky, Rudolf. *Mohammedanische Traditionen über das jüngste Gericht: Eine vergleichende Studie zur jüdisch-christlichen und mohammedanischen Eschatologie*. Kirchhain N.-L.: Schmersow, 1909.

Levi Della Vida, G. *Elenco dei manoscritti arabi islamici della Biblio-*

teca Vaticana, Vaticani, Barberiniani, Borgiani, Rossiani. Studi e Testi, 67. Vatican, 1935.

Lichtenstadter, Ilse. "Origin and Interpretation of Some Koranic Symbols." In *Arabic and Islamic Studies in Honor of Hamilton A. R. Gibb,* edited by G. Makdisi. Leiden, 1965.

Lidzbarski, Marcellus. *De propheticis, quae dicuntur, legendis arabicis.* Leipzig: Typis Guilelmi Drugulini, 1893.

*Majlisī, Muḥammad-Bāqir. *Ḥayāt al-qulūb dar qiṣaṣ wa-aḥwālāt-i payghambarān-i ʿizām wa-awṣiyā'-i īshān.* 3 vols. Teheran: Chāpkhāna-i Islāmiyya, 1373.

Malan, S. C., trans. *The Book of Adam and Eve, or the Conflict of Adam with Satan.* London, 1882.

Malov, S. "Musul'manskie skazania o propokakh po Rabguzi (Légendes musulmanes relatives aux prophètes, d'après Rabghuzi). *Zapiski Kollegii Vostokovedov* 5 (1930): 507–526.

al-Maqdisī, al-Muṭahhar ibn al-Ṭāhir. (Also attributed to Abū Zayd Aḥmad ibn Sahl al-Balkhī.) *Kitāb al-bad' wa'l-tārīkh.* Edited by Cl. Huart. 6 parts. Paris: Ernest Leroux, 1903. Reprinted at Baghdad: al-Muthannā, 196?.

Margoliouth, D. S. "Harut and Marut." *Moslem World* 18 (1928): 73–79.

Martin, François. *Le Livre apocryphe d'Hénoch.* Paris, 1906.

Massé, Henri. *Croyances et coutumes persanes, suivies de contes et chansons populaires.* Vol. 1, Paris: G. P. Maisonneuve, 1938. English translation, *Persian Beliefs and Customs.* Translated by C. A. Messner. New Haven: Human Relations Area Files, 1954.

Massignon, Louis. *Essai sur les origines du lexique technique de la mystique musulmane.* Études Musulmanes, 2. Paris: J. Vrin, 1954.

Meʿārath gazzē. See C. Bezold and also E. A. W. Budge.

Meyer, Abraham, ed. *Légendes juives apocryphes sur la vie de Moïse.* Paris: P. Geuthner, 1925.

Muḥammad ibn Ḥabīb. *Kitāb al-muḥabbar.* Edited by Ilse Lichtenstadter. Hyderabad, Deccan: Dā'irat al-Maʿārif, 1942.

Nagel, Tilman. *Die Qiṣaṣ al-Anbiyā': Ein Beitrag zur arabischen Literaturgeschichte.* Bonn, 1967.

*al-Najjār, ʿAbd al-Wahhāb. *Qiṣaṣ al-anbiyā'.* 3rd edn. Beirut: Dār Iḥyā' al-Turāth al-ʿArabī, n. d.

Norden, Eduard. *Die Geburt des Kindes, Geschichte einer religiösen Idee.* Leipzig: Teubner, 1924.

al-Nuwayrī, Aḥmad ibn ʿAbd al-Wahhāb. *Nihāyat al-arab fī funūn al-adab.* 18 vols. Cairo: Dār al-Kutub, 1923ff.

O'Leary, de Lacy. *The Saints of Egypt*. London & New York: Macmillan, 1937.

Oppenheim, Gustav, trans. *Fabula Josephi et Asenathæ apocrypha e libro syriaco latine versa*. Berlin, 1886.

O'Shaughnessy, T. "The Seven Names for Hell in the Qur'an." *Bulletin of the School of Oriental and African Studies* 24 (1961): 444–469.

Paret, R. *Die Geschichte des Islams im Spiegel der arabischen Volksliteratur*. Tübingen: J. C. B. Mohr, 1927.

Parrinder, Geoffrey, *Jesus in the Qur'ān*. New York: Barnes & Noble, 1965.

Pedersen, Johs. "The Criticism of the Islamic Preacher." *Die Welt des Islams*, new series 2 (1953): 215–231.

——————. "The Islamic Preacher: *wā'iz, mudhakkir, qāṣṣ*." In *Ignace Goldziher Memorial Volume*, edited by S. Löwinger & J. Somogyi, pp. 226–251. Budapest, 1948.

al-Qazwīnī, Zakariyā ibn Muḥammad. *'Ajā'ib al-makhlūqāt wa'l-ḥayawānāt wa-gharā'ib al-mawjūdāt*. In margin of Kamāl al-Dīn al-Damīrī, *Ḥayāt al-ḥayawān al-kubrā*. 2 vols. Beirut: Dār al-Qāmūs al-Ḥadīth, reprint of 1309 edn.

*al-Rabghūzi, Nāṣir al-Dīn ibn Burhān al-Dīn. *Narrationes de prophetis: Qiṣaṣ al-anbiyā'*. Copenhagen: Munksgaard, 1948.

Rappoport, Angelo Solomon. *Myth and Legend of Ancient Israel*. 3 vols. New York: Ktav Publishing House, 1966.

*al-Rāzī, Fakhr al-Dīn. *'Iṣmat al-anbiyā'*. Silsilat al-Thaqāfa al-Islāmiyya, 47. Cairo, 1383/1964.

Rieu, C. *Supplement to the Catalogue of the Arabic Manuscripts in the British Museum*. London, 1894.

Robinson, Forbes, tr. *Coptic Apocryphal Gospels*. Cambridge: Cambridge Univ. Press, 1896.

Rost, L. *Die Ueberlieferung von der Thronnachfolge Davids*. Stuttgart, 1926.

Sale, George. See Koran.

Salzberger, Georg. *Salomos Tempelbau und Thron in der semitischen Sagenliteratur*. Berlin: Mayer & Müller, 1912.

——————. *Die Salomosage in der semitischen Literatur: Ein Beitrag zur vergleichenden Sagenkunde*. Berlin, 1907.

Schapiro, Israel. *Die Haggadischen Elemente im erzählenden Teil des Korans*. Leipzig: G. Fock, 1907.

Schimmel, Annemarie. *Sindhi Literature*. A History of Indian Literature, edited by Jan Gonda, vol. 8. Wiesbaden: Harrassowitz, 1974.

Schützinger, Heinrich. "Die Arabische Legende von Nebukadnezar und Johannes dem Täufer." *Der Islam* 40 (1965): 113–141.

———. *Ursprung und Entwicklung der arabischen Abraham-Nimrod-Legende.* Bonner orientalistische Studien, new series 11. Bonn, 1961.

Sezgin, Fuat. *Geschichte des arabischen Schrifttums.* Vol. 1. Leiden: E. J. Brill, 1967.

al-Shahrastānī, Abū'l-Fatḥ Aḥmad. *al-Milal wa'l-niḥal.* Edited by 'Abd al-'Azīz Muḥ. al-Wakīl. 2 pts. in 1 vol. Cairo: al-Ḥalabī, 1387/1968.

Sidersky, David. *Les Origines des légendes musulmanes dans le Coran et dans les Vies de Prophètes.* Paris: P. Geuthner, 1933.

Speyer, H. *Die Biblischen Erzählungen im Qoran.* Grafenhainichen, n. d.

Steinschneider, Moritz. *Die Arabische Literatur der Juden: Ein Beitrag zur Literaturgeschichte der Araber.* Frankfurt, 1902.

Storey, C. A. *Persian Literature: A Bio-bibliographical Survey.* Volume 1, part 1. London: Royal Asiatic Society, 1927. Repr. 1970.

Sulaymān, Mūsā. *al-Adab al-qaṣaṣī 'ind al-'arab.* 3rd edn. Beirut: Maktabat al-Madrasa, 1960.

al-Ṭabarī, Muḥammad ibn Jarīr. *Tārīkh al-rusul wa'l-mulūk.* Edited by Muḥammad Abū'l-Faḍl Ibrāhīm. 10 vols. Cairo: Dār al-Ma'ārif, 1960–69.

*al-Tha'labī, Aḥmad ibn Muḥammad. *'Arā'is al-majālis: Qiṣaṣ al-anbiyā'.* Beirut: al-Maktaba al-Thaqāfiyya, n. d.

Thilo, Johann Karl. *Codex apocryphus Novi Testamenti e libris editis et manuscriptis.* Volume 1, Leipzig, 1832.

de Tischendorf, Constantinus. *Evangelia apocrypha.* Leipzig: Hermann Mendelssohn, 1876.

Vajda, G. "Observations sur quelques citations bibliques chez Ibn Qutayba." *Revue des Études Juives* 99 (1935): 68–80.

Walker, Alexander, tr. *Apocryphal Gospels, Acts, and Revelations.* Edinburgh: T. & T. Clark, 1873.

Walker, John. "Asiya: The Wife of Pharaoh." *Moslem World* 18 (1928): 45–48.

———. *Bible Characters in the Koran.* Paiseley, 1931.

Weil, Gustav, *Biblische Legenden der Muselmänner.* Frankfurt am Main, 1845. Translated by the author as *Biblical Legends of the Mussulmans.* London: Longman, Brown, Green, and Longmans, 1846.

Wensinck, A. J. *Handbook of Early Muhammadan Tradition, Alphabetically Arranged.* Leiden: E. J. Brill, 1927. Repr. 1960.

——. *The Muslim Creed: Its Genesis and Historical Development.* London: Frank Cass, 1965.
Westermarck, E. *Survivances païennes dans la civilisation mahométane.* Translated by R. Godet. Paris: Payot, 1935.
Widengren, Geo. "Oral Tradition and Written Literature." *Acta Orientalia* 23 (1959): 201–262.
Wolfensohn, I. *Ka'b al-Aḥbār und seine Stellung im Ḥadīṯ und in der islamischen Legendenliteratur.* Frankfurt am Main, 1933.
Wright, William. *Contributions to the Apocryphal Literature of the New Testament.* London, 1865.
Yāqūt al-Rumī, Shihāb al-Dīn. *Irshād al-arīb ilā ma'rifat al-adīb: Mu'jam al-udabā' aw Ṭabaqāt al-udabā'.* Edited by D. S. Margoliouth. 2nd edn. Cairo: Maṭba'at Hindiyya, 1930.
——. *Mu'jam al-buldān.* N. p.: Maṭba'at al-Sa'āda, 1323.

General Index

Index to Koranic Quotation